# Land Use Law in Florida

*Land Use Law in Florida* presents an in-depth analysis of land use law common to many states across the United States, using Florida cases and statutes as examples.

Florida case law is an important course of study for planners, as the state has its own legal framework that governs how people may use land, with regulation that has evolved to include state-directed urban and regional planning. The book addresses issues in a case format, including planning, land development regulation, property rights, real estate development and land use, transportation, and environmental regulation. Each chapter summarizes the rules that a reader should draw from the cases, making it useful as a reference for practicing professionals and as a teaching tool for planning students who do not have experience in reading law.

This text is invaluable for attorneys; professional planners; environmental, property rights, and neighborhood activists; and local government employees who need to understand the rules that govern how property owners may use land in Florida and around the country.

**W. Thomas Hawkins** is a Lecturer in the University of Florida's Department of Urban and Regional Planning and is Program Director of the university's online Master of Urban and Regional Planning. In addition to teaching courses in land use law, planning administration and ethics, and development review for the department, Thomas has taught land use law for the Levin College of Law and for Florida State University. Prior to joining the department, he was Policy & Planning Director of 1000 Friends of Florida—the state's leading advocate for planning and growth management in the public interest—where he addressed land use and transportation policy. Thomas also served two terms as a Gainesville City Commissioner. He has a law degree from the Emory University School of Law, a Master of Science in Real Estate from the Hough Graduate School of Business at the University of Florida, is a member of the American Institute of Certified Planners, and a member of the Florida Bar.

# Land Use Law in Florida

W. Thomas Hawkins

Routledge
Taylor & Francis Group
NEW YORK AND LONDON

First published 2021
by Routledge
605 Third Avenue, New York, NY 10158

and by Routledge
2 Park Square, Milton Park, Abingdon, Oxon OX14 4RN

*Routledge is an imprint of the Taylor & Francis Group, an informa business*



Library of Congress Cataloging-in-Publication Data
Names: Hawkins, W. Thomas, author.
Title: Land use law in Florida / W. Thomas Hawkins.
Description: Milton Park, Abingdon, Oxon ; New York, NY : Routledge, 2021. |
Includes bibliographical references and index. |
Identifiers: LCCN 2020055331 (print) | LCCN 2020055332 (ebook) |
ISBN 9780367622602 (hardback) | ISBN 9780367622596 (paperback) |
ISBN 9781003108603 (ebook)
Subjects: LCSH: Land use—Law and legislation—Florida. | Land use—
Planning—Florida.
Classification: LCC KFF458 .H39 2021 (print) | LCC KFF458 (ebook) |
DDC 346.75904/5—dc23
LC record available at https://lccn.loc.gov/2020055331
LC ebook record available at https://lccn.loc.gov/2020055332

ISBN: 978-0-367-62260-2 (hbk)
ISBN: 978-0-367-62259-6 (pbk)
ISBN: 978-1-003-10860-3 (ebk)

Typeset in Bembo
by Apex CoVantage, LLC

# Contents

# Acknowledgements

Matthew J. Ossorio is a skilled lawyer whose research and edits improved this book. I am grateful for his talents and his time.

David Coffey introduced me to the new urbanism and to the practice of local government law. I value his years of friendship and mentorship.

1000 Friends of Florida, our state's leading advocate for planning in the public interest, deepened my passion for planning. The employees and volunteers of this organization have given a tremendous amount to Florida and to me.

Sara and Rowan remind me every day what truly matters.

# Citation and text

I have formatted Florida Statutes, non-Florida cases, and secondary sources according to The Bluebook. I have omitted dates for cited statutes; all were current as of 2020. I have formatted citations to Florida cases according to The Bluebook—for case name abbreviations and pincites—and according to Fla. R. App. P. 9.800—for Florida administrative hearings, agency orders, and appellate court names.

To facilitate typesetting, I have avoided small caps. Author names and periodical titles are in ordinary type. Book titles are in italics.

I have edited cases for length and clarity. Ellipses indicate deleted material except that I have removed or edited citations without indication.

# 1 Introduction

This book presents a collection of significant concepts in land use law. I have written this book to be a useful tool for all of attorneys, professional planners, and students.

I have included cases from federal and Florida courts to present U.S. Constitutional issues, Florida common law, and Florida statutory issues. Although this text focuses on Florida land use law, most states have comparable laws. In every jurisdiction, always consult state and local government laws.

In addition to cases and explanatory materials, I have included hypothetical land use conflicts. I wrote these fact patterns to provide you with an opportunity to test your learning.

Florida has its own legal framework for regulating how people may use land. An ever-growing population, booming real estate development, and the lure of a beautiful-but-fragile environment have defined the Sunshine State for more than a century. These factors have led to constant change in Florida communities and to chronic concern about the repercussions of real estate development. The state and local governments have responded in part by creating a unique system to regulate and manage growth.

While this text focuses on land use regulation, Florida has also served as a laboratory for city design and development. From Henry Flagler's railroad opening the Atlantic Coast to Walt Disney's global tourist attraction, Florida's industry has been the business of building itself.

Although the sixteenth-century establishment of St. Augustine seems distant from modern Florida, the city illustrates the relationship between real estate, land use regulation, and community. St. Augustine began as a planned community, designed according to the Laws of the Indies—rules prescribing the form of Spanish settlements in the Americas.[1] Land use rules determined St. Augustine's original design, including its main square, streets, and building sites. Centuries later, people continue to live in the place shaped by those rules. This is the essence of land use regulation: rules combine with urban design and the business of real estate development to build the places people live, likely for generations to come.

In Florida, examples of the relationships between law, design, and business abound. For example, developer and politician George E. Merrick developed Coral Gables in 1921. His business venture failed, brought down by the cost of providing public infrastructure.[2] But Coral Gables has since become its own city and succeeded as an enduring community, beloved for its beauty.

Some Florida developers, pursuing short-term profit over a legacy of town-building, created zombie subdivisions.[3] Local governments continue to struggle to provide public services to these subdivided but largely undeveloped tracts of land. Consider Lehigh Acres in Lee County, where 62,000 acres (or 97 square miles) of land subdivided in the 1950s and 1960s consists of single-family homesites remote from other land uses or urban services.[4] It remains sparsely populated, a failure as a community even if initially profitable.

Other large-scale developments, such as the Arvida Corporation's City of Weston, were successful business ventures and have become functioning cities that efficiently provide services to residents.[5] But they are banal, lacking charm and vibrant public spaces.

In recent decades, perhaps learning from past mistakes, some Florida developers have refocused on designing and building complete communities. This movement, called the New Urbanism, sees many social, civic, and environmental problems as symptoms of poor urban design. Robert Davis, the developer of the new urban Seaside, helped begin this trend not just in Florida, but in the United States. Town planners Andres Duany and Elizabeth Plater-Zyberk designed Seaside and credit Davis with prioritizing place over profit.[6] Yet Seaside and the surrounding developments it inspired have succeeded financially.

Land use law lies at the intersection of community needs and preferences for the character of communities, the real estate market, and private property rights. This is the field that determines how we will build and maintain the places in which people will live their lives for generations to come.

Consider a built place you love. This may be your childhood home. It may be an open space in the neighborhood where you work. It may be a civic space in a favorite city you have visited. In any case, real estate development built these places and a local government's regulations undoubtedly impacted their character. Land use law matters because where and how we live matter.

## Land use as a practice area

Generally, land use law is the field of law answering the question, "How may a person use this real property?" Land use law differs from real estate law in that real estate law answers the question, "Who owns this real property?" Land use has at least three characteristics that color the routine work of the land use practitioner: land use decisions are based in local government and politics; land use practice is interdisciplinary; and land use law regulates real estate development. This list is written from an attorney's perspective, rather than from that of a professional planner. But planners should consider these characteristics to help them relate to a lawyer's perspective on land use.

### *Land use is local government and local politics*

Land use law is based in local government and local politics.[7] This has two implications for the practice area. First, decision-makers are typically laypeople. The legislators adopting the ordinances with which land use practitioners work are local government officials—sometimes elected from a pool of just a few hundred registered voters.

Moreover, the decision-makers applying those rules to determine whether a property owner may take a certain action are often volunteers—serving on a board like an historic preservation board, a development review board, or a board of adjustment. A land use lawyer might corral the expert opinions of trained architects, planners, and engineers only to provide them to a layperson—like a neighborhood activist—who has no professional training that gives context to the information the attorney seeks to provide.

Second, because land use is political, the decision-makers—whether they admit it or not—pay attention to the identity of applicants and of parties opposed to applicants. Are people with opinions about a land use matter voters or donors to political campaigns? Does a particular developer have a good or bad track record? Is a neighborhood association opposed to a project also politically active, holding an influential candidate forum?

In local government, elected officials and applicants often have close personal relationships. And few elected officials or lay decision-makers will be as skilled at focusing on the relevant facts and the applicable law as are judges.

### *Land use practice is interdisciplinary*

Land use practitioners work with professionals in many other disciplines. Land use lawyers and planners work together. And both work with architects, engineers, financiers, and environmental scientists. To succeed, a land use practitioner must be able to communicate with these other professionals about their areas of expertise.

Working collaboratively through an application process is likely to be a more valuable skill to a practicing land use attorney than prowess in civil litigation. Of course, this does not mean that a land use practitioner needs to be an expert in any other subject matter. Still, a working knowledge of the issues with which these experts deal and how they approach problems is essential. A land use practitioner must understand enough about these related fields to know what questions to ask and to appreciate what he or she doesn't know.

### *Land use law regulates real estate development*

Land use law regulates the business of real estate development. As a result, time matters. If a requested development approval is litigated, rather than reaching final disposition quickly before a local government, the applicant may lose because of the delay—regardless of the ultimate outcome.

At least two reasons make *timely* approval significant. One reason is that markets change over time. Real estate developers formulate projects for the market at a specific point in time considering the prices at which they can sell or lease space. If a development project is delayed several years, other developers may fulfill that market demand. Because supply and demand are constantly in flux, undue delays can change the economic feasibility of a development proposal.

Another reason time matters is that keeping a potential real estate development in play costs money over time. Most real estate developers do not propose projects for land they own outright. Instead, developers and landowners are often separate parties.

When a developer does not own the property he or she seeks to develop, that developer will secure a contract with the owner of the real estate, giving the developer the option to purchase the property for a set period of time, pending development approval. Even when a developer does own land, that property is often encumbered with debt. In either case, the developer must pay over time to keep the land available for development.

## Notes

1 Richard RuBino & Earl M. Starnes, *Lessons Learned? The History of Planning in Florida* 2–3 (Sentry Press, Inc. 2008).
2 *Id.* at 71.
3 "Zombie subdivision" is a particularly evocative planning term. The Florida Statutes refer to these developments by the more staid "antiquated subdivision." Fla Stat. § 163.3164(5).
4 Sheridan v. Lee Cnty., Case No. 90-007791GM para. 49 (Fla. DOAH Jan. 27, 1993) (recommended order).
5 *The History of the City of Weston*, The City of Weston, FL, www.westonfl.org/about/city-history (last visited Aug. 4, 2020).
6 Andres Duany et al., *Suburban Nation: The Rise of Sprawl and the Decline of the American Dream* 113 (North Point Press 2000).
7 Cross Key Waterways v. Askew, 351 So. 2d 1062, 1065 (Fla. 1st DCA 1977) (acknowledging "[t]he primacy of local government jurisdiction in land development regulation"), *aff'd*, 372 So. 2d 913 (Fla. 1978).

# Part I

# How governments regulate land use

# 2 Nuisance

Nuisance is a common law cause of action that gives people the right to sue others over the use to which they put their land.[1] The general rule on nuisance is that any use of land which substantially and unreasonably disturbs a person in the free use, possession, or enjoyment of his or her property may be a nuisance.[2] Several limitations in the concept of nuisance, however, make it narrower in practice than the general rule implies.

## Causation

Causation refers to the causal relationship between a defendant's conduct and the harm to a plaintiff. Causation may limit liability for nuisance when the causal relationship is too tenuous. In the case of *Shamhart v. Morrison Cafeteria Co.*, the majority opinion and that of the dissenting justice disagree on what is the true cause of the harm experienced by the plaintiff.

### Florida Supreme Court

### *Shamhart v. Morrison Cafeteria Co.*[3]

### 1947

ADAMS, Justice.

Morrison's Cafeteria in West Palm Beach fronts west on Olive Street with an alley on the north side. One hundred eight feet to the south is appellant's corner drug store with entrances on Olive Street and also on Datura Street. During the noon and evening meals, customers of the cafeteria form lines on the sidewalk which frequently result in most of the entrances to appellant's drug store being virtually closed to its customers for long periods of time. Appellant sued the cafeteria to enjoin the nuisance and sought damages for loss of business. The cause was referred to a master who recommended a decree for appellant and found the damage to date amounted to $2896.57. Exceptions were filed to the report.

On consideration of the master's report, the chancellor found no basis for injunctive relief; dismissed the bill and therefore did not pass on the amount or the question of damages.

The rule has long been settled at common law that no man shall use his property as to injure another. The general rule is settled by good authority to the effect that abutting property owners may not use the sidewalk in an unreasonable manner and where such unreasonable use is made it is both a public and private nuisance. Where another suffers a special injury as a result thereof he may have appropriate relief. *Jacksonville, Tampa & Key West Railway Co. v.*

*Thompson*, 16 So. 282 (Fla. 1894); 25 Am. Jur., pages 606, 607; 39 Am. Jur., page 280; Eugene McQuillin, *The Law of Municipal Corporations* § 1489 (2d. ed., rev. vol. 4, 1943).

A late case somewhat analogous to this is that of *Tushbant v. Greenfield's, Inc.*, 14 N.W.2d 520, 521 (Mich. 1944), wherein it was held that:

> If a nuisance is private, infringes on the rights of others, and arises out of the manner of conducting a legitimate business, equity will point out the nuisance and decree the adoption of methods calculated to eliminate or minimize the injurious features.

The same rule is generally approved by the English authorities.

This case presents a clear case where appellee has utilized the sidewalk as a waiting room for its customers rather than provide a place upon its own premises.

The nature of the use employed, surrounding appellant's entrances, is such as to cause appellant an injury different in kind and degree from the public in general. It is not incumbent on the appellant to solve appellee's problem of how or where to place the customers. Neither will the court devise a plan or suggest a method. The appellee created his problem by utilizing the entire space of his premises for cooking food and seating customers, therefore he cannot constantly make use of the public sidewalk as a waiting room to the special injury of appellant.

As to the amount of damages, we will not pass upon that because the chancellor naturally did not get to that question. Upon the mandate going down, the chancellor will ascertain what damages the appellant has sustained.

The decree is reversed.

THOMAS, C. J., and TERRELL and CHAPMAN, JJ., concur.

BUFORD and BARNS, JJ., and PARKS, A. J., dissent.

BARNS, Justice (dissenting).

I regret that I am compelled to dissent to the Court's opinion prepared by Mr. Justice ADAMS.

I am unable to conclude that Morrison Cafeteria is doing anything wrong toward plaintiff.

It is a maxim of law that one should so use his property as to not injure another but every inconvenience, discomfort, and annoyance is not a nuisance.

The annoyance to the plaintiff is not from the restaurateur but from the public who are the patrons apparently because of the excellent qualities of the food served.

I fail to see that Morrison Cafeteria has done more than use its property as others in like businesses should be encouraged to do-to-wit: serve food so good, wholesome and delectable as to cause the public to be willing, if necessary, to stand in line and wait for the opportunity to enter and satisfy their hunger. Some competition seems to be the only justified interference.

It is the people of the street who are using the sidewalk in the manner complained of and not Morrison Cafeteria. The Cafeteria's act is the remote cause but not the proximate. The regulation of traffic on the sidewalk is one for the municipality and not for the Cafeteria nor a court of equity.

The plaintiff may be suffering some damages because of the great patronage of Morrison Cafeteria but this damage is not the proximate result of any wrongful act of the Cafeteria. The Cafeteria's acts are the remote and not the proximate cause-Morrison Cafeteria's act being only to make its food wanted.

As stated in the opinion of *Paty v. Town of Palm Beach, Fla.*, 29 So. 2d 363, 364 (Fla. 1947): "It appears that the appellee is sued for doing of an authorized act and the exercise of a lawful right and that the damages were without wrong." ...

### Right protected by law

In *Fontainebleau Hotel Corp. v. Forty-Five Twenty-Five, Inc.*, the court considers whether nuisance protects the rights of the plaintiff on which the defendant infringes. In determining that nuisance does not protect plaintiffs, the court suggests that land use regulations are the appropriate means for addressing the harms.

## Florida Third District Court of Appeal

### *Fontainebleau Hotel Corp. v. Forty-Five Twenty-Five, Inc.*[4]

### 1959

PER CURIAM.

This is an interlocutory appeal from an order temporarily enjoining the appellants from continuing with the construction of a fourteen-story addition to the Fontainebleau Hotel, owned and operated by the appellants. Appellee, plaintiff below, owns the Eden Roc Hotel, which was constructed in 1955, about a year after the Fontainebleau, and adjoins the Fontainebleau on the north. Both are luxury hotels, facing the Atlantic Ocean. The proposed addition to Fontainebleau is being constructed twenty feet from its north property line, 130 feet from the mean high water mark of the Atlantic Ocean, and 76 feet 8 inches from the ocean bulkhead line. The 14-story tower will extend 160 feet above grade in height and is 416 feet long from east to west. During the winter months, from around two o'clock in the afternoon for the remainder of the day, the shadow of the addition will extend over the cabana, swimming pool, and sunbathing areas of the Eden Roc, which are located in the southern portion of its property.

In this action, plaintiff-appellee sought to enjoin the defendants-appellants from proceeding with the construction of the addition to the Fontainebleau (it appears to have been roughly eight stories high at the time suit was filed), alleging that the construction would interfere with the light and air on the beach in front of the Eden Roc and cast a shadow of such size as to render the beach wholly unfitted for the use and enjoyment of its guests, to the irreparable injury of the plaintiff; further, that the construction of such addition on the north side of defendants' property, rather than the south side, was actuated by malice and ill will on the part of the defendants' president toward the plaintiff's president; and that the construction was in violation of a building ordinance requiring a 100-foot setback from the ocean. It was also alleged that the construction would interfere with the easements of light and air enjoyed by plaintiff and its predecessors in title for more than twenty years and "impliedly granted by virtue of the acts of the plaintiff's predecessors in title, as well as under the common law and the express recognition of such rights by virtue of Chapter 9837, Laws of Florida 1923 * * *." Some attempt was also made to allege an easement by implication in favor of the plaintiff's property, as the dominant, and against the defendants' property, as the servient, tenement.

The defendants' answer denied the material allegations of the complaint ... .

The chancellor heard considerable testimony on the issues made by the complaint and the answer and, as noted, entered a temporary injunction restraining the defendants from continuing with the construction of the addition. His reason for so doing was stated by him, in a memorandum opinion, as follows:

> In granting the temporary injunction in this case the Court wishes to make several things very clear. The ruling is not based on any alleged presumptive title nor prescriptive right of the plaintiff to light and air nor is it based on any deed restrictions nor recorded plats in the title of the plaintiff nor of the defendant nor of any plat of record. It is not based

> on any zoning ordinance nor on any provision of the building code of the City of Miami Beach nor on the decision of any court, nisi prius or appellate. It is based solely on the proposition that no one has a right to use his property to the injury of another. In this case it is clear from the evidence that the proposed use by the Fontainebleau will materially damage the Eden Roc. There is evidence indicating that the construction of the proposed annex by the Fontainebleau is malicious or deliberate for the purpose of injuring the Eden Roc, but it is scarcely sufficient, standing alone, to afford a basis for equitable relief.

This is indeed a novel application of the maxim *sic utere tuo ut alienum non laedas*. This maxim does not mean that one must never use his own property in such a way as to do any injury to his neighbor. *Beckman v. Marshall*, 85 So. 2d 552 (Fla. 1956). It means only that one must use his property so as not to injure the lawful *rights* of another. *Cason v. Florida Power Co.*, 76 So. 535 (Fla. 1917). In *Reaver v. Martin Theatres*, 52 So. 2d 682, 683 (Fla. 1951), under this maxim, it was stated that "it is well settled that a property owner may put his own property to any reasonable and lawful use, so long as he does not thereby deprive the adjoining landowner of any right of enjoyment of his property *which is recognized and protected by law, and so long as his use is not such a one as the law will pronounce a nuisance*." [Emphasis added]. No American decision has been cited, and independent research has revealed none, in which it has been held that—in the absence of some contractual or statutory obligation—a landowner has a legal right to the free flow of light and air across the adjoining land of his neighbor. Even at common law, the landowner had no legal right, in the absence of an easement or uninterrupted use and enjoyment for a period of 20 years, to unobstructed light and air from the adjoining land. *Blumberg v. Weiss*, 17 A.2d 823 (N.J. 1941); 1 Am. Jur. *Adjoining Landowners* § 51. And the English doctrine of "ancient lights" has been unanimously repudiated in this country. 1 Am. Jur. *Adjoining Landowners* § 49, p. 533; *Lynch v. Hill*, 6 A.2d 614 (Del. Ch. 1939), overruling *Clawson v. Primrose*, 4 Del. Ch. 643 (Del. Ch. 1873).

There being, then, no legal right to the free flow of light and air from the adjoining land, it is universally held that where a structure serves a useful and beneficial purpose, it does not give rise to a cause of action, either for damages or for an injunction under the maxim *sic utere tuo ut alienum non laedas*, even though it causes injury to another by cutting off the light and air and interfering with the view that would otherwise be available over adjoining land in its natural state, regardless of the fact that the structure may have been erected partly for spite. See the cases collected in the annotation in *Hornsby v. Smith*, 13 S.E.2d 20 (Ga. 1941); 1 Am. Jur. *Adjoining Landowners* § 54, p. 536; *Taliaferro v. Salyer*, 328 P.2d 799 (Cal. Dist. Ct. App. 1958); *Musumeci v. Leonardo*, 75 A.2d 175 (R.I. 1950); *Harrison v. Langlinais*, 312 S.W.2d 286 (Tex. Civ. App. 1958); *Granberry v. Jones*, 216 S.W.2d 721 (Tenn. 1949); *Letts v. Kessler*, 42 N.E. 765 (Ohio 1896); *Kulbitsky v. Zimnoch*, 77 A.2d 14 (Md. 1950); *Southern Advertising Co. v. Sherman*, 308 S.W.2d 491 (Tenn. Ct. App. 1957).

We see no reason for departing from this universal rule. If, as contended on behalf of plaintiff, public policy demands that a landowner in the Miami Beach area refrain from constructing buildings on his premises that will cast a shadow on the adjoining premises, an amendment of its comprehensive planning and zoning ordinance, applicable to the public as a whole, is the means by which such purpose should be achieved … . [T]o change the universal rule—and the custom followed in this state since its inception—that adjoining landowners have an equal right under the law to build to the line of their respective tracts and to such a height as is desired by them (in the absence, of course, of building restrictions or regulations) amounts, in our opinion, to judicial legislation. As stated in *Musumeci v. Leonardo*, [75 A.2d at 177], "So use your own as not to injure another's property is, indeed, a sound and salutary principle for the promotion of justice, but it may not and should not be applied so as gratuitously to confer upon an adjacent property owner incorporeal rights incidental to his ownership of land which the law does not sanction." ...

Since it affirmatively appears that the plaintiff has not established a cause of action against the defendants by reason of the structure here in question, the order granting a temporary injunction should be and it is hereby reversed with directions to dismiss the complaint.

Reversed with directions.

HORTON, C. J., and CARROLL, CHAS., J., and CABOT, TED, Associate Judge concur.

## Private nuisance and public nuisance

A nuisance may be a private nuisance or a public nuisance. A private nuisance causes harm to one or a few property owners and is addressed through a civil action.[5] A public nuisance, however, is a use of land that causes harm broadly to all or many members of a community.[6] If a use of land is a public nuisance, it may also constitute a private nuisance.[7]

Private nuisance and public nuisance also differ in who has the ability to sue to redress the wrong. The harm caused by a public nuisance will be common to many people.[8] But, to have standing to redress a public nuisance, a plaintiff must suffer some harm that is different in *kind* and in *degree* from the public in general.[9] Not every harmed person can sue to redress a public nuisance.

Further, a private nuisance requires the plaintiff to have suffered an interference with his or her use of land.[10] Therefore, the plaintiff must have an interest in land.[11] A plaintiff in a public nuisance case does not need to have an interest in land.

Finally, some statutes and local government ordinances define certain uses of land as public nuisances.[12] As a result, a governmental enforcement action is sometimes a way to remedy a public nuisance.

### Florida Supreme Court

### *Page v. Niagara Chem. Div. of Food Mach. & Chem. Corp.*[13]

### 1953

SEBRING, Justice.

The plaintiffs below have appealed from an order granting the defendant's motion to dismiss their second amended complaint.

As shown by the complaint, this is a suit instituted by 20 employees of the Atlantic Coast Line Railroad Company employed at the A. C. L. export yard in Jacksonville, Florida, to restrain the defendant from operating its plant lying adjacent to the export yard in such a manner as to cause or permit dangerous insecticide chemicals, dusts, stenches, odors and noxious gases to escape therefrom and descend upon and injure plaintiffs at their place of work.

As the basis for the relief prayed the complaint alleges, in substance, that the plaintiffs are long-time employees of the Railroad Company and by reason thereof have acquired valuable "seniority rights"; that the A. C. L. yard is a particularly desirable place to work and only employees with long service are enabled to work there; that in its plant adjacent to the railroad yard the defendant manufactures various chemicals and insecticides, the dusts of some of which when expelled into the air are dangerous, poisonous, toxic and harmful to the plaintiffs; that these conditions, although not continuous, frequently exist with the result that the dusts descend into the railroad yard at which the plaintiffs work and cause personal injury to the workmen. The prayer of the complaint is for a decree declaring that the defendant is guilty, either of maintaining a private nuisance which the plaintiffs are entitled to have abated, or of maintaining a public nuisance which causes the plaintiffs such special injury and damage as to entitle them to maintain an action for abatement and damages for personal injuries.

We think it is plain that the plaintiffs have not alleged a case entitling them to an injunction on the "private-nuisance theory." As we understand their claim it is based upon the proposition that by reason of their seniority rights, which have given them the privilege of choosing as their place of employment the A. C. L. export yard, "each of said plaintiffs is a lawful occupant of said Atlantic Coast Line export yard during their working hours." We cannot accept the thesis. While the plaintiffs, as employees of the railroad company, may have a cause of action for personal injuries resulting from the operations of the defendant upon adjacent property, their assertion that they are "occupants" of the Coast Line property during working hours is not sufficient to show that they have such an interest in or relation to their employer's property as would entitle them to maintain a suit to enjoin the defendant's operation as for a private nuisance. *See* 39 Am. Jur. *Nuisances* § 9; Restatement of the Law of Torts §§ 822, 823, ch. 40, pp. 219–20; *Prosser on Torts*, pp. 575–77. "The chancellor's opinion, we think, lays down the correct rule as to the character of the estate the complainant must have to entitle him to injunctive relief against a nuisance." * * * "The complainant here owns no interest in the real property affected. * * * He is a mere employee occupant at will * * *. A person must have some estate, be it ever so little, such as that of a tenant at will, or on sufferance, to be a tenant. Occupation as servant, or licensee, does not make one a tenant. *Presby v. Benjamin*, 62 N.E. 430 (N.Y. 1902)." *Reber v. Illinois Cent. R. Co.*, 138 So. 574, 577 (Miss. 1932) … .

As to the right of the plaintiffs to enjoin the defendant upon the theory of the maintenance of a public nuisance, the complaint is equally deficient. To entitle private individuals to maintain actions to enjoin public nuisances, it must be shown that they have sustained special or peculiar injuries different in *kind*, not merely in *degree*, from the injury to the public at large. *Brown v. Florida Chautauqua Association*, 52 So. 802 (Fla. 1910); *Deering v. Martin*, 116 So. 54 (Fla. 1928); *Biscayne Co. v. Martin*, 116 So. 66 (Fla. 1927). The plaintiffs have failed to make such showing. The same fumes, dust and gases which the plaintiffs allege are objectionable to them, would also affect the members of the general public in that area, the pedestrians and motorists traveling in the district, and many other employees who spend their working hours in the area. The fact that plaintiffs might be affected to a greater degree would not, under the above decisions, entitle them to injunctive relief.

A private individual may sue to abate a public nuisance where, and only where, he suffers special injury from its maintenance different from that suffered by the public generally * * * because the public wrong must be redressed at the suit of the state. * * *

*Cooley on Torts* § 447 (4th ed., vol. 3). "To prevent multiplicity of actions, promote justice, and secure the public tranquility, courts refuse to entertain private actions" in such cases. *Woods v. Rock Hill Fertilizer Co.*, 86 S.E. 817, 819 (N.C. 1915). Compare sec. Fla. Stat. § 64.11(1951), *with F.S.A. National Container Corporation v. State ex rel. Stockton*, 189 So. 4 (Fla. 1939).

Accordingly, the decree appealed from should be affirmed.

It is so ordered.

ROBERTS, C. J., and TERRELL and MATHEWS, JJ., concur.

## Reasonable man doctrine

A use of land must be unreasonable to constitute a nuisance. The *reasonable man doctrine* and the *reasonable use doctrine* are two measures of reasonableness.

The reasonable man doctrine is a limit on the concept of nuisance that looks to the sensitivity of the party whom the nuisance bothers. In circumstances where that party is unusually sensitive, the complained-of action will not be a nuisance, even though it is a use that annoys or disturbs another person.

Under the reasonable man doctrine, evaluate whether that complaining person is an ordinary person—with a reasonable disposition, in ordinary health, and possessing the average and normal sensibilities—or is a person of delicate sensibility—who is particularly sensitive to annoyance or disturbance.

If the bothered person is of normal sensitivity, then the reasonable man doctrine will not preclude the land use from being a nuisance. If the person is more sensitive than is typical, then the reasonable man doctrine makes the land use less likely to be a nuisance.

## Florida Supreme Court

### *Beckman v. Marshall*[14]

### 1956

DICKINSON, Associate Justice, and DREW, Chief Justice.

This is a squabble between two neighbors.

Plaintiffs below, operators of a guest house on Ridgewood Avenue in Daytona Beach (four-lane U.S. Highway No. 1) brought this action against the four defendants alleging that they were maintaining a private nuisance on their property in that they were conducting a day nursery thereon five days a week for children from two to six years of age from about 8:00 a.m. to about 5:00 p.m ...

[P]laintiffs bought this property in 1940 and have operated it as a guest house ever since ... . No one other than the plaintiff is complaining. As a matter of fact, the owner of the guest house on the other side of defendants' nursery testified that she was not annoyed by it. Plaintiffs are elderly people ... . [T]he matter boils down to whether this is a private nuisance or not.

From the testimony it appears that these children begin to arrive about 8:00 a.m. and leave about 5:00 p.m., taking a nap after being fed their lunch. The school here is well supervised by the defendant and an assistant, that is as well supervised as an institution of this kind can be. The playing of the children outside is limited and supervised. Their actions and singing inside is supervised and everything that can be done is being done to minimize the noise. Since this is an unrestricted area so far as zoning against schools is concerned, the school would have to qualify as a private nuisance for equity to intervene. True, the children make a certain amount of noise, but there must be some relationship of their noise to the surrounding noises for equity to act. It is inconceivable to see how ... the pitter patter of little feet and the noises of children singing and at play, even though there may be twenty-five of them, can become a nuisance to plaintiffs and be enjoinable in a court of equity.

The following language from the case of *Antonik v. Chamberlain*, 78 N.E.2d 752, 758 (Ohio Ct. App. 1947), which we hereby adopt and approve, is particularly applicable and we think largely determinative of the questions involved in this case:

> Nuisance, in law, for the most part consists in so using one's property as to injure the land or some incorporeal right of one's neighbor. An act which is wrongful in itself may be adjudged wrongful before it is committed, as well as afterwards. But an act which is in itself rightful, and may become wrongful only because of some effect which it produces, is generally not proved wrongful by a priori reasoning. Even when it appears that a given act or acts done in a certain way are wrongful, it does not follow that some part of the

act or acts may not be rightfully done, or even that the entire operation may not be later done in such a way as to be rightful. It is often found that the damage to the defendant which the interference of a court, through injunction, would cause, will be out of all proportion to the damage to the plaintiff or to the public in general.

The law of nuisance plays between two antithetical extremes: The principle that every person is entitled to use his property for any purpose that he sees fit, and the opposing principle that everyone is bound to use his property in such a manner as not to injure the property or rights of his neighbor. For generations, courts, in their tasks of judging, have ruled on these extremes according to the wisdom of the day, and many have recognized that the contemporary view of public policy shifts from generation to generation.

The necessities of a social state, especially in a great industrial community, compel the rule that no one has absolute freedom in the use of his property, because he must be restrained in his use by the existence of equal rights in his neighbor to the use of his property. This rule has sometimes been erroneously interpreted as a prohibition of all use of one's property which annoys or disturbs his neighbor in the enjoyment of his property. The question for decision is not simply whether the neighbor is annoyed or disturbed, but is whether there is an injury to a legal right of the neighbor. The law of private nuisance is a law of degree; it generally turns on the factual question whether the use to which the property is put is a reasonable use under the circumstances, and whether there is "an appreciable, substantial, tangible injury resulting in actual, material, physical discomfort, and not merely a tendency to injure. It must be real and not fanciful or imaginary, or such as results merely in a trifling annoyance, inconvenience, or discomfort." * * *

It is not everything in the nature of a nuisance which is prohibited. There are many acts which the owner of land may lawfully do, although it brings annoyance, discomfort, or injury to his neighbor, which are damnum absque injuria * * * ... .

All systems of jurisprudence recognize the requirement of compromises in the social state. Members of society must submit to annoyances consequent upon the reasonable use of property. "Sic Utere tuo ut alienum non laedas" is an old maxim which has a broad application. If such rule were held to mean that one must never use his own property in such a way as to do any injury to his neighbor or his property, it could not be enforced in civilized society. People who live in organized communities must of necessity suffer some damage, inconvenience and annoyance from their neighbors. For these annoyances, inconveniences and damages, they are generally compensated by the advantages incident to living in a civilized state.

We are not unmindful of the fact that this record does show the operation of the nursery to be offensive and annoying to the appellees. This, however, is not the test. Obviously the appellees, so to speak, are simply allergic to children and the noises they make. In dealing with the question of what constitutes a nuisance, the characteristics and temperament of the affected person or persons must be taken into consideration. The test to be applied is the effect of the condition complained of on ordinary persons with a reasonable disposition in ordinary health and possessing the average and normal sensibilities. It is a well-settled principle of law that:

> The test is not what the effect of the matters complained of would be on persons of delicate or dainty habits of living, or of fanciful or fastidious tastes; or on persons who are delicate, or invalids, afflicted with disease, bodily ills, or abnormal physical conditions; or on persons who are of nervous temperament, or peculiarly sensitive to annoyance

> or disturbance of the character complained of; or on persons who use their land for purposes which require exceptional freedom from deleterious influences. 66 C.J.S. *Nuisances* § 18(c), p. 765 … .

Measured by the above standards, the decree appealed from is erroneous and is hereby reversed with instructions to dismiss the cause at the cost of the plaintiffs below.

TERRELL and THORNAL, JJ., concur.

## Reasonable use doctrine

Another doctrine that limits the concept of nuisance is the reasonable use doctrine. Unlike the reasonable man doctrine—which focuses on the reasonableness of the person who is bothered by a particular use—the reasonable use doctrine focuses on the reasonableness of the use of the property.[15]

One must determine the reasonableness of a use of property from the circumstances of each instance. The following are criteria courts might evaluate to determine whether a use of property is a reasonable use:[16]

- whether the person conducting the alleged nuisance is using due care and skill (i.e. taking reasonable actions to minimize annoyance);
- whether the alleged nuisance is allowed under applicable zoning regulations;
- whether the alleged nuisance is similar to prevailing uses in the area;
- whether the alleged nuisance is consistent with an existing policy established by the community (e.g. a local government comprehensive plan or economic development plan);
- whether the alleged nuisance is beneficial to the local economy (e.g. does it provide jobs or a necessary good or service?); and
- whether the alleged nuisance is consistent with prevailing social mores (e.g. opinions on environmental or social equity matters).

The reasonable use doctrine considers reasonableness broadly and none of the criteria above is necessarily dispositive. This includes whether the law allows the use that is potentially a nuisance.[17]

## Florida First District Court of Appeal

### *Lee v. Florida Pub. Util. Co.*[18]

### 1962

WIGGINTON, Judge.

[The court explained that this was an appeal by the Plaintiffs' after the trial court directed a verdict for the Defendant] … Plaintiffs' action is at law for recovery of damages suffered as a result of a private nuisance alleged to have been created and now maintained by defendant. The evidence, when considered in a light most favorable to plaintiff, reveals the following factual situation.

Plaintiffs own and operate a fuel oil business in a building which also includes their home. This property is located in a section of Fernandina devoted essentially to commercial enterprises. Located within the area adjacent or in close proximity to plaintiffs' property is a lumber yard, an ice plant, a plumbing shop, an upholstery business and the electrical generating plant owned by defendant. Although not zoned as such, the area may properly be characterized as commercial or industrial.

Plaintiffs have lived upon and operated their business at its present location for a period of approximately eight years. During this time defendant has operated its electrical generating plant in a large building located on property adjacent to that owned by plaintiffs. This plant generates electricity which supplies the community of Fernandina. Although the generating units located within the building owned by defendant created a certain amount of noise, they have never become particularly objectionable to those living and maintaining businesses in that area. The generating units are powered by diesel fuel, the fumes from which are emitted from a tall chimney or smoke stack of sufficient height to carry them off into the atmosphere, and have never proved offensive.

Commencing approximately three years prior to the filing of this action defendant installed on a spur railroad track located between its plant and plaintiffs' property three railroad boxcars, each containing an electrical generating unit operated by diesel fuel. Since their installation these units have been operated on a constant twenty-four hour a day basis. The fumes from the fuel used to power these units are emitted from openings in the top of the boxcars through relatively short smoke stacks. The noise resulting from the operation of these mobile units is so intense that plaintiff is unable to transact business with his customers in a normal fashion, for in order to communicate it is necessary that they shout at each other in order to be heard. The noise is so loud that plaintiff and his family are unable to sleep at nights, which condition has had an adverse effect upon their health. At certain periods of day and night the odors from the fumes exhausted by the mobile units become extremely strong and highly noxious. The operation of the generating units causes the surrounding land to vibrate in such a marked degree as to shake the springs of the beds on which plaintiff and his family sleep, as well as rattle the windows in the house and the dishes in the cupboard. Plaintiffs complained to defendant concerning the foregoing conditions created by its operation of the mobile generating units, and was told that steps would be taken to minimize the noise, vibration and odors resulting therefrom. Despite such request the conditions above enumerated have continued uninterruptedly.

It is appellants' position that under the applicable principles of law relating to the creation and maintenance of a private nuisance, the foregoing facts are sufficient to establish at least a prima facie case entitling plaintiff to no less than nominal damages. It is appellee's position that this evidence fails to make out a prima facie case of unreasonable use of its property on the one hand, or unreasonable harm to plaintiffs on the other, and hence entitled appellee to the directed verdict on which is based the judgment appealed.

It appears to be well settled that if one voluntarily elects to live in an industrial area, he cannot complain of noise, noxious odors or any other unpleasant factors that may arise from the normal operation of businesses in the area merely because they may interfere with his personal satisfaction or aesthetic enjoyment. It is said that no one can move into an area given over to foundries and boiler shops and demand the quiet of a farm.

The test to be applied in determining whether one operating a business in an industrial area is guilty of maintaining an actionable nuisance is the rule of reasonableness. As said by the Supreme Court of Florida in the *Cason* case,

> All property is owned and used subject to the laws of the land. Under our system of government property may be used as its owner desires within the limitations imposed by law for the protection of the public and private rights of others. Those who own real estate may use it as desired so long as the rights of others are not thereby invaded. And there is no such invasion when the use is authorized by law and is reasonable with reference to the rights of others. Legality and reasonableness in the use of property, as such use affects the public and private rights of others, mark the limitations of the owner's rights. The reasonableness of the use of property by its owner must of necessity be determined from the facts and circumstances of particular cases as they arise, by

> the application of appropriate provisions or principles of law and the dictates of mutual or reciprocal justice. Property owned by one party may be so situated and conditioned with reference to the property of another as that the rights of ownership and the uses of such properties are interdependent or correlative. In such cases each owner should so reasonably use his property as not to injure the property rights of others.
>
> 76 So. 535, 536 (Fla. 1917)

In *Beckman*, 85 So. 2d 552 (Fla. 1956), the Supreme Court quoted with approval from *Antonik v. Chamberlain*, 78 N.E.2d 752, 758 (Ohio Ct. App. 1947), as follows: "The test of the permissible use of one's own land is not whether the use or the act causes injury to his neighbor's property, or that the injury was the natural consequence, or that the act is in the nature of a nuisance, but the inquiry is, Was the act or use a reasonable exercise of the dominion which the owner of property has by virtue of his ownership over his property? having regard to all interests affected, his own and those of his neighbors, and having in view, also, public policy." * * *

In emphasizing the test of reasonableness the Third District Court of Appeal in the *Barfield Instrument Corporation* case, 102 So. 2d 740, 741 (Fla. 3d DCA 1958) said:

> A lawful business may be conducted in such an unreasonable manner, that as a result thereof, a neighbor is deprived of the free use or enjoyment of his adjoining property. * * * We are also cognizant of the fact that in an industrial area a reasonable use of property often places some burden upon the property of one's neighbor, and that these burdens must be considered carefully in the light of the circumstances presented in order to determine the reasonableness of the particular use. *Beckman v. Marshall*, 85 So. 2d 552 (Fla. 1956). The reasonableness of each use must be determined from the circumstances of each case. *Reaver v. Martin Theatres of Florida*, 52 So. 2d 682 (Fla. 1951); *McClosky v. Martin*, 56 So. 2d 916 (Fla. 1951). * * *

Based upon the foregoing authorities it is our opinion that the evidence adduced by plaintiff was wholly sufficient to create a jury question as to whether defendant's use of its property was reasonable under the circumstances. It would be for the jury to say whether defendant had done everything reasonably required of it to minimize the noise, noxious odors and vibration resulting from its operation of the mobile generating units maintained by it. It would be the jury's further prerogative to determine whether defendant's use of its property is unreasonable under the circumstances, and whether such use has resulted in injury of damage to plaintiff for which he is entitled to compensation. Since the verdict in this case was directed in favor of defendant at the conclusion of plaintiffs' evidence, defendant has not yet availed itself of the opportunity of showing that its use of its property is reasonable under all the circumstances, and that such use results in no unreasonable harm or injury to plaintiffs. Plaintiffs' evidence having made out a prima facie case of nuisance, the court erred in directing the verdict on which it based its final judgment ... .

The judgment appealed is reversed and the cause remanded for a new trial.

Reversed.

CARROLL, DONALD K., C. J., and STURGIS, J., concur.

**Box 2.1 Practice problem: Dumme Ahze Rocks, Inc.**

Winston Dumme and Carl Ahze moved to South County in 1942. They purchased land and founded Dumme Ahze Rocks, Inc., a rock-mining business. The ground in South County is limestone with large amounts of silica deposited by several iterations of the sea rising and receding over South County across millennia. This large amount of silica makes the limestone in South County harder than most other limestone and ideal for the construction of roads.

The state department of transportation's standard agreement with road construction contractors requires contractors to use limestone rock from South County in road construction "whenever feasible." Currently, about one-half of all road beds constructed in the state use South County limestone. Roads built on limestone from other mines in the state deteriorate more quickly and require more expensive repairs than roads built on South County limestone.

Mining limestone entails detonating explosives and digging with heavy machinery. These activities have several effects which are noticeable away from a quarry. For example, the aquifer in South County is shallow. Rock-mining pits hold groundwater that flows between the pit and the surrounding ground. The explosives pollute this water. In fact, the South County utility company has detected chemicals used in explosives at the South County wellfield more than 20 miles from an active mining operation. Also, the explosions and the machinery create noise and vibrations.

The Bureau of Prisons operates a low security corrections institute on land adjacent to a rock quarry owned and operated by Dumme Ahze Rocks, Inc. The rock mine impacts the corrections institute in several ways. First, the water from wells at the corrections institute has a chemical odor and a metallic taste caused by the pollution from the nearby mine. Second, people at the corrections institute can hear noises from the quarry that are sometimes so loud they must shout to one another in order to communicate. Finally, because the corrections institute is the closest neighbor to the quarry, people at the corrections institute can feel vibrations from the quarry that people on other properties cannot feel. These vibrations disrupt the sleep of many inmates at the corrections institute.

Gaia Law Center is a not-for-profit legal services provider focused on environmental justice issues. It files a lawsuit against Dumme Ahze Rocks, Inc. on behalf of the inmates at the corrections institute alleging that the rock mine is a nuisance. Evaluate the inmates' claim. Include in your response whether Gaia Law Center should allege the rock mine is a public or a private nuisance.

## Notes

1 *Nuisance*, *Black's Law Dictionary* (11th edn 2019) (mentioning that "Nuisance is really a field of tortious liability rather than a single type of tortious conduct: the feature which gives it unity is the interest invaded—that of the use and enjoyment of land").

2 *Id.* (defining nuisance as "[a] condition, activity, situation (such as a loud noise or foul odor) that interferes with the use or enjoyment of property ... Liability might or might not arise from the condition or situation").

3 32 So. 2d 727 (Fla. 1947) (en banc).

4 114 So. 2d 357 (Fla. 3d DCA 1959).

5 *Nuisance*, *Black's Law Dictionary* (11th edn 2019) (commenting that this nuisance "affects a private right not common to the public or causes a special injury to a person"); *see* 38 Fla. Jur. 2d *Nuisances* § 6 (2020) (stating that since a private nuisance "produces damages to one or a few persons ... as such, [it] must be redressed by private action").

6 *Nuisance*, *Black's Law Dictionary* (11th edn 2019) (highlighting that this is also termed *common nuisance*).

7 38 Fla. Jur. 2d *Nuisances* § 5 (2020) ("Often, a nuisance is both private and public").

8 *Id.* (stating that "[t]he damage resulting from a public nuisance is common to the whole community").

9 *See* Brown v. Fla. Chautauqua Ass'n, 52 So. 802, 804 (Fla. 1910) (explaining the rationale for the special injury standing rule).

10 38 Fla. Jur. 2d *Nuisances* § 6 (2020) (summarizing that a private nuisance "is a wrong only to those who have property rights and privileges in the land").

11 *See* City of Lakeland v. Douglass, 197 So. 467, 469 (Fla. 1940) (concluding that in a suit for damages the plaintiff only must show possession and enjoyment of the property at the time of the alleged tortious act).
12 *See, e.g.,* Fla. Stat. ch. 823.
13 68 So. 2d 382 (Fla. 1953).
14 85 So. 2d 552 (Fla. 1956).
15 *See* 38 Fla. Jur. 2d *Nuisances* § 6 (2020).
16 *See* 58 Am. Jur. 2d *Nuisances* § 59 (2020); *see also* Restatement (Second) of Torts § 827 (Am. L. Inst. 1979).
17 *See* Cason v. Fla. Power Co., 76 So. 535 (Fla. 1917) (holding that explicit federal government permission to use land a certain way is not necessarily a defense to nuisance).
18 145 So. 2d 299 (Fla. 1st DCA 1962).

# 3 Local government land use powers

## Police powers

Most Americans are generally familiar with the relationship between the several states and the United States. That is, each state is an independent government that has ceded some power to the Federal Government for the purpose of joining the United States.

The Tenth Amendment to the U.S. Constitution says that "[t]he powers not delegated to the United States by the Constitution, nor prohibited by it to the States, are reserved to the States respectively, or to the people."[1] This amendment is the general rule for determining whether a state government or the federal government (or both) may exercise a particular power.

One power the U.S. Constitution does not delegate from the states to the Federal Government is the police power. The police power is "[t]he inherent and plenary power of a sovereign to make all laws necessary and proper to preserve the public security, order, health, morality, and justice."[2] This power is broad and justifies a variety of state actions, including land use regulation. The Supreme Court famously commented on the wide breadth of the police power in the 1954 case *Berman v. Parker*:

> An attempt to define [the police power's] reach or trace its outer limits is fruitless ... . Public safety, public health, morality, peace and quiet, law and order—these are some of the more conspicuous examples of the traditional application of the police power to municipal affairs. Yet they merely illustrate the scope of the power and do not delimit it ... . The concept of the public welfare is broad and inclusive ... . The values it represents are spiritual as well as physical, aesthetic as well as monetary. It is within the power of the legislature to determine that the community should be beautiful as well as healthy, spacious as well as clean, well-balanced as well as carefully patrolled. In the present case, the Congress and its authorized agencies have made determinations that take into account a wide variety of values. It is not for us to reappraise them. If those who govern the District of Columbia decide that the Nation's Capital should be beautiful as well as sanitary, there is nothing in the Fifth Amendment that stands in the way.[3]

## Dillon's Rule

While the police power is the authority that allows government to regulate the use of land, that power is inherent to states, not to local governments. Understanding how local governments exercise the police power requires consideration of Dillon's Rule, which reads as follows:

> It is a general and undisputed proposition of law that a municipal corporation possesses and can exercise the following powers, and no others: First, those granted in express words; second, those necessarily or fairly implied in or incident to the powers expressly granted;

third, those essential to the declared objects and purposes of the corporation—not simply convenient, but indispensable.[4]

Florida courts have adopted Dillon's Rule and given guidance that it be applied to the benefit of the rights of citizens, not of local governments.

> The doctrines are well established in the state relating to municipal corporations that the existence of authority for a municipality to act cannot be assumed. If a reasonable doubt exists as to a particular power, it should be resolved against the city … . Any ambiguity or doubt as to the extent of a power attempted to be exercised by a city out of the usual range or which may affect the common law right of a citizen should be resolved against the city.[5]

When determining whether a state has delegated authority to a local government, first identify the state law—called an enabling statute—that grants powers from the state to the local government. Then, review that enabling statute using Dillon's Rule to determine whether the state has actually delegated the specific power that the local government is attempting to exercise.

### *Home rule*

While Dillon's Rule limits local governments' abilities to act independently of their respective states, many states—through their constitutions or through legislative acts—have broadly delegated power to their municipalities. *Home rule* is the name for the circumstance in which a state has broadly delegated power to its local governments.[6]

Note that this delegation of authority from the state to its local governments is not an *alternative* to Dillon's Rule. Rather, home rule is a *condition under* Dillon's Rule. Always use Dillon's Rule to evaluate a delegation of power from a state to a local government.

## Model state enabling acts

By the first decades of the twentieth century, many state governments had adopted enabling statutes that delegated some police powers to local governments for the purposes of regulating land use. Believing that uniform rules on land use would benefit the economy and encourage good city planning, the U.S. Commerce Department developed model state-enabling statutes named the Standard State Zoning Enabling Act and the Standard City Planning Enabling Act.[7] These model acts were not legislation themselves. Recall that states possess police powers and may grant these powers to their municipalities. The Commerce Department, a part of the Federal Government, drafted these model acts. The Commerce Department intended these documents to be examples for the states to follow, not federal laws.

The model acts established at least two characteristics of land use regulation that still define the way local governments regulate the use of land today. First, the model acts established zoning (or dividing communities into different districts based upon the uses of land allowed in each district) as the principal tool of land use regulation.[8] Today, zoning is so ubiquitous that making use-segregation the basic component of city planning feels as natural as making driver convenience the basic component of transportation planning. Before the twentieth century, however, use-segregated communities were as new an idea as a transportation system dependent on the automobile.

Second, the model acts established a two-tiered regulatory process. The two tiers are, first, planning—an action that results in the drafting of a comprehensive plan—and, second, creating more detailed land development regulations to implement the comprehensive plan.[9] This two-step process has had implications on procedural due process which the drafters of the model acts likely did not anticipate and which this text will address in greater detail.

## Florida is a home rule state

The Florida Constitution and Florida Statutes generally grant broad powers to the local governments most directly involved in regulating land use: cities and counties. The specifics of this delegation, however, are slightly different for cities and counties.

### *Home rule for cities*

Cities, also called municipalities, are local governments the state may create. Florida has 410 cities ranging in population from eight people to more than 800,000 people.[10] Only some land in Florida is within a municipality.

The Florida Constitution states:

> Municipalities shall have governmental, corporate and proprietary powers to enable them to conduct municipal government, perform municipal functions and render municipal services, and may exercise any power for municipal purposes except as otherwise provided by law.[11]

This language is a broad delegation of power from the state to its municipalities. Therefore, under the Florida Constitution, Florida cities have home rule authority.

### *Home rule for counties*

Counties are political subdivisions of the state. Florida has 67 counties and all land in the state is within a county. Of these 67 counties, 20 are *charter counties*, meaning a locally adopted charter sets out the organization and powers of county government.[12]

The Florida Constitution grants home-rule authority to charter counties, but not to non-charter counties.[13] However, the Florida Legislature has granted home-rule authority to *all* Florida counties: "The legislative and governing body of a county shall have the power to carry on county government."[14] Further, "[t]he provisions of this section shall be liberally construed in order to effectively carry out the purpose of this section and to secure for the counties the broad exercise of home rule powers authorized by the State Constitution."[15]

Still, charter counties have a slightly different suite of powers than non-charter counties. Specifically, a charter county's charter may authorize the county to regulate some activities on a countywide basis. In this circumstance, "[t]he charter shall provide which shall prevail in the event of conflict between county and municipal ordinances."[16] Essentially—if the charter so stipulates for a particular matter—a charter county can pre-empt municipal regulation.

The Seminole County charter provides an example of when a municipal ordinance is pre-empted by a county ordinance. The charter expressly defines "rural areas" and gives the county land use authority over those areas.[17] The charter explicitly makes this authority exclusive and supersedes all municipal ordinances to the extent of conflict.[18]

### *Limits of home rule authority*

In addition to the grants of home rule authority from the state of Florida to Florida local governments, other provisions of Florida law retain some powers. An example is the power to tax, which Florida does not give liberally to cities or to counties.[19]

The state also routinely *pre-empts* both cities and counties by adopting laws on specific topics that supersede local government ordinances. This pre-emption may be *express* or *implied*.

> In Florida, a municipality is given broad authority to enact ordinances under its municipal home rule powers. Under its broad home rule powers, a municipality may legislate concurrently with the Legislature on any subject which has not been expressly preempted to the State. "Preemption essentially takes a topic or a field in which local government might otherwise establish appropriate local laws and reserves that topic for regulation exclusively by the legislature." "Express pre-emption requires a specific statement; the pre-emption cannot be made by implication nor by inference." However, "[t]he preemption need not be explicit [(i.e. it may be *implied*)] so long as it is clear that the legislature has clearly preempted local regulation of the subject."[20]

Further, "[i]mplied preemption occurs if a legislative scheme is so pervasive that it occupies the entire field, creating a danger of conflict between local and state laws."[21]

Finally, that Florida is a home rule state does not mean Florida's local governments have unfettered authority to regulate land use. To the contrary, this text is fundamentally an explanation of how (and whether) local governments may regulate the use of land.

### Box 3.1 Practice problem: Downtown Chic

The state in which Collegeborough is located does not have a general grant of police powers to its municipalities in its constitution. To allow its communities to adopt growth management legislation, therefore, the state has adopted zoning-enabling legislation that says, in its entirety:

> To protect public safety, local governments have the ability to encourage the most appropriate use of land, water, and resources within their jurisdictions. Through the process of comprehensive planning, local governments can improve the public safety by improving: efficiency of law enforcement and fire prevention; provision of transportation, water, sewerage, schools, parks, recreational facilities, and housing; and conservation of natural resources within their jurisdictions.

Having the authority to regulate the use of land, the City of Collegeborough solicited community input on what land use regulations it would adopt. The Collegeborough Downtown Association, a trade group of business owners in downtown Collegeborough, petitioned the city to adopt regulations regulating the building materials of new structures in downtown.

Most buildings in downtown are historic and are built of brick in traditional architectural styles. Several newer buildings, however, are made of cheaper materials, including metal siding on their exteriors. The Collegeborough Downtown Association expects that too many new structures that do not match the aesthetics of the older downtown structures will diminish the charm and character of downtown. In turn, they fear a decline in business.

Based on the request of the Collegeborough Downtown Association, the City of Collegeborough adopted a requirement that new buildings in downtown Collegeborough have brick facades. Concurrent with adoption of this rule, the city council made two findings. First, that new buildings with metal siding would harm the aesthetics of Collegeborough by diminishing the charm of downtown. And, second, that new buildings with metal sidings would harm the economy of Collegeborough by damaging the marketplace for downtown merchants.

After these rules were adopted, Chic Hampton, a downtown business owner who is not a member of the Collegeborough Downtown Association, applied to build a metal-clad building. Collegeborough denied Mr. Hampton's permit application citing the new ordinance. Mr. Hampton has sued, claiming that Collegeborough does not have the authority to regulate the type of siding on his building.

Evaluate Mr. Hampton's claim.

## Notes

1 U.S. Const. amend. X.
2 *Police Power, Black's Law Dictionary* (11th edn 2019).
3 Berman v. Parker, 348 U.S. 26, 32–3 (1954) (citations omitted)
4 John F. Dillon, *Commentaries on The Law of Municipal Corporations* § 89, at 115 (3rd edn 1881).
5 Loeb v. City of Jacksonville, 134 So. 205, 208 (Fla. 1931).
6 *See* Richard Briffault, *Home Rule and Local Political Innovation*, 22 J.L. & Pol. 1, 19 (2006) (mentioning the state can delegate power through enactment of a constitutional provision or statute).
7 Ruth Knack, Stuart Meck, & Israel Stollman, *The Real Story behind the Standard Planning and Zoning Acts of the 1920s*, 48 Land Use L. & Zoning Dig. 3, 3 (1996).
8 *Id.* at 5–6.
9 *See id.* at 8–9.
10 *Florida Is Her Cities*, Fla. League of Cities, Inc., www.floridaleagueofcities.com (last visited May 18, 2020).
11 Fla. Const. art. VIII, § 2(b).
12 *About Florida's Counties*, Fla. Assoc. of Cntys., www.fl-counties.com (last visited Aug. 5, 2020).
13 *See* Fla. Const. art. VIII, §§ 1(f), 1(g).
14 Fla. Stat. § 125.01(1).
15 *Id.* § 125.01(3)(b).
16 Fla. Const. art. VIII, § 1(g).
17 Seminole Cnty. Home Rule Charter art. V, § 5.2(A).
18 *Id.* § 5.2(D).
19 Fla. Const. art. VII, § 1(a).
20 City of Hollywood v. Mulligan, 934 So. 2d 1238, 1243 (Fla. 2006) (emphasis added) (citations omitted).
21 Santa Rosa Cnty. v. Gulf Power Co., 635 So. 2d 96, 101 (Fla. 1st DCA 1994).

# 4 Substantive due process

Due process is one limit on the power of state and local governments to regulate the use of land. The Florida Constitution, the Fifth Amendment to the U.S. Constitution, and the Fourteenth Amendment to the U.S. Constitution each contain a due process clause.

- The Florida constitution provides: "No person shall be deprived of ... property without due process of law."[1]
- The Fifth Amendment provides: "No person shall ... be deprived of ... property, without due process of law ... ."[2] This protection limits the power of the federal government, not of state and local governments.[3]
- And the Fourteenth Amendment provides: "No State shall ... deprive any person of ... property, without due process of law ... ."[4] This protection limits the power of all federal, state, and local governments.

Cases that discuss the due process limitations placed by the U.S. Constitution on land use regulation may refer to both, or to either of, the Fifth Amendment and the Fourteenth Amendment due process clauses.

Two kinds of due process exist: substantive due process and procedural due process. Generally, substantive due process sets limits on the *content or subject* of state and federal laws to "protect[] 'the full panoply of individual rights from unwarranted encroachment by the government.'"[5] In contrast, procedural due process governs *how governments administer* their laws to ensure fair treatment.[6]

Recall that the Standard State Zoning Enabling Act and the Standard City Planning Enabling Act established a two-tiered regulatory process. Under those model acts, local governments first engage in planning. Then, they implement plans through more specific regulations.

Florida courts recognize two kinds of land use decisions that generally mirror the separate *planning* and *implementing* activities. These two kinds of decisions have the names *legislative* and *quasi-judicial*. Whether the character of the decision made by a local government is in the nature of policy *formulation* or the nature of policy *implementation* determines whether the decision is legislative or quasi-judicial. Courts subject each kind of decision to a different standard of review and afford participants in each kind of hearing a different degree of procedural protection.

In this chapter, you will learn to associate substantive due process requirements with legislative land use decisions. Chapter 5 will associate procedural due process requirements with quasi-judicial land use decisions.

**Box 4.1 Connecting concepts to practice**

Knowing some local government nomenclature will help you connect the concept of due process to state and local government practices.

First, state laws are *statutes*. A significant Florida statute related to land use is the Community Planning Act, which is—among many other things—Florida's zoning-enabling legislation.

Second, local government laws are *ordinances*. A local government's comprehensive plan and implementing regulations are ordinances. Different local governments give their comprehensive plans different names. For example, Miami-Dade County calls its comprehensive plan the Comprehensive Development Master Plan and the city of Miami calls its comprehensive plan the Miami Comprehensive Neighborhood Plan. Similarly, local governments refer to their implementing regulations by different names. Common names are: land development regulations, land use code, unified land development code, and zoning ordinance.

Finally, local governments do not need to adopt an ordinance to make a decision. And local governments may make many land use decisions which do not involve changing their comprehensive plans or land development regulations.

Generally, most local government decisions to approve or deny individual development proposals do not involve changes to the law. These decisions are called *development orders*.

## Legislative decisions

*Hadacheck v. Sebastian*[7] is an early twentieth-century U.S. Supreme Court decision relating to a city of Los Angeles ordinance banning brickmaking at certain locations in the city. Clearly, making bricks—which requires excavating clay, firing bricks, and transporting bricks—in an urban area could constitute a nuisance. Based on your existing knowledge of land use, you should be able to imagine the city's rationale for regulating brickmaking.

The owner of a brickmaking operation sued the city, asserting that the ordinance ended an existing and valuable use of his land and violated his due process rights. In resolving the dispute, the Court sided with Los Angeles, deferring to the city's judgment.

> [W]e cannot declare invalid the exertion of a power which the city undoubtedly has because of a charge that it does not exactly accommodate the conditions, or that some other exercise would have been better or less harsh. We must accord good faith to the city in the absence of a clear showing to the contrary and an honest exercise of judgment upon the circumstances which induced its action.[8]

This judicial deference to local government legislative decision-making is a hallmark of substantive due process. Eleven years after it decided *Hadacheck*, the U.S. Supreme Court considered another land use case, *Euclid v. Ambler Realty Co.*, which opened the door for more prescriptive land use regulation across the United States.

In *Euclid*, the court evaluated whether a Village of Euclid, Ohio ordinance was "in derogation of section 1 of the Fourteenth Amendment to the federal Constitution in that it deprive[d] appellee of liberty and property without due process of law."[9] While this issue is the same as that in *Hadacheck*, the cases are different in a significant way. Brickmaking, the regulated activity in *Hadacheck*, could clearly constitute a nuisance. The city ordinance at issue in *Euclid*, however, prohibited uses of land which were not so obviously nuisances.

## Supreme Court of the United States

### *Vill. of Euclid v. Ambler Realty Co.*[10]

### 1926

Mr. Justice SUTHERLAND delivered the opinion of the Court.

The village of Euclid is an Ohio municipal corporation. It adjoins and practically is a suburb of the city of Cleveland. Its estimated population is between 5,000 and 10,000, and its area from 12 to 14 square miles, the greater part of which is farm lands or unimproved acreage. It lies, roughly, in the form of a parallelogram measuring approximately 3 1/2 miles each way. East and west it is traversed by three principal highways: Euclid avenue, through the southerly border, St. Clair avenue, through the central portion, and Lake Shore boulevard, through the northerly border, in close proximity to the shore of Lake Erie. The Nickel Plate Railroad lies from 1,500 to 1,800 feet north of Euclid avenue, and the Lake Shore Railroad 1,600 feet farther to the north. The three highways and the two railroads are substantially parallel.

Appellee is the owner of a tract of land containing 68 acres, situated in the westerly end of the village, abutting on Euclid avenue to the south and the Nickel Plate Railroad to the north. Adjoining this tract, both on the east and on the west, there have been laid out restricted residential plats upon which residences have been erected.

On November 13, 1922, an ordinance was adopted by the village council, establishing a comprehensive zoning plan for regulating and restricting the location of trades, industries, apartment houses, two-family houses, single family houses, etc ... .

The entire area of the village is divided by the ordinance into six classes of use districts, denominated U-1 to U-6, inclusive; ... . The use districts are classified in respect of the buildings which may be erected within their respective limits, as follows: U-1 is restricted to single family dwellings, public parks, water towers and reservoirs, suburban and interurban electric railway passenger stations and rights of way, and farming, non-commercial greenhouse nurseries, and truck gardening; U-2 is extended to include two-family dwellings; U-3 is further extended to include apartment houses, hotels, churches, schools, public libraries, museums, private clubs, community center buildings, hospitals, sanitariums, public playgrounds, and recreation buildings, and a city hall and courthouse; U-4 is further extended to include banks, offices, studios, telephone exchanges, fire and police stations, restaurants, theaters and moving picture shows, retail stores and shops, sales offices, sample rooms, wholesale stores for hardware, drugs, and groceries, stations for gasoline and oil (not exceeding 1,000 gallons storage) and for ice delivery, skating rinks and dance halls, electric substations, job and newspaper printing, public garages for motor vehicles, stables and wagon sheds (not exceeding five horses, wagons or motor trucks), and distributing stations for central store and commercial enterprises; U-5 is further extended to include billboards and advertising signs (if permitted), warehouses, ice and ice cream manufacturing and cold storage plants, bottling works milk bottling and central distribution stations, laundries, carpet cleaning, dry cleaning, and dyeing establishments, blacksmith, horseshoeing, wagon and motor vehicle repair shops, freight stations, street car barns, stables and wagon sheds (for more than five horses, wagons or motor trucks), and wholesale produce markets and salesroom; U-6 is further extended to include plants for sewage disposal and for producing gas, garbage and refuse incineration, scrap iron, junk, scrap paper, and rag storage, aviation fields, cemeteries, crematories, penal and correctional institutions, insane and feeble-minded institutions, storage of oil and gasoline (not to exceed 25,000 gallons), and manufacturing and industrial operations of any kind other than, and any public utility not included in, a class U-1, U-2, U-3, U-4, or U-5 use. There is a seventh class of uses which is prohibited altogether.

Class U-1 is the only district in which buildings are restricted to those enumerated. In the other classes the uses are cumulative-that is to say, uses in class U-2 include those enumerated in the preceding class U-1; class U-3 includes uses enumerated in the preceding classes, U-2, and U-1; and so on. In addition to the enumerated uses, the ordinance provides for accessory uses; that is, for uses customarily incident to the principal use, such as private garages. Many regulations are provided in respect of such accessory uses ... .

Appellee's tract of land comes under U-2, U-3 and U-6. The first strip of 620 feet immediately north of Euclid avenue falls in class U-2, the next 130 feet to the north, in U-3, and the remainder in U-6. The uses of the first 620 feet, therefore, do not include apartment houses, hotels, churches, schools, or other public and semipublic buildings, or other uses enumerated in respect of U-3 to U-6, inclusive. The uses of the next 130 feet include all of these, but exclude industries, theaters, banks, shops, and the various other uses set forth in respect of U-4 to U-6, inclusive ... .

The ordinance is assailed on the grounds that it is in derogation of section 1 of the Fourteenth Amendment to the federal Constitution in that it deprives appellee of liberty and property without due process of law ... . The prayer of the bill is for an injunction restraining the enforcement of the ordinance and all attempts to impose or maintain as to appellee's property any of the restrictions, limitations or conditions. The court below held the ordinance to be unconstitutional and void, and enjoined its enforcement, *Ambler Realty Co. v. Vill. of Euclid*, 297 F. 307 (N.D. Ohio 1924) ... .

The bill alleges that the tract of land in question is vacant and has been held for years for the purpose of selling and developing it for industrial uses, for which it is especially adapted, being immediately in the path or progressive industrial development; that for such uses it has a market value of about $10,000 per acre, but if the use be limited to residential purposes the market value is not in excess of $2,500 per acre; that the first 200 feet of the parcel back from Euclid avenue, if unrestricted in respect of use, has a value of $150 per front foot, but if limited to residential uses, and ordinary mercantile business be excluded therefrom, its value is not in excess of $50 per front foot ... .

The record goes no farther than to show, as the lower court found, that the normal and reasonably to be expected use and development of that part of appellee's land adjoining Euclid avenue is for general trade and commercial purposes, particularly retail stores and like establishments, and that the normal and reasonably to be expected use and development of the residue of the land is for industrial and trade purposes. Whatever injury is inflicted by the mere existence and threatened enforcement of the ordinance is due to restrictions in respect of these and similar uses, to which perhaps should be added-if not included in the foregoing-restrictions in respect of apartment houses. Specifically there is nothing in the record to suggest that any damage results from the presence in the ordinance of those restrictions relating to churches, schools, libraries, and other public and semipublic buildings. It is neither alleged nor proved that there is or may be a demand for any part of appellee's land for any of the last-named uses, and we cannot assume the existence of facts which would justify an injunction upon this record in respect to this class of restrictions. For present purposes the provisions of the ordinance in respect of these uses may therefore be put aside as unnecessary to be considered. It is also unnecessary to consider the effect of the restrictions in respect of U-1 districts, since none of appellee's land falls within that class.

We proceed, then, to a consideration of those provisions of the ordinance ... . The question is ... as stated by appellee: Is the ordinance invalid, in that it violates the constitutional protection "to the right of property in the appellee by attempted regulations under the guise of the police power, which are unreasonable and confiscatory"?

Building zone laws are of modern origin. They began in this country about 25 years ago. Until recent years, urban life was comparatively simple; but, with the great increase and concentration of population, problems have developed, and constantly are developing, which require, and will continue to require, additional restrictions in respect of the use and occupation of private lands in urban communities. Regulations, the wisdom, necessity, and validity of which, as applied to existing conditions, are so apparent that they are now uniformly sustained, a century ago, or even half a century ago, probably would have been rejected as arbitrary and oppressive. Such regulations are sustained, under the complex conditions of our day, for reasons analogous to those which justify traffic regulations, which, before the advent of automobiles and rapid transit street railways, would have been condemned as fatally arbitrary and unreasonable. And in this there is no inconsistency, for, while the meaning of constitutional guaranties never varies, the scope of their application must expand or contract to meet the new and different conditions which are constantly coming within the field of their operation. In a changing world it is impossible that it should be otherwise. But although a degree of elasticity is thus imparted, not to the meaning, but to the application of constitutional principles, statutes and ordinances, which, after giving due weight to the new conditions, are found clearly not to conform to the Constitution, of course, must fall.

The ordinance now under review, and all similar laws and regulations, must find their justification in some aspect of the police power, asserted for the public welfare. The line which in this field separates the legitimate from the illegitimate assumption of power is not capable of precise delimitation. It varies with circumstances and conditions. A regulatory zoning ordinance, which would be clearly valid as applied to the great cities, might be clearly invalid as applied to rural communities. In solving doubts, the maxim "sic utere tuo ut alienum non laedas," which lies at the foundation of so much of the common low [sic] of nuisances, ordinarily will furnish a fairly helpful clew. And the law of nuisances, likewise, may be consulted, not for the purpose of controlling, but for the helpful aid of its analogies in the process of ascertaining the scope of, the power. Thus the question whether the power exists to forbid the erection of a building of a particular kind or for a particular use, like the question whether a particular thing is a nuisance, is to be determined, not by an abstract consideration of the building or of the thing considered apart, but by considering it in connection with the circumstances and the locality. *Sturgis v. Bridgeman*, L. R. 11 Ch. 852, 865. A nuisance may be merely a right thing in the wrong place, like a pig in the parlor instead of the barnyard. If the validity of the legislative classification for zoning purposes be fairly debatable, the legislative judgment must be allowed to control. *Radice v. New York*, 264 U.S. 292, 294 (1924).

There is no serious difference of opinion in respect of the validity of laws and regulations fixing the height of buildings within reasonable limits, the character of materials and methods of construction, and the adjoining area which must be left open, in order to minimize the danger of fire or collapse, the evils of overcrowding and the like, and excluding from residential sections offensive trades, industries and structures likely to create nuisances. *See Welch v. Swasey*, 214 U.S. 91 (1909); *Hadacheck v. Los Angeles*, 239 U.S. 394 (1915); *Reinman v. Little Rock*, 237 U.S. 171 (1915); *Cusack Co. v. City of Chicago*, 242 U.S. 526, 529–30 (1917).

Here, however, the exclusion is in general terms of all industrial establishments, and it may thereby happen that not only offensive or dangerous industries will be excluded, but those which are neither offensive nor dangerous will share the same fate. But this is no more than happens in respect of many practice-forbidding laws which this court has upheld, although drawn in general terms so as to include individual cases that may turn out to be innocuous in themselves. *Hebe Co. v. Shaw*, 248 U.S. 297, 303 (1919); *Pierce Oil Corp. v. City of Hope*, 248 U.S. 498, 500 (1919). The inclusion of a reasonable margin, to insure effective enforcement, will not put upon a law, otherwise valid, the stamp of invalidity. Such laws may also find their justification in the fact that, in some fields, the bad fades into the good by such insensible degrees that the two are not capable of being readily distinguished and separated in terms of legislation. In the light of these considerations, we are not prepared to say that the end in view was not sufficient to justify the general rule of the ordinance, although some industries of an innocent character might fall within the proscribed class. It cannot be said that the ordinance in this respect "passes the bounds of reason and assumes the character of a merely arbitrary fiat." *Purity Extract Co. v. Lynch*, 226 U.S. 192, 204 (1912). Moreover, the restrictive provisions of the ordinance in this particular may be sustained upon the principles applicable to the broader exclusion from residential districts of all business and trade structures, presently to be discussed ... .

If it be a proper exercise of the police power to relegate industrial establishments to localities separated from residential sections, it is not easy to find a sufficient reason for denying the power because the effect of its exercise is to divert an industrial flow from the course which it would follow, to the injury of the residential public, if left alone, to another course where such injury will be obviated ... .

We find no difficulty in sustaining restrictions of the kind thus far reviewed. The serious question in the case arises over the provisions of the ordinance excluding from residential districts apartment houses, business houses, retail stores and shops, and other like establishments. This question involves the validity of what is really the crux of the more recent zoning legislation, namely, the creation and maintenance of residential districts, from which business and trade of every sort, including hotels and apartment houses, are excluded. Upon that question this court has not thus far spoken ... .

[T]he exclusion of buildings devoted to business, trade, etc., from residential districts, bears a rational relation to the health and safety of the community. Some of the grounds for this conclusion are promotion of the health and security from injury of children and others by separating dwelling houses from territory devoted to trade and industry; suppression and prevention of disorder; facilitating the extinguishment of fires, and the enforcement of street traffic regulations and other general welfare ordinances; aiding the health and safety of the community, by excluding from residential areas the confusion and danger of fire, contagion, and disorder, which in greater or less degree attach to the location of stores, shops, and factories. Another ground is that the construction and repair of streets may be rendered easier and less expensive, by confining the greater part of the heavy traffic to the streets where business is carried on.

The Supreme Court of Illinois, in *City of Aurora v. Burns*, *supra*, 149 N.E. 784, 788 (Ill. 1925), in sustaining a comprehensive building zone ordinance dividing the city into eight districts, including exclusive residential districts for one and two family dwellings, churches, educational institutions, and schools, said:

> The constantly increasing density of our urban populations, the multiplying forms of industry and the growing complexity of our civilization make it necessary for the state, either directly or through some public agency by its sanction, to limit individual activities to a greater extent than formerly. With the growth and development of the state the police power necessarily develops, within reasonable bounds, to meet the changing conditions. * * *
>
> * * * The harmless may sometimes be brought within the regulation or prohibition in order to abate or destroy the harmful. The segregation of industries, commercial pursuits, and dwellings to particular districts in a city, when exercised reasonably, may bear a rational relation to the health, morals, safety, and general welfare of the community. The establishment of such districts or zones may, among other things, prevent congestion of population, secure quiet residence districts, expedite local transportation, and facilitate the suppression of disorder, the extinguishment of fires, and the enforcement of traffic and sanitary regulations. The danger of fire and the of contagion are often lessened by

the exclusion of stores and factories from areas devoted to residences, and, in consequence, the safety and health of the community may be promoted. * * *

* * * The exclusion of places of business from residential districts is not a declaration that such places are nuisances or that they are to be suppressed as such, but it is a part of the general plan by which the city's territory is allotted to different uses, in order to prevent, or at least to reduce, the congestion, disorder, and dangers which often inhere in unregulated municipal development.

The Supreme Court of Louisiana, in *State ex rel. Civello v. City of New Orleans, supra,* 97 So. 440, 444 (La. 1923), said:

> In the first place, the exclusion of business establishments from residence districts might enable the municipal government to give better police protection. Patrolmen's beats are larger, and therefore fewer, in residence neighborhoods than in business neighborhoods. A place of business in a residence neighborhood furnishes an excuse for any criminal to go into the neighborhood, where, otherwise, a stranger would be under the ban of suspicion. Besides, open shops invite loiterers and idlers to congregate; and the places of such congregations need police protection. In the second place, the zoning of a city into residence districts and commercial districts is a matter of economy is street paving. Heavy trucks, hauling freight to and from places of business in residence districts, require the city to maintain the same costly pavement in such districts that is required for business districts; whereas, in the residence districts, where business establishments are excluded, a cheaper pavement serves the purpose. * * *
>
> Aside from considerations of economic administration, in the matter of police and fire protection, street paving, etc., any business establishment is likely to be a genuine nuisance in a neighborhood of residences. Places of business are noisy; they are apt to be disturbing at night; some of them are malodorous; some are unsightly; some are apt to breed rats, mice, roaches, flies, ants, etc. * * *
>
> If the municipal council deemed any of the reasons which have been suggested, or any other substantial reason, a sufficient reason for adopting the ordinance in question, it is not the province of the courts to take issue with the council. We have nothing to do with the question of the wisdom or good policy of municipal ordinances. If they are not satisfying to a majority of the citizens, their recourse is to the ballot-not the courts.

The matter of zoning has received much attention at the hands of commissions and experts, and the results of their investigations have been set forth in comprehensive reports. These reports which bear every evidence of painstaking consideration, concur in the view that the segregation of residential, business and industrial buildings will make it easier to provide fire apparatus suitable for the character and intensity of the development in each section; that it will increase the safety and security of home life, greatly tend to prevent street accidents, especially to children, by reducing the traffic and resulting confusion in residential sections, decrease noise and other conditions which produce or intensify nervous disorders, preserve a more favorable environment in which to rear children, etc. With particular reference to apartment houses, it is pointed out that the development of detached house sections is greatly retarded by the coming of apartment houses, which has sometimes resulted in destroying the entire section for private house purposes; that in such sections very often the apartment house is a mere parasite, constructed in order to take advantage of the open spaces and attractive surroundings created by the residential character of the district. Moreover, the coming of one apartment house is followed by others, interfering by their height and bulk with the free circulation of air and monopolizing the rays of the sun which otherwise would fall upon the smaller homes, and bringing, as their necessary accompaniments, the disturbing noises incident to increased traffic and business, and the occupation, by means of moving and parked automobiles, of larger portions of the streets, thus detracting from their safety and depriving children of the privilege of quiet and open spaces for play, enjoyed by those in more favored localities-until, finally, the residential character of the neighborhood and its desirability as a place of detached residences are utterly destroyed. Under these circumstances, apartment houses, which in a different environment would be not only entirely unobjectionable but highly desirable, come very near to being nuisances.

If these reasons, thus summarized, do not demonstrate the wisdom or sound policy in all respects of those restrictions which we have indicated as pertinent to the inquiry, at least, the reasons are sufficiently cogent to preclude us from saying, as it must be said before the ordinance can be declared unconstitutional, that such provisions are clearly arbitrary and unreasonable, having no substantial relation to the public health, safety, morals, or general welfare. *Cusack Co. v. City of Chicago, supra*, 242 U.S. 526, 530–31 (1917); *Jacobson v. Massachusetts*, 197 U.S. 11, 30–31 (1905).

It is true that when, if ever, the provisions set forth in the ordinance in tedious and minute detail, come to be concretely applied to particular premises, including those of the appellee, or to particular conditions, or to be considered in connection with specific complaints, some of them, or even many of them, may be found to be clearly arbitrary and unreasonable. But where the equitable remedy of injunction is sought, as it is here, not upon the ground of a present infringement or denial of a specific right, or of a particular injury in process of actual execution, but upon the broad ground that the mere existence and threatened enforcement of the ordinance, by materially and adversely affecting values and curtailing the opportunities of the market, constitute a present and irreparable injury, the court will not scrutinize its provisions, sentence by sentence, to ascertain by a process of piecemeal dissection whether there may be, here and there, provisions of a minor character, or relating to matters of administration, or not shown to contribute to the injury complained of, which, if attacked separately, might not withstand the test of constitutionality … .

The relief sought here is … an injunction against the enforcement of any of the restrictions, limitations, or conditions of the ordinance. And the gravamen of the complaint is that a portion of the land of the appellee cannot be sold for certain enumerated uses because of the general and broad restraints of the ordinance. What would be the effect of a restraint imposed by one or more or the innumerable provisions of the ordinance, considered apart, upon the value or marketability of the lands, is neither disclosed by the bill nor by the evidence, and we are afforded no basis, apart from mere speculation, upon which to rest a conclusion that it or they would have any appreciable effect upon those matters. Under these circumstances, therefore, it is enough for us to determine, as we do, that the ordinance in its general scope and dominant features, so far as its provisions are here involved, is a valid exercise of authority, leaving other provisions to be dealt with as cases arise directly involving them … .

Decree reversed.

Mr. Justice VAN DEVANTER, Mr. Justice McREYNOLDS, and Mr. Justice BUTLER dissent.

### *U.S. Constitution allows use-segregated zoning*

For urban and regional planning, the most significant consequence of *Euclid v. Ambler* was the advent of "Euclidean zoning." That term refers to land use regulations that—like the Village of Euclid's—organize a community into zones differentiated by area controls (such as building height and building placement on land) and by land use (such as commercial, residential, etc.).

The Court only considered one aspect of the city's ordinance critically: the segregation of uses into different zones, even when these uses were not likely to be nuisances.[11] In upholding the ordinance, the Court specifically recognized use-segregated zoning as constitutionally permitted practice. Today, Euclidean zoning is so pervasive that many take for granted a principle purpose of local government regulation is segregating communities by land use.

### *Fairly debatable standard*

For law, the most significant consequence of *Euclid v. Ambler* was the advent of the fairly debatable standard, a test used to determine whether local government legislative land use decisions violate property owners' substantive due process rights. Under the fairly debatable standard, local government land use regulations satisfy due process unless "such provisions are clearly arbitrary and unreasonable, having no substantial relation to the public health, safety, morals, or general welfare."[12]

Consistent with the analysis in *Hadacheck*, the fairly debatable standard is chiefly characterized by its deference to legislative decision-making. When you consider whether a local government's land use regulation runs afoul of the fairly debatable standard, know that courts defer to the judgment of legislative bodies (like a local government commission or council) in determining whether a given ordinance meets the standard.

The fairly debatable standard has two parts. First, a local government land use regulation must have a substantial relation to the public health, safety, morals, or general welfare. This is a statement that local government regulation must be an exercise of that government's police powers. Because police powers are broad, having a substantial relation to them is a low bar for a local government to meet in imposing land use regulations.[13]

Second, the land use regulation must not be clearly arbitrary. This means that the alleged connection between the local government's regulation and the police power must be plausible.[14] In other words, one's expectation that the regulation will have the intended outcome must at least be rational. This prong also is a very low bar for a local government to meet. Any amount of evidence or rational argument will pass muster under the fairly debatable standard[15] because this is "a highly deferential standard requiring approval of a planning action if reasonable persons could differ as to its propriety."[16]

The Florida Supreme Court adopted the fairly debatable standard in *City of Miami Beach v. Ocean & Inland Co.*[17] Citing *Euclid*, the court acknowledged the "accepted rules that the court will not substitute its judgment for that of the city council; that the ordinance is presumed valid and that the legislative intent will be sustained if 'fairly debatable.'"[18]

## Notes

1 Fla. Const. art. I, § 9.
2 U.S. Const. amend. V.
3 *See* Feldman v. United States, 322 U.S. 487, 490 (1944) (citations omited) (finding that "one of the settled principles of our Constitution has been that these Amendments [the Fourth and the Fifth] protect only against invasion of civil liberties by the Government ...") *overruled in part by* Murphy v. Waterfront Comm'n of N.Y. Harbor, 378 U.S. 52 (1964).
4 U.S. Const. amend. XIV, § 1.
5 Haire v. Fla. Dept. of Agric. & Consumer Servs., 870 So. 2d 774, 781 (Fla. 2004) (citing Dep't of L. Enf't v. Real Prop., 588 So. 2d 957, 960 (Fla. 1991)).
6 *Haire*, 870 So. 2d at 787; *see* Keys Citizens for Responsible Gov't, Inc. v. Fla. Keys Aqueduct Auth., 795 So. 2d 940, 948 (Fla. 2001).
7 239 U.S. 394 (1915).
8 Hadacheck v. Sebastian, 239 U.S. 394, 413–14 (1915).
9 Vill. of Euclid v. Ambler Realty Co., 272 U.S. 365, 384 (1926).

10 272 U.S. 365, 384 (1926).
11 *Id.* at 390.
12 *Id.* at 395 (citations omitted).
13 *See* Vill. of Belle Terre v. Boraas, 416 U.S. 1, 4 (1974) (listing "considerations bearing on the constitutionality of zoning ordinances [as] the danger of fire or collapse of building, the evils of overcrowding people, and the possibility that 'offensive trades, industries, & structures' might 'create nuisance' to residential sections").
14 Moore v. City of E. Cleveland, 431 U.S. 494, 498 n.6 (1977) ("But our cases have not departed from the requirement that the government's chosen means must rationally further some legitimate state purpose").
15 *Belle Terre*, 416 U.S. at 5 (explaining the reasoning behind the holding in *Euclid* as the "ordinance was sanctioned because the validity of the legislative classification was 'fairly debatable' and therefore could not be said to be wholly arbitrary").
16 Coastal Dev. of N. Fla., Inc. v. City of Jacksonville Beach, 788 So. 2d 204, 205 n.1 (Fla. 2001) (citations omitted).
17 3 So. 2d 364, 366–67 (Fla. 1941).
18 City of Miami Beach v. Ocean & Inland Co., 3 So. 2d 364, 366 (Fla. 1941) (citations omitted).

# 5 Quasi-judicial decision-making

While the fairly debatable standard remains the rule by which courts judge local governments' legislative decisions on land use regulation, when Florida courts apply those rules to particular circumstances, they are not so deferential to local government judgments.

*Euclid v. Ambler* concluded with a discussion in which the Court drew a distinction between a facial challenge to a land use regulation and an as-applied challenge to a land use regulation.[1] The decision implied that the appropriate test for a due process challenge may be different in each circumstance. Indeed, just two years following its *Euclid* decision, the Court heard another land use dispute in *Nectow v. City of Cambridge*.[2] The Court there said:

> The governmental power to interfere by zoning regulations with the general rights of the land owner by restricting the character of his use, is not unlimited, and, other questions aside, such restriction cannot be imposed if it does not bear a substantial relation to the public health, safety, morals, or general welfare. Here, the express finding of the master, already quoted, confirmed by the court below, is that the health, safety, convenience, and general welfare of the inhabitants of the part of the city affected will not be promoted by the disposition made by the ordinance of the locus in question.[3]

The Florida Supreme Court applied this reasoning as early as 1930 to strike down a city of Vero Beach land use action.[4] But Florida courts would take decades to clearly articulate when the fairly debatable standard should not apply to review of local government land use decisions.

Today, Florida courts call as-applied land use actions *quasi-judicial* and subject those decisions to strict scrutiny, a standard which—in this context—requires competent and substantial evidence and testimony showing that the decision meets applicable requirements of law. Additionally, parties affected by quasi-judicial decisions are entitled to procedural due process protections to which parties affected by legislative decisions are not entitled. The following case, *Machado v. Musgrove*, discusses the strict scrutiny standard.

## Florida Third District Court of Appeals

### *Machado v. Musgrove*[5]

### 1988

PER CURIAM.

Petitioners sought to have their property rezoned from GU (interim zoning) to RU-5A (professional offices) in an area designated by the comprehensive land use plan as estate residential-up to two units per gross acre. They seek certiorari review of a circuit court decision reversing the County Commission's grant of the requested change. Applying the "fairly debatable" standard the circuit court held the proposed 140,000 square foot office complex incompatible with other uses in the area and violative of the land use plan.

The 8.5 acre site of the proposed commercial use is within the area covered by a neighborhood study called the West Dade Ranch Area Study which limits the area to ranchlands, nurseries and croplands. The neighborhood study, an element of the land use plan, is the subject of an ordinance now codified at section 2–116.7, Dade County Code.

This application came before the County Commission on two occasions. In the first appearance, on November 21, 1985, both the Planning Director and the Zoning Director recommended that the application be denied. The Zoning Director expressed an opinion that the proposed RU-5A zoning would be incompatible with the Area Study and the agricultural and institutional uses on the east side of S.W. 127th Avenue.[1] He was specifically concerned that "approval of semi-professional office uses in this area could prompt similar or commercial uses on other properties in the area which could be detrimental." Administrative action was deferred.

When the matter came before the County Commission a second time on January 23, 1986, the Planning Director was still firmly of the view that office zoning on the site would set a precedent for similar requests on undeveloped sites in the area causing erosion of an already dwindling area set aside for ranches and farmland. However, the Zoning Director had changed his view, recommending approval primarily because "the property to the east across S.W. 125th Avenue has been approved for a temple and property to the northeast has been approved for a private school."

Testimony was heard from long-time area residents-farmers, ranchers, and single-family homeowners—who opposed the proposed zoning for fear that it would bring burdensome traffic and alter the character of the area. The applicant presented exhibits and legal argument. In a session closed to the public, County Commissioners thereafter approved the zoning request on a 3–2 vote.

At the outset we note that the Zoning Director's reason in support of a recommendation for approval of the commercial project—that properties to the east had been approved for a school and temple—was totally irrelevant to the land use plan consistency question. The recommendation was thus entitled to no consideration. *Cf. Hall v. Korth*, 244 So. 2d 766 (Fla. 3d DCA 1971). Schools and churches as defined in section 33–18, Dade County Code, unlike commercial offices, are contemplated in estate residential zones so long as they satisfy the impact requirements of that section and section 33–311(d), for unusual uses. See *Metropolitan Dade County. v. Fuller*, 497 So. 2d 1322 (Fla. 3d DCA 1986), and *Board of County Comm'rs v. First Free Will Baptist Church*, 374 So. 2d 1055 (Fla. 3d DCA 1979).

*I*

*Planning and Zoning As Separate Functions*

Application of the fairly debatable standard to both the land use and zoning questions, as is often done, tends to obscure the difference between their distinct functions. Land use planning and zoning are different exercises of sovereign power, *Baker v. City of Milwaukie*, 533 P.2d 772 (Or. 1975); Charles M. Haar, *In Accordance with a Comprehensive Plan*, 68 Harv. L.

1 The site is at the southwest corner of S.W. 127th Avenue and Sunset Drive in Dade County. Surrounding property includes two churches to the north, a plant nursery to the south, and single family homes (RU-1) to the west. Lands immediately west are unimproved. Dade County and the applicant describe the plant nursery as a commercial use. Both the Planning Director and Zoning Director treat it as consistent with an agricultural use.

Rev. 1154 (1955); therefore, a proper analysis, for review purposes, requires that they be considered separately.

A local comprehensive land use plan is a statutorily mandated legislative plan to control and direct the use and development of property within a county or municipality. Fla. Stat. § 163.3167(1) (1985); *Southwest Ranches Homeowners Ass'n, Inc. v. Broward County*, 502 So. 2d 931 (Fla. 4th DCA 1987). The plan is likened to a constitution for all future development within the governmental boundary. *O'Loane v. O'Rourke*, 42 Cal. Rptr. 283, 288 (Cal. Ct. App. 1965).

Zoning, on the other hand, is the means by which the comprehensive plan is implemented, *City of Jacksonville Beach v. Grubbs*, 461 So. 2d 160 (Fla. 1st DCA 1984), and involves the exercise of discretionary powers within limits imposed by the plan. *Baker*, 533 P.2d at 775. It is said that a zoning action not in accordance with a comprehensive plan is ultra vires. Haar, *In Accordance With A Comprehensive Plan*, at 1156.

## *II*

### *Standard of Review; Burden of Proof*

It is well settled that a zoning action is an exercise of legislative power to which a reviewing court applies the deferential fairly debatable test. *See*, e.g., *Southwest Ranches*, 502 So. 2d at 935. If the zoning action is one where reasonable people could differ as to its propriety, i.e., whether the action is arbitrary, capricious, or otherwise an abuse of discretion, the administrative decision will not be disturbed by a reviewing court. *Dade Savings & Loan Ass'n v. City of North Miami*, 458 So. 2d 861 (Fla. 3d DCA 1984).

Part II of Chapter 163, Florida Statutes, called the Local Government Comprehensive Planning and Land Development Regulation Act, and the local comprehensive plans which it mandates, are not zoning laws. The statute's requirement that all zoning action conform to an approved land use plan is, in effect, a limitation on a local government's otherwise broad zoning powers. *Maryland-National Capital Park & Planning Comm'n v. Mayor & Council of Rockville*, 325 A.2d 748 (Md. 1974). The purpose of the statute is to accomplish, *inter alia*, orderly growth, protection of resources and stability of land use throughout the state. Fla. Stat. § 163.3161(7) (1985).[2]

The test in reviewing a challenge to a zoning action on grounds that a proposed project is inconsistent with the comprehensive land use plan is whether the zoning authority's determination that a proposed development conforms to each element and the objectives of the land use plan is supported by competent and substantial evidence. The traditional and non-deferential standard of strict judicial scrutiny applies.

Strict scrutiny is not defined in the land use cases which use the phrase but its meaning can be ascertained from the common definition of the separate words. Strict implies rigid exactness, *People ex rel. Flood v. Gardiner*, 53 N.Y.S. 451 (N.Y. App. Div. 1898), or precision, *Black's Law Dictionary* 1275 (5th ed. 1979). A thing scrutinized has been subjected to minute investigation. *Commonwealth v. White*, 115 A. 870 (Pa. 1922). Strict scrutiny is thus

2 That the land use plan does restrict local zoning power becomes increasingly clear with each legislative session. Section 163.3177(6), Florida Statutes (1985), requires that the future land use map designate the exact location and extent of all proposed commercial uses. Sections 163.3167, 163.3177, and 163.3184, Florida Statutes (Supp. 1986), mandate that local comprehensive plans coordinate with regional and state plans, subject to review for compliance with state and regional land use plans. *See* deHaven-Smith & Paterson, *The 1986 Glitch Bill-Missing Links in Growth Management*, Fla. Envtl. & Urban Issues, October 1986, at 4.

the process whereby a court makes a detailed examination of a statute, rule or order of a tribunal for exact compliance with, or adherence to, a standard or norm. It is the antithesis of a deferential review.

Analogously where a zoning action is challenged as violative of the comprehensive land use plan the burden of proof is on the one seeking a change to show by competent and substantial evidence that the proposed development conforms strictly to the comprehensive plan and its elements. *See Fasano v. Board of County Comm'rs*, 507 P.2d 23 (Or. 1973) (en banc). *See also* Carl J. Peckinpaugh, Jr., Comment, *Burden of Proof in Land Use Regulations: A Unified Approach and Application to Florida*, 8 Fla. St. U.L. Rev. 499 (1980) (the proof of conformity of the zoning action to the land use plan must be discernible to a reviewing court on a verbatim record). Where the record is silent, or the evidence shows nonconformity with the plan, e.g., that a proposed project constitutes a greater intensity of use, *Baker v. Milwaukie*; *Maryland-National Capital Park & Planning Comm'n v. Mayor & Council of Rockville*, a lesser intensity of use, *City of Cape Canaveral v. Mosher*, 467 So. 2d 468 (Fla. 5th DCA 1985), a different and incompatible character of use, *Alachua County v. Eagle's Nest Farms, Inc.*, 473 So. 2d 257 (Fla. 1st DCA 1985), or a failure to comply with the plan's mandatory procedures, *Hillsborough County v. Putney*, 495 So. 2d 224 (Fla. 2d DCA 1986), the requested rezoning will be denied as inconsistent with the comprehensive plan ... .

### *III*

#### *Consistency With Land Use Plan*

The tests for consistency of a development project with a land use plan have been, until recently, conflicting or imprecise primarily because the word consistency lacked definition. In 1985 the legislature added a definition of consistency at section 163.3194(3)(a), Florida Statutes (1985):

> A development order or land development regulation shall be consistent with the comprehensive plan if the land uses, densities or intensities, and other aspects of development permitted by such order or regulation are compatible with and further the objectives, policies, land uses, and densities or intensities in the comprehensive plan and if it meets all other criteria enumerated by the local government.

The legislation implies, as one writer has noted in a thoughtful examination of the subject, that application of a fairly debatable, or for that matter any other deferential or discretionary standard, is not the correct standard of review of an administrative determination that a development order is consistent with the local comprehensive plan. John K. McPherson, Note, *Cumulative Zoning and the Developing Law of Consistency with Local Comprehensive Plans*, 61 Fla. B.J. 71 (1987).

Writing a concurring opinion in *City of Cape Canaveral v. Mosher*, 467 So. 2d 468 (Fla. 5th DCA 1985), Judge Cowart gave the term consistency a working definition which squares with the statute:

> The word "consistent" implies the idea or existence of some type or form of model, standard, guideline, point, mark or measure as a norm and a comparison of items or actions against that norm. Consistency is the fundamental relation between the norm and the compared item. If the compared item is in accordance with, or in agreement with, or within the parameters specified, or exemplified, by the norm, it is "consistent" with it but if the compared item deviates or departs in any direction or degree from the parameters of the norm, the compared item or action is not "consistent" with the norm.

*Mosher*, 467 So. 2d at 471.

Further, in reasoning which we adopt, he wrote:

> A comprehensive land use plan legislatively sets a zoning norm for each zone. Under Section 163.3194(1), Fla. Stat., after adoption of such a plan, zoning changes should be made only when existing zoning is inconsistent with the plan; otherwise, the plan should be legislatively amended as to the area of the entire zone or as to the uses permitted within the entire zone. This is ... the only way to (1) regulate and maintain land use by zones; (2) make individual zoning changes, which are essentially executive action, conform to a legislated plan; and (3) avoid arbitrary "spot zoning" change that permits the use of individual parcels to depart from a plan.

*Mosher*, 467 So. 2d at 471.

Dade County is critical of *Mosher* and its requirement for strict adherence to the land use plan, contending that it would deprive local government of the flexibility needed to respond to rapidly changing conditions in Dade County. In response the opponents, neighboring land-owners, contend that conditions change in rapid and uncontrolled fashion in Dade County, increasing the need for costly public services and facilities, due to loose enforcement of the land use planning scheme. We briefly examine the three elements of the Land Use Plan in light of the arguments.

The Land Use Plan consists of a color-coded map which separates uses of all county lands into roughly thirteen categories including residential (six densities), industrial and office, agricultural, and parks and recreation. Textual material on the reverse side of the map constitutes the second element of the plan. Neighborhood and functional studies and plans, as adopted pursuant to ordinance, make up the third element of the comprehensive plan.

The pertinent textual material provides:

> The residential designations [on the map] only indicate the overall maximum residential density for an area. *Non-residential uses that are permitted in these areas are not shown.* Decisions by the County relative to when, where and how these areas are to be developed with respect to non-residential uses *will be* guided through the use of the policies and written guidelines of the Comprehensive Development Master Plan. *The application of these policies and guidelines for planning ... of ... nonresidential permitted use is most appropriate and beneficial at the neighborhood level.*

[Emphasis added].

Dade County argues that the plan's textual language states a general policy which it is not bound to follow. We agree with respondents that if that is the case then there are no standards or parameters to guide when, where, what kind and how much commercial use will be permitted in a planned residential zone, leaving the zoning authority free to approve, *ad hoc*, commercial zoning in a residential zone subject only to a deferential court review. We have previously rejected that philosophy:

> [T]he law of Florida is committed to the doctrine of the requirement that zoning ordinances ... must be predicated upon legislative standards which can be applied to all cases, rather than to the theory of granting an administrative board or even a legislative body the power to arbitrarily decide each case entirely within the discretion of the members of the administrative board or legislative body.

*City of Homestead v. Schild*, 227 So. 2d 540, 543 (Fla. 3d DCA 1969).

A Comprehensive Land Use Plan is not a "vest-pocket tool," *Baker,* 533 P. 2d at 775, for making individual zoning changes based on political vagary, *see* Haar & Kayden, *Zoning Laws Reflect Our Values and Priorities*, N.Y. Times, Nov. 24, 1986, at 17, col. 1, *noted in Southwest Ranches*. Instead, it is a broad statement of a legislative objective "to protect human, environmental, social, and economic resources; and to maintain, through orderly growth and development, *the character and stability of present and future land use and development in this state.*" Fla. Stat. § 163.3161(7) (1985) [emphasis added]. *See* 1979 Op. Fla. Att'y Gen. 079-88 (Sept. 28, 1979).

Further, a neighborhood study, when adopted by ordinance, becomes a law and an integral element of the land use plan. To accept Dade County's argument, that it is not bound by the neighborhood study element of the plan, would render useless the costly and time-consuming processes of formulating a comprehensive plan, and adopting neighborhood area studies. Uselessness will not be attributed to legislative acts. *Allied Fidelity Ins. Co. v. State*, 415 So. 2d 109 (Fla. 3d DCA 1982). Finally, and significantly, the neighborhood study once adopted by ordinance is no longer an expression of general policy. The study becomes a permanent law of local government which continues in force until repealed. Fla. Stat. § 166.041(1)(a) (1985). We know of no rule and petitioners have offered none, which allows government, acting in its executive capacity, to disregard its own laws.

Section 163.3194(4)(a), Florida Statutes (1985),[6] relied upon by the petitioners in support of the argument that the plan is a flexible instrument, does not compel a different result. We read the provision, in context, as a recognition of the court's inherent power to take into account fundamental fairness questions as may arise from a strict application of the plan-not as a license to second-guess the legislative body where there is simply the to-be-expected collision of the plan with private interests. The record reflects no contention or showing below that the plan is totally unreasonable as applied to the development involved in the litigation, or that the plan is incomplete or internally inconsistent, or that the plan, in its application, would constitute a taking of private property without due process or fair compensation. Even where there is some basis for consideration by the court pursuant to section 163.3194, its actions must be consistent with the overall purpose and intent of the Act as expressed in section 163.3161.

### *Conclusion*

Whether a proposed development project is consistent with a local comprehensive land use plan and all of its elements is tested on review by a standard of strict scrutiny; the burden is on the applicant for rezoning to show by competent and substantial evidence that the requested rezoning conforms to the legislative plan.

A neighborhood area study is a critical element of Dade County's land use plan; without it there are no legislative standards to guide where, when, what kind and the amount of nonresidential uses will be allowed in a residential zone. The requested rezoning for a nonresidential use is on a site within a residential zone which is the subject of a neighborhood

6 Fla. Stat. § 163.3194(4)(a) provides:

> A court, in reviewing local governmental action ... under this act, may consider, among other things, the reasonableness of the comprehensive plan, or element or elements thereof, relating to the issue justiciably raised or the appropriateness and completeness of the comprehensive plan, or element or elements thereof, in relation to the governmental action ... under consideration. The court may consider the relationship of the comprehensive plan, or element or elements thereof, to the governmental action taken ... but private property shall not be taken without due process of law and the payment of just compensation.

area study. That study, now codified at section 2-116.7, Dade County Code, as the West Dade Ranch Study Area, limits non-residential development in the zone to ranchlands, nurseries and croplands.

Because the applicants were unable to show that their proposed commercial project was consistent with each element of the land use plan and furthered its objectives, the circuit court was eminently correct in voiding the rezoning.

In light of our determination on the land use plan issue we need not reach the separate zoning question.

Certiorari denied.

Before SCHWARTZ, C.J., and BARKDULL, HENDRY, HUBBART, NESBITT, BASKIN, DANIEL S. PEARSON, and FERGUSON, JJ.

On Rehearing En Banc

Upon consideration of this cause en banc, the court unanimously adopts the panel opinion herein filed July 14, 1987, as its own. Accordingly, the petition for writ of certiorari is denied.

## Discussion

The *Machado* case provides that the strict scrutiny standard requires a court to determine whether "competent, substantial evidence" and testimony supports a local government's quasi-judicial land use decision.[6] The Florida Supreme Court expounded on the character of evidence sufficient to support a quasi-judicial decision in *De Groot v. Sheffield*.[7]

> We have used the term "competent substantial evidence" advisedly. Substantial evidence has been described as such evidence as will establish a substantial basis of fact from which the fact at issue can be reasonably inferred. We have stated it to be such relevant evidence as a reasonable mind would accept as adequate to support a conclusion. In employing the adjective "competent" to modify the word "substantial," we are aware of the familiar rule that in administrative proceedings the formalities in the introduction of testimony common to the courts of justice are not strictly employed. We are of the view, however, that the evidence relied upon to sustain the ultimate finding should be sufficiently relevant and material that a reasonable mind would accept it as adequate to support the conclusion reached. To this extent the "substantial" evidence should also be "competent."[8]

Given that the strict scrutiny standard, as opposed to the fairly debatable standard, is the correct judicial standard of review for a local government's quasi-judicial land use decision, determining whether a decision is legislative or quasi-judicial is the first step in evaluating whether the decision violates due process rights.

In deciding *Brevard Cnty. v. Snyder*, the Florida Supreme Court described the difference between legislative and quasi-judicial decisions. This seminal case follows *Fasano v. Wash. Cnty.*,[9] in which the Supreme Court of Oregon established a clear distinction between legislative and quasi-judicial land use decisions. Florida courts have summarized the *Snyder* test[10] to distinguish legislative action from quasi-judicial action as "whether the [local government] decision on the petition formulates a 'general rule of policy' and, thus, will affect many people, or whether it merely applies an existing general rule of policy to a specific parcel."[11]

Quasi-judicial decisions are akin to, and borrow aspects from, the judicial decision-making process. Judicial decisions involve "enforcing" an existing law,[12] whereas legislative decisions formulate policy.[13]

> [A] judicial inquiry investigates, declares, and enforces liabilities as they stand on present facts and under laws supposed already to exist … . Legislation … looks to the future and

> changes existing conditions by making a new rule to be applied thereafter to all or some part of those subject to its power.[14]

In a quasi-judicial hearing, a local government asks, does "the law allow the party to do what it wants?"[15] In contrast, legislation "*changes* the existing law"[16] to "meet[] the future land use and needs of the community."[17]

## Florida Supreme Court

### *Brevard Cnty. v. Snyder*[18]

### 1993

GRIMES, Justice.

We review *Snyder v. Board of County Commissioners*, 595 So. 2d 65 (Fla. 5th DCA 1991) … . Jack and Gail Snyder owned a one-half acre parcel of property on Merritt Island in the unincorporated area of Brevard County. The property is zoned GU (general use) which allows construction of a single-family residence. The Snyders filed an application to rezone their property to the RU-2-15 zoning classification which allows the construction of fifteen units per acre. The area is designated for residential use under the 1988 Brevard County Comprehensive Plan Future Land Use Map. Twenty-nine zoning classifications are considered potentially consistent with this land use designation, including both the GU and the RU-2-15 classifications.

After the application for rezoning was filed, the Brevard County Planning and Zoning staff reviewed the application and completed the county's standard "rezoning review worksheet." The worksheet indicated that the proposed multifamily use of the Snyders' property was consistent with all aspects of the comprehensive plan except for the fact that it was located in the one-hundred-year flood plain in which a maximum of only two units per acre was permitted. For this reason, the staff recommended that the request be denied.

At the planning and zoning board meeting, the county planning and zoning director indicated that when the property was developed the land elevation would be raised to the point where the one-hundred-year-flood plain restriction would no longer be applicable. Thus, the director stated that the staff no longer opposed the application. The planning and zoning board voted to approve the Snyders' rezoning request.

When the matter came before the board of county commissioners, Snyder stated that he intended to build only five or six units on the property. However, a number of citizens spoke in opposition to the rezoning request. Their primary concern was the increase in traffic which would be caused by the development. Ultimately, the commission voted to deny the rezoning request without stating a reason for the denial.

The Snyders filed a petition for certiorari in the circuit court. Three circuit judges, sitting en banc, reviewed the petition and denied it by a two-to-one decision. The Snyders then filed a petition for certiorari in the Fifth District Court of Appeal.

The district court of appeal acknowledged that zoning decisions have traditionally been considered legislative in nature. Therefore, courts were required to uphold them if they could be justified as being "fairly debatable." Drawing heavily on *Fasano v. Board of County Commissioners*, 507 P.2d 23 (Or. 1973) (en banc), however, the court concluded that, unlike initial zoning enactments and comprehensive rezonings or rezonings affecting a large portion of the public, a rezoning action which entails the application of a general rule or policy to specific individuals, interests, or activities is quasi-judicial in nature. Under the latter circumstances, the court reasoned that a stricter standard of judicial review of the rezoning decision was required. The court went on to hold:

> ... Since a property owner's right to own and use his property is constitutionally protected, review of any governmental action denying or abridging that right is subject to close judicial scrutiny ... .

*Snyder v. Board of County Commissioners*, 595 So. 2d at 81 (footnotes omitted).

Applying these principles to the facts of the case, the court found (1) that the Snyders' petition for rezoning was consistent with the comprehensive plan; (2) that there was no assertion or evidence that a more restrictive zoning classification was necessary to protect the health, safety, morals, or welfare of the general public; and (3) that the denial of the requested zoning classification without reasons supported by facts was, as a matter of law, arbitrary and unreasonable. The court granted the petition for certiorari.

Before this Court, the county contends that the standard of review for the county's denial of the Snyders' rezoning application is whether or not the decision was fairly debatable ... .

The Snyders contend that their rezoning application was consistent with the comprehensive plan ... .

Historically, local governments have exercised the zoning power pursuant to a broad delegation of state legislative power subject only to constitutional limitations. Both federal and state courts adopted a highly deferential standard of judicial review early in the history of local zoning. In *Village of Euclid v. Ambler Realty Co.*, 272 U.S. 365 (1926), the United States Supreme Court held that "[i]f the validity of the legislative classification for zoning purposes be fairly debatable, the legislative judgment must be allowed to control." 272 U.S. at 388. This Court expressly adopted the fairly debatable principle in *City of Miami Beach v. Ocean & Inland Co.*, 3 So. 2d 364 (Fla. 1941).

Inhibited only by the loose judicial scrutiny afforded by the fairly debatable rule, local zoning systems developed in a markedly inconsistent manner. Many land use experts and practitioners have been critical of the local zoning system. Richard Babcock deplored the effect of "neighborhoodism" and rank political influence on the local decision-making process. Richard F. Babcock, *The Zoning Game* (1966). Mandelker and Tarlock recently stated that "zoning decisions are too often ad hoc, sloppy and self-serving decisions with well-defined adverse consequences without off-setting benefits." Daniel R. Mandelker & A. Dan Tarlock, *Shifting the Presumption of Constitutionality in Land-Use Law*, 24 Urb. Law. 1, 2 (1992).

Professor Charles Harr, a leading proponent of zoning reform, was an early advocate of requiring that local land use regulation be consistent with a legally binding comprehensive plan which would serve long range goals, counteract local pressures for preferential treatment, and provide courts with a meaningful standard of review. Charles M. Harr, *In Accordance with a Comprehensive Plan*, 68 Harv. L. Rev. 1154 (1955). In 1975, the American Law Institute adopted the Model Land Development Code, which provided for procedural and planning reforms at the local level and increased state participation in land use decision-making for developments of regional impact and areas of critical state concern.

Reacting to the increasing calls for reform, numerous states have adopted legislation to change the local land use decision-making process. As one of the leaders of this national reform, Florida adopted the Local Government Comprehensive Planning Act of 1975. Ch. 75-257, Laws of Fla. This law was substantially strengthened in 1985 by the Growth Management Act. Ch. 85-55, Laws of Fla.

Pursuant to the Growth Management Act, each county and municipality is required to prepare a comprehensive plan for approval by the Department of Community Affairs. The adopted local plan must include "principles, guidelines, and standards for the orderly and balanced future economic, social, physical, environmental, and fiscal development" of the local government's jurisdictional area. Fla. Stat. § 163.3177(1) (1991). At the minimum, the local plan must include elements covering future land use; capital improvements generally;

sanitary sewer, solid waste, drainage, potable water, and natural ground water aquifer protection specifically; conservation; recreation and open space; housing; traffic circulation; intergovernmental coordination; coastal management (for local government in the coastal zone); and mass transit (for local jurisdictions with 50,000 or more people). *Id.* § 163.3177(6).

Of special relevance to local rezoning actions, the future land use plan element of the local plan must contain both a future land use map and goals, policies, and measurable objectives to guide future land use decisions. This plan element must designate the "proposed future general distribution, location, and extent of the uses of land" for various purposes. *Id.* § 163.3177(6)(a). It must include standards to be utilized in the control and distribution of densities and intensities of development. In addition, the future land use plan must be based on adequate data and analysis concerning the local jurisdiction, including the projected population, the amount of land needed to accommodate the estimated population, the availability of public services and facilities, and the character of undeveloped land. *Id.* § 163.3177(6)(a).

The local plan must be implemented through the adoption of land development regulations that are consistent with the plan. *Id.* § 163.3202. In addition, all development, both public and private, and all development orders approved by local governments must be consistent with the adopted local plan. *Id.* § 163.3194(1)(a). Fla. Stat. § 163.3194(3)(1991), explains consistency as follows:

> (a) A development order or land development regulation shall be consistent with the comprehensive plan if the land uses, densities or intensities, and other aspects of development permitted by such order or regulation are compatible with and further the objectives, policies, land uses, and densities or intensities in the comprehensive plan and if it meets all other criteria enumerated by the local government.

Fla. Stat. § 163.3164 (1991) reads in pertinent part:

> (6) "Development order" means any order granting, denying, or granting with conditions an application for a development permit.
> (7) "Development permit" includes any building permit, zoning permit, subdivision approval, rezoning, certification, special exception, variance, or any other official action of local government having the effect of permitting the development of land.

Because an order granting or denying rezoning constitutes a development order and development orders must be consistent with the comprehensive plan, it is clear that orders on rezoning applications must be consistent with the comprehensive plan.

The first issue we must decide is whether the Board's action on Snyder's rezoning application was legislative or quasi-judicial. A board's legislative action is subject to attack in circuit court. *Hirt v. Polk County Bd. of County Comm'rs*, 578 So. 2d 415 (Fla. 2d DCA 1991). However, in deference to the policy-making function of a board when acting in a legislative capacity, its actions will be sustained as long as they are fairly debatable. *Nance v. Town of Indialantic*, 419 So. 2d 1041 (Fla. 1982). On the other hand, the rulings of a board acting in its quasi-judicial capacity are subject to review by certiorari and will be upheld only if they are supported by substantial competent evidence. *De Groot v. Sheffield*, 95 So. 2d 912 (Fla. 1957).

Enactments of original zoning ordinances have always been considered legislative. *Gulf & Eastern Dev. Corp. v. City of Fort Lauderdale*, 354 So. 2d 57 (Fla. 1978); *County of Pasco v. J. Dico, Inc.*, 343 So. 2d 83 (Fla. 2d DCA 1977). In *Schauer v. City of Miami Beach*, this Court held that the passage of an amending zoning ordinance was the exercise of a legislative function. 112 So. 2d at 839. However, the amendment in that case was comprehensive in nature in that it effected a change in the zoning of a large area so as to permit it to be used as locations for multiple family buildings and hotels. *Id.* In *City of Jacksonville Beach v. Grubbs* and *Palm Beach County v. Tinnerman*, the district courts of appeal went further and held that board action on specific rezoning applications of individual property owners was also legislative. *Grubbs*, 461 So. 2d at 163; *Tinnerman*, 517 So. 2d at 700.

... Generally speaking, legislative action results in the formulation of a general rule of policy, whereas judicial action results in the application of a general rule of policy. Carl J. Peckingpaugh, Jr., Comment, *Burden of Proof in Land Use Regulations: A Unified Approach and Application to Florida*, 8 Fla. St. U.L. Rev. 499, 504 (1980). In *West Flagler Amusement Co. v. State Racing Commission*, 165 So. 64, 65 (1935), we explained:

> A judicial or quasi-judicial act determines the rules of law applicable, and the rights affected by them, in relation to past transactions. On the other hand, a quasi-legislative or administrative order prescribes what the rule or requirement of administratively determined duty shall be with respect to transactions to be executed in the future, in order that same shall be considered lawful ... .

Applying this criterion, it is evident that comprehensive rezonings affecting a large portion of the public are legislative in nature. However, we agree with the court below when it said:

> [R]ezoning actions which have an impact on a limited number of persons or property owners, on identifiable parties and interests, where the decision is contingent on a fact or facts arrived at from distinct alternatives presented at a hearing, and where the decision can be functionally viewed as policy application, rather than policy setting, are in the nature of ... quasi-judicial action ... .

*Snyder*, 595 So. 2d at 78.

Therefore, the board's action on Snyder's application was in the nature of a quasi-judicial proceeding and properly reviewable by petition for certiorari.

We also agree with the court below that the review is subject to strict scrutiny. In practical effect, the review by strict scrutiny in zoning cases appears to be the same as that given in the review of other quasi-judicial decisions. *See Lee County v. Sunbelt Equities, II, Ltd. Partnership*, 619 So. 2d 996 (Fla. 2d DCA 1993) (the term "strict scrutiny" arises from the necessity of strict compliance with comprehensive plan). This term as used in the review of land use decisions must be distinguished from the type of strict scrutiny review afforded in some constitutional cases. *Compare Snyder v. Board of County Comm'rs*, 595 So. 2d 65, 75–76 (Fla. 5th DCA 1991) (land use), and *Machado v. Musgrove*, 519 So. 2d 629, 632 (Fla. 3d DCA 1987), review denied, 529 So. 2d 693 (Fla. 1988), *and review denied*, 529 So. 2d 694 (Fla. 1988) (land use), *with In re Estate of Greenberg*, 390 So. 2d 40, 42–43 (Fla. 1980) (general discussion of strict scrutiny review in context of fundamental rights), *appeal dismissed*, 450 U.S. 961 (1981), *Florida High Sch. Activities Ass'n v. Thomas*, 434 So. 2d 306 (Fla. 1983) (equal protection), *and Department of Revenue v. Magazine Publishers of America, Inc.*, 604 So. 2d 459 (Fla. 1992) (First Amendment).

At this point, we depart from the rationale of the court below. In the first place, the opinion overlooks the premise that the comprehensive plan is intended to provide for the future use of land, which contemplates a gradual and ordered growth. *See City of Jacksonville Beach*, 461 So. 2d at 163, in which the following statement from *Marracci v. City of Scappoose*, 552 P.2d 552, 553 (Or. Ct. App. 1976), was approved:

> [A] comprehensive plan only establishes a long-range maximum limit on the possible intensity of land use; a plan does not simultaneously establish an immediate minimum

limit on the possible intensity of land use. The present use of land may, by zoning ordinance, continue to be more limited than the future use contemplated by the comprehensive plan.

Even where a denial of a zoning application would be inconsistent with the plan, the local government should have the discretion to decide that the maximum development density should not be allowed provided the governmental body approves some development that is consistent with the plan and the government's decision is supported by substantial, competent evidence.

Further, we cannot accept the proposition that once the landowner demonstrates that the proposed use is consistent with the comprehensive plan, he is presumptively entitled to this use unless the opposing governmental agency proves by clear and convincing evidence that specifically stated public necessity requires a more restricted use. We do not believe that a property owner is necessarily entitled to relief by proving consistency when the board action is also consistent with the plan. As noted in *Lee County v. Sunbelt Equities II, Limited Partnership*:

> [A]bsent the assertion of some enforceable property right, an application for rezoning appeals at least in part to local officials' discretion to accept or reject the applicant's argument that change is desirable. The *right* [emphasis in the original] of judicial review does not *ipso facto* ease the burden on a party seeking to overturn a decision made by a local government, and certainly does not confer any property-based right upon the owner where none previously existed ... .
>
> Moreover, when it is the zoning classification that is challenged, the comprehensive plan is relevant only when the suggested use is inconsistent with that plan. Where any of several zoning classifications is consistent with the plan, the applicant seeking a change from one to the other is not entitled to judicial relief absent proof the *status quo* is no longer reasonable. It is not enough simply to be "consistent"; the proposed change cannot be *inconsistent* [emphasis in the original], and will be subject to the "strict scrutiny" of *Machado* to insure this does not happen.

619 So. 2d at 1005–06.

This raises a question of whether the Growth Management Act provides any comfort to the landowner when the denial of the rezoning request is consistent with the comprehensive plan. It could be argued that the only recourse is to pursue the traditional remedy of attempting to prove that the denial of the application was arbitrary, discriminatory, or unreasonable. *Burritt v. Harris*, 172 So. 2d 820 (Fla. 1965); *City of Naples v. Central Plaza of Naples, Inc.*, 303 So. 2d 423 (Fla. 2d DCA 1974). Yet, the fact that a proposed use is consistent with the plan means that the planners contemplated that that use would be acceptable at some point in the future. We do not believe the Growth Management Act was intended to preclude development but only to insure that it proceed in an orderly manner.

Upon consideration, we hold that a landowner seeking to rezone property has the burden of proving that the proposal is consistent with the comprehensive plan and complies with all procedural requirements of the zoning ordinance. At this point, the burden shifts to the governmental board to demonstrate that maintaining the existing zoning classification with respect to the property accomplishes a legitimate public purpose. In effect, the landowners' traditional remedies will be subsumed within this rule, and the board will now have the burden of showing that the refusal to rezone the property is not arbitrary, discriminatory, or unreasonable. If the board carries its burden, the application should be denied.

While they may be useful, the board will not be required to make findings of fact. However, in order to sustain the board's action, upon review by certiorari in the circuit court it must be shown that there was competent substantial evidence presented to the board to support its ruling. Further review in the district court of appeal will continue to be governed by the principles of *City of Deerfield Beach v. Vaillant*, 419 So. 2d 624 (Fla. 1982).

Based on the foregoing, we quash the decision below and disapprove *City of Jacksonville Beach v. Grubbs* and *Palm Beach County v. Tinnerman*, to the extent they are inconsistent with this opinion ... .

It is so ordered.

BARKETT, C.J., and OVERTON, McDONALD, KOGAN and HARDING, JJ., concur.

SHAW, J., dissents.

## Procedural due process in quasi-judicial land use hearings

As discussed, substantive due process sets limits on the *content or subject* of laws to protect individual rights. And procedural due process governs *how governments administer* their laws to ensure fair treatment. People whose rights are affected in quasi-judicial hearings have procedural due process rights that parties affected by legislative decisions do not have.

Procedural due process "serve[s] as a vehicle to ensure fair treatment through proper administration of justice where substantive rights are at issue."[19] The "core" of procedural due process "is the right to notice and a meaningful opportunity to be heard."[20] And the opportunity to be heard requires "a meaningful opportunity to contest [a possible government deprivation], usually before it is imposed."[21]

In Florida, case law dictates how local governments must conduct quasi-judicial hearings. Parties to quasi-judicial hearings are generally entitled to: (1) receive notice of the hearing; (2) an opportunity to be heard; (3) present and rebut evidence; (4) cross-examine witnesses; (5) a tribunal which is impartial in the matter; and (6) be informed of all the facts on which the commission acts.[22] The following decision, *Jennings v. Dade Cnty.*, elaborates on these procedural due process rights and on the appropriateness of local government decision-makers engaging in ex parte communications (i.e. engaging in communications outside of a hearing).

## Florida Third District Court of Appeal

### *Jennings v. Dade Cnty.*[23]

### 1991

NESBITT, Judge.

The issue we confront is the effect of an ex parte communication upon a decision emanating from a quasi-judicial proceeding of the Dade County Commission. We hold that upon proof that a quasi-judicial officer received an ex parte contact, a presumption arises, pursuant to section 90.304, Florida Statutes (1989), that the contact was prejudicial. The aggrieved party will be entitled to a new and complete hearing before the commission unless the defendant proves that the communication was not, in fact, prejudicial. For the reasons that follow, we quash the order under review with directions.

Respondent Schatzman applied for a variance to permit him to operate a quick oil change business on his property adjacent to that of petitioner Jennings. The Zoning Appeals Board granted Schatzman's request. The county commission upheld the board's decision. Six days prior to the commission's action, a lobbyist Schatzman employed to assist him in connection with the proceedings registered his identity as required by section 2–11.1(s) of the Dade County Ordinances. Jennings did not attempt to determine the content of any communication between the lobbyist and the commission or otherwise challenge the propriety of any communication prior to or at the hearing.

Following the commission order, Jennings filed an action for declaratory and injunctive relief in circuit court wherein he alleged that Schatzman's lobbyist communicated with some or all of the county commissioners prior to the vote, thus denying Jennings due process both under the United States and Florida constitutions as well as section (A)(8) of the Citizens' Bill of Rights, Dade County Charter. Jennings requested the court to conduct a hearing to establish the truth of the allegations of the complaint and upon a favorable determination then to issue an injunction prohibiting use of the property as allowed by the county. Based upon the identical allegations, Jennings also claimed in the second count of his complaint that Schatzman's use of the permitted variance constituted a nuisance which he requested the court to enjoin. The trial court dismissed Count I of the complaint, against both Dade County and Schatzman. The court gave Jennings leave only against Dade County to amend the complaint and to transfer the matter to the appellate division of the circuit court. The trial court denied Schatzman's motion to dismiss Count II and required him to file an answer. Jennings then timely filed this application for common law certiorari … .

At the outset of our review of the trial court's dismissal, we note that the quality of due process required in a quasi-judicial hearing is not the same as that to which a party to full judicial hearing is entitled. *See Goss v. Lopez*, 419 U.S. 565 (1975); *Hadley v. Department of Admin.*, 411 So. 2d 184 (Fla. 1982). Quasi-judicial proceedings are not controlled by strict rules of evidence and procedure. *See Astore v. Florida Real Estate Comm'n*, 374 So. 2d 40 (Fla. 3d DCA 1979); *Woodham v. Williams*, 207 So. 2d 320 (Fla. 1st DCA 1968). Nonetheless, certain standards of basic fairness must be adhered to in order to afford due process. *See Hadley*, 411 So. 2d at 184; *City of Miami v. Jervis*, 139 So. 2d 513 (Fla. 3d DCA 1962). Consequently, a quasi-judicial decision based upon the record is not conclusive if minimal standards of due process are denied. *See Morgan v. United States*, 298 U.S. 468, 480–81 (1936); *Western Gillette, Inc. v. Arizona Corp. Comm'n*, 592 P.2d 375 (Ariz. Ct. App. 1979). A quasi-judicial hearing generally meets basic due process requirements if the parties are provided notice of the hearing and an opportunity to be heard. In quasi-judicial zoning proceedings, the parties must be able to present evidence, cross-examine witnesses, and be informed of all the facts upon which the commission acts. *Coral Reef Nurseries, Inc. v. Babcock Co.*, 410 So. 2d 648, 652 (Fla. 3d DCA 1982) … .

The county … argues that Jennings was not denied due process because he either knew or should have known of an ex parte communication due to the mandatory registration required of lobbyists. The county further contends that Jennings failed to avail himself of section 33–316 of the Dade County Code to subpoena the lobbyist to testify at the hearing so as to detect and refute the content of any ex parte communication. We disagree with the county's position.

Ex parte communications are inherently improper and are anathema to quasi-judicial proceedings. Quasi-judicial officers should avoid all such contacts where they are identifiable. However, we recognize the reality that commissioners are elected officials in which capacity they may unavoidably be the recipients of unsolicited ex parte communications regarding quasi-judicial matters they are to decide. The occurrence of such a communication in a quasi-judicial proceeding does not mandate automatic reversal. Nevertheless, we hold that the allegation of prejudice resulting from ex parte contacts with the decision makers in a quasi-judicial proceeding states a cause of action. E.g., *Waste Management of Illinois, Inc. v. Pollution Control Bd.*, 530 N.E.2d 682 (Ill. App. Ct. 1988); *PATCO*, 685 F.2d 547 (D.C. Cir. 1982). Upon the aggrieved party's proof that an ex parte contact occurred, its effect is presumed to be prejudicial unless the defendant proves the contrary by competent evidence. § 90.304. *See generally Caldwell v. Division of Retirement*, 372 So. 2d 438 (Fla. 1979) (for discussion of rebuttable presumption affecting the burden of proof). Because knowledge and evidence of the contact's impact are peculiarly in the hands of the defendant quasi-judicial officer(s), we find such a burden appropriate. *See Technicable Video Sys. v. Americable*, 479 So. 2d 810 (Fla. 3d DCA 1985); *Allstate Finance Corp. v. Zimmerman*, 330 F.2d 740 (5th Cir. 1964).

In determining the prejudicial effect of an ex parte communication, the trial court should consider the following criteria which we adopt from *PATCO*, 685 F.2d at 564–65:

> [w]hether, as a result of improper ex parte communications, the agency's decisionmaking [sic] process was irrevocably tainted so as to make the ultimate judgment of the agency unfair, either as to an innocent party or to the public interest that the agency was obliged to protect. In making this determination, a number of considerations may be relevant: the gravity of the ex parte communications; whether the contacts may have influenced the agency's ultimate decision; whether the party making the improper contacts benefited from the agency's ultimate decision; whether the contents of the communications were unknown to opposing parties, who therefore had no opportunity to respond; and whether vacation of the agency's decision and remand for new proceedings would serve a useful purpose. Since the principal concerns of the court are the integrity of the process and the fairness of the result, mechanical rules have little place in a judicial decision whether to vacate a voidable agency proceeding. Instead, any such decision must of necessity be an exercise of equitable discretion.

*Accord E & E Hauling, Inc. v. Pollution Control Bd.*, 451 N.E.2d 555, 571 (Ct.App.1983), *aff'd*, 481 N.E.2d 664 (1985).

Accordingly, we hold that the allegation of a prejudicial ex parte communication in a quasi-judicial proceeding before the Dade County Commission will enable a party to maintain an original equitable cause of action to establish its claim. Once established, the offending party will be required to prove an absence of prejudice.

In the present case, Jennings' complaint does not allege that any communication which did occur caused him prejudice. Consequently, we direct that upon remand Jennings shall be afforded an opportunity to amend his complaint. Upon such an amendment, Jennings shall be provided an evidentiary hearing to present his prima facie case that ex parte contacts occurred. Upon such proof, prejudice shall be presumed. The burden will then shift to the respondents to rebut the presumption that prejudice occurred to the claimant. Should the respondents produce enough evidence to dispel the presumption, then it will become the duty of the trial judge to determine the claim in light of all the evidence in the case.

For the foregoing reasons, the application for common law certiorari is granted. The orders of the circuit court are quashed and remanded with directions.

BARKDULL, J., concurs.

FERGUSON, Judge (concurring).

I concur in the result and write separately to address [an argument of Dade County] ... .

[Dade County's] argument is made for the purpose of brining this case within what the respondents describe as a legislative-function exception to the rule against ex parte communications. Indeed, there is language in the *Coral Reef* opinion, particularly the dicta that "it is the character of the administrative hearing leading to the action of the administrative body that determines the label" as legislative or quasi-judicial, *Coral Reef*, 410 So. 2d at 652, which, when read out of context, lends support to Dade County's contentions. As an abstract proposition, the statement is inaccurate.

Whereas the character of an administrative hearing will determine whether the proceeding is quasi-judicial or executive ... it is the nature of the act performed that determines its character as legislative or otherwise. *Suburban Medical Center v. Olathe Community Hosp.*, 597 P.2d 654, 661 (1979). *See also Walgreen Co. v. Polk County*, 524 So. 2d 1119, 1120 (Fla. 2d DCA 1988) ("The quasi-judicial nature of a proceeding is not altered by mere procedural flaws.").

> A judicial inquiry investigates, declares and enforces liabilities as they stand on present facts and under laws supposed already to exist. That is its purpose and end. Legislation, on the other hand, looks to the future and changes existing conditions by making a new rule to be applied thereafter to all or some part of those subject to its power.

*Suburban Medical Center*, 597 P.2d at 661 (quoting *Prentis v. Atlantic Coast Line Co.*, 211 U.S. 210, 226 (1908))[1] … .

### *Discussion*

*Jenning*'s holding can be impractical in application. Land use decisions take place in the context of local politics and most local elected officials will want to interact with constituents who have opinions about pending land use decisions.

When a voter contacts his or her elected official to share an opinion on a proposed development, the elected official responding "I cannot have this conversation with you because I will consider that matter in a quasi-judicial hearing and it just wouldn't be fair to the developer of the project to hear your opinion" is not the response the constituent seeks.

The Florida Legislature has responded to this reality by allowing ex parte communications when local governments adopt a process for disclosure.

> A county or municipality may adopt an ordinance or resolution removing the presumption of prejudice from ex parte communications with local public officials by establishing a process to disclose ex parte communications with such officials pursuant to this subsection or by adopting an alternative process for such disclosure.[24]

This section of Florida Statutes continues by describing the requirements of an ordinance sufficient to remove the presumption of prejudice from ex parte communications.

Another challenge in granting procedural due process in quasi-judicial hearings is identifying *whom* due process protects. Florida local governments typically invite public participation in their meetings. And quasi-judicial hearings often attract broad interest.

> Oftentimes, however, such quasi-judicial hearings are attended by more than just the parties. They are open to the public. In the case of rezoning hearings, neighboring landowners may attend and want to be heard on a proposed zoning change to a nearby property. Our court has previously stated that "[a] participant in a quasi-judicial proceeding is clearly entitled to some measure of due process … The issue of what process is due depends on the function of the proceeding as well as the nature of the interests affected."[25]

Recognizing this issue, the decision *Carillon Cmty. Residential v. Seminole Cnty.* distinguishes between *parties* and *participants* and holds that only parties to quasi-judicial hearings are entitled to a full suite of procedural due process protections.[26]

1 Relying on *Coral Reef*, the majority opinion refers to "quasi-judicial zoning proceedings," a confounding phrase which has its genesis in Rinker Materials Corp. v. Dade County, 528 So. 2d 904, 906, n. 2 (Fla. 3d DCA 1987). There, Dade County argued to this court that the according of "procedural due process" converts a legislative proceeding into a quasi-judicial proceeding, citing *Coral Reef*. That proposition runs afoul of an entire body of administrative law. If an act is in essence legislative in character, the fact of a notice and a hearing does not transform it into a judicial act. If it would be a legislative act without notice and a hearing, it is still a legislative act with notice and a hearing. *See* Prentis v. Atlantic Coast Line Co., 211 U.S. 210 (1908); Reagan v. Farmers' Loan & Trust Co., 154 U.S. 362 (1894).

Each local government may establish its own rules to determine who may be a party to a quasi-judicial hearing and is therefore entitled to due process protections. These rules are often patterned off the common law standing requirement that the plaintiff suffer a harm which is distinct in kind and in degree from the community at-large. For example, the city of Gainesville has adopted the following rule governing quasi-judicial hearings by the city's local planning agency.

> The following persons may participate as an affected party in a quasi-judicial hearing: 1) the applicant; 2) city staff; and 3) other affected parties. Other affected parties may include persons who are either: 1) entitled to mailed notice of the petition before the Board in accordance with the Land Development Code; or 2) have applied for such status no less than seven days prior to the hearing and have been determined by the Board to be an affected party because the person may, depending on the result of the quasi- judicial hearing, suffer an injury distinct in kind and degree from that shared by the general public.
> ... Although the general public may not participate as an affected party, quasi-judicial hearings shall provide an opportunity for public comment.[27]

Note that the city of Gainesville rules include a deadline (of seven days before a hearing) by which people affected by a quasi-judicial hearing must apply in order to protect their due process rights. Practitioners should always take care to ensure they follow local rules to protect clients' rights.

*Table 5.1* Key characteristics of legislative and quasi-judicial decision-making

| | *Legislative* | *Quasi-judicial* |
|---|---|---|
| Character of decision | Legislative actions create a general rule or policy which will be applicable to an open class of individuals, interests, or situations. | Quasi-judicial actions apply an existing general rule or policy to specific individuals, interests, or situations. |
| Examples | • Comprehensive plan adoption<br>• Comprehensive plan amendment (including 'small-scale' amendment)<br>• Adopting land development code<br>• Rezoning many properties | • Rezoning one property<br>• Development order or development permit<br>• Variance<br>• Special exception |
| Standard of review (rule) | Courts review legislative decisions using the fairly debatable standard. This standard has two parts. First, laws must bear a substantial relation to a legitimate police power purpose. Second, the connection between that rule and its purported purpose may not be clearly arbitrary and unreasonable. | Courts reviewing quasi-judicial decisions use strict scrutiny. The strict scrutiny standard requires local governments to make a decision that substantial competent evidence shows is consistent with applicable laws. |
| Procedural requirements | Provided by legislature in statute rather than by the courts in case law. Practitioners should consult applicable statutes to determine what procedure should be afforded parties to legislative hearings. | *Parties* at the hearing are entitled to: (1) receive notice of the hearing; (2) an opportunity to be heard; (3) present and rebut evidence; (4) cross-examine witnesses; (5) a tribunal which is impartial in the matter—i.e. having had no ex parte communications; and (6) be informed of all the facts on which the commission acts. |

### Box 5.1 Practice problem: Airport entrance road

The entrance to the Collegeborough Regional Airport in the City of Collegeborough was off of County Road, across from County Jail. The Collegeborough Regional Airport Authority (CRAA), the owner of the airport, believed an entrance across from the jail was harming the airport's prospects and developed a new entrance road. That new entrance road comes from another direction, off of State Highway, and also provides access to undeveloped land adjacent to the airport's main terminal and runways.

The CRAA hired a real estate market consulting firm named Seinewell to develop a plan for marketing this newly accessible land to businesses which like to locate near airports, such as hotels, distribution centers, and car rental agencies.

One of Seinewell's recommendations was to increase the size of the airport's monument sign at this new location. A monument sign is a sign that is constructed flush with the ground rather than on a pole. Pursuant to the Collegeborough Land Development Code, the maximum allowed monument sign size is 20 square feet (about five feet tall and four feet wide). Seinewell advised the CRAA to construct a sign at least five times that size to appeal to tenants.

The Collegeborough Comprehensive Plan includes the following policy in its future land-use element: "To prevent blight and protect public safety, signs shall be regulated in the community by size, number and method of illumination. The city shall not permit new signs that constitute blight or are a distraction for motorists."

The CRAA applied for an amendment to the Collegeborough Land Development Code to create a new class of regulated facilities under the sign portion of that code. The new group of "facilities which are regionally unique and significant the local economy"—a class that would include only the Collegeborough Regional Airport, State University, and Central Hospital—would be allowed to have monument signs up to 120 square feet in size. If the city adopted the new rule, the CRAA planned to submit an administrative application for its new monument sign.

At the hearing where the Collegeborough City Council considered adopting the proposed changes to the Collegeborough Land Development Code, the councillors examined renderings of the CRAA's planned sign. Mayor Jackson opposed the sign's "garish" colors. Another councilperson did not like that the sign was lit internally, so that it would cause glare and distract motorists. A third member of the council did not like the image of the plane on the sign, which was "cartoonish" and "not in the character of a university city."

The president of the Collegeborough Beautification Society, Dr. Autumn, also attended the hearing. Dr. Autumn spoke at length of how the sign would constitute just the sort of blight prohibited by the Collegeborough Comprehensive Plan.

The CRAA's attorney got up immediately after Dr. Autumn's comments and requested the opportunity to cross-examine her. The attorney knew that Dr. Autumn had a PhD in entomology, not planning, and simply wasn't qualified to testify as to the sign's adherence to the requirements of the comprehensive plan.

Mayor Jackson said to the attorney, "No sir. We do not have cross-examination at these sorts of hearings. We want everyone to feel comfortable speaking here. We are not going to let you big-city lawyers drive over from Bay Town and intimidate our residents." Then, he called for a vote and the Collegeborough City Council denied the CRAA's application.

The CRAA wants to seek judicial review of whether the denial of cross-examination violated CRAA's right to due process. Evaluate the CRAA's claim.

## Notes

1 Vill. of Euclid v. Ambler Realty Co., 272 U.S. 365, 395 (1926).
2 277 U.S. 183 (1928).
3 Nectow v. City of Cambridge, 277 U.S. 183, 188 (1928) (citations omitted).
4 *See* State *ex rel.* Helseth v. Dubose, 128 So. 40 (Fla. 1930).
5 519 So. 2d 629 (Fla. 3d DCA 1987).
6 Machado v. Musgrove, 519 So. 2d 629, 632 (Fla. 3d DCA 1987).
7 95 So. 2d 912 (Fla. 1957).
8 De Groot v. Sheffield, 95 So. 2d 912, 916 (Fla. 1957) (citations omitted).
9 Fasano v. Wash. Cnty., 507 P.2d 23, 30 (Or. 1973).
10 Brevard Cnty. v. Snyder, 627 So. 2d 469, 474 (Fla. 1993).
11 Kahana v. City of Tampa, 683 So. 2d 618, 620 (Fla. 2d DCA 1996) (citations omitted).
12 Lee Cnty. v. Sunbelt Equities, II, Ltd. P'ship, 619 So. 2d 996, 1000 (Fla. 2d DCA 1993).
13 Minnaugh v. Broward Cnty., 752 So. 2d 1263, 1265 (Fla. 4th DCA 2000), *aff'd*, 783 So. 2d 1054 (Fla. 2001).
14 Jennings v. Dade Cnty., 589 So. 2d 1337, 1343 (Fla. 3d DCA 1991) (Ferguson, J., concurring) (quoting Prentis v. Atlantic Coast Line Co., 211 U.S. 210, 226 (1908)).
15 *Sunbelt Equities, II*, 619 So. 2d at 1000.
16 *Id.*
17 *Minnaugh*, 752 So. 2d at 1265 (citations omitted) (concluding that such considerations are left to the discretion of the legislative body).
18 627 So. 2d 469 (Fla. 1993).
19 Haire v. Fla. Dept. of Agric. & Consumer Servs., 870 So. 2d 774, 787 (Fla. 2004) (citations omitted).
20 LaChance v. Erickson, 522 U.S. 262, 266 (1998).
21 State v. Robinson, 873 So. 2d 1205, 1212 (Fla. 2004).
22 Lee Cnty. v. Sunbelt Equities, II, Ltd. P'ship, 619 So. 2d 996, 1002 (Fla. 2d DCA 1993) (quoting Jennings v. Dade Cnty., 589 So. 2d 1337, 1340 (Fla. 3d DCA 1991)).
23 589 So. 2d 1337 (1991).
24 Fla. Stat. § 286.0115(1)(a).
25 Carillon Cmty. Residential v. Seminole Cnty., 45 So. 3d 7, 10 (Fla. 5th DCA 2010) (citations omitted).
26 *Id.* at 11.
27 City of Gainesville, Fla., Rules of the City Plan Bd. no. 170287A 4–5 (2017).

# 6 Florida's planning statutes

## Timeline

Florida adopted its first zoning law, the Florida General Zoning Statute, in 1939.[1] The state patterned that early statute after the model acts promulgated by the U.S. Department of Commerce in the 1920s.[2] The state did not initially delegate zoning powers to all local governments.[3] So, prior to the passage of the General Zoning Statute, every city and county in Florida required a special act of the legislature to enable that city or county to regulate land use.[4]

In the 1970s, the state began to reassess its role in growth management. And Florida has been conducting an experiment in state-led planning for land use and development since that decade. But the experiment parameters have not been static. They have changed constantly along the way. The following are some of the significant events in the evolution of modern growth management laws in Florida.

- In 1971, Governor Rueben Askew appointed the Task Force on Resource Management.
- In 1972, the Legislature adopted state regulation of large-scale developments called developments of regional impact and of areas of critical state concern. During that session, the Legislature also created the Environmental Land Management Study Committee, called the ELMS Committee.
- In 1975, the Legislature adopted the Local Government Comprehensive Planning Act,[5] which—for the first time—required local governments to adopt comprehensive plans.
- In 1982, Governor Bob Graham created another Environmental Land Management Study Committee, ELMS II.
- In 1984, the Legislature adopted the Florida State and Regional Planning Act, which provided standards and procedures for adoption of a state comprehensive plan.[6]
- In 1985, the Legislature adopted the Local Government Comprehensive Planning and Land Development Regulation Act.[7] That enactment is commonly referred to as the Growth Management Act. The law remains the most significant to Florida land use. It was a noted improvement over the 1975 Local Government Comprehensive Planning Act because, for the first time, the law provided two requirements that form the backbone of Florida's integrated system of land use regulation: *compliance* and *consistency*.

*Compliance* is a requirement that every local government comprehensive plan meet standards established in Florida statutes.[8] The Growth Management Act provided a process for state review of local government comprehensive plans to ensure they complied with state law.[9] *Consistency* is a requirement that local government decisions on development orders be consistent with the respective local government's adopted land use rules, including its comprehensive plan.[10]

Thomas Pelham, a former head of the state land planning agency, wrote about the Growth Management Act's significance:

> The greatest success of the [Growth Management Act] may be the establishment of local planning processes at the local level. Prior to enactment of the 1985 [Growth Management Act], many of Florida's local governments did not have or did not implement local plans, and some had no zoning or other land use regulations. Now every local government has adopted a local plan approved by the state, and all but the smallest of them have planning departments and an institutionalized ongoing local planning process to address growth and development issues.[11]

The Legislature achieved that outcome through the complex task of incorporating local, regional, and state governmental entities into a comprehensive land use regulation scheme.

> The product of the cooperative—though not easily achieved—executive and legislative initiatives of the mid-1980s is the most complex intergovernmental development management system in the nation. The system is complex because virtually every type of local, regional, and state public entity involved in any aspect of development is in some manner tied to the development management process. Adding to this complexity is that Florida's development management system does not stem from a single law: it is a combination of several associated laws and administrative rules enacted over time. These laws and rules affect private and even public development proposals.[12]

Subsequent changes in law have amended fundamental components of the Growth Management Act to simplify and weaken land use regulation in Florida. However, planning—as Florida does it today—largely follows the framework set out in the 1985 Growth Management Act.

- In 1991, Governor Lawton Chiles empaneled the third Environmental Land Management Study Committee, ELMS III. The Legislature adopted some revisions to the Growth Management Act as recommended by ELMS III in 1993. A significant revision to the statute in 1993 was the introduction of concurrency, a requirement that public infrastructure be available to serve new development as a precondition for that development occurring.[13]
- In 1995, the Legislature adopted the Bert J. Harris, Jr., Private Property Rights Protection Act.[14] Governor Lawton Chiles had convened a working group that drafted an early version of the bill. The law created a cause of action for property owners to recover monetary damages when their property was inordinately burdened by land use regulation.[15] This support for private property rights responded to concerns that the comprehensive planning in place since the adoption of the Growth Management Act led to onerous restrictions on property owners.
- In 2005, the Legislature adopted the Growth Management Reform Act. That law made significant changes to how infrastructure is planned and funded.[16] It lessened developers' obligations to provide new transportation infrastructure needed to serve developments by allowing exceptions to transportation concurrency, a transportation planning tool mandated by the Growth Management Act.
- In 2011, the Legislature adopted the Community Planning Act,[17] which significantly overhauled the Growth Management Act. The most significant change brought by the Community Planning Act was a new emphasis on protecting resources of important statewide significance.[18] These resources could be anything, including environmentally significant lands or transportation infrastructure.

This shift in focus came at the expense of reviewing comprehensive plans for *compliance*, or ensuring local government plans complied with state law. The Community Planning Act revised the procedures by which the state land planning agency would review local government comprehensive plans. It called the new process "expedited review" and it focused on speed.[19] Only a small number of comprehensive plan amendments go through a more detailed review called state coordinated review.[20] These changes effectively ended the state oversight of local government comprehensive planning that Thomas Pelham had hailed as the greatest success of the Growth Management Act.

Moreover, the 2011 act failed to be clear as to what are resources of important statewide significance.

> [T]he [Community Planning Act]'s fundamental terms, important state resources and facilities are not statutorily defined and [the Department of Economic Opportunity] is not authorized to define or refine these expansive terms by rule. Instead, for every proposed local plan amendment, up to ten state and regional government agencies may review the amendment and in the context of their statutory jurisdiction may determine what is an important state resource and facility and whether the amendment would adversely impact them.[21]

This failure to define a key statutory term has created a regulatory scheme which can be subjective, unreliable, and unpredictable.[22]

Two other changes to growth management which occurred in 2011 will also be significant to your reading of Florida land use cases and commentary. First, the Community Planning Act repealed Rule 9J-5 of the Florida Administrative Code. That rule had provided the administrative rules for the state land planning agency. Second, the Legislature eliminated the state-government agency called the Department of Community Affairs, which had been the state land planning agency, and created the Department of Economic Opportunity, which became the new state land planning agency. Cases decided before 2011 and articles authored before 2011 may reference Rule 9J-5 or the Department of Community Affairs.

- In 2016 and in 2018, the Legislature practically repealed all remaining requirements related to developments of regional impact, which had pre-dated even the Growth Management Act. Extant provisions of Florida Statutes section 380.06 govern those outstanding developments of regional impact approved by local governments before 2016.
- In 2019, the Legislature imposed timelines on local government review of development orders. This created deadlines for local governments to conduct reviews of applications for development. That year, the Legislature also changed statutory provisions governing the *consistency challenge*, the only tool available at law to enforce consistency. Recall that consistency is the statutory requirement that local government decisions on development orders be consistent with the respective local government's adopted land use rules, including its comprehensive plan. The change specifically made by the Legislature was providing an award of attorney fees to prevailing parties in consistency challenges.[23] In other words, any plaintiff who seeks to enforce a local government comprehensive plan will be liable for attorney fees of the local government—and any party intervening in the litigation—if that plaintiff does not prevail in the case.

## Comprehensive planning requirements

Every local government in Florida *must* plan for future growth and *must* adopt and maintain a comprehensive plan.[24] Despite the Community Planning Act reducing state oversight of local governments, the state continues to play a formal role in the adoption and amendment of local government comprehensive plans. A state agency, the Department of Economic Opportunity, is Florida's state land planning agency and reviews most local plans and proposed amendments to local plans before local governments may adopt them.[25]

Florida Statutes section 163.3177 speaks most specifically to how local governments must draft their comprehensive plans. Below are some of its significant requirements. Note that the administrative decisions cited by this text to edify these statutory requirements generally come from cases that precede the 2011 adoption of the Community Planning Act. As a result, they do not always apply the text of Florida Statutes section 163.3177 in their analyses. Instead, they sometimes apply identical (or very similar) language that existed in Florida Administrative Code Rule 9J-5. Recall that the Florida Legislature repealed Rule 9J-5 and simultaneously moved many of its substantive requirements for comprehensive planning into Florida Statutes Chapter 163 by enacting the Community Planning Act in 2011.

### *Meaningful and predictable standards*

Comprehensive plans must establish *meaningful and predictable standards* for the use and development of land. "The plan shall establish meaningful and predictable standards for the use and development of land and provide meaningful guidelines for the content of more detailed land development and use regulations."[26]

The requirement for meaningful and predictable standards does "not mean that objectives must eliminate all possibility [sic] ambiguity or be amenable to quantitative measurement."[27] Instead, a comprehensive plan must "be specific and measurable in the sense that it can be determined when the 'intermediate end' [set out in plan objectives] is reached."[28]

### *Relevant and appropriate data and analysis*

Comprehensive plans must be based on relevant and appropriate data and analysis.

> [T]he comprehensive plan and plan amendments shall be based upon relevant and appropriate data and an analysis by the local government that may include, but not be limited to, surveys, studies, community goals and vision, and other data available at the time of adoption of the comprehensive plan or plan amendment. To be based on data means to react to it in an appropriate way and to the extent necessary indicated by the data available on that particular subject at the time of adoption of the plan or plan amendment at issue.[29]

And:

> Data must be taken from professionally accepted sources. The application of a methodology utilized in data collection or whether a particular methodology is professionally accepted may be evaluated. However, the evaluation may not include whether one accepted methodology is better than another. Original data collection by local governments is not required. However, local governments may use original data so long as methodologies are professionally accepted.[30]

A challenge to comprehensive plan adoption or amendment occurs in a *de novo* hearing. Therefore, new data and new analysis (i.e. data and analysis created or identified *after* the adoption of the challenged comprehensive plan amendment) will almost certainly be part of the record in a comprehensive plan challenge. This raises the question of *when* data and analysis must exist to support a local government action on its comprehensive plan.

Data which support a comprehensive planning decision must exist at the time of the decision.[31] Analysis, on the other hand, may occur after the local government decision.

> [T]he data and analysis which may support a plan amendment are not limited to those identified or actually relied upon by a local government. All data available to a local government in existence at the time of the adoption of the plan amendment may be relied upon to support an amendment in a *de novo* proceeding … . Analysis which may support a plan amendment, however, need not be in existence at the time of the adoption of a plan amendment … . Data which existed at the time of the adoption of a plan amendment may be subject to new or even first-time analysis at the time of an administrative hearing challenging a plan amendment.[32]

The state has also interpreted the requirement that decisions be based on data and analysis as not requiring a set quality or quantity of data for all decisions. Rather, big decisions require more data and analysis, while less significant decisions require less data and analysis.

> In determining whether a plan amendment complies with [the requirement that it be based on relevant and appropriate data and analyses], the [state land planning agency] reviews each amendment on a case-by-case basis. In doing so, it does not require the same amount or type of data for all plan amendments … . For example, if amendments merely represent a policy or directional change and depend on future activities and assessments (i.e., further analyses and decision-making by the local government), the Department does not require the degree of data and analyses that other amendments require (these amendments have sometimes been referred to as aspirational amendments …). Conversely, amendments which are mandatory in nature, that is, amendments which are required to be implemented by Chapter 163, Florida Statutes … require more data and analyses.[33]

### *Internally consistent*

Comprehensive plans must be *internally consistent.*

> Coordination of the several elements of the local comprehensive plan shall be a major objective of the planning process. The several elements of the comprehensive plan shall be consistent. Where data is relevant to several elements, consistent data shall be used … .[34]

Administrative decisions have identified *conflict* as the essence of internal inconsistency. "To be 'internally consistent,' comprehensive plan elements must not conflict. If the objectives do not conflict, then they are coordinated, related, and consistent."[35]

However, comprehensive plans may allow waivers or exceptions to their own policies without causing an internal inconsistency.

> A plan amendment creates an internal inconsistency when it has the effect of conflicting with an existing provision of the comprehensive plan. If an amendment expressly creates an exception or waiver to a general rule set forth in the plan, it does not create an internal inconsistency.[36]

Nonetheless, having an internal inconsistency is a likely reason that a comprehensive plan might be not in compliance with the Community Planning Act. Local government comprehensive plans are lengthy documents—comprising hundreds of pages—written by many different authors across decades. Changing planning preferences of transient elected officials or planning officials sometimes leads to a local government adopting new policies that are in conflict with existing parts of a plan.

### *Required elements*

Florida Statutes section 163.3177 also identifies and describes the required elements of local government comprehensive plans. Elements are the components of the comprehensive plan, like chapters in a textbook.

The required elements are:

- a capital improvements element;[37]
- a future land use plan element;[38]
- a transportation element;[39]
- a general sanitary sewer, solid waste, drainage, potable water, and natural groundwater aquifer recharge element;[40]
- a conservation element for the conservation, use, and protection of natural resources in the area;[41]
- a recreation and open space element;[42]
- a housing element;[43]
- an intergovernmental coordination element;[44] and
- for coastal counties, a coastal management element.[45]

Of these several elements, section 163.3177 provides the most detailed requirements for the future land use plan element and the transportation element. This book discusses the requirements for the future land use plan element in this chapter. This book discusses the capital improvements element and the transportation element in greater detail in a subsequent chapter on infrastructure finance. In addition to the required elements, local governments may adopt optional elements on other subjects as they prefer.[46]

## Policy considerations for future land use plan element

A comprehensive plan's future land use plan element (FLUE) is the pithiest part of the plan. The Community Planning Act provides that every FLUE must show "future general distribution, location, and extent of the uses of land for residential uses, commercial uses, industry, agriculture, recreation, conservation, education, public facilities, and other categories of the public and private uses of land."[47] These future land use categories, much like zoning categories, identify how land can be used throughout a city or a county.

Each FLUE has a future land use map (FLUM) that visually represents all of the property in the local government's jurisdiction designated with a future land use category.[48] FLUE text policies control development in a community in conjunction with implementing regulations and other portions of the comprehensive plan.

Every local government's FLUE policies are unique. Understanding the intricacies of how any one local government regulates development requires reading its distinct rules.

### *Density and intensity*

Every local government comprehensive plan must accommodate *at least* ten years' worth of anticipated growth, as will be explained further on. Local governments may not use their comprehensive plans to plan for less growth or for no growth.

> The plan must be based on at least the minimum amount of land required to accommodate the medium projections ... for at least a 10-year planning period ... . Absent physical limitations on population growth, population projections for each municipality, and the unincorporated area within a county must, at a minimum, be reflective of each area's proportional share of the total county population and the total county population growth.[49]

Local governments coordinate their future land use elements with population projections. This is accomplished in part by requiring every future land use category to include standards for *density* and *intensity*.

> Each future land use category must be defined in terms of uses included, and must include standards to be followed in the control and distribution of population *densities* and building and structure *intensities*. The proposed distribution, location, and extent of the various categories of land use shall be shown on a land use map or map series which shall be supplemented by goals, policies, and measurable objectives.[50]

Density measures how many people are allowed per unit of land. "'Density' means an objective measurement of the number of people or residential units allowed per unit of land, such as residents or employees per acre."[51] Intensity measures how much non-residential development is allowed per unit of land.

> "Intensity" means an objective measurement of the extent to which land may be developed or used, including the consumption or use of the space above, on, or below ground; the measurement of the use of or demand on natural resources; and the measurement of the use of or demand on facilities and services.[52]

Multiplying allowed densities and intensities in a comprehensive plan's several future land use categories, by the amount of land the FLUM designates with those future land use categories, produces a measure of what population and what amount of non-residential development a comprehensive plan accommodates.[53]

### *Sprawl rule*

One of the specific policy directions in the Community Planning Act to which local governments must adhere when adopting or amending their comprehensive plans is the sprawl rule. Every comprehensive plan's FLUE must "discourage the proliferation of urban sprawl."[54] At more than 500 words, the sprawl rule is substantial. It defines sprawl with a list of 13 indicators of sprawl and a list of eight criteria showing that a plan discourages sprawl.

These 21 standards emphasize conserving natural resources[55] and agricultural areas,[56] efficiently providing public services,[57] and "[p]romot[ing] walkable and connected communities and provid[ing] for compact development and a mix of uses at densities and intensities that will support a range of housing choices and a multimodal transportation system, including pedestrian, bicycle, and transit, if available."[58]

The sprawl rule provides substantial direction to local governments on how they may organize land uses on the future land use maps. The rule contrasts with much of the Community Planning Act which directs the planning process, but leaves ultimate planning policy to local governments. Despite this, the structure of the rule renders it practically weak. A FLUE can comply with the sprawl rule, while only meeting a few of the listed criteria.[59] The Legislature has simultaneously acknowledged the importance of preventing urban sprawl, while practically leaving land use policy decisions at the discretion of local governments.

## Coastal management element

Erosion, risk of floods, severe storms, and the growing effects of sea level rise create unique concerns for coastal development. The Community Planning Act's direction to local governments for drafting comprehensive plans includes specific direction regarding such construction.

> [I]t is the intent of the Legislature that local government comprehensive plans restrict development activities where such activities would damage or destroy coastal resources, and that such plans protect human life and limit public expenditures in areas that are subject to destruction by natural disaster.[60]

Statutes implement this intent in part by requiring that coastal counties engage in specific planning activities. For example, "local government[s] abutting the Gulf of Mexico or the Atlantic Ocean" must include a coastal management element in their comprehensive plans.[61]

The Community Planning Act's criteria for the coastal management element outlines those policy issues that coastal development raises, such as protecting coastal aesthetics and ecology, limiting public subsidies for vulnerable coastal development, safety from extreme weather, and protecting ports.[62] In addition, Florida's coastal local governments *may* adopt an adaptation action area.[63] An adaptation action area is a geographic area that is vulnerable to sea level rise and for which a local government adopts specific planning policies "to improve resilience to coastal flooding resulting from high-tide events, storm surge, flash floods, stormwater runoff, and related impacts of sea-level rise."[64]

## Process for adopting and amending comprehensive plans

The Community Planning Act provides three separate processes for reviewing and adopting proposed comprehensive plans and plan amendments. They are: the expedited state review process, the state coordinated review process, and the process for adoption of a small-scale comprehensive plan amendment.[65] In addition to these three processes, Florida Statutes instruct cities and counties on how to provide adequate notice and on how to adopt ordinances and resolutions implementing their decisions.[66]

The expedited state review process is the default process and is used for all comprehensive plan amendments which do not qualify for the other two processes.[67] The scope of the expedited state review process is only to "comment on important state resources and facilities that will be adversely impacted by the amendment if adopted."[68]

The state coordinated review process is the most involved process and is used in specific circumstances identified by the Community Planning Act. Those specific circumstances are adoption of a comprehensive plan or plan amendment that:

- is in an area of critical state concern;
- proposes a rural land stewardship area;
- proposes a sector plan or amends an adopted sector plan;
- updates a comprehensive plan based on an evaluation and appraisal process;
- proposes a development that meets the extant thresholds to be a development of regional impact; or
- is for a newly incorporated municipality.[69]

The scope of state coordinated review is to determine *both* "whether the plan or plan amendment is in compliance *and* whether the plan or plan amendment will adversely impact important state resources and facilities."[70]

The process for adoption of a small-scale comprehensive plan amendment is only available to small-scale comprehensive plan amendments. Generally, a small-scale comprehensive plan amendment is an amendment of the future land use map for ten or fewer acres of land.[71] The small-scale comprehensive plan amendment process does not include state review.[72]

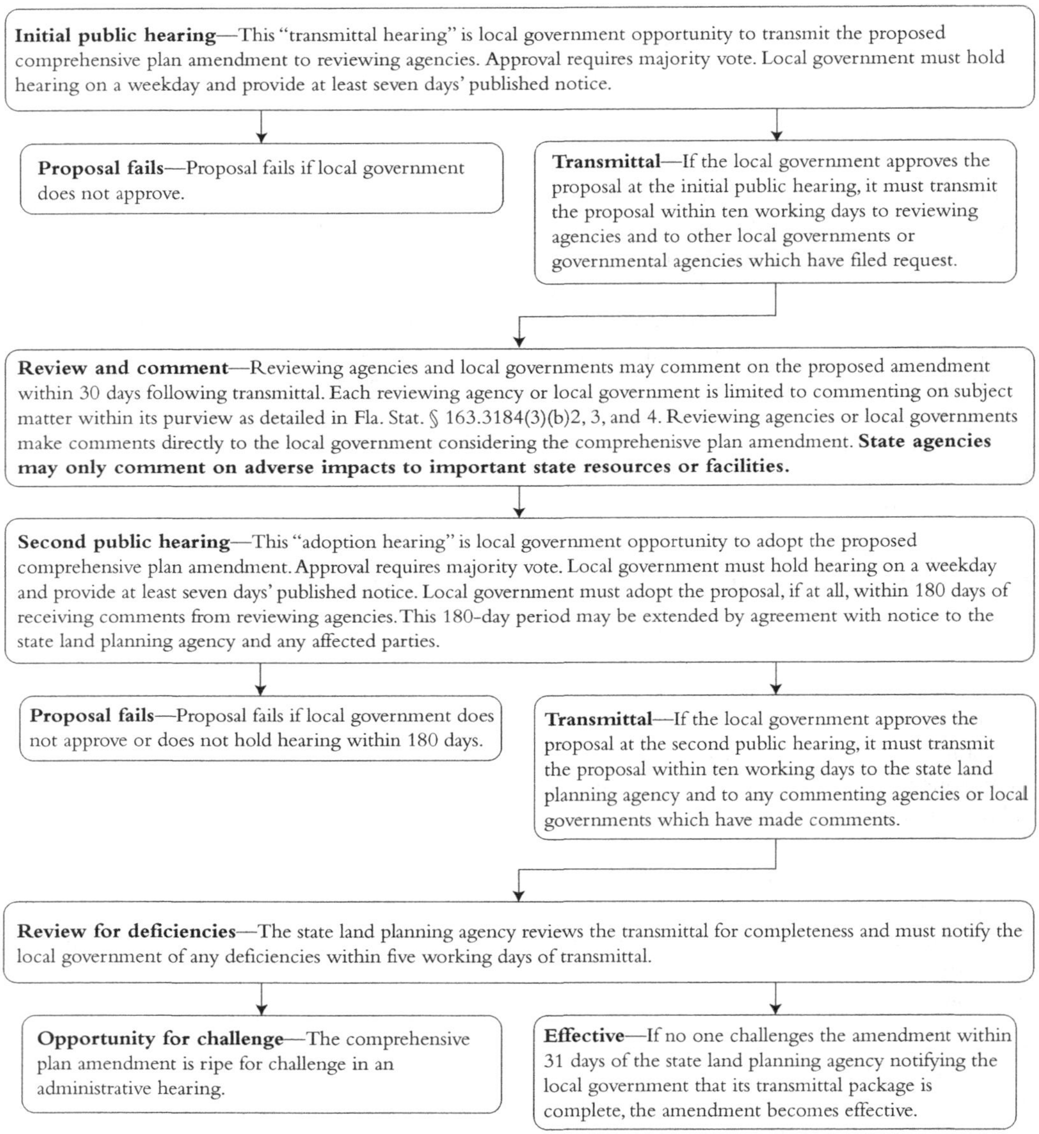


*Figure 6.1* Flow chart describing the expedited state review process for amending a comprehensive plan

Note: *see* Fla. Stat. § 163.3184(3)

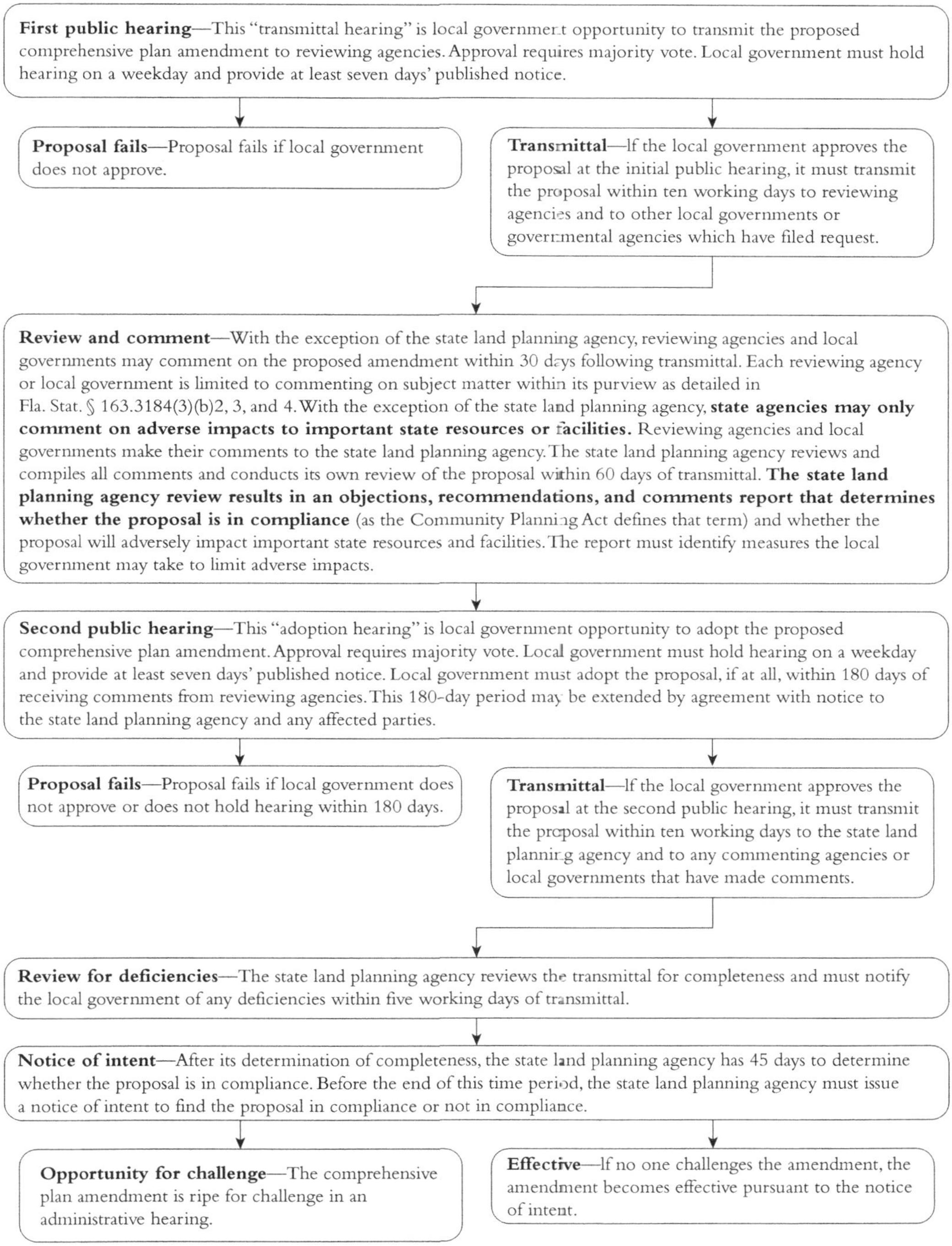


*Figure 6.2* Flow chart describing the state-coordinated review process for adopting or amending a comprehensive plan

Note: *see* Fla. Stat. § 163.3184(4)

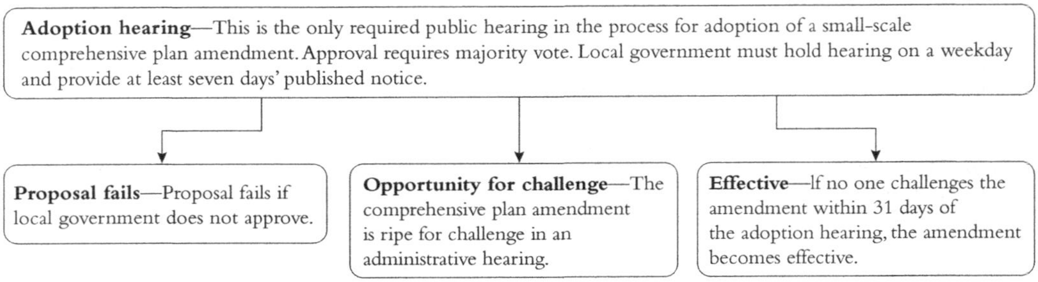


*Figure 6.3* Flow chart describing the small-scale comprehensive plan amendment review process for amending a comprehensive plan

Note: *see* Fla. Stat. § 163.3187

Both the expedited state review process and the state coordinated review process refer to *reviewing agencies*.[73] That phrase is a term of art meaning the following agencies and local governments:

- the state land planning agency;
- the appropriate regional planning council;
- the appropriate water management district;
- the Department of Environmental Protection;
- the Department of State;
- the Department of Transportation;
- in the case of plan amendments relating to public schools, the Department of Education;
- in the case of plans or plan amendments that affect a military installation listed in s. 163.3175, the commanding officer of the affected military installation;
- in the case of county plans and plan amendments, the Fish and Wildlife Conservation Commission and the Department of Agriculture and Consumer Services; and
- in the case of municipal plans and plan amendments, the county in which the municipality is located.[74]

These agencies review and may comment on local government comprehensive plans and comprehensive plan amendments during the expedited state review process and the state coordinated review process.[75]

## Local planning agencies

The Community Planning Act requires every Florida local government to have a local planning agency to advise it on planning matters.[76] A local governing body (i.e. a city commission or a county commission) may designate itself as its own local planning agency.[77] The specific responsibilities of a local planning agency under the law are: to prepare comprehensive plans and plan amendments; to oversee the effectiveness of the comprehensive plan and to recommend changes; and to review proposed land development regulations.[78]

While local planning agencies are a necessary part of the planning process—because the local government body cannot make a final decision on a plan or a plan amendment without first receiving a recommendation from its local planning agency—none of the descriptions of the expedited state review process, the state coordinated review process, or the process for adoption of a small-scale comprehensive plan amendment includes the role of the local planning agency. Each of these processes, as this text describes them, begins after the local planning agency recommends action.

In addition to these statutorily assigned responsibilities, local governments may charge their local planning agencies with additional roles.[79] Many local planning agencies are also responsible for quasi-judicial land use decisions—either as advisory boards to the local governing body or as final decision-makers. Local governments give their local planning agencies a variety of names, such as plan board, planning commission, or zoning board.

## Evaluation and appraisal

The Community Planning Act anticipates that comprehensive plans will not be static, but will change over time in response to changing conditions and evolving public preferences. To facilitate this continual improvement, the act requires communities to undergo a periodic evaluation and appraisal of their comprehensive plans.[80] Local governments must conduct this monitoring at least once every seven years.[81] If a local government's assessment concludes that it must update its comprehensive plan to reflect changes in state requirements, the local government must prepare the needed comprehensive plan amendments for review within one year.[82]

## Land development regulations

Florida statutes require local governments to implement their comprehensive plans by adopting land development regulations.[83] "[A]dopted comprehensive plans or elements thereof shall be implemented, in part, by the adoption and enforcement of appropriate local regulations on the development of lands and waters within an area."[84] These regulations must be "specific and detailed" and the statutes list topics the regulations must address at a minimum.[85] These required topics include subdivision of land, compatibility between adjacent land uses, protection of water and environmentally sensitive lands, signage, and availability of public services.[86] Each local government must codify its land development regulations into a single code.[87]

## Areas of critical state concern

Even before requiring comprehensive planning statewide, Florida created a program to plan for so-called areas of critical state concern (ACSCs). An ACSC is an area the Administration Commission—a body comprising the Governor and members of the Florida Cabinet—has designated as such.[88] Areas eligible to be ACSCs are parts of Florida that are susceptible to intense development and that have environmental, natural, or historical resources with statewide significance.[89] After it designates an area as an ACSC, the Administration Commission plays a formal role in the adoption or amendment of local government comprehensive plans for the area.[90]

## Sector plans

Sector planning is a process for changing local land use laws and state laws to accommodate long-range private development plans.[91] To be eligible for approval as a sector plan, a development proposal must plan for *at least* 15,000 acres,[92] or more than 23 square miles. This threshold is a large amount of land. For reference, the entire city of Miami Beach has a land area of fewer than eight square miles.[93]

The sector planning process has two steps.

> Sector planning encompasses two levels: adoption pursuant to s. 163.3184 of a long-term master plan for the entire planning area as part of the comprehensive plan, and adoption by local development order of two or more detailed specific area plans that implement the long-term master plan … .[94]

The long-term master plan governs the entire sector plan area. Once approved, a long-term master plan becomes a part of the respective local government's comprehensive plan. If a local government approves a long-term master plan, it may then consider adopting detailed specific area plans (DSAPs) for subareas within the sector planning area. Each DSAP implements the long-term master plan for the subarea governed by the DSAP.[95]

## Rural land stewardship areas

A rural land stewardship area is a transferable development rights tool that "accommodate[s] future land uses in a manner that protects the natural environment, stimulate[s] economic growth and diversification, and encourage[s] the retention of land for agriculture and other traditional rural land uses."[96]

Transferable development rights are permissions to develop land that a government allows to be exchanged and moved to different properties. Landscape planner Randal Arendt explains that the transferable development rights technique

> involves a density swap in which all or a part of the development potential of one property (the "sending parcel") is shifted to another property (the "receiving parcel"), thereby preserving all or part of the former by densifying the latter. After the transaction is completed, the ability to develop the sending parcel is reduced or ended, ensuring its permanent preservation.[97]

The beneficial purpose of such a technique is that it "conserves farmland and upland wooded habitat," while it "promotes compact development and redevelopment."[98] Across a landscape, a transferable development rights program acts to cluster development so that developed areas are distinctly urban and undeveloped areas are distinctly rural or agricultural.[99] In the long term, "this approach should not only preserve environmental resources and agricultural land, but should also lead to higher quality built places and less expensive urban services."[100]

A rural land stewardship area in Florida must be at least 10,000 acres in area.[101] A county applies a rural land stewardship area to land as a future land use overlay.[102] This means that the rural land stewardship area designation applies to land *in addition* to some other land use designation shown on the adopted land use map. A property owner may therefore use its land as the county allows for that underlying land use designation *or* as the county allows for the rural land stewardship overlay.

## University campus master plans

Each Florida university board of trustees must adopt a campus master plan.[103] A campus master plan is a land use plan and is analogous to a local government comprehensive plan.

> The master plan must identify general land uses and address the need for and plans for provision of roads, parking, public transportation, solid waste, drainage, sewer, potable water, and recreation and open space during the coming 10 to 20 years. The plans must contain elements relating to future land use, intergovernmental coordination, capital improvements, recreation and open space, general infrastructure, housing, and conservation. Each element must address compatibility with the surrounding community. The master plan must identify specific land uses, general location of structures, densities and intensities of use, and contain standards for onsite development, site design, environmental management, and the preservation of historic and archaeological resources. The transportation element must address reasonable transportation demand management techniques to minimize offsite impacts where possible.[104]

Each university must update its campus master plan at least once every five years[105] and "a campus master plan must not be in conflict with the comprehensive plan of the host local government and the comprehensive plan of any affected local governments."[106]

Unlike local government comprehensive plans, a university may adopt a campus master plan without complying with either the expedited state review process or the state coordinated review process. Instead, Florida Statutes provide for a separate adoption process that requires review by the state land planning agency, other state and regional agencies, and some local governments.[107]

## Notes

1 Floyd A. Wright, *Zoning under the Florida Law*, 7 Miami L.Q. 324, 327 & n.17 (1953).

2 Daniel R. Mandelker, *The Role of the Local Comprehensive Plan in Land Use Regulation*, 74 Mich. L. Rev. 899, 901–2 (1976) (discussing the two major model acts: the 1928 Standard City Planning Enabling Act and the 1926 Standard State Zoning Enabling Act).

3 *See* Floyd A. Wright, *Zoning under the Florida Law*, 7 Miami L.Q. 324, 325–27 (1953).

4 Floyd A. Wright, *Zoning under the Florida Law*, 7 Miami L.Q. 324, 329 (1953), noting that

> [t]he general law terminated the need for further zoning authorization by special acts and, in adopting more recent zoning ordinances, municipalities have relied upon it for the necessary delegated powers. Prior thereto Florida municipalities received their general zoning authority from special statutes.

5 Ch. 75–257, Laws of Fla., §§ 1, 4(2).

6 *See generally* Robert M. Rhodes & Robert C. Apgar, *Charting Florida's Course: The State and Regional Planning Act of 1984*, 12 Fla. St. U.L. Rev. 583 (1984).

7 Ch. 85–55, Laws of Fla.

8 *See* Fla. Stat. § 163.3184(b) (defining "In compliance"). Some commenters also use the term "vertical consistency" to describe local plans which meet state standards; but "vertical consistency" may also mean local plans being consistent with a state plan. *See*, e.g., Jerry Weitz, *Retrenchment and Demise of State Growth Management Programs*, 4 J. Compar. Urb. L. & Pol'y 46 (2020).

9 *See* Fla. Stat. §§ 163.3184(4)(a)–(4)(e) (explaining the state coordinated review process).

10 *Id.* §§ 163.3194(1)(a), (1)(b).

11 Thomas G. Pelham, *A Historical Perspective for Evaluating Florida's Growth Management Process*, in *Growth Management in Florida: Planning for Paradise* 15 (Timothy S. Chapin et al. eds, 2007).

12 Richard G. RuBino & Earl M. Starnes, *Lessons Learned? The History of Planning in Florida* 274 (Sentry Press 2008).

13 Ch. 93–206, Laws of Fla. § 8.

14 Ch. 95–181, Laws of Fla.

15 *See generally* Amber L. Ketterer & Rafael E. Suarez-Rivas, *The Bert J. Harris, Jr. Private Property Rights Protection Act: An Overview, Recent Developments, and What the Future May Hold*, 89 Fla. B.J. 49 (2015).

16 *See* Ch. 2005–290, Laws of Fla.

17 Ch. 2011–139, Laws of Fla., §§ 4–32.

18 *See generally* Fla. Stat. § 163.3184 (mentioning that various agencies are limited in their comments, in either review process, to just issues relating to important state resources).

19 *Id.* § 163.3184(3).
20 *Id.* § 163.3184(4); *see id.* § 163.3184(2)(c) (describing the types of comprehensive plans and plan amendments that must follow the state coordinated review process).
21 Robert M. Rhodes, *Florida's Growth Management Odyssey: Revolution, Evolution, Devolution, Resolution*, in 4 J. Compar. Urb. L. & Pol'y 56, 61 (2020).
22 *Id.*
23 Fla. Stat. § 163.3215(8)(c).
24 *Id.* §§ 163.3167(1)(a), (1)(b).
25 *See id.* § 163.3184(3), (1)(c).
26 *Id.* § 163.3177(1).
27 Fla. Wildlife Fed'n Inc. v. Town of Marineland, Case No. 05-4402GM, para. 72 (Fla. DOAH Apr. 28, 2006) (recommended order); *see also* Izaak Walton Invs., LLC v. Town of Yankeetown, Case No. 08-2451GM, para. 82 (DOAH Oct. 30, 2009) (recommended order) (a comprehensive plan "need not address every possible or potential set of facts and circumstances").
28 *Fla. Wildlife Fed'n Inc.*, *supra* note 27.
29 Fla. Stat. § 163.3177(1)(f).
30 *Id.* § 163.3177(1)(f)(2).
31 *See*, e.g., Zemel v. Lee Cnty., Case No. 90-7793GM, 15 F.A.L.R. 2735, para. 137 (DOAH Dec. 16 22, 1992) (recommended order).
32 Sutterfield v. City of Rockledge, Case No. 02-1630GM, para. 91 (DOAH Sept. 16, 2002) (recommended order) (citations omitted).
33 City of W. Palm Beach v. Dep't of Cmty. Affs., Case No. 04-4336GM, para. 46 (DOAH July 18, 2005) (recommended order) (citations omitted).
34 Fla. Stat. § 163.3177(2).
35 Melzer v. Martin Cnty., Case Nos. 02-1014GM & 02-1015GM, para. 194 (DOAH July 1, 2003) (recommended order).
36 *Id.* para. 195.
37 Fla. Stat. § 163.3177(3)(a).
38 *Id.* § 163.3177(6)(a).
39 *Id.* § 163.3177(6)(b).
40 *Id.* § 163.3177(6)(c).
41 *Id.* § 163.3177(6)(d).
42 *Id.* § 163.3177(6)(e).
43 Fla. Stat. § 163.3177(6)(f)(1).
44 *Id.* § 163.3177(6)(h)(1).
45 *Id.* § 163.3177(6)(g).
46 *Id.* § 163.3177(1)(a).
47 *Id.* §163.3177(6)(a).
48 *Id.* § 163.3177(6)(a)(1); *see also* Coastal Dev. of N. Fla., Inc. v. City of Jacksonville Beach, 788 So. 2d 204, 208 (Fla. 2001) (describing the FLUM as the "pictorial depiction of the future land use element").
49 Fla. Stat. § 163.3177(1)(f)(3).
50 *Id.* § 163.3177(6)(a)(1) (emphasis added).
51 *Id.* § 163.3164(12).
52 *Id.* § 163.3164(22).
53 *See id.* §§ 163.3177(6)(a)1, (a)(2), (a)4.
54 *Id.* § 163.3177(6)(a)9.
55 Fla. Stat. §§ 163.3177(6)(a)9.a.(IV), b.(I), b.(IV), b.(VI).
56 *Id.* §§ 163.3177(6)(a)9.a.(V), b.(V).
57 *Id.* §§ 163.3177(6)(a)9.a.(VI), a.(VII), a.(VIII), b.(II).
58 *Id.* § 163.3177(6)(a)9.b.(III).
59 *Id.* §§ 163.3177(6)(a)9.b.
60 *Id.* § 163.3178(1).
61 Fla. Stat. §§ 380.24, 163.3177 (6)(g).
62 *Id.* § 163.3177 (6)(g).
63 *Id.* § 163.3177 (6)(g)10.
64 *Id.*
65 *Id.* §§ 163.3184(3), 163.3184(4), and 163.3187(1), respectively.
66 *Id.* § 125.66 (providing notice and adoption requirements for county ordinances and resolutions); *id.* § 166.041 (providing notice and adoption requirements for city ordinances and resolutions).
67 Fla. Stat. § 163.3184(2)(a).

68 *Id.* § 163.3184(3)(b)2.
69 *Id.* § 163.3184(2)(c).
70 *Id.* § 163.3184(4)(d)1 (emphasis added).
71 *Id.* § 163.3187(1)(a).
72 *See id.* § 163.3187.
73 Fla. Stat. §§ 163.3184(3)(b)(1)–(b)(2), 163.3184(4)(b)–(4)(c), respectively.
74 *Id.* § 163.3184(1)(c).
75 *Id.* §§ 163.3184(3)(b)(2), 163.3184(4)(c).
76 *Id.* § 163.3174(1).
77 *Id.* §§ 163.3174(1), (2).
78 *Id.* §§ 163.3174(4)(a)–(4)(c).
79 Fla. Stat. § 163.3174(4)(d).
80 *Id.* § 163.3191(3).
81 *Id.* § 163.3191(1).
82 *Id.* § 163.3191(2).
83 *Id.* § 163.3201.
84 *Id.*
85 Fla. Stat. § 163.3202(2).
86 *Id.*
87 *Id.* § 163.3202(3).
88 *Id.* §§ 380.045(2)–(3).
89 *Id.* § 380.05(2)(a) (giving a non-exhaustive list, including state or federal parks, forests, and aquatic preserves).
90 *Id.* § 380.05(11) (highlighting that the Administration Commission may amend or rescind the amendment of local government comprehensive plans).
91 *See* Fla. Stat. § 163.3245(1).
92 *Id.* § 163.3245(10).
93 QuickFacts Miami Beach city, Florida, U.S. Census Bureau (2010), www.census.gov/ (reporting the land area as 7.63 square miles) (last visited April 13, 2021).
94 Fla. Stat. § 163.3245(3).
95 *See id.* §§ 163.3245(3)(b)(1)–(b)(9).
96 *Id.* § 163.3248(1).
97 Randall Arendt, *Rural by Design: Planning for Town and Country* 297 (2nd edn, Am. Plan. Ass'n Planners Press 2015).
98 *Id.*
99 *Id.*
100 *Id.*
101 Fla. Stat. § 163.3248(5).
102 *Id.* § 163.3248(2).
103 *Id.* § 1013.30(3).
104 *Id.*
105 *Id.*
106 *Id.* § 1013.30(5).
107 Fla. Stat. § 1013.30(6).

# 7 Judicial treatment of comprehensive plans

The following case, *Martin Cnty. v. Yusem*, develops the bright-line rule that local government comprehensive planning decisions are legislative. As a result, under *Brevard Cnty. v. Snyder*, the appropriate due process standard for comprehensive planning decisions is the fairly debatable standard.

## Florida Supreme Court

### *Martin Cnty. v. Yusem*[1]

### 1997

WELLS, Justice.

We have for review a decision addressing the following question certified to be of great public importance:

> CAN A REZONING DECISION WHICH HAS LIMITED IMPACT UNDER SNYDER, BUT DOES REQUIRE AN AMENDMENT OF THE COMPREHENSIVE LAND USE PLAN, STILL BE A QUASI-JUDICIAL DECISION SUBJECT TO STRICT SCRUTINY REVIEW?

*Martin County v. Yusem*, 664 So. 2d 976, 982 (Fla. 4th DCA 1995) (on motions for rehearing and certification) ... . We answer the certified question in the negative and hold that amendments to a comprehensive land use plan which was adopted pursuant to Chapter 163, Florida Statutes, are legislative decisions subject to the "fairly debatable" standard of review ... .

Melvyn Yusem owns fifty-four acres of land in Martin County. In 1982, Martin County (County) adopted by ordinance a comprehensive plan for land use planning in the county. Subsequently, in 1990, the County replaced its earlier plan by adopting a comprehensive land use plan (Plan) pursuant to the 1985 Local Government Comprehensive Planning Act. *See generally* Fla. Stat. § 163.3184 (1985). Under the Plan, Yusem's fifty-four acres are part of a 900-acre tract which was included within the Plan's Primary Urban Service District (PUSD). Although up to two units per acre were allowed in the PUSD under the Plan, the future land use map, a component of the Plan, restricted this 900-acre tract to only one residential unit per two acres. *See* Fla. Stat. § 163.3177(6)(a) (1989).

Yusem requested an amendment to the future land use map for his property from "Rural Density," which allows development of .5 units per acre, to "Estate Density," which allows development of up to two units per acre. In conjunction with this amendment, Yusem requested a rezoning of his property from "A-1" (agricultural) to "Planned Unit Development" (residential) ... .

[T]he Board voted three to two to deny Yusem's proposal.

Yusem then sought relief in the circuit court. Yusem first filed a petition for certiorari but voluntarily dismissed it, choosing instead to file a complaint for declaratory and injunctive relief. In finding in Yusem's favor, the trial court relied upon *Snyder v. Board of County Commissioners*, 595 So. 2d 65 (Fla. 5th DCA 1991) (*Snyder I*), quashed, 627 So. 2d 469 (Fla. 1993). The trial court noted that *Snyder I* involved a rezoning question; however, it found the basic rationale of that case to apply in the plan-amendment context. The trial court then found that when a planning decision has an impact on a limited number of persons or property or identifiable parties and is contingent on a fact or facts, the action is quasi-judicial. Consequently, the trial court framed the issue in the case as follows:

> whether or not the requested land use amendment is consistent with the Martin County Comprehensive Plan and whether or not the requested land use amendment is a logical and consistent extension of present uses in the general area of Plaintiff's land.

Since resolution of the issue was contingent upon facts, the court applied the strict-scrutiny standard of review and concluded that the County improperly denied Yusem's requested amendment.

On appeal, the Fourth District reversed the trial court's ruling based upon a determination that the court was without jurisdiction to decide the merits of the action. However, in its opinion, the panel divided, with the majority agreeing that the County's decision was subject to a strict-scrutiny standard of review. *Martin County v. Yusem*, 664 So. 2d 976 (Fla. 4th DCA 1995) ... . The district court, similar to the trial court, concluded that the County's action was essentially a quasi-judicial rezoning decision because to increase the density on Yusem's fifty-four acres would have a limited impact on the public ... . Further, the district court ... conclud[ed] that amendments to comprehensive plans are not necessarily legislative ... .

Judge Pariente dissented, writing that the adoption of a comprehensive land use plan, which required the county to determine whether it should alter its overall plan for managed growth, local services, and capital expenditures as embodied in the future land use map, was a legislative act; therefore, decisions concerning the amendment of a comprehensive plan should similarly be treated as legislative acts. 664 So. 2d at 979. Further, Judge Pariente distinguished this case from our decision in *Snyder*, in which we found the denial of a request to rezone a particular parcel of land to a designation which was consistent with the policies of the plan was a quasi-judicial decision, because the rezoning request in this case was inconsistent with the plan and required a plan amendment. Judge Pariente noted that a bright-line rule finding that all plan amendments were legislative acts would provide clarity to the procedures involved in this otherwise confusing area of the law. *Id.* at 982. Therefore, Judge Pariente would have found that the trial court should have reviewed the county's action in a trial *de novo* under the deferential "fairly debatable" standard of review. *Id.*

On motion for rehearing and clarification, the court certified the foregoing question, asking us to clarify whether a rezoning decision which has a limited impact under *Snyder II* but requires an amendment to the comprehensive plan is still a quasi-judicial decision subject to strict-scrutiny review. *Yusem*, 664 So. 2d at 982 (on motions for rehearing and certification).

To resolve this question, the County advocates that we adopt the dissent's view and find that amendments to a comprehensive plan are legislative decisions subject to a fairly debatable standard of review. The County notes that this proceeding was clearly a legislative proceeding because Yusem's request was to change, rather than apply, the existing plan. It is on this basis that the County distinguishes the case involving a request for a plan amendment from *Snyder II* involving a request for rezoning.

Yusem responds by arguing that the hearing before the Board was clearly quasi-judicial because during the hearing, he presented detailed evidence in support of his request; the hearing was directed at one specific property owner and one 54-acre parcel of land; and the County reviewed the facts and applied the standards contained in the plan. Yusem argues that there is no logical or factual reason to distinguish this case from *Snyder II*, and the trial court should strictly scrutinize this plan-amendment proceeding, which also involved a rezoning request. Several other parties have submitted amicus briefs in support of their positions.

Chapter 163, part II, Florida Statutes (1989) (Local Government Comprehensive Planning and Land Development Regulation Act) (the Act), was intended to enhance present advantages and encourage appropriate uses of land and resources. *See* Fla. Stat. § 163.3161(3) (1989). In furtherance of these goals, the Act requires each local government to adopt a comprehensive plan to prescribe the "principles, guidelines, and standards for the orderly and balanced future economic, social, physical, environmental, and fiscal development of the area." Fla. Stat. § 163.3177(1) (1989); *see Snyder II*, at 475 (stating that a comprehensive plan is intended to provide for the future use of land, which contemplates a gradual and ordered growth). A comprehensive plan includes several elements including a future land use element. *See* Fla. Stat. § 163.3177(1989). With reference to this element, we have noted:

> [T]he future land use plan element of the local plan must contain both a future land use map and goals, policies, and measurable objectives to guide future land use decisions. This plan element must designate the "proposed future general distribution, location, and extent of the uses of land" for various purposes. *Id.* § 163.3177(6)(a). It must include standards to be utilized in the control and distribution of densities and intensities of development. In addition, the future land use plan must be based on adequate data and analysis concerning the local jurisdiction, including the projected population, the amount of land needed to accommodate the estimated population, the availability of public services and facilities, and the character of undeveloped land. *Id.* § 163.3177(6)(a).

*Snyder II*, at 473.

In *Snyder II*, in the rezoning context, we distinguished legislative actions which result in the formulation of a general rule of policy and quasi-judicial actions which result in the application of a general rule of policy. *Id.* at 474. We recognized that comprehensive rezonings which affect a large portion of the public are legislative determinations; however, we also recognized that rezonings which impact a limited number of persons and in which the decision is contingent upon evidence presented at a hearing are quasi-judicial proceedings properly reviewable by petition for certiorari. *Id.* at 474–75. In reaching this decision, we stressed that in a quasi-judicial rezoning proceeding, the landowner has the burden of proving that the proposal is consistent with the comprehensive plan and complies with all procedural requirements of the zoning ordinance before the burden shifts to the government to demonstrate that maintaining the existing zoning classification accomplishes a legitimate public purpose. *Id.* at 476. In *Snyder II*, we plainly did not deal with the issue of the appropriate standard of review for amendments to a comprehensive land use plan … .

We … recognize that subsequent to *Snyder* … several district courts have employed a functional analysis in determining whether a plan amendment is either quasi-judicial or legislative. In some cases, the district courts have concluded that amendments to comprehensive plans are legislative decisions subject to the fairly debatable rule. *See, e.g., City Envtl. Servs. Landfill, Inc. v. Holmes County*, 677 So. 2d 1327 (Fla. 1st DCA 1996) (county's decision to deny amendment creating new land use classification based on environmental risks, traffic, and road repair was legislative); *Martin County v. Section 28 Partnership, Ltd.*, 676 So. 2d 532 (Fla. 4th DCA), review denied, 686 So. 2d 581 (Fla. 1996); *Board of County Comm'rs v. Karp*, 662 So. 2d 718 (Fla. 2d DCA 1995) (finding amendment to comprehensive plan for 5.5-mile corridor affecting 179 acres and 48 parcels was legislative); *Section 28 Partnership, Ltd. v. Martin County*, 642 So. 2d 609 (Fla. 4th DCA 1994) (finding plan amendment requiring creation of new classification of property allowing development of land near headwaters of Loxahatchee River and state park was legislative), review denied, 654 So. 2d 920 (Fla. 1995). Whereas in this case, the trial court and the district court used a functional analysis to reach the opposite conclusion: that an amendment to the comprehensive plan was a quasi-judicial decision subject to strict-scrutiny review. The district court concluded that the decision by the County should be functionally viewed as having limited impact on the public since the Board hearing addressed the change in land use designation for a particular piece of property.

While we continue to adhere to our analysis in *Snyder* with respect to the type of rezonings at issue in that case, we do not extend that analysis or endorse a functional, fact-intensive approach to determining whether amendments to local comprehensive land use plans are legislative decisions. Rather, we expressly conclude that amendments to comprehensive land use plans are legislative decisions. This conclusion is not affected by the fact that the amendments to comprehensive land use plans are being sought as part of a rezoning application in respect to only one piece of property.[6]

As this Court noted in *Snyder II*, a comprehensive land use plan must be based upon adequate data and analysis in providing for gradual and ordered growth in the future use of land. *Snyder II*, 627 So. 2d at 475; *see also Machado v. Musgrove*, 519 So. 2d 629 (Fla. 3d DCA 1987) (finding that a local land use plan is like a constitution for all future development within the governmental boundary). Consequently, we agree with Judge Pariente's dissent below that *Snyder*'s functional analysis in rezoning cases is not applicable in comprehensive plan amendment cases:

> [I]n contrast to the rezonings at issue in *Snyder*, the review of the proposed amendment here required the County to engage in policy reformulation of its comprehensive plan and to determine whether it now desired to retreat from the policies embodied in its future land use map for the orderly development of the County's future growth. The county was required to evaluate the likely impact such amendment would have on the county's provision of local services, capital expenditures, and its overall plan for growth and future development of the surrounding area. The decision whether to allow the proposed amendment to the land use plan to proceed to the DCA for its review and then whether to adopt the amendment involved considerations well beyond the landowner's 54 acres.

*Yusem*, 664 So. 2d at 981 (Pariente, J., dissenting). We also agree with Judge Stone's concurring opinion in *Section 28 Partnership* that there is no reason to treat a county's decision rejecting a proposed modification of a previously adopted land use plan as any less legislative in nature than the decision initially adopting the plan. *See Section 28 Partnership*, 642 So. 2d at 613 (Stone, J., concurring).

6 We do note that in 1995, the legislature amended section 163.3187(1)(c), Florida Statutes, which provides special treatment for comprehensive plan amendments directly related to proposed small-scale development activities. Ch. 95–396, § 5, Laws of Fla. We do not make any findings concerning the appropriate standard of review for these small-scale development activities.

Our conclusion that amendments to comprehensive plans are legislative decisions is further supported by the procedures for effecting such amendments under the Act. Amendments to comprehensive plans are evaluated on several levels of government to ensure consistency with the Act and to provide ordered development. *See* § Fla. Stat. 163.3184(8).

The Act provides for a two-stage process for amending a comprehensive plan: transmittal and adoption. In the first stage, the local government determines whether to transmit the proposed amendment to the Department for further review. *See* § Fla. Stat. 163.3184(3). If the local government transmits the proposed amendment, the process moves into the second stage. The Department, after receiving the amendment, provides the local government with its objections, recommendations for modifications, and comments of any other regional agencies. *See* § Fla. Stat. 163.3184(4). At this point, the local government has three options: (1) adopt the amendment; (2) adopt the amendment with changes; or (3) not adopt the amendment. *See* Fla. Stat. § 163.3184(7) (1989).

Upon adoption of the amendment by the local government, the Department again reviews the amendment. *See* Fla. Stat. § 163.3184(8) (1989). After this review and an administrative hearing, if an amendment is determined not to be in compliance with the Act, the State Comprehensive Plan, and the Department's minimum criteria rule, *see* § Fla. Stat. 163.3184(1)(b), then the matter is referred to the Administration Commission. *See* Fla. Stat. §§ 163.3184(9)(b), (10)(b). The Administration Commission, composed of the Governor and the Cabinet, *see* Fla. Stat. § 163.3164(1), is then empowered to levy sanctions against a local government, including directing state agencies not to provide the local government with funding for future projects. *See* Fla. Stat. § 163.3184(11)(a) (1989).

This integrated review process ensures that the policies and goals of the Act are followed. The strict oversight on the several levels of government to further the goals of the Act is evidence that when a local government is amending its comprehensive plan, it is engaging in a policy decision. This is in contrast to a rezoning proceeding, which is only evaluated on the local level. *See Snyder.*

Moreover, our conclusion today that amendments to a comprehensive plan are legislative decisions subject to the fairly debatable rule is consistent with section 163.3184, Florida Statutes (1989). As noted above, once a local government decides to adopt an amendment, the Department issues a notice of intent to find whether an amendment is in compliance with state law, see Fla. Stat. § 163.3184(9)(a), or is not compliance with state law, *see* Fla. Stat. § 163.3184(10)(a)t. In this proceeding, the determination of compliance is made using the fairly debatable rule. *Id.* By our decision today, we make clear that this standard applies at any stage in such proceedings.

Additionally, our decision today will further the proper administration of justice in Florida. Currently in Florida, there is much confusion surrounding the proper procedural vehicle for challenging a local government's decision concerning an amendment to a comprehensive plan. *See, e.g., Yusem; Martin County v. Section 28 Partnership, Ltd.*, 676 So. 2d 532 (Fla. 4th DCA 1996) (original action); *Section 28 Partnership, Ltd. v. Martin County*, 642 So. 2d 609 (Fla. 4th DCA 1994) (petition for certiorari). By our holding that all amendments to comprehensive plans are legislative activities subject to the fairly debatable standard, parties will know to file such challenges as original actions in the circuit court. *See Hirt v. Polk County Board of County Comm'rs*, 578 So. 2d 415, 416 (Fla. 2d DCA 1991).

...

Last, we note the following. The fairly debatable standard of review is a highly deferential standard requiring approval of a planning action if reasonable persons could differ as to its propriety. *See B & H Travel Corp. v. State Dep't of Community Affairs*, 602 So. 2d 1362 (Fla. 1st DCA 1992). In other words, "[a]n ordinance may be said to be fairly debatable when for any reason it is open to dispute or controversy on grounds that make sense or point to a logical deduction that in no way involves its constitutional validity." *City of Miami Beach v. Lachman*, 71 So. 2d 148, 152 (Fla. 1953). The procedural requirements inuring to a quasi-judicial proceeding are distinct from those inuring to a legislative proceeding. *See generally City Envtl. Servs. Landfill, Inc. v. Holmes County*, 677 So. 2d 1327 (Fla. 1st DCA 1996). However, we do point out that even with the deferential review of legislative action afforded by the fairly debatable rule, local government action still must be in accord with the procedures required by Chapter 163, part II, Florida Statutes, and local ordinances. Cf. *David v. City of Dunedin*, 473 So. 2d 304 (Fla. 2d DCA 1985) (finding null and void an ordinance enacted in violation of the notice provisions of the relevant statutes).

Accordingly, we hold that all comprehensive plan amendments are legislative decisions subject to the fairly debatable standard of review. We find that amendments to a comprehensive plan, like the adoption of the plan itself, result in the formulation of policy ... .

It is so ordered.

KOGAN, C.J., and OVERTON, SHAW, GRIMES and HARDING, JJ., concur.

ANSTEAD, J., recused.

### *Discussion*

In deciding *Martin Cnty. v. Yusem*, the Florida Supreme Court declined to extend its holding that comprehensive planning decisions are legislative to small-scale comprehensive plan amendments.[2] In *Coastal Dev. of N. Fla., Inc. v. City of Jacksonville Beach*, however, the court considered that precise question.[3] It resolved the issue by extending its bright-line rule to all comprehensive planning decisions, concluding "small-scale development amendments ... are legislative decisions which are subject to the fairly debatable standard of review."[4]

The following case, *1000 Friends of Fla., Inc. v. Palm Beach Cnty.*, evaluates the meaning of a local government comprehensive plan provision as legislation, using normal rules of statutory construction.

## Florida Fourth District Court of Appeal

## *1000 Friends of Florida, Inc. v. Palm Beach Cnty.*[5]

## 2011

LEVINE, J.

... The issue presented for our review is whether the trial court erred in upholding a development order issued by the Palm Beach County Commission permitting mining in the Everglades. The trial court interpreted the relevant land use policy in the comprehensive plan as non-exclusive, thereby permitting mining in an area zoned for agriculture for a purpose that was not enumerated in the land use policy. We find the trial court erred by failing to define "only" as restrictive and thereby failing to limit mining to the purposes enumerated in the future land use element policy. We reverse.

The Palm Beach County Commission issued a development order to Bergeron Sand and Rock Mine Aggregates, Inc., granting the corporation the right to mine within the "Everglades Agricultural Area" in western Palm Beach County. Bergeron sought to expand its mining operations on property designated as "agricultural production" in the comprehensive plan. After a public hearing, the Palm Beach County Commission unanimously granted conditional approval for the development order and subsequently adopted Bergeron's application, finding the mining proposal to be consistent with the comprehensive plan.

After the order issued, appellants filed a complaint for declaratory and injunctive relief to challenge the development order, claiming that the order was inconsistent with a Future

Land Use Element ("FLUE") policy of the comprehensive plan. The specific FLUE policy, 2.3–e.3, states that "[m]ining and excavation activities, as applicable, shall be restricted" as follows:

> Within the Agricultural Production Future Land Use designation, mining may be permitted only to support public roadway projects or agricultural activities or water management projects associated with ecosystem restoration, regional water supply or flood protection, on sites identified by the South Florida Water Management District or the U.S. Army Corps of engineers where such uses provide viable alternate technologies for water management.

Both at the public hearing and later at trial, the parties admitted that aggregate mined from the property designated as agricultural production within the Everglades Agricultural Area could be used for purposes other than to "support public roadway projects."[1] The county submitted to the trial court a staff analysis which stated that "limestone aggregate from the subject property will be marketed to FDOT for road building and construction." The staff analysis further recommended that Bergeron be required to report annually regarding the amount of material mined and that Bergeron be required to provide "[d]ocumentation as to the intended use of the material" and whether the usage of the material "complies with the County requirements, such as but not limited to the quarry's status with FDOT and other usages for the mined aggregate." When the county commission approved the application, it adopted the staff recommendation that Bergeron submit such an annual report documenting compliance with the comprehensive plan.

Appellants argued at trial that Bergeron intended to sell the aggregate mined from the property on the open market. Lonnie Bergeron, in his deposition, conceded that he had no control over whether the material excavated would, in fact, be used for the construction of public highways. Appellants argued that the sale of the excavated material on the open markets without any controls, runs afoul of the comprehensive plan. Because any development order issued by a local government "shall be consistent" with the comprehensive plan, appellants sought to have the development order quashed. Fla. Stat. § 163.3194(1)(a).

The trial court entered a final summary judgment concluding that the proposed mining was proper since "some portion of the material produced by the proposed mine will be FDOT certified material that will be used in road projects." The court concluded that the use of some material by FDOT was sufficient to "support" public road construction. This appeal ensues from the trial court's granting of a final summary judgment on behalf of the county and Bergeron.

We review de novo an order on a motion for summary judgment. *Volusia County v. Aberdeen at Ormond Beach, L.P.*, 760 So. 2d 126, 130 (Fla. 2000). Summary judgment is proper if there is no genuine issue of material fact and the moving party is entitled to judgment as a matter of law. *Id.*

The trial court need not defer to the county's interpretation of the comprehensive plan. *Pinecrest Lakes, Inc. v. Shidel*, 795 So. 2d 191, 197–98 (Fla. 4th DCA 2001). The parties have

1 On appeal, the parties' briefs and oral argument focused on public roadway projects. To the extent that the parties raised other claims of compliance with FLUE police 2.3–e.3 below, but did not fully address such claims on appeal, those claims have essentially been abandoned. See, e.g., Johnson v. State, 795 So. 2d 82, 89–90 (Fla. 5th DCA 2000) (finding an issue abandoned where, even if briefs could be construed as raising the issue, the argument was not developed).

agreed that the order permitting Bergeron's conditional use of the agricultural property in the Everglades is a development order.[2] The parties have further agreed that the sole issue on appeal is whether the development order, authorizing Bergeron's mining of the "agricultural production" area in the Everglades Agricultural Area, is consistent with FLUE policy 2.3–e.3, which states that mining may be permitted "only to support" public roadways, agricultural activities, or water management projects.

In order to determine if the development order is consistent with the policy of the comprehensive plan, we have to look at the plain language of the policy. We apply the same rules of construction to a comprehensive plan that we would apply to other statutes. *Rinker Materials Corp. v. City of N. Miami*, 286 So. 2d 552, 553 (Fla. 1973). If the terms of the comprehensive plan are not defined, then the language of the plan "should usually be given its plain and ordinary meaning." *Fla. Birth-Related Neurological Injury Comp. Ass'n v. Fla. Div. of Admin. Hearings*, 686 So. 2d 1349, 1354 (Fla. 1997).[3] The plain and ordinary meaning of "only" has been explained as "[s]olely; merely; for no other purpose; at no other time; in no otherwise; along; of or by itself; without anything more; exclusive; nothing else or more." *Black's Law Dictionary* 982 (5th ed. 1979). "It is appropriate to refer to dictionary definitions when construing statutes or rules." *Barco v. Sch. Bd. of Pinellas Cnty.*, 975 So. 2d 1116, 1122 (Fla. 2008).

The Florida Supreme Court has determined in a case involving restrictive covenants on real property that "only" can mean "solely" and "nothing else." *Moore v. Stevens*, 106 So. 901, 904 (Fla. 1925). In *Moore*, the Florida Supreme Court found that the covenant, "to be used for residence purposes only," meant that the residence can be used solely for one type of occupancy. *Id.* "The word 'only' is a limiting term which qualifies the word with which it is grammatically connected ... . It qualifies the phrase 'to be used,' with like effect as if the covenant had read that the property 'is to be used only for residence purposes.'" *Id.* As recognized in other Florida cases, "the word 'only' is synonymous with the word 'solely' and is the equivalent of the phrase 'and nothing else.'" *White v. Metro. Dade County*, 563 So. 2d 117, 124 (Fla. 3d DCA 1990) (quoting *Thompson v. Squibb*, 183 So. 2d 30, 32 (Fla. 2d DCA 1966)). In the present case, the word "only" limits mining in the Everglades Agricultural Area to the three enumerated activities: public roadway projects, agricultural activities, and water management projects.

We are persuaded that mining is permitted "only" to support the restricted and exclusive list of activities outlined in the FLUE within the comprehensive plan.[4] As aptly stated by another court, "[o]nly means only." *Union Station Assocs., LLC v. Puget Sound Energy, Inc.*, 238 F. Supp. 2d 1218, 1225 (W.D. Wash. 2002); *accord Nicklos Drilling Co. v. Cowart*, 907 F. 2d 1552, 1554 (5th Cir. 1990).

2 A "development order" is defined as an "order granting, denying, or granting with conditions an application for a development permit." § 163.3164(7), Fla. Stat. (2008). A "development permit" constitutes "any other official action of local government having the effect of permitting the development of land," such as rezoning, special exception, or variance. § 163.3164(8), Fla. Stat. (2008).

3 As Justice Scalia commented: "Words do have a limited range of meaning, and no interpretation that goes beyond that range is permissible." Antonin Scalia, *Common-Law Courts in a Civil-Law System: The Role of United States Federal Courts in Interpreting the Constitution & Laws*, in *A Matter of Interpretation: Federal Courts & the Law* 24 (Amy Gutmann ed. 1997).

4 Appellees contend that their interpretation of FLUE policy 2.3–e.3 requires only that the mining must "support" road building. The trial court adopted this position by finding that as long as some of the aggregate was used to "support" public road construction then the development order was consistent with the comprehensive plan. We reject this position which elevates the word "support" to the detriment of the word "only."

The plain language of the text is controlling. "A text should not be construed strictly, and it should not be construed leniently; it should be construed reasonably, to contain all that it fairly means." Scalia, *supra*, at 23. At oral argument, the county argued that the language requiring mined aggregate to be used "only to support" public roadway projects would conceivably allow mining where only one percent of aggregate is used for public roads (or another enumerated use). We find that particular interpretation of the text in the FLUE policy of the comprehensive plan to be unreasonable in light of the plain language of the text. It would undercut the plain language, as well as the spirit, of the comprehensive plan if only one percent of the aggregate would need to go to public roads while the other ninety-nine percent could go to non-enumerated activities. This construct of the comprehensive plan would eviscerate the clear restrictions outlined in the text, denoted by the word "only."

We find the plain language controlling, but we also point to the canons of construction for further support. One rule of construction, for example, is "expressio unius est exclusio alterius" or "to express or include one thing implies the exclusion of the other." *Black's Law Dictionary* (9th ed. 2009). This maxim supports the argument that the comprehensive plan lists a restrictive and exclusive list of three activities, which excludes other activities by virtue of the fact they were not included in the enumerated list. Thus, if the FLUE policy permitted mining in the Everglades Agricultural Area to support private building construction, policy 2.3–e.3 would explicitly reference private building construction. Because private construction is not listed in the policy, we assume it is not permissible by the fact that it is not enumerated or listed.

Further, "[a]s a fundamental rule of statutory interpretation, 'courts should avoid readings that would render part of a statute meaningless.'" *Unruh v. State*, 669 So. 2d 242, 245 (Fla. 1996) (citation omitted). If we accepted the trial court's interpretation, then the word "only" would be superfluous, since "mining may be permitted ... to support" public roadways, agricultural activities, or water management projects. The removal of the word "only" would make the list of activities non-exclusive since mining would only be required to "support" the enumerated activities.

In summary, we find the development order permitting mining in the agricultural production area of the Everglades Agricultural Area is inconsistent with FLUE policy 2.3–e.3 of the comprehensive plan. As Justice Oliver Wendell Holmes concluded over one hundred years ago, "[w]hatever the consequences, we must accept the plain meaning of plain words." *United States v. Brown*, 206 U.S. 240, 244 (1907). Therefore, we reverse the judgment in favor of appellees and remand with instructions for the trial court to declare the development order inconsistent with the comprehensive plan and to enjoin enforcement of the order.

*Reversed and remanded with instructions.*

WARNER and CONNER, JJ., concur.

## Notes

1 690 So. 2d 1288 (Fla. 1997).
2 Martin Cnty. v. Yusem, 690 So. 2d 1288, 1293, n.6 (Fla. 1997).
3 788 So. 2d 204 (Fla. 2001).
4 *Id.* at 210.
5 69 So. 3d 1123 (Fla. 4th DCA 2011).

# 8 Local variation

Local politics and locally preferred approaches dictate how communities regulate land.[1] This is true even though police powers are inherent to the state and Florida's legislature extensively directs local governments on how to plan and regulate land use. Due to this local primacy, just about every city and county has some unique aspect to its regulatory approach. This chapter presents examples of uncommon techniques to show the existing variety. These examples are certainly not exhaustive, underscoring the need for the land use practitioner to closely review the rules in each jurisdiction where he or she works.

## Monroe County rate of growth ordinance

Monroe County is the southernmost county in Florida. The Florida Keys—a long chain of small islands on the southern tip of Florida—are within Monroe County. For several reasons, the number of people living in the Florida Keys is of great public importance. First, the Florida Keys are a fragile and unique natural system. While the natural environment sustains the local tourist economy and quality of life, it is also vulnerable to the human population. Second, providing potable water and sewer service to the islands is challenging. Keeping public services available in pace with growing demand requires diligence. Finally, the Florida Keys are vulnerable to deadly storms. A 2017 storm, Hurricane Irma, destroyed approximately 4,000 homes in the Keys.[2] No hurricane shelters for Category 3 to 5 storms are available in the Keys.[3] When a severe storm is approaching, people living in the Keys must leave using a single road, US 1. Maintaining an ability for people to safely evacuate from the Keys is essential.

In recognition of the need to carefully plan for the number of people in the Florida Keys, the Florida Keys Area Protection Act[4] provides particular standards for local government comprehensive plans in the Keys. This state law requires the state land planning agency to review amendments to comprehensive plans for local governments in the Florida Keys to ensure they "protect public safety and welfare in the event of a natural disaster by maintaining a hurricane evacuation clearance time for permanent residents of no more than 24 hours."[5]

The comprehensive plans of the several local governments in the Keys and the Florida Administrative Code maintain this required evacuation time from the Keys by carefully limiting new dwelling unit permits in the Keys. For example, Monroe County uses a rate of growth ordinance (ROGO) that limits the number of residential development permits to an annual cap of 197.[6] Similarly, the cities of Marathon and Islamorada use a residential building permit allocation system to cap the number of new dwelling units permitted by those cities.[7]

These local ordinances implement the safety standards set by the state of Florida by limiting permits for *new* dwelling units and do not apply to permits for rehabilitating homes or replacing homes destroyed by storms.[8] Despite this tightly knit framework including state law, local law, and carefully prepared data, high demand for housing in the Keys maintains constant political pressure for eroding the ROGO system.

Monroe County's system of rationing permission to develop based on a predetermined allotment of permits may seem like an extreme approach to land use regulation. But other jurisdictions have used the ROGO approach and federal courts have evaluated whether it violates the U.S. Constitution. Petaluma, California is a city in Sonoma County, to the north of San Francisco. In the 1960s and 1970s, the city was growing rapidly. In response, the city adopted a ROGO it called the "Petaluma Plan."

After landowners in Petaluma sued the city, a federal court considered whether the Petaluma Plan violated property owners' due process rights. The court said the following:

> Although we assume that some persons desirous of living in Petaluma will be excluded under the housing permit limitation and that, thus, the Plan may frustrate some legitimate regional housing needs, the Plan is not arbitrary or unreasonable. We agree with appellees that unlike the situation in the past most municipalities today are neither isolated nor wholly independent from neighboring municipalities and that, consequently, unilateral land use decisions by one local entity affect the needs and resources of an entire region. It does not necessarily follow, however, that the Due process rights of builders and landowners are violated merely because a local entity exercises in its own self-interest the police power lawfully delegated to it by the state. If the present system of delegated zoning power does not effectively serve the state interest in furthering the general welfare of the region or entire state, it is the state legislature's and not the federal courts' role to intervene and adjust the system ... [T]he federal court is not a super zoning board and should not be called on to mark the point at which legitimate local interests in promoting the welfare of the community are outweighed by legitimate regional interests.
>
> We conclude therefore that ... the concept of the public welfare is sufficiently broad to uphold Petaluma's desire to preserve its small town character, its open spaces and low density of population, and to grow at an orderly and deliberate pace.[9]

The ROGO approach, therefore, is within the bounds of the U.S. Constitution's constraints on local government land use regulation.

## County-wide planning

Generally, each Florida municipality has exclusive jurisdiction to plan for land within its corporate limits.[10] And each county plans for just the unincorporated lands within its boundaries.[11] Several Florida counties depart from this general framework, however, and plan for land that is inside municipalities within those counties.[12]

Pinellas County comprises the peninsula between Tampa Bay and the Gulf of Mexico. The county has a Pinellas County Planning Council created by the Florida Legislature through a special act.[13] Per the Legislature's direction, the council adopts a "countywide plan" analogous to a comprehensive plan as described in Florida Statutes Chapter 163.[14] In addition to meeting other requirements of law, Pinellas County and each of the 24 municipalities in Pinellas County must conform their comprehensive plans to the countywide comprehensive plan drafted by the Pinellas County Planning Council.[15]

The city of Tallahassee and Leon County regulate land use inside the city and in the unincorporated area of the county with one document, the Tallahassee-Leon County 2030 Comprehensive Plan. Unlike Pinellas County, where state law requires joint planning, Leon County and the city of Tallahassee cooperatively fund a single planning department and respectively adopt their shared comprehensive plan of their own volition. Tallahassee is the only city in Leon County.

### Supermajority vote required

Generally, governmental bodies make decisions by majority vote.[16] Some Florida local governments, however, require a vote by more than a simple majority of their governing body in order to make certain land use decisions.[17]

For example, a special act of the Florida Legislature applicable to Collier County and the three cities within Collier County requires a four-fifths majority vote for those local governments to change their zoning ordinances.[18] Also, Gadsden County requires a supermajority vote for some land use decisions. The relevant county ordinance provides the following:

> Votes for ALL COMPREHENSIVE PLAN amendments, and Major Land Development Reviews including but not limited to variances, special exceptions, major site plans and major subdivision shall require a "super majority" vote of the BOCC. A super majority vote of the BOCC is required to amend or repeal this ordinance.[19]

Similar restrictions exist in Sarasota County;[20] the village of Wellington;[21] the city of Lauderhill;[22] the town of Loxahatchee Groves;[23] the town of Ponce Inlet;[24] and the city of Sarasota.[25]

### Miami-Dade County community councils

In 1996, Miami-Dade County created a system of ten community councils to make planning and land development decisions closer to the people affected by those decisions. County voters elect members of each community council to four-year terms.[26] The community councils make many final land use decisions, including whether to approve special exceptions, variances, proposed changes to zoning district boundaries, and site plans.[27]

### Florida law doesn't require zoning

The city of Cedar Key is a fishing and tourist village in Levy County, on Florida's gulf coast. The city is somewhat unique among Florida cities from a land use regulation perspective because it has no zoning. Instead, this island city relies on just its future land use map to organize land uses, densities, and intensities.[28] While the Community Planning Act provides detailed standards for comprehensive planning, it has few standards for land development regulations. One land use regulation practice that Florida law does not require local governments to use is zoning.[29]

### Regulating land use in a charter

Many Florida local governments include land use restrictions in their charters. Examples include urban growth boundaries in both Seminole County[30] and Sarasota County.[31] Placing a land use regulation in a charter insulates that rule from political changes favoring particular property owners or interest groups because amending a city or county charter requires a referendum (i.e. requires a vote of the electors).[32] This added barrier to amending rules will also make a community less responsive to changes in the environment or economy that affect land use planning.

Two specific examples of charter-level land use restrictions show how this approach works. First, the town of Yankeetown is a small community in Levy County, on Florida's gulf coast. The town charter includes several provisions relating to land use. One section requires voter approval for any comprehensive plan amendment affecting more than five parcels.[33] Another section allows the town council to amend the comprehensive plan for fewer than five parcels of land, but only by a super-majority vote.[34] Second, the town of Lauderdale-By-The-Sea lies on a barrier island north of Fort Lauderdale in Broward County. The town charter sets a maximum height for buildings in the town of 44 feet or four stories.[35]

Communities having charters that do not currently require referenda for planning decisions, however, cannot now add those provisions. Florida statutes now generally prohibit local governments from regulating land use by referendum.[36] The Legislature added this provision to state law after a statewide 2010 referendum on a constitutional amendment proposed requiring all comprehensive planning to occur by referenda.[37] That proposed constitutional amendment failed by a two-thirds vote.[38]

## Notes

1 Cross Key Waterways v. Askew, 351 So. 2d 1062, 1065 (Fla. 1st DCA 1977) ("The primacy of local government jurisdiction in land development regulation has traditionally been, in this country, a corollary of the people's right of access to government. In a sense, therefore, the jurisdictional claim of local governments in these matters is based on historical preferences stronger than law.") *aff'd*, 372 So. 2d 913 (Fla. 1978).

2 *Hurricane Irma*, Monroe Cnty. Emergency Mgmt., www.monroecounty-fl.gov/982/Hurricane-Irma (last visited February 5, 2021).

3 *Shelters*, Monroe Cnty. Emergency Mgmt., www.monroecounty-fl.gov/992/Shelters (last visited June 2, 2020).

4 Fla. Stat. § 380.0552(1).

5 *Id.* § 380.0552(9)(a)(2).

6 Fla. Admin. Code Ann. r. 28–20.140(2)(b) (2020).

7 *See id.* rr. 28–18.400(2)(a), 28–19.310(2)(a) (2020).

8 *See* Monroe Cnty. Land Dev. Code § 138–22(a) (2016).

9 Constr. Indus. Ass'n of Sonoma Cnty. v. City of Petaluma, 522 F.2d 897, 908–9 (9th Cir. 1975) (citations omitted).

10 Fla. Stat. § 163.3171(1).

11 *Id.* § 163.3171(2).

12 *Id.* § 163.3171(1) (granting municipalities this authority if "the governing bodies of the municipality and the county in which the area is located agree on the boundaries of such additional areas" agree to various additional procedures, and the involved governing bodies approve the joint agreement).

13 Ch. 2012–245, Laws of Fla., § 3(4).

14 *Id.* § 3(1).

15 *Id.* § 10(1)(e).

16 Fla. Stat. § 380.0664; *see generally* Osborne M. Reynolds, Jr., *Voting Requirements in Municipal Governing Bodies: Minority Rule or Legislative Stalemate?*, 27 Urb. L. 87 (1995).

17 *See*, e.g., Palm Beach Cnty. Ordinance 2018–002 (2018) (requiring a supermajority vote of the Board of County Commissioners (BCC) for additional large and small scale amendments outside of the scheduled intake dates).

18 Collier Cnty. Land Dev. Code § 2.03.07(D)(4)(b)(iv) (2019) (mentioning a super-majority vote is required to approve the transfer of residential development rights); *see also* Ch. 2001–344, Laws of Fla., § 11.

19 Gadsden Cnty. Ordinance No. 2010–005, § 7001.1(D) (2010) (emphasis in the original).

20 Sarasota Cnty. Charter § 2.2A(1) (requiring an affirmative vote "of a majority plus one" for any ordinance amending the county's comprehensive plan that increases allowable land use, density, or intensity).

21 Vill. of Wellington Charter, § 10(F)(1) (require an "affirmative vote of not less than four members of the council" for zoning amendments).

22 City of Lauderhill Land Dev. Reg. § 3.5(E)(3) (2020) (requiring a "super-majority vote" for a special use exception).

23 Town of Loxahatchee Groves Charter § 9(10) (requiring an "affirmative vote of no fewer than four members of the town council" for any change to the town's future land use map or to the zoning designation for any parcel within the town).

24 Town of Ponce Inlet Land Use & Dev. Code § 6.6.1(C)(3)(b) (2020) (requiring an affirmative vote of "at least four members of the town council" to a legislative amendment to the official zoning map).

25 Sarasota Cnty. Charter art. IV, §§ 2(i), (j) (requiring a "super-majority" vote requirement of four city commissioners to adopt a successor statute providing for amendments to a local comprehensive plan or to approve small-scale plan amendments).
26 Miami-Dade Cnty. Code § 20–43(A)(2) (2020).
27 *See id.* §§ 33–311(A)(3), (A)(4), (A)(6), (A)(8), (A)(10) (2020).
28 Laws of Cedar Key Comprehensive Plan, Ch. 3 §§ 1–2.1, 1–2.2 (2018).
29 *See* Fla. Stat. § 163.3202(3) ("A general zoning code shall not be required if a local government's adopted land development regulations meet the requirements of this section").
30 Seminole Cnty. Home Rule Charter art. V, § 5.2(A).
31 Sarasota Cnty. Charter § 2.2A(2) (relating to ordinances that amend the county's comprehensive plan and affect the urban service area boundary).
32 *See* 21 Fla. Jur. 2d *Elections* § 232 (2021) (explaining that the term "referendum" also "encompasses the power of the people to approve or reject legislation that has been referred to them by the legislature").
33 Town of Yankeetown Charter § 11 (2019).
34 *Id.* § 16.
35 Town of Lauderdale-By-The-Sea Charter § 7.1(1).
36 Fla. Stat. § 163.3167(8).
37 Ch. 2011–139, Laws of Fla., § 7.
38 Fla. Dep't of State, Div. of Elections, November 2, 2010 Gen. Election Off. Results, Const. Amend.: Referenda Required for Adoption and Amend. of Loc. Gov't Comprehensive Land Use Plans (2010).

# 9 Specific quasi-judicial decisions

Local governments make many kinds of quasi-judicial decisions. From quasi-judicial changes in zoning to approvals for individual developments, these land use approvals are plentiful and varied. *Exceptions*, *variances*, and *spot zoning* are each a kind of quasi-judicial decision with its own unique treatment on judicial review.

## Exceptions

Although sometimes conflated, exceptions and variances are different. An exception is a grant of a deviation from a general requirement of a code when a development meets predetermined requirements.[1] The code itself anticipates the exception and provides the criteria on which the local government may grant it.[2] A variance, on the other hand, is permission to deviate from the requirements of code that the rule does not anticipate.[3] Instead, the basis of the grant of a variance is a showing of hardship.[4]

One Florida court explained the distinction as follows:

> A "variance" is the relief granted from the literal enforcement of a zoning ordinance permitting the use of property in a manner otherwise forbidden upon a finding that enforcement of the ordinance as written would inflict practical difficulty or unnecessary hardship on a property owner. An "exception" is a departure from the general provisions of a zoning ordinance granted by legislative process under express provision of the enactment itself. If certain facts or circumstances specified in the ordinance are found to exist, then either on a direct application, or on an appeal from an administrative order enforcing the zoning ordinance, a Board of Adjustment may grant an exception. A variance is entirely different from an exception although the terms are sometimes, in error, used synonymously. In the absence of a specific provision of law requiring it, one need not show unusual hardships to secure an exception. An ordinance granting the power to make exceptions must contain proper standards or rules of guidance. ...[5]

Local governments utilize exceptions when a use is potentially problematic, but can occur without conflict if subject to heightened development standards and additional governmental review. A local government therefore anticipates permitting this potentially problematic use and provides specialized standards a development proposal must meet to address those potential problems. Local governments give exceptions a variety of names, such as special exceptions, special use permits, and conditional use permits. In the following case, *City of Naples v. Cent. Plaza of Naples, Inc.*, a reviewing court holds that a local government may not deny a request for an exception based on some criterion not adopted by law.

## Florida Second District Court of Appeal

### *City of Naples v. Cent. Plaza of Naples, Inc.*[6]

### 1974

GRIMES, Judge.

This is an appeal from an order directing the City of Naples to grant a special exception to the City Zoning Code so as to permit the appellee to construct certain multifamily housing.

Appellee is the owner of an essentially square piece of property which is located between the Gordon River and Goodlette Road in the City of Naples. The property protrudes into the river to the extent that it is bordered by water on three sides. A large shopping center fronting west on Goodlette Road occupies the bulk of the property. Appellee desires to build three four-story multifamily residences on the balance of the property which faces the river. According to the plans, access to the residential complex would be directly into Goodlette Road by means of a boulevard built along the north edge of the property so that there would be no direct vehicle access between the residential area and the shopping center. A row of pine trees would serve as a buffer between the shopping center and the apartments. The appellee agreed to limit permanent residency in the units to persons over the age of sixteen years.

Appellee's entire property is zoned K-a Industrial. The ordinance provides that as a special exception in this zone multiple family residences "may be permitted by the City Council after a joint public hearing with due public notice has been held and a recommendation from the Planning Board has been submitted to the City Council." Appellee filed a petition for a special exception and provided the necessary supporting documents. A joint public hearing was held by the Planning Board and the Naples City Council, at which time there was comprehensive discussion concerning the advisability of granting the exception. Ultimately, the Planning Board by a vote of four to one recommended approval of the exception. Three of the six members of the Council present voted in favor of the exception; the other three voted against it. Upon the advice of the City Attorney, the Mayor declared that the motion for approval had failed by virtue of the tie vote.

Appellee thereafter filed suit seeking a variety of remedies including declaratory relief and a mandatory injunction. The parties agreed to allow the court to decide the case solely upon the transcript of the testimony taken at the joint public hearing and certain exhibits which were stipulated into evidence. The court found that the City's evidence did not substantially controvert the evidence presented by appellee ... . [The trial court held that the city should have granted the request for the exception.]

With respect to special exceptions, the City Zoning Code provides:

> (C) *Standards*: Prior to granting a special exception, the Planning Board and City Council shall find that the proposed special exception is necessary and/or appropriate to the area in which it is proposed, that it will be reasonably compatible with surrounding uses; that any nuisance or hazardous feature involved is suitably separated and buffered from adjacent uses; that it will no [sic] hinder development of nearby vacant properties; that excessive traffic will not be generated on minor residential streets; that a parking problem will not be created; and that the land and/or building which are involved is adequate.
>
> District standards for lots, yards, floor area, height, etc., are designed for permitted uses, not special exceptions. Appropriate standards shall be determined and made a part of a permit for a special exception.

Neither party questions the validity of these standards. Therefore, this case is unlike *The City of St. Petersburg v. Schweitzer*, 297 So. 2d 74 (Fla. 2d DCA 1974), in which a portion of the zoning code which permitted the granting of special exceptions was held invalid for the failure to include sufficient guidelines to be followed in the granting of these exceptions. The position of appellee below and on this appeal is that its petition for special exception fully complied with all of the applicable standards ... .

In support of its argument that there was a reasonable basis for the denial of appellee's petition, the City points to the evidence presented which indicated that the erection of these apartments would substantially increase the amount of traffic travelling on Goodlette Road. Likewise, there was also some evidence that the construction could result in an overpopulation of the area creating excessive demands on utilities and other services. Yet, as pertinent as these matters may seem to be, the City Council did not have a right to consider them in making its determination. *See* 2 A. Rathkopf, *The Law of Zoning and Planning* 54–27 (3d ed. 1972). The only criteria upon which the Council could legally base its decision were those set forth in the ordinance. *North Bay Village v. Blackwell*, 88 So. 2d 524 (Fla. 1956).

The only reference to traffic among the enumerated standards is with respect to minor residential streets. The record clearly shows that Goodlette Road is a main commercial artery and not a minor residential street. There is no reference whatever to the effect that a proposed exception might have upon the ability of the City to furnish utilities and other supporting services. Therefore, the impact of the proposed project on these matters was legally irrelevant.

It has not been seriously argued that the project is inappropriate to the area in which it is proposed. There was no evidence that a properly appointed multiresidential complex bounded on three sides by water and catering to older people would be incompatible with a shopping center where these people might be expected to obtain their necessities. Since the evidence reflects that appellee's petition was in full compliance with all of the standards which were prescribed for the granting of the exception, it should have been granted.

The judgment is affirmed.

McNULTY, C.J., and SIDWELL, BENJAMIN C., Associate Judge, concur.

### *Discussion*

A corollary to the holding in *City of Naples v. Cent. Plaza of Naples, Inc.* is that ordinances which provide for exceptions must provide meaningful standards or guidelines that a local government can use to determine whether an applicant has met the required criteria to receive the exception. An exception without standards would allow a local government to make land use decisions ad hoc, without necessarily relating its decision to a legitimate police power purpose. Courts view standardless exceptions as "whimsical and capricious" and impermissible "unreasonable restrictions."[7]

In a local government hearing on a special exception, the applicant for the exception first has the burden of demonstrating by competent substantial evidence that the exception meets applicable standards.[8] For the local government to deny the exception, someone opposed to the exception—a third party or the government itself—then has the burden of showing "by competent substantial evidence that the proposed exception does not meet the published criteria."[9]

## Variances

A variance is a permit that allows a property owner to use property in a way that a local government's land development regulations specifically do not allow. The Florida Supreme Court first acknowledged variances in Florida law in *Josephson v. Autrey*.[10] In that decision, the court addressed both the practical need for variances and the necessity of limitations on the authority to grant variances.

Variances are practically useful because "situations [exist] where strict adherence to the letter of the ordinance would produce a unique or special hardship on the particular property owner."[11] A risk of variances, however, is that they may delegate legislative authority to administrative boards.[12] Therefore, boards with authority to grant variances must be "circumscribed by reasonable bounds."[13]

Courts generally recognize three limitations on the authority of local governments to grant variances. First, complying with the law must cause an unnecessary hardship which cannot be self-created.[14] Second, the problem must arise from unique circumstances peculiar to the property, not from general conditions in the neighborhood.[15] And, third, the use or development the variance allows must not alter the essential character of the neighborhood.[16] This third criterion is admittedly somewhat subjective.[17]

All variances fall into one of two categories: use or area. Use variances allow a property owner to use the subject property in a way the law does not allow (e.g. a residentially zoned property might be used for commercial purposes). For use variances, unnecessary hardship means that a property cannot earn a reasonable return if used as authorized in the applicable zoning ordinance.

Area variances allow a property owner to develop the subject property in a way that violates some dimensional requirement of applicable law, like a height or a setback standard. For area variances, unnecessary hardship means that it would be physically impossible to develop a property while complying with all applicable rules.

Note that the requirement that hardship not be self-created plays out differently for use variances than for area variances. Because hardship in the context of a use variance is an inability to earn a reasonable return, the price one pays for property may determine whether a hardship exists. Therefore, when requesting a use variance, one cannot have purchased a property for an above-market price with knowledge that he or she will need a use variance to make use of the property. Allowing the property owner to use that overpayment as justification for receiving a variance would be allowing a variance for a self-created hardship, as the following case illustrates.

In contrast, hardship in the context of an area variance is a practical difficulty in using the property because of its physical characteristics. With this sort of variance, the hardship is unique to the property and remains with the property without regard to who owns it. In the case of an area variance, purchasing a property with knowledge that one must acquire a variance to use the property is not a barrier to receiving a variance

*Table 9.1* Key characteristics distinguishing use and area variances

| | *Use* | *Area* |
|---|---|---|
| Definition | Variance from use requirement of code (e.g. a residentially zoned property might be used for commercial purposes). | Variance from dimensional requirement of code, such as height or setback standard. |
| Nature of hardship | Property cannot earn a reasonable return if used as zoned. | Developing property in compliance with all dimensional requirements is not possible. |
| Consequence of purchasing with knowledge of need for variance | Constitutes self-created hardship if purchase price is above market value as zoned. | Has no consequence, hardship runs with the land. |

The following three cases—*Elwyn v. City of Miami*, *City of Coral Gables v. Geary*, and *Town of Indialantic v. Nance*—elaborate on, and exemplify, these variance requirements.

## Florida Third District Court of Appeal

## *Elwyn v. City of Miami*[18]

## 1959

CARROLL, CHAS, Chief Judge.

Appellants, plaintiffs below, appeal from an order of the circuit court dismissing their complaint by which they sought a decree to invalidate an ordinance allowing a zoning variance. The question for our determination is whether the complaint stated a cause of action.

The complaint, summarized, showed the following:

The City Commission of the City of Miami granted a variance permit, on the application of the appellee Elgene, Inc., for the construction and operation of a gasoline service station on certain property in the City of Miami, fronting on South Dixie Highway (U. S. No. 1) at the intersection of Southwest 30th Court. The property involved consisted of Lots 13, 14 and 15 of Block 2, Highway Park Sub., according to a plat thereof recorded in Plat Book 40, Page 29, of the Public Records of Dade County. For some years the property along the highway in that area had been zoned R2 (duplex). While it was so zoned, Mary Loi acquired the subject parcel. On May 15, 1957, property in that area for a number of blocks fronting on the highway was rezoned to the more liberal classification of R3, which was alleged to include the uses of "apartment, hotel, motel, private club, community garage, parking lot, public art gallery, public museum."

Some nine months later, and while the subject parcel was owned by Mary Loi, an application was made by the appellee Elgene, Inc., for a "hardship" variance to allow the construction and operation of a gasoline service station on the property, being a use not authorized by the R3 zoning. The hardship claimed by the applicant was that the character of the neighborhood had changed; that two of the lots were not directly accessible to the highway; and that the property was no longer usable for residential purposes.

Appellants, who were owners and residents of adjoining properties, and numerous other owners of properties nearby, filed objections. The City Planning & Zoning Board heard and denied the Elgene, Inc., application for a hardship variance.

After its application had been denied, Elgene, Inc. purchased the property and took a conveyance from Mary Loi. Then Elgene, Inc. appealed the zoning board's ruling to the city commission.

Under § 72(t) of the charter of the city (Chapter 10847, Laws of Florida, Special Acts of 1925, as amended), variance permits were authorized and restricted as follows:

> A variance of the restrictions, regulations and boundaries established by the zoning ordinance may be granted under the same terms and conditions as an addition to, amendment, supplement, change, modification, or repeal of the Zoning Ordinance. No variance permit shall be issued, however, except in instances where practical difficulties and unnecessary hardship shall be incurred by the applicant if said permit were refused.

The city commission reversed the action of the zoning board, and granted the variance to authorize use of the property as a gasoline service station, by enacting ordinance No. 6174, dated April 16, 1958. The reason given in the ordinance for granting the variance was: "Because it has been shown that the restrictions of the above described property under an R3 use will cause undue and unnecessary hardship."

The appellants in their complaint contended that the ordinance was invalid because (1) any hardship which the applicant Elgene, Inc. might claim was self-imposed [and] (2) there was no hardship basis to justify a variance ... and (4) the variance would result in injury and depreciation in value of plaintiffs' adjoining properties, and destroy the use and enjoyment thereof ... .

"[U]nnecessary hardship" as used in the city charter, and as contemplated in this sense, has been given a special and limited meaning. The authorities seem uniform on the proposition that the difficulties or hardships relied on must be unique to the parcel involved in the application for the variance. They must be peculiar to that particular property, and not general in character, since difficulties or hardships shared with others in the area go to the reasonableness of the zoning generally, and will not support a variance. If the hardship is one which is common to the area the remedy is to seek a change of the zoning for the neighborhood rather than to seek a change through a variance for an individual owner. Thus some exceptional and undue hardship to the individual land owner, unique to that parcel of property and not shared by property owners in the area, is an essential prerequisite to the granting of such a variance. 58 Am. Jur., *Zoning*, §§ 203–204; 101 C.J.S. *Zoning* §§ 290–294; 8 McQuillin, Municipal Corporations, §§ 25.166–25.169 (3d ed. rev. 1957); 1 Yokley, *Zoning Law and Practice*, §§ 138–139 (2d ed. 1953).

A variance should not be granted where the use to be authorized thereby will alter the essential character of the locality, or interfere with the zoning plan for the area and with rights of owners of other property; and a variance which permits a use not authorized by an existing zoning classification fixed under a planned zoning of the area or neighborhood, generally is not justified unless the land cannot yield a reasonable return when used only for purposes authorized in its present zoning. From the complaint it appears that the variance was sought for the economic advantage of the applicant, and not because the property was not reasonably and profitably usable for one or another of the purposes for which it was zoned.

The complaint in this case adequately raised the question of the existence *vel non* of any exceptional and undue hardship pertaining to the particular property involved, so as to justify or permit the ordinance for the variance, and therefore was sufficient to withstand the challenge of a motion to dismiss.

Moreover, the complaint showed that the hardship claimed was self-created and self-imposed. One who purchases property while it is in a certain known zoning classification, ordinarily will not be heard to claim as a hardship a factor or factors which existed at the time he acquired the property. That point is stronger in this case because here the purchaser of the property, aware of the permitted uses, sought to obtain a variance therefrom before it acquired the property, and the appellee corporation took conveyance of the property after the city zoning board had ruled against its application for a variance. A self-imposed or self-acquired hardship (such as by purchasing property under existing zoning and then applying for a variance) is not the kind of hardship for which variance should be granted. See *Kazlow v. Peters*, 53 So. 2d 321 (Fla. 1951); *Josephson v. Autrey*, 96 So. 2d 784 (Fla. 1957); *Green v. City of Miami*, 107 So. 2d 390 (Fla. 3d DCA 1958); *City of Miami Beach v. Greater Miami Hebrew Academy*, 108 So. 2d 50 (Fla. 3d DCA 1958).

In *Josephson v. Autrey*, *supra* [96 So. 2d 786], the Supreme Court dealt with the question of "the effect of a zoning restriction existing when property is acquired on the claim of the property owner that a hardship exists by virtue of such zoning restriction." With reference thereto the Supreme Court there said (96 So. 2d at pages 789–790):

> *** In the instant case the appellees Cunningham acquired the land with full knowledge of the existing zoning restrictions. As a matter of fact, they paid to the seller a substantial

> profit over and above the amount paid for the land by the seller a short time before. They purchased the property burdened with the provision of the zoning ordinance that restricted its use to tourist accommodations and similar uses. They then appeared before the appeals board and contended "hardship" solely on the basis that the land was not worth what they paid for it burdened by the use restriction which they knew to be in existence when they bought the property.
>
> The authorities are generally in accord on the proposition that in seeking a variance on the ground of a unique or unnecessary hardship, a property owner cannot assert the benefit of a "self-created" hardship. Appellee cites our cases where we have held that a property owner will not be precluded from attacking the basic validity of a zoning ordinance merely because the ordinance was in force when he acquired the property. The situation is entirely different. The invalid ordinance can have no effect whatsoever and its invalidity can be assaulted at any time. The application for a variance permit recognizes the basic validity of the ordinance and seeks the grant of a variance purely on the basis of some hardship peculiar to his particular property. When the owner himself by his own conduct creates the exact hardship which he alleges to exist, he certainly should not be permitted to take advantage of it ... .

The showing in the complaint was sufficient to state a cause of action to invalidate the challenged variance ordinance. The dismissal order appealed from is reversed, and the cause is remanded for further proceedings not inconsistent with this opinion.

Reversed.

HORTON and PEARSON, JJ., concur.

## Florida Third District Court of Appeal

### *City of Coral Gables v. Geary*[19]

### 1980

SCHWARTZ, Judge.

Coral Gables appeals from a final judgment requiring it to grant the plaintiff-appellee four variances from building restrictions imposed by the city's zoning code. The variances, which deal with set-back requirements and building and wall height limitations, were ordered because, as appeared without contradiction below, the unusual triangular shape of the plaintiff's property rendered it simply and practicably impossible for it to be developed in accordance with the existing regulations.

It is, of course, well-recognized that the irregular shape or other peculiar physical characteristic of a particular parcel constitutes a classic "hardship" unique to an individual owner which justifies, and in some cases requires the granting of a variance. *Forde v. City of Miami Beach*, 1 So. 2d 642 (Fla. 1941); see *Leveille v. Zoning Board of Appeals*, 144 A.2d 45 (Conn. 1958); *Downey v. Grimshaw*, 101 N.E.2d 275 (Ill. 1951); *City of Baltimore v. Sapero*, 186 A.2d 884 (Md. 1962); 3 Anderson, *American Law of Zoning* s 18.34 (2nd ed. 1977). The appellant does not really take issue with this rule or with its clear application to the case at bar.

The city does contend, however, relying primarily upon *Elwyn v. City of Miami*, 113 So. 2d 849 (Fla. 3d DCA 1959), *cert. denied*, 116 So. 2d 773 (Fla. 1959), that the alleged hardship was "self-created," thus precluding relief, because the plaintiff purchased the property in its present configuration with knowledge of the already-imposed building restrictions. See *Allstate Mortgage Corp. of Fla. v. City of Miami Beach*, 308 So. 2d 629 (Fla. 3d DCA 1975), *cert. denied*, 317 So. 2d 763 (Fla. 1975); *Crossroads Lounge, Inc. v. City of Miami*, 195 So. 2d 232 (Fla. 3d DCA 1967), *cert. denied*, 201 So. 2d 459 (Fla. 1967); *Friedland v. City of Hollywood*, 130 So.

2d 306 (Fla. 2nd DCA 1961). We do not agree with this position. Unlike the situation in each of the cited decisions, the hardship involved here arose from circumstances peculiar to the realty alone, unrelated to the conduct or to the self-originated expectations of any of its owners or buyers. See the discussion of the cases on this issue from other jurisdictions in 3 Rathkopf, *Law of Zoning and Planning*, s 39.02 (4th ed. 1979).[1] In this case, therefore, as the court observed in *Murphy v. Kraemer*, 16 Misc.2d 374, 182 N.Y.S.2d 205, 206 (Sup.Ct. 1958), "since it is not the act of the purchaser which brings the hardship into being, it is incorrect to charge him with having created it." It is undisputed that the appellee's predecessor in title, who held the property when the restrictions were initially imposed, would then have been entitled to the variances in question. Compare *Duval Productions, Inc. v. City of Tampa*, 307 So. 2d 493 (Fla. 2d DCA 1975), *cert. denied*, 317 So. 2d 78 (Fla. 1975) (predecessor compensated for "hardship" created by condemnation). The "self-imposed" hardship doctrine thus does not apply. We endorse the principle stated in *Harrington Glen, Inc. v. Municipal Board of Adjustment*, 243 A.2d 233, 237 (N.J. 1968):

> As we indicated in *Wilson v. Borough of Mountainside*, 201 A.2d 540 (N.J. 1964), when neither the owner of the lot at the time of adoption of the zoning ordinance ... nor a subsequent owner, did anything to create the condition ... for which the variance is sought, a right to relief possessed by the original owner passes to the successor in title. Such right is not lost simply because the succeeding owner bought or contracted to buy with knowledge of the ... restriction. See 2 Rathkopf, *Law of Zoning & Planning*, c. 48, p. 48–20 (3d ed. 1966). (e. s.)
>
> Accord, *Landmark Universal, Inc. v. Pitkin County Board of Adjustment*, 579 P.2d 1184, 1185 (Colo. App. 1978) ("If a prior owner would have been entitled to a variance at the time the zoning ordinance was passed, that right is not lost to a purchaser simply because he bought with knowledge of the zoning regulation involved."); *School Committee v. Zoning Board of Review*, 133 A.2d 734, 737 (R.I. 1957) ("The zoning law deals with the use of land. The time when the land was acquired is not pertinent in determining its proper use."); *Denton v. Zoning Board of Review*, 133 A.2d 718, 720 (R.I. 1957) ("The question of whether an applicant is entitled to a variance because of hardship flowing from a literal application of the terms of the ordinance is in no way dependent upon his knowledge or lack of knowledge of the existence of zoning restrictions affecting the land.").

Affirmed.

## Florida Fifth District Court of Appeal

### *Town of Indialantic v. Nance*[20]

### 1981

COBB, Judge.

The Town of Indialantic (Indialantic) denied appellee Nance's request for a zoning variance based on hardship. A three-judge circuit court panel sitting in review of Indialantic's decision

1 Rathkopf's summary of these decisions at s 39.02(3) aptly characterizes the Florida cases as well:

> Despite the fact that some courts have used language which, taken upon its face, would indicate that even where a unique hardship existed with respect to land which would have warranted the person owning that property prior to the enactment of the ordinance to apply for and receive a variance, the mere act of purchase with knowledge of the ordinance may alone bar the purchaser

granted Nance's petition for certiorari and ordered Indialantic to grant the requested variance. Indialantic appeals the final judgment of the circuit court, and we reverse.

In July, 1978, Nance purchased Lots 8 and 9 of Indialantic-By-The-Sea, the two contiguous lots in question. The property was oceanfront property, bounded to the north by an existing three-story motel and to the south by six contiguous lots owed in whole or in part by Nance. The motel to the north, built before mean high-water and dune set-backs were required, is nonconforming to the extent that a portion of it lies east of the dune line. Over three hundred feet to the south on Lots 14 and 15, a contractual restriction required a motel to be built, if anything.

In August, 1978, Nance submitted a plan with Indialantic's Zoning Board, proposing construction of dual, three-story buildings. The two buildings were to provide a total of twenty-four dwelling units. Because of the plan's vagueness and also because it lacked the requisite number of off-street parking units, the Zoning Board rejected the plan suggesting that Nance file for a variance with Indialantic's Board of Adjustment.

Other than the parking deficiency, the dual three-story plan met all other Indialantic zoning requirements, including a thirty-five-foot height restriction. The Zoning Board was required to deny the site plan, however, because it lacked the authority to grant a variance as to the parking deficiency.

Instead of filing an application for a parking variance on the dual three-story proposal, Nance applied to the Board of Adjustment for a height and parking variance for a single six-story building. Though containing twenty-four dwelling units, the same as the original plan, the six-story proposal provided four less parking units than the already parking-deficient original plan. The Board of Adjustment rejected Nance's six-story plan, finding, among other things, that Nance had not demonstrated hardship, nor had he demonstrated the property at issue to be of an unusual nature.

Nance appealed the Board's decision to Indialantic's Town Council. During the Town Council hearing, Nance argued that Indialantic's set-back, breeze-way parking, and landscape requirements, the state coastal, set-back restriction, the narrow shape of the subject property, the existence of the three-story motel to the north, and the requirement that a motel be built, if anything, three hundred feet to the south (on land also owned by Nance), combined to create such a hardship that he should be granted a height and parking variance. When questioned by council members, Nance admitted being aware of the thirty-five-foot height restriction at the time he purchased Lots 8 and 9. Nance's architect admitted that the single six-story building would be less expensive to construct than the dual, three-story version. The council unanimously rejected Nance's hardship contention, and denied the requested height and parking variances.

Subsequent to the Town Council's rejection, Nance petitioned the Circuit Court of Brevard County for review of the council's decision. The circuit court found that the height restriction combined with other Indialantic zoning requirements to create an unusual and unnecessary hardship to Nance, and that the hardship was not self-created. Finding additionally that the variance requested did not violate any conditions or limitations to the granting of the variance, the court reversed Indialantic's rejection of the six-story plan, and ordered Indialantic to grant Nance's application for variance. Indialantic petitioned this court for writ of certiorari to review the circuit court's decision; we treat the petition for certiorari as a timely notice of appeal ... .

from the same relief, it is apparent that few higher court decisions have actually so decided. In each case in which the refusal of a variance was upheld and in which such language was used, the facts showed either that there was an affirmative act which created the hardship peculiar to the property involved or that there was insufficient evidence as to at least one of the elements required for the grant of a variance.

[T]he task of the court reviewing a zoning variance decision is to insure that the authority's decision is based on evidence a reasonable mind would accept to support a conclusion. *Compare De Groot*, 95 So. 2d at 916, with *Wolff v. Dade County*, 370 So. 2d at 841–842. If there was such evidence presented, the authority's determination must stand. *Martin v. First Apostolic Church*, 321 So. 2d 471 (Fla. 4th DCA 1975). A prerequisite to the granting of a hardship zoning variance is the presence of an exceptional and unique hardship to the individual landowner, unique to that parcel and not shared by other property owners in the area. *City of Miami v. Franklin Leslie, Inc.*, 179 So. 2d 622 (Fla. 3d DCA 1965). In the instant case, the evidence reasonably supports Indialantic's conclusion that Nance did not suffer the requisite hardship. The lots at issue are typical of Indialantic oceanfront lots in size, shape and topography; the town's height, set-back, breezeway, parking, and landscape requirements, as well as the state coastal construction set-back restriction, apply equally to all beachfront property situated in Indialantic. Indialantic's zoning restrictions are common difficulties shared by all other oceanfront lot owners in the area, and are therefore not the unique hardship required to support a variance.

Additionally, Nance possessed a viable, dual, three-story plan that, with the exception of the parking deficiency, met all Indialantic zoning requirements, including the height restriction. Nance never presented this plan to the Board of Adjustment, the body vested with the authority to grant such variance. The viability of this dual three-story plan itself illustrates a lack of hardship.

Nance, however, maintains that the motel to the north and the possibility of a motel being built three hundred feet to the south make his land unique. He contends that the nonconforming motel materially blocks the view to the north, and the possibility of a motel to the south threatens his view in that direction, and that this entitles him to a height variance. In ordering the variance to be granted, the circuit court placed central emphasis on the uniqueness of Nance's asserted lack of view. We find the circuit court erred by considering the impaired view to be such a hardship that reversal of the determination by the Town Council was mandated as a matter of law. In the absence of some contractual or statutory obligation, a landowner has no absolute legal right to unobstructed air and light from the adjoining land. *Fontainebleau Hotel Corp. v. Forty-Five Twenty-Five, Inc.*, 114 So. 2d 357 (Fla. 3d DCA 1959), *cert. denied*, 117 So. 2d 842 (Fla. 1960).

The evidence before the Town Council reasonably supported its conclusion that Nance does not suffer the unique and unnecessary hardship required for the issuance of a variance. The circuit court erroneously substituted Indialantic's reasonable finding that Nance suffers no legal hardship with its own finding that he does ... . We reverse the circuit court below and remand the case to it with directions to reinstate Indialantic's decision.

REVERSED and REMANDED with instructions.

DAUKSCH, C. J., and ORFINGER, J., concur.

**Box 9.1 Practice problem: Burt's Store**

Burt owns Burt's Store across the street from State University's law school in Collegeborough. The store is a small neighborhood market—about 2,000 square feet in size—that sells groceries and convenience items to folks in the surrounding neighborhood.

Twenty years ago, Collegeborough rezoned Burt's Store from a zoning designation that allowed retail uses to a zoning designation that only allows residential uses. The rezoning made sense because then, like today, Burt's property was the only commercial property in the neighborhood. All of the other lots are developed with houses. Only Burt's lot has the frontage on the street that makes it right for commercial uses.

To prevent Burt from suing over the zoning change, the city included a "grandfathering clause" in the rezoning ordinance. The grandfathering clause allowed Burt to keep operating his store. The residential-only use restriction was not to go into effect unless Burt closed his store and kept it closed for more than six months.

Last year, Burt decided to retire. Since a supermarket opened up about a mile away, customers stopped shopping at Burt's Store. Also, Burt just thinks he is too old to keep operating a neighborhood market. He closed Burt's Store.

Jacob just graduated from State University's law school, but doesn't want to be an attorney. Too many rules! He considered getting another degree in planning, but decided instead he would like to operate his own business. When Burt's Store was still open, Jacob thought Burt could make much more money by catering to law students. Specifically, Jacob thought Burt's Store should have sold beer, law text books, and office supplies. With that product mix, Jacob thought people would walk from the law school across the street every day to shop at Burt's Store.

Now that Burt has retired, Jacob decides that owning Burt's Store is his dream job. Jacob negotiates with Burt and buys Burt's Store at a price he can afford with the projected profits from the updated product mix. That negotiated price is much higher than the price at which surrounding residential properties have sold in recent years. Because Burt's Store was closed for more than six months before Jacob bought the property, Jacob knows he must apply for a variance in order to reopen the store.

Evaluate Jacob's eligibility for a variance.

## Spot zoning

The Florida Supreme Court has called illegal spot zoning "a practice which we and all other courts have universally condemned."[21] Spot zoning is a zoning action that gives a small area privileges which are not extended to other land in the vicinity. Not all spot zoning is impermissible. Spot zoning is justified when in furtherance of a general plan and in the best interests of the community as a whole. Spot zoning is not allowed when it solely benefits a particular property owner.[22]

A Florida court has said: "The power to amend [zoning] is not arbitrary. It cannot be exercised merely because certain individuals want it done or think it ought to be done. The change must be necessary for the public good."[23] *Sw. Ranches Homeowners Assoc. v. Broward Cnty.* presents the principle that the public necessity for a land use can support a finding that a zoning action is not impermissible spot zoning.

## Florida Fourth District Court of Appeal

### *Sw. Ranches Homeowners Ass'n v. Broward Cnty.*[24]

### 1987

ANSTEAD, Judge.

This is an appeal from a final judgment declaring valid two zoning ordinances enacted by Broward County in order to facilitate the location of a sanitary landfill and resource recovery plant in an unincorporated area of the County. We affirm.

In 1981, Broward County began to search for an appropriate location, and secure necessary zoning, for a large scale sanitary landfill and resource recovery plant. After a long period of search and negotiations including the consideration of some 100 prospective sites, the County settled upon a 588 acre parcel of land adjacent to the Broward Correctional Institution (BCI), a women's prison located in an unincorporated portion of agricultural southwest Broward County. It was determined that two land use code changes would be necessary to locate the project on that site. First, an application would be required to change the BCI site from a limited agricultural A–1 zoning district, which permits a variety of agricultural, low intensity uses but prohibits dumps, sanitary fill or incinerators, to an agricultural-disposal A–6 zoning district, which permits sanitary fill and incinerators. Second, in order to permit the large scale solid waste disposal facility contemplated, the text of the A–6 district provision needed to be changed to allow landfill up to 125 feet above ground level, to provide for a resource recovery facility, to allow structures to be 200 feet high, and to permit incineration on an area of 20 acres or less. These changes were accomplished by enactment of ... ordinances declared valid below.

The Southwest Ranches Homeowners Association, Inc. sought to enjoin the County from locating the project on the BCI site, claiming ... that the rezoning constituted improper spot zoning and conflicted with the Broward County land use plan. At trial, the Association called several expert witnesses. ... [The Association] presented the testimony of an urban planner to the effect that the proposed use is incompatible with the general agricultural character of the region, and inconsistent with several other elements of the Broward County Comprehensive Plan. In particular, the Association attempted to demonstrate that the proposed use was inconsistent with the coastal zone protection conservation element, the potable water element, and the solid waste element of the plan. Finally, the Association presented evidence that this same site had previously been rejected as a location for an industrial and office use, in light of existing land use policy to keep development in the area to a minimum.

The County presented evidence which controverted the claims of the Association in virtually every material regard. The County put on evidence demonstrating the critical need for the facility and the lengthy search for a suitable site ... . In response to the Association's evidence that the project would be inconsistent with certain elements of the comprehensive plan, the County contended that the facility was consistent with the land use elements of the plan and also consistent with the overall objective of the plan to provide an adequate level of services to support future growth in the County without endangering environmental resources. The project was described as providing for a 40 acre park, initially, with the landfill itself to have a 20 year life during the course of which it would be converted entirely into a public park. A County planning official also testified that pursuant to the County Code, the petition for rezoning had been reviewed and approved for consistency with the comprehensive plan by all of the County agencies with expertise in their respective fields, such as pollution and drainage control. It was also demonstrated that the project was subject to the scrutiny and approval of numerous other federal, state and local governmental entities concerned with water pollution and flood control.

The court concluded in its final order ... that the ordinances did not constitute spot zoning and would be upheld as "fairly debatable."...

We ... reject the Association's claim that the trial court erred in holding that the ordinances in question did not constitute illegal "spot zoning." Spot zoning is the name given to the piecemeal rezoning of small parcels of land to a greater density, leading to disharmony with the surrounding area. *See Dade County v. Inversiones Rafamar, S.A.*, 360 So. 2d 1130, 1133 (Fla. 3d DCA 1978). Spot zoning is usually thought of as giving preferential treatment to one parcel at the expense of the zoning scheme as a whole. *See Allapattah Community Ass'n, Inc. of Florida v. City of Miami*, 379 So. 2d 387, 394 (Fla. 3d DCA 1980). Moreover, the term is generally applied to the rezoning of only one or a few lots. *Cf. Allapattah*, 379 So. 2d at 395 n. 9. The ordinances in question do not give preferential treatment to one group of property owners in the area over another. Nor is the pattern of development in the area such that its character will be destroyed by the waste disposal facility. The site in question is not completely surrounded by low density rural uses; rather, it will be adjoined by the prison on its eastern edge. More importantly, perhaps, the BCI site is 588 acres in size, substantially larger than a few lots.

...

Taking all the relevant considerations into account, we can find no basis for setting aside the trial court's conclusion that the proposed ordinances are consistent with the overall provisions and purposes of the comprehensive plan ... .

... Obviously, waste, if not disposed of in a proper manner, constitutes a substantial threat to the environment and public health. While it may appear that we have come a long way from the time when sewage was indiscriminately dumped in our waterways and piled on our lands, legitimate concerns continue and must be addressed on an ongoing basis. The record reflects the County's near exhaustion of available waste disposal facilities, an immediate need for the project in question, and an absence of any ultimate weapon against waste accumulation and its effects.

Therefore, we conclude that the trial court did not err in finding that [the change in zoning] was a permissible exercise of the County's authority ... .

DOWNEY, J., and WILLIS, BEN C., Associate Judge (Retired), concur.

*Discussion*

For a colorful description of spot zoning as "'melanoma zoning' or, for short, 'melazoning,'" see *Bird-Kendall Homeowners Ass'n v. Metro. Dade Cnty.*[25]

**Box 9.2 Practice problem: Windsor Heights Neighborhood Association**

John owns a parcel of property in the Windsor Heights neighborhood. Windsor Heights is a large historic neighborhood in the city of Collegeborough.

The Collegeborough Comprehensive Plan says this about the Windsor Heights neighborhood:

> Windsor Heights is an appropriate area for a variety of residential uses including single family homes, duplexes, apartment buildings of up to eight units and bed and breakfast type inns. Windsor Heights is not an appropriate location for commercial uses except those commercial uses which are compatible with residential uses.

The Collegeborough zoning code has designated the entire Windsor Heights neighborhood RHD or Residential Historic District. That zoning category allows single family homes, duplexes, apartment buildings up to eight units, bed and breakfast type inns, and home-based professional offices.

The Collegeborough zoning code has another residential zoning category called RG or Residential General. That zoning category allows all of the uses allowed in the RHD district plus places of religious assembly, schools, and day-care centers. Places of religious assembly, schools, and day-care centers are commercial uses the zoning code calls "compatible with residential uses."

John would like to operate a day-care center on his property in Windsor Heights. He applies for a change in the zoning of his property from RHD to RG. John hires Paul, a professional planner, to process the application.

At the hearing to consider this change, Paul testifies that "use of John's property as a day care center would benefit the residents of the neighborhood because many have young children and are currently traveling outside of the neighborhood for day care services." Also, he testifies "the zoning change would reduce traffic by keeping these folks in the neighborhood and would therefore be a benefit to the whole community."

Collegeborough approves John's rezoning request. George, a member of the Windsor Heights Neighborhood Association, is unhappy about the change in zoning and sues Collegeborough. George alleges that granting the approval was impermissible spot zoning.

Evaluate George's claim.

## Notes

1 7 Fla. Jur. 2d *Building, Zoning, and Land Controls* § 245 (2020).
2 *Id.*
3 *Id.* § 246.
4 As to the requirement that unusual hardship be shown to obtain a variance, *see* 7 Fla. Jur. 2d *Building, Zoning, and Land Controls* §§ 251–55 (2020).
5 Mayflower Prop., Inc. v. City of Fort Lauderdale, 137 So. 2d 849, 852–53 (Fla. 2d DCA 1962).
6 303 So. 2d 423 (Fla. 2d DCA 1974).
7 Cap's-on-the-Water, Inc. v. St. Johns Cnty., 841 So. 2d 507, 509 (Fla. 5th DCA 2003).
8 Dusseau v. Metro. Dade Cnty., 794 So. 2d 1270, 1273 (Fla. 2001) (quoting Irvine v. Duval Cnty., 495 So. 2d 167, 167 (Fla. 1986)).
9 *Dusseau*, 794 So. 2d at 1274 (quoting Fla. Power & Light Co. v. City of Dania, 761 So. 2d 1089, 1092 (Fla. 2000)).
10 96 So. 2d 784 (Fla. 1957) (en banc).
11 Josephson v. Autrey, 96 So. 2d 784, 788 (Fla. 1957) (en banc).
12 *Id.* ("To endow such a board with the authority to amend the zoning ordinance in particular instances by authorizing a use of property prohibited by the ordinance itself would be to convey to the appeals board the authority to enact legislation, nullify the decision of the municipal legislative body, and in effect destroy the beneficient results to be obtained by comprehensive zoning.")
13 *Id.*
14 7 Fla. Jur. 2d *Building, Zoning, and Land Controls* § 255 (2020).
15 *Id.* at § 253.
16 Elwyn v. City of Miami, 113 So. 2d 849, 852 (Fla. 3d DCA 1959).
17 It is true that a "local government's evaluation of 'neighborhood compatibility' necessarily includes subjective elements ... [and] is to some degree a question of taste and aesthetics." AT&T Wireless Servs. of Fla., Inc. v. Orange Cnty., 23 F. Supp. 2d 1355, 1362 (M.D. Fla. 1998) (interpreting Florida land use law).
18 113 So. 2d 849 (Fla. 3d DCA 1959).
19 383 So. 2d 1127 (Fla. 3d DCA 1980).
20 400 So. 2d 37 (Fla. 5th DCA 1981), *aff'd*, 419 So. 2d 1041 (Fla. 1982).
21 Parking Facilities, Inc. v. City of Miami Beach, 88 So. 2d 141, 143 (Fla. 1956).

22 In other words, illegal spot zoning is a "rezoning which creates a small island of property with restrictions on its use different from that of surrounding properties-solely for the benefit of a particular property owner." Bird-Kendall Homeowners Ass'n v. Metro. Dade Cnty., 695 So. 2d 908, 909 n.2 (Fla. 3d DCA 1997) (citing City Comm'n of Miami v. Woodlawn Park Cemetery Co., 553 So. 2d 1227, 1240 (Fla. 3d DCA 1989) (Ferguson, J., dissenting)).

23 Allapattah Cmty. Ass'n of Fla. v. City of Miami, 379 So. 2d 387, 395 (Fla. 3d DCA 1980) (citing Kennedy v. City of Evanston, 181 N.E. 312, 314 (Ill. 1932)).

24 502 So. 2d 931 (Fla. 4th DCA 1987).

25 Bird-Kendall Homeowners Ass'n v. Metro. Dade Cnty., 695 So. 2d 908, 909 n.1 (Fla. 3d DCA 1997).

# Part II

# Challenging land use decisions

# 10 Administrative hearing

## Overview of causes of action

Florida law provides different opportunities for landowners, developers, or other affected parties to challenge land use decisions. These are the principal tools available to challenge local government land use decisions under Florida law. Note that these options do not include enforcement of U.S. Constitutional protections or federal laws. The tools are:

- *petitioning for hearing by the Division of Administrative Hearings* to challenge comprehensive plan adoption or amendment on the grounds the decision is not in compliance with certain requirements of law;
- filing a *writ of certiorari* to state circuit court which is how one appeals a quasi-judicial decision on grounds other than consistency with the comprehensive plan;
- making a *consistency challenge* in state circuit court which is appropriate for challenging a decision on the grounds that it is not consistent with the comprehensive plan; and
- seeking a *declaratory judgment* in state circuit court which is appropriate for challenging an administrative action or a legislative action when neither petitioning for a hearing by the Division of Administrative Hearings, nor making a consistency challenge, is the prescribed cause of action.

In addition to each cause of action below, note that this text addresses the Florida Land Use and Environmental Dispute Resolution Act—a process for mediating settlements to land use disputes with local governments—and the Bert J. Harris Private Property Rights Protection Act—a law giving property owners the right to seek damages for some local government restrictions on land use—in Chapter 17.

## Petition for hearing by the Division of Administrative Hearings

As previously discussed, the Department of Economic Opportunity, Florida's state land planning agency, reviews proposed amendments to local plans before local governments may adopt them.[1] To challenge plan adoptions and plan amendments, one may petition for a hearing before the Division of Administrative Hearings (DOAH) pursuant to the Administrative Procedure Act, Chapter 120 of Florida Statutes.[2] A petition for hearing by DOAH is appropriate for challenging adoption or amendment of a comprehensive plan on the grounds that the plan is not "in compliance" with specific requirements of the Community Planning Act.[3] This text presents a flow chart to graphically present the process for an administrative challenge to a comprehensive plan adoption or plan amendment.

The following statutory provisions create this avenue for relief and describe who has standing to appeal comprehensive planning decisions to DOAH.

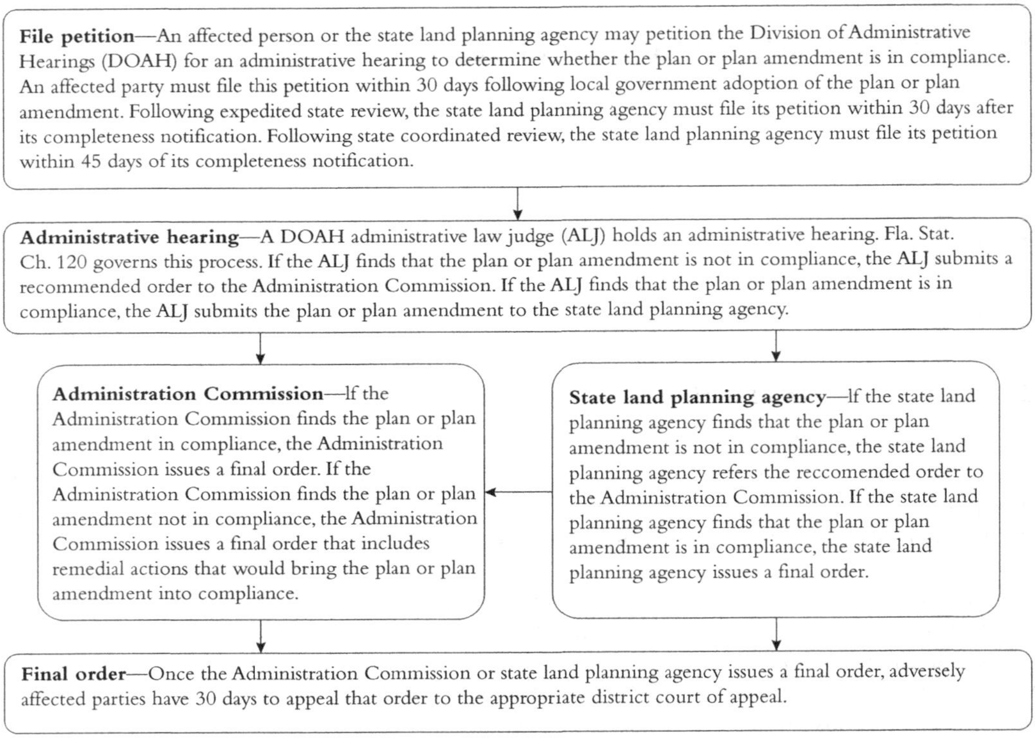


*Figure 10.1* Flow chart describing the process of an administrative challenge to comprehensive plan adoption or amendment

Note: *see* Fla. Stat. § 163.3184(5) and (8)

> (5) ADMINISTRATIVE CHALLENGES TO PLANS AND PLAN AMENDMENTS.—
>
> (a) Any affected person as defined in paragraph (1)(a) may file a petition with the Division of Administrative Hearings pursuant to ss. 120.569 and 120.57, with a copy served on the affected local government, to request a formal hearing to challenge whether the plan or plan amendments are in compliance as defined in paragraph (1)(b). This petition must be filed with the division within 30 days after the local government adopts the amendment. The state land planning agency may not intervene in a proceeding initiated by an affected person.[4]

Further, statutes define an "affected person" as follows:

> "Affected person" includes the affected local government; persons owning property, residing, or owning or operating a business within the boundaries of the local government whose plan is the subject of the review; owners of real property abutting real property that is the subject of a proposed change to a future land use map; and adjoining local governments that can demonstrate that the plan or plan amendment will produce substantial impacts on the increased need for publicly funded infrastructure or substantial impacts on areas designated for protection or special treatment within their jurisdiction.

> Each person, other than an adjoining local government, in order to qualify under this definition, shall also have submitted oral or written comments, recommendations, or objections to the local government during the period of time beginning with the transmittal hearing for the plan or plan amendment and ending with the adoption of the plan or plan amendment.[5]

The liberal definition of "affected person" in the statute grants standing to challenge comprehensive plans broadly. In addition, the state land planning agency may petition DOAH for a hearing on whether a local plan or plan amendment is "in compliance."[6]

Note, however, that not all parties who have standing to file an initial petition to DOAH will have standing to subsequently appeal the DOAH decision. The DOAH hearing before an administrative law judge results in a recommended order for consideration by the state land planning agency or the Administration Commission (comprising the Governor and the members of the Florida Cabinet), which will subsequently issue a final order.[7] If the recommended order includes a finding that the plan amendment is not in compliance, the Administration Commission issues the final order.[8] If the recommended order includes a finding that the plan amendment is in compliance, the state land planning agency issues the final order.[9] Appeal from a final order, in turn, is properly made to the appellate district court "where the agency maintains its headquarters or where a party resides or as otherwise provided by law."[10]

Only parties who are "adversely affected" by final agency action have standing to appeal to the district court.[11] That standard is less generous than the one in Chapter 163.[12] The First District Court of Appeals has recognized that these requirementss for standing differ.

> The fact that a person may have the requisite standing to appear as a party before an agency at a de novo proceeding does not mean that the party automatically has standing to appeal. The [Administrative Procedures Act's] definition of a party recognizes the need for a much broader zone of party representation at the administrative level than at the appellate level.[13]

Another relevant detail of standing requirements, particularly given the interest in land use and environmental matters from organizations, is associational standing. The Florida Supreme Court has explicitly found that organizations may have associational standing—that is standing to represent the interests of their members—in administrative appeals.

For a court to recognize associational standing,

> [1] an association must demonstrate that a substantial number of its members, although not necessarily a majority, are "substantially affected" by the challenged rule. Further, [2] the subject matter of the rule must be within the association's general scope of interest and activity, and [3] the relief requested must be of the type appropriate for a trade association to receive on behalf of its members.[14]

In the administrative hearing, DOAH has jurisdiction to determine whether the comprehensive planning decision is in compliance where

> "[i]n compliance" means consistent with the requirements of ss. 163.3177, 163.3178, 163.3180, 163.3191, 163.3245, and 163.3248, with the appropriate strategic regional policy plan, and with the principles for guiding development in designated areas of critical state concern and with part III of chapter 369, where applicable.[15]

Of course, this definition has little meaning without a review of the many statutory cross-references. Note that this text discusses the most significant of these compliance standards in the chapter regarding statutory comprehensive planning requirements. Generally, they are that comprehensive plans: must establish meaningful and predictable standards for the use and development of land; must be based on relevant and appropriate data and analysis; and must be internally consistent.[16]

When considering whether to challenge a comprehensive plan through an administrative appeal to DOAH or a declaratory judgment in circuit court, review the previously cited provisions of Chapter 163 to determine which cause of action is appropriate.

Whereas a due process challenge to a local government's legislative land use decision is always subject to the fairly debatable standard of review,[17] Florida Statutes provide different standards of review for a DOAH consideration of local government comprehensive planning decisions.

What standard of review applies depends on two factors: the identity of the petitioner and the scope of review requested. The following provisions of Florida Statutes present the several potentially applicable standards of review, and when each applies.

1. In challenges filed by an affected person, the comprehensive plan or plan amendment shall be determined to be in compliance if the local government's determination of compliance is fairly debatable.
2. a. In challenges filed by the state land planning agency, the local government's determination that the comprehensive plan or plan amendment is in compliance is presumed to be correct, and the local government's determination shall be sustained unless it is shown by a preponderance of the evidence that the comprehensive plan or plan amendment is not in compliance.
   b. In challenges filed by the state land planning agency, the local government's determination that elements of its plan are related to and consistent with each other shall be sustained if the determination is fairly debatable.
3. In challenges filed by the state land planning agency that require a determination by the agency that an important state resource or facility will be adversely impacted by the adopted plan or plan amendment, the local government may contest the agency's determination of an important state resource or facility. The state land planning agency shall prove its determination by clear and convincing evidence.[18]

The state land planning agency, therefore, has a much stronger position in an administrative hearing to challenge a local government land use decision than does an affected person making the same claim. Whether the inclination of the state is to intervene in local government planning decisions is often the determining factor in whether local governments are compelled to follow Florida laws governing comprehensive planning. When administrative challenges are left to affected parties, potential violations of the law are resolved using the fairly debatable standard. In these situations, state law requires DOAH to give greater deference to the local government's judgment.

The following case, *Martin Cnty. v. Dep't of Cmty. Affs.*, resolves a petition alleging that comprehensive plan amendments by the city of Stuart were not in compliance. The court's discussions on the posture of the case and of the basis for the allegation that the amendments were not in compliance give context to this discussion of the petition for a hearing by DOAH.

## Florida Fourth District Court of Appeals

## *Martin Cnty. v. Dep't of Cmty. Affs.*[19]

## 2000

STEVENSON, J.

The Board of County Commissioners of Martin County and 1000 Friends of Florida, Inc., an interested not-for-profit organization, appeal a final order of the Department of Community Affairs finding a number of amendments to the City of Stuart's comprehensive plan to be "in compliance" with the Florida Interlocal Cooperation Act, the Growth Policy Act, the Florida Local Government Development Agreement Act, the Local Government Planning and Land Development Regulation Act, and other applicable rules and regulations outlined in Chapter 163, Florida Statutes. We affirm in part and reverse in part.

The facts and history underlying the instant appeal are somewhat lengthy and complex. In late 1996 / early 1997, Martin County determined that a number of its roads were over capacity and, as a result, in certain areas of the county there was a moratorium on development. In 1997, the City of Stuart began receiving petitions for voluntary annexation of parcels of real property. Ultimately, some 1,200 acres were annexed into the City. Despite the annexation, however, pursuant to section 171.062(2), Florida Statutes (1997), the parcels remained subject to Martin County's land use plan and/or zoning and subdivision regulations until such time as the City adopted comprehensive plan amendments that included the annexed parcels. In late 1997, the City of Stuart began the process of amending its comprehensive plan to include the newly annexed parcels. When the smoke cleared, the City of Stuart had amended its comprehensive plan, assigning a land use designation to each of the newly annexed parcels, creating a new land use category, and revising the text of virtually all of the elements of its plan, including the intergovernmental coordination element.

From the outset, Martin County challenged the plan amendments. In short, the County contended that the amendments were not "in compliance" as defined in section 163.3184(1)(b), Florida Statutes, that the amendments failed to discourage urban sprawl, that the amendments were not consistent with the County's comprehensive plan, that the intergovernmental coordination element was inadequate to meet the requirements of Chapter 163, that the amendments were not based on adequate data and analysis, and that the City failed to demonstrate a need for the annexed parcels. 1000 Friends joined the litigation, siding with Martin County. The five cases that had resulted from Martin County's serial petitions to challenge the amendments were consolidated and a hearing was held before an administrative law judge. By the time of the hearing, the Department of Community Affairs (the "Department"), who had initially indicated an intent to find some of the amendments not "in compliance," and the City of Stuart were on the same side—defending the amendments. The Department's final order adopted the vast majority of the findings in the administrative law judge's eighty-seven page order and upheld the amendments.

For the most part, the appellants challenge generally the Department's decision that the amendments are "in compliance," arguing that the Department did not properly harmonize the statutory growth management policies with state policies governing municipal annexation, Chapters 163 and 171, Florida Statutes, respectively. In addition, appellants specifically challenge the City's amendment to its intergovernmental coordination element, arguing that it failed to comply with section 163.3177(6)(h)1.a., as required, and the City's inclusion of a Future Annexation Area Map in its plan, contending that the map is not supported by adequate data and analysis. We affirm as to all issues, except the challenge to the Future Annexation Area Map.

The administrative law judge described the Future Annexation Area Map as "identif[ying] approximately 8,000 additional acres of land which the City may consider annexing through the year 2015." During the proceedings below and here on appeal, the appellants contended that the map represented an amendment to the comprehensive plan and the amendment was not supported by adequate data and analysis. The Department rejected these arguments, finding that the map was data and analysis, which need not be supported by other data and analysis, and not an amendment to the comprehensive plan or, alternatively, that even if the map "is considered to be an operative policy of the City Plan" the map is not required, does not conflict with any provision of Chapter 163 or Chapter 9J–5 and, thus, may be upheld. We respectfully disagree.

The first issue that must be addressed is whether the map is, in fact, an amendment to the comprehensive plan since amendments must be supported by adequate data and analysis. See § 163.3177(8), Fla. Stat. ("All elements of the comprehensive plan, whether mandatory or optional, shall be based upon data appropriate to the element involved."). Contrary to the Department's finding that the map is nothing more than data and analysis, the ordinance adopting the map characterizes it as part of the City's comprehensive plan. Section 10 of Ordinance 1628–97 provides that:

> In addition to the foregoing amendments to the Plan, the maps designated on "Attachment B" as "EXISTING CONDITIONS MAPS" and "FUTURE CONDITIONS MAPS" [including the Future Annexation Area Map] are hereby adopted as amendments to the Plan. The City Manager shall cause each of the maps adopted hereby to be codified within the text of the Plan at an appropriate place to facilitate an understanding of the Plan provisions.

In the face of this statement of intent on the part of the City of Stuart, we simply cannot concur in the Department's conclusion that the Future Annexation Area Map does not represent an amendment to the comprehensive plan and is merely data and analysis. And, our review of the record convinces us that the appellants are correct in their assertion that no data or analysis was offered in support of the map and its boundaries. Accordingly, on this issue alone, we reverse.

AFFIRMED in part and REVERSED in part.

POLEN and TAYLOR, JJ., concur.

## Administrative review of land development regulations

In addition to adoption or amendment of a comprehensive plan, administrative hearings are available to consider whether local government land use regulations are consistent with a comprehensive plan. Pursuant to section 163.3213, any person who is affected by the adoption of a local government land use regulation can administratively appeal that adoption on the grounds that the adoption is not consistent with the relevant comprehensive plan.[20]

This option to challenge a land use rule is different from the consistency challenge available under section 163.3215. As this chapter will discuss, while a consistency challenge allows affected parties to challenge a development order (i.e. a decision on a specific development permit),[21] a request for review under section 163.3213 is available to challenge a legislative decision adopting or amending a local government's generally applicable land use regulations.[22] Further, this administrative relief is the only proceeding available to challenge a land use regulation as inconsistent with the applicable comprehensive plan.[23]

A party affected by the land use regulation initiates the process by filing a petition with the state land planning agency within one year of the date the local government adopted the land use regulation.[24] Then, the state land planning agency holds an informal hearing.[25]

From this point, the process generally proceeds to a hearing by DOAH, a final decision by the Administration Commission or the state land planning agency, and an optional appeal to the appropriate district court of appeal.[26] Procedurally, an administrative challenge to land development regulations is similar to an administrative challenge to comprehensive plan adoption or amendment.

## Notes

1 *See* Fla. Stat. §§ 163.3184(2)(a), 163.3184(3).
2 *Id.* § 163.3184(5)(a).
3 Florida Statutes identify the specific requirements of law that can be the subject of a finding that a comprehensive plan is not in compliance at section 163.3184(1)(6).
4 Fla. Stat. § 163.3184(5).
5 *Id.* § 163.3184(1)(a).
6 *Id.* § 163.3184(1)(b).
7 *Id.* §§ 164.3184(5)(e)(1), (e)(2).
8 *Id.* § 164.3184(5)(d).
9 *Id.* § 164.3184(5)(e)(2).
10 Fla. Stat. § 120.68(2)(a).
11 *Id.* § 120.68(1)(a).
12 *Cf.* Fla. Stat. § 120.68(1)(a), *with* Fla. Stat. § 163.3184(1)(a), *and* Fla. Stat. § 163.3184(5)(a).
13 Martin Cnty. Conservation All. v. Martin Cnty., 73 So. 3d 856, 862 (Fla. 1st DCA 2011) (citation omitted), *appeal dismissed* 122 So. 3d 243 (Fla. 2013) (per curiam) (mem.).
14 Fla. Home Builders, Ass'n v. Dep't of Lab. & Emp. Sec., 412 So. 2d 351, 353–54 (Fla. 1982).
15 Fla. Stat. § 163.3184(1)(b).
16 *Id.* §§ 163.3177(1), (1)(f), 163.3177(2).
17 Brevard Cnty. v. Snyder, 627 So. 2d 469, 474 (Fla. 1993).
18 Fla. Stat. § 163.3184(5)(c).
19 771 So. 2d 1268 (Fla. 4th DCA 2000).
20 *See* Fla. Stat. § 163.3213(3) (stating that "a substantially affected person ... may challenge a land development regulation on the basis that it is inconsistent with the local comprehensive plan").
21 "'Development permit' includes any building permit, zoning permit, subdivision approval, rezoning, certification, special exception, variance, or any other official action of local government having the effect of permitting the development of land." Fla. Stat. § 163.3164(16).
22 Also note that this method of appeal for administrative review does not apply to "a zoning map, an action which results in zoning or a rezoning of land, or any building construction standard ... ." *Id.* § 163.3213(2)(b).
23 *Id.* § 163.3213(7).
24 *Id.* § 163.3213(3).
25 *Id.* § 163.3213(4).
26 *See id.* §§ 163.3213(5), (6).

# 11 Writ of certiorari

One may appeal a local government quasi-judicial decision to the courts by filing a writ of certiorari.[1] Generally, "Florida courts have adapted the common law writ of certiorari for use in various scenarios, including ... to review actions of local government agencies."[2] Review by a writ of certiorari is not available for legislative decisions.[3]

Note that both the writ of certiorari and a consistency challenge made pursuant to Florida Statutes section 163.3215(3) are available to seek review of quasi-judicial decisions. However, Florida Statutes make the consistency challenge the only available remedy for local government land use decisions which are not consistent with the corresponding comprehensive plan.[4] A writ of certiorari is appropriate for the remaining challenges to quasi-judicial decisions (i.e. a writ of certiorari is appropriate when a consistency challenge is not). These remaining challenges might allege a violation of common law—such as the rules on variances, special exceptions, and spot zoning—or a local government failure to provide due process.

## First-tier certiorari review

First-tier certiorari review is the appeal of a local government quasi-judicial decision to the circuit court pursuant to the certiorari procedures found in Fla. R. App. P. 9.100.[5]

A party must make an appeal "within 30 days of rendition of the order to be reviewed."[6] Rendition is the triggering event that begins the tolling of time for seeking appellate relief.[7] Florida's Rules of Appellate Procedure control what constitutes rendition.[8] The rules provide "[a]n order is rendered when a signed, written order is filed with the clerk of the lower tribunal."[9] In the context of a local government quasi-judicial decision, a decision is filed with the clerk when filed "with a government clerk or the person who most closely resembles a clerk in functions performed."[10] Local governments do not always have clear and consistent practices for rendition, which can create uncertainty for parties seeking to protect their rights through certiorari appeal.

In first-tier certiorari review, the scope of the circuit court's authority is limited to a three-part standard of review:

> Where a party is entitled as a matter of right to seek review in the circuit court from administrative action, the circuit court must determine whether [1] procedural due process is accorded, [2] whether the essential requirements of the law have been observed, and [3] whether the administrative findings and judgment are supported by competent substantial evidence.[11]

Under the first prong, the circuit court determines "whether the specific quasi-judicial decision under review was derived from a proceeding which itself afforded procedural due process."[12]

While a court will not hold a local government hearing to the same procedural due process standard as a judicial hearing, "[i]n quasi-judicial proceedings, the parties must be able to present evidence, cross-examine witnesses, and be informed of all the facts upon which the commission acts."[13] In addition:

> Although strict compliance with statutory notice requirements is mandatory, a contesting party's right to assert a defect in such notice may be waived if the party appeared at the hearing and was able to fully and adequately present his or her objections.[14]

And a violation of procedural due process rights must be "more than mere political bias or an unfriendly political atmosphere" to invalidate a quasi-judicial proceeding.[15]

Under the second prong, the court evaluates whether the local government departed from the essential requirements of the law. This phrase means more than "the mere existence of legal error."[16] A circuit court cannot grant relief to an appellant simply because the district court disagrees with a local government decision, or even if the local government has misapplied the correct law.[17] Instead, "a violation of [a] clearly established principle of law resulting in a miscarriage of justice" must exist.[18] The correct law, however, "may derive from a variety of sources including local governmental ordinances."[19]

Under the third prong, the court evaluates "whether the [local government] decision [is] supported by competent substantial evidence."[20] Substantial evidence is "evidence that provides a factual basis from which a fact at issue may reasonably be inferred."[21] And "[c]ompetent substantial evidence is tantamount to legally sufficient evidence."[22] In other words, competent substantial evidence "sufficient to sustain a finding of an administrative agency, is evidence that is sufficiently relevant and material that a reasonable mind would accept it as adequate to support the conclusion reached."[23]

The following are examples of what courts have found to be competent, substantial evidence:

- the application for development review;[24]
- relevant fact-based statements made by experts *or citizens*;[25]
- recommendations from the local planning agency;[26] and
- the applicable land development regulations and the local government's interpretation of them.[27]

The following are examples of what courts have found not to be competent substantial evidence:

- "generalized statements in opposition to a land use proposal, even those from an expert";[28]
- legal arguments;[29] and
- opinions and speculation from lay witnesses.[30]

If the circuit court finds that the local government's decision is not supported by competent substantial evidence, then the agency's decision "must be quashed."[31]

### *Standing*

The Florida Supreme Court described the standard for a plaintiff to have standing to enforce a valid zoning ordinance applicable to a local government land use decision in *Renard v. Dade County*.[32]

> [O]ne seeking redress, either preventive or corrective, against an *alleged violation of a municipal zoning ordinance* must allege and prove special damages peculiar to himself differing in kind as distinguished from damages differing in degree suffered by the community as a whole. [This] "special damage" rule of the *Boucher* case is an outgrowth of the law of public nuisance. Zoning violations have historically been treated as public nuisances not subject to suit by an individual unless that individual has suffered damages different in kind and degree from the rest of the community.[33]

This standard is more stringent than the statutory standard adopted by the Florida Legislature for consistency challenges.[34]

The following are examples of appellants whom courts have found to have standing to appeal a local government quasi-judicial decision by writ of certiorari:

- neighboring property owners;[35]
- abutting homeowners;[36]
- homeowners' associations representing "residents, who border or are in close proximity to the proposed development";[37]
- property owners who are adjacent to a development, but also "across [a] waterway";[38] and
- property owners who "share [a] private road" with a proposed development.[39]

### *Preserving the record for appeal*

First-tier certiorari review is an appellate proceeding. And review "is not possible without a record upon which to predicate such a review."[40] In its appellate capacity, "the circuit court is not permitted to reweigh the evidence nor to substitute its judgment for that of the agency."[41] Rather, the "question of the weight and credibility of the evidence is for the [local government] and not the reviewing court, even though the court may have reached a different conclusion on the same testimony."[42] Thus, the circuit court's task is to "review the record for evidence that *supports* the [local government]'s decision, not that *rebuts* it—for the court cannot reweigh the evidence."[43] The circuit court simply may not make factual findings in certiorari review.[44]

Given the necessity of a record for appeal, a practitioner representing a party to a quasi-judicial hearing *must ensure that the record of the local government decision is adequate* in order to preserve his or her client's right to appeal.[45] If the circuit court finds that the record is "incomplete, confusing and contradictory," then the appeal cannot proceed; if the record is incomplete, the appellant "will not be able to demonstrate error and he will fail on the merits."[46]

This requirement for a complete record is relevant to standing. *An appellant must establish his or her standing as part of the local government's quasi-judicial proceedings.*[47] The circuit court cannot later make a de novo determination as to standing.[48]

## Second-tier certiorari review

Second-tier certiorari review is an appeal from the circuit court to a district court of appeal.[49] Second-tier certiorari review is "necessarily narrower" than first-tier certiorari review.[50]

The district court of appeals' review "is limited to whether the circuit court afforded procedural due process and whether the circuit court applied the correct law, or, as otherwise stated, departed from the essential requirements of law."[51]

Upon its review, the district court may decide "either to quash the writ of certiorari or to quash the order reviewed."[52] The Florida Supreme Court has discussed the limited impact available from these options.

> When the order is quashed, as it was in this case, it leaves the subject matter, that is, the controversy pending before the tribunal, commission, or administrative authority, as if no order or judgment had been entered and the parties stand upon the pleadings and proof as it existed when the order was made with the rights of all parties to proceed further as they may be advised to protect or obtain the enjoyment of their rights under the law in the same manner and to the same extent which they might have proceeded had the order reviewed not been entered.
>
> The appellate court has no power in exercising its jurisdiction in certiorari to enter a judgment on the merits of the controversy under consideration nor to direct the respondent to enter any particular order or judgment.[53]

For litigants in land use disputes, this resolution (or lack thereof) is certain to seem anticlimactic.

The following case, *City of Fort Myers v. Splitt*, presents many of the procedural issues related to filing a writ of certiorari to appeal a local government land use action.

## Florida Second District Court of Appeal

### *City of Fort Myers v. Splitt*[54]

### 2008

CANADY, Judge.

In this certiorari proceeding initiated by the City of Fort Myers, we consider whether the circuit court applied the wrong law regarding standing in issuing a writ of certiorari quashing an ordinance adopted by the City. For the reasons we explain, we conclude that the City is entitled to relief.

#### *I. Background*

The respondents here, Virginia Splitt, Caloosahatchee River Citizens Association, Inc., and Responsible Growth Management Coalition, Inc. (referred to hereafter collectively as Mrs. Splitt et al.), appeared in the course of proceedings before the City related to a proposed planned unit development (PUD) for a multiuse project known as "The Vue" to be located on riverfront lands adjacent to Centennial Park. The interest asserted by Mrs. Splitt et al. in the proceedings before the City related primarily to their concerns regarding the public enjoyment of Centennial Park. At the hearings before the City, Mrs. Splitt personally only argued (1) that a tree had been planted in the park in memory of her husband and she did not want it moved and (2) that no part of the park should be turned over to private enterprise. The Caloosahatchee River Citizens Association argued in turn that it was concerned that people who purchased condominiums in the buildings which were part of the PUD would object to noise and traffic from festivals held in the park. The Association also asserted that it was "echoing" the objections raised by other citizens. The Association did not specify which objections it was adopting, but the objections made related to (1) the size of the PUD, (2) the fact that people would complain about noise and traffic, (3) increases in intensity and density, (4) elimination of public use of the land since the park would be in the backyard of the condominium purchasers, (5) overburdening of the city's street system, and (6) overburdening of the wastewater treatment system. The Responsible Growth Management Coalition objected only on the basis of the size of the PUD and the fact that city garbage trucks would have to use access roads to pick up the trash at the PUD.

Mrs. Splitt et al. filed a certiorari petition in the circuit court challenging three ordinances adopted by the City concerning "The Vue" PUD project. Initially, Mrs. Splitt et al. also filed a declaratory judgment action seeking a determination that the ordinances were inconsistent with the City's comprehensive plan. That action was, however, voluntarily dismissed. The thrust of the certiorari petition was that the ordinances did not comply with the PUD criteria and other requirements applicable under the City's zoning ordinances. The circuit court denied the petition with respect to two of the challenged ordinances but granted it with respect to the third ordinance, ordinance 3366, which was adopted January 11, 2007.

In the circuit court, the City challenged the standing of Mrs. Splitt et al. on the ground that they had failed to establish in the record of the proceedings before the City that they had standing under the "special damages" standing test articulated in *Renard v. Dade County*, 261 So. 2d 832, 837 (Fla.1972), for challenges seeking to enforce valid zoning ordinances.

Mrs. Splitt et al. conceded that the *Renard* standard was applicable but contended that the allegations of their petition were sufficient to establish their standing under *Renard*. The circuit court concluded, however, that the question of standing was governed not by the *Renard* standard but by the provisions of section 163.3215, Florida Statutes (2006), regarding challenges to the consistency of a development order with a comprehensive plan. Based on the application of section 163.3215, the circuit court determined that—according to the allegations of their petition in the circuit court—Mrs. Splitt et al. had the requisite standing.

The City now contends that the circuit court's decision granting relief with respect to ordinance 3366 should be quashed because the circuit court applied the wrong law with respect to the test for standing and thus departed from the essential requirements of law. The City also contends that the circuit court applied the wrong law by not requiring that the facts establishing standing appear in the record of the proceedings before the City.

### *II. Analysis*

Both parties acknowledge that the decision of the City at issue here was a quasi-judicial decision rather than a legislative decision and thus subject to challenge in the circuit court by way of certiorari. *See Park of Commerce Assocs. v. City of Delray Beach*, 636 So. 2d 12 (Fla.1994).

#### *A. Standard of Review*

In a second-tier certiorari proceeding with respect to a quasi-judicial decision of a local governmental entity, the district court's review of the circuit court's judgment is limited to "[1] whether the circuit court afforded procedural due process and [2] applied the correct law." *Broward County v. G.B.V. Int'l, Ltd.*, 787 So. 2d 838, 843 (Fla.2001) (alterations in original) (quoting *City of Deerfield Beach v. Vaillant*, 419 So. 2d 624, 626 (Fla.1982)). In utilizing this two-part standard, a district court is simply "deciding whether the lower court 'departed from the essential requirements of law.'" *Id.* at 843 n. 16 (quoting *Haines City Cmty. Dev. v. Heggs*, 658 So. 2d 523, 530 (Fla.1995)).

"The appellate court has no power in exercising its jurisdiction in certiorari to enter a judgment on the merits of the controversy under consideration nor to direct the [entry of] any particular order or judgment." *G.B.V. Int'l, Ltd.*, 787 So. 2d at 844 (quoting *Tamiami Trail Tours v. R.R. Comm'n*, 128 Fla. 25, 174 So. 451, 454 (1937) (on rehearing)).

#### *B. The Applicable Law of Standing*

The section 163.3215 standard for standing applied by the trial court governs de novo challenges to "the consistency of a development order with a comprehensive plan." 163.3215(1). Under the statute, "[a]ny aggrieved or adversely affected party may maintain a de novo action for declaratory, injunctive, or other relief" with regard to "a development order ... which materially alters the use or density or intensity of use on a particular piece of property which is not consistent with the comprehensive plan." § 163.3215(3).

The statute defines "aggrieved or adversely affected party" to mean

> any person or local government that will suffer an adverse effect to an interest protected or furthered by the local government comprehensive plan, including interests related to health and safety, police and fire protection service systems, densities or intensities of development, transportation facilities, health care facilities, equipment or services, and environmental or natural resources. The alleged adverse interest may be shared in common with other members of the community at large but must *exceed in degree* the general interest in community good shared by all persons. The term includes the owner, developer, or applicant for a development order. § 163.3215(2) [emphasis added].

The *Renard* standard for "standing to enforce a valid zoning ordinance" requires a showing of "special damages." 261 So. 2d at 837. The "special damages" rule is derived from "the law of public nuisance." *Id.* at 835 (citing *Boucher v. Novotny*, 102 So. 2d 132 (Fla.1958)). Under this standard, an individual does not have standing to sue unless he can show "special damages peculiar to himself differing in kind as distinguished from damages differing in degree suffered by the community as a whole." *Renard*, 61 So. 2d at 835 (quoting *Boucher*, 102 So. 2d at 135).

It has repeatedly been acknowledged that the standing provisions of section 163.3215 were adopted to liberalize the standing requirements that would otherwise be applicable. *See Parker v. Leon County*, 627 So. 2d 476, 479 (Fla.1993); *Stranahan House, Inc. v. City of Fort Lauderdale*, 967 So. 2d 427, 433 (Fla. 4th DCA 2007); *Payne v. City of Miami*, 927 So. 2d 904, 907 (Fla. 3d DCA 2005); *Pinecrest Lakes, Inc. v. Shidel*, 795 So. 2d 191, 200 (Fla. 4th DCA 2001); *Putnam County Envtl. Council, Inc. v. Bd. of County Comm'rs*, 757 So. 2d 590, 593 (Fla. 5th DCA 2000); *Sw. Ranches Homeowners Ass'n v. Broward County*, 502 So. 2d 931, 935 (Fla. 4th DCA 1987).

The difference between the section 163.3215 standard and the *Renard* special damages test is immediately apparent. Under section 163.3215(2), standing may be based on the showing of an adverse effect on an interest that "*exceed[s] in degree* the general interest in community good shared by all persons" [emphasis added]. The more restrictive *Renard* standard requires a showing of special damages "*differing in kind* as distinguished from damages differing in degree suffered by the community as a whole." 261 So. 2d at 835 [emphasis added] (quoting *Boucher*, 102 So. 2d at 135).

Here, Mrs. Splitt et al. voluntarily abandoned any comprehensive plan consistency challenge to the ordinance. Once they did so, Mrs. Splitt et al. were foreclosed from obtaining the advantage of the more liberal standing provisions applicable under section 163.3215. In determining the standing issue on the basis of section 163.3215, the circuit court failed to apply the correct law.

### *C. Determining Standing in Certiorari Proceedings*

The circuit court similarly failed to apply the correct law when it determined the standing issue on the basis of the allegations of Mrs. Splitt et al. in their certiorari petition rather than on the basis of the record made in the proceedings before the City. "[T]he well[-]established rule applicable to ... certiorari proceedings[s][is] that the reviewing court's consideration shall be confined strictly and solely to the record of proceedings by the agency or board on which the questioned order is based." *Dade County v. Marca, S.A.*, 326 So. 2d 183, 184 (Fla.1976). This rule controls the determination of the factual basis establishing standing to initiate a certiorari proceeding in the circuit court. *See Battaglia Fruit Co. v. City of Maitland*, 530 So. 2d 940, 943 (Fla. 5th DCA 1988) (holding that where city as certiorari petitioner failed to establish the basis for city's standing in the record of the county zoning proceedings, "the circuit court departed from the essential requirements of law in not dismissing the City's petition for lack of standing").

### *D. Prejudicial Error*

We reject any suggestion that Mrs. Splitt et al. had standing even under the more restrictive requirements of *Renard* and that the circuit court's failure to apply the correct law therefore was harmless error. Standing under the *Renard* special damages test is typically based on some impact on the litigant's interest as an owner of property. *See, e.g., Kagan v. West*, 677 So. 2d 905, 908 (Fla. 4th DCA 1996); *Pichette v. City of N. Miami*, 642 So. 2d 1165, 1165–66 (Fla. 3d DCA 1994); *State ex rel. Gardner v. Sailboat Key, Inc.*, 306 So. 2d 616, 618 (Fla. 3d DCA 1974). There is no warrant for concluding that if the circuit court had applied the correct law, it would have determined that Mrs. Splitt et al. established their standing under the special damages test.

### ***III. Conclusion***

Because the circuit court applied the wrong law, we grant the City's petition for certiorari. The order of the circuit court is quashed to the extent that it granted relief with respect to ordinance 3366.

Petition granted; order quashed in part.

FULMER and VILLANTI, JJ., Concur.

## Notes

1 Fla. R. App. P. 9.100(c)(2).
2 Broward Cnty. v. G.B.V. Int'l, Ltd., 787 So. 2d 838, 843 (Fla. 2001).
3 *G.B.V. Int'l, Ltd.*, 787 So. 2d at 843 & nn.12–13.
4 Fla. Stat. § 163.3213(7).
5 Fla. R. App. P. 9.100(c)(2), (f).
6 Fla. R. App. P. 9.100(c)(2).
7 Pettway v. City of Jacksonville, 264 So. 3d 210, 211 (Fla. 1st DCA 2018).
8 Smull v. Town of Jupiter, 854 So. 2d 780 (Fla. 5th DCA 2003).
9 Fla. R. App. P. 9.020(h).
10 *Pettway*, 264 So. 3d at 212 (citations omitted) (citing President's Council of SD, Inc. v. Walton Cnty., 36 So. 3d 764 (Fla. 1st DCA 2010)).
11 City of Deerfield Beach v. Vaillant, 419 So. 2d 624, 626 (Fla. 1982).
12 Evergreen Tree Treasurers of Charlotte Cnty., Inc. v. Charlotte Cnty., 810 So. 2d 526, 531 (Fla. 2d DCA 2002).
13 Kupke v. Orange Cnty., 838 So. 2d 598, 599 (Fla. 5th DCA 2003) (citing Lee Cnty. v. Sunbelt Equities, II, Ltd. P'ship, 619 So. 2d 996, 1002 (Fla. 2d DCA 1993)).
14 City of Jacksonville v. Huffman, 764 So. 2d 695, 696–97 (Fla. 1st DCA 2000).
15 Seminole Ent., Inc. v. City of Casselberry, 811 So. 2d 693, 696 (Fla. 5th DCA 2001).
16 Combs v. State, 436 So. 2d 93, 95 (Fla. 1983).
17 Stilson v. Allstate Ins. Co., 692 So. 2d 979, 982 (Fla. 2d DCA 1997).
18 Ivey v. Allstate Ins. Co., 774 So. 2d 679, 682–83 (Fla. 2000) (citing Haines City Cmty. Dev. v. Heggs, 658 So. 2d 523, 528 (Fla. 1995)).
19 Wolk v. Seminole Cnty., 117 So. 3d 1219, 1224 (Fla. 5th DCA 2013).
20 *See* Broward Cnty. v. G.B.V. Int'l, Ltd., 787 So. 2d 838, 845 (Fla. 2001) (finding that when the circuit "court combed the record and extracted its own factual finding," the "court ... exceeded the scope of its authority under *Valliant*").

21 City of Hialeah Gardens v. Miami-Dade Charter Found., Inc., 857 So. 2d 202, 204 (Fla. 3d DCA 2003) (citing De Groot v. Sheffield, 95 So. 2d 912, 916 (Fla. 1957)).

22 Dusseau v. Metro. Dade Cnty., 794 So. 2d 1270, 1274 (Fla. 2001). Stated differently, the rulings "of a board acting in its quasi-judicial capacity are subject to review by certiorari and will be upheld only if they are supported by substantial competent evidence." Brevard Cnty. v. Snyder, 627 So. 2d 469, 474 (Fla. 1993).

23 Sch. Bd. Of Hillsborough Cnty. v. Tampa Sch. Dev. Corp., 113 So. 3d 919, 923 (Fla. 2d DCA 2013) (citing *De Groot*, 95 So. 2d at 916 (Fla. 1957)); *see also* Lee Cnty. v. Sunbelt Equities, II, Ltd. P'ship, 619 So. 2d 996, 1002–3 (Fla. 2d DCA 1993) (quoting Town of Indialantic v. Nance, 400 So. 2d 37, 40 (Fla. 5th DCA 1981), *aff'd*, 419 So. 2d 1041 (Fla. 1982)).

24 ABG Real Estate Dev. Co. v. St. Johns Cnty., 608 So. 2d 59, 61 (Fla. 5th DCA 1992).

25 *City of Hialeah Gardens*, 857 So. 2d at 205 (citing Metro. Dade Cnty. v. Blumenthal, 675 So. 2d 598, 607 (Fla. 3d DCA 1995) (Cope, J., dissenting)); Katherine's Bay, LLC v. Fagan, 52 So. 3d 19, 30 (Fla. 1st DCA 2010) (citing *Blumenthal*, 675 So. 3d at 601).

26 Palm Beach Cnty. v. Allen Morris Co., 547 So. 2d 690, 694 (Fla. 4th DCA 1989).

27 Town of Longboat Key v. Islandside Prop. Owners Coal., LLC, 95 So. 3d 1037, 1042 (Fla. 2d DCA 2012).

28 Payne v. City of Miami, 52 So. 3d 707, 762 (Fla. 3d DCA 2010) (Wells, J., dissenting) (citing City of Hialeah Gardens v. Miami-Dade Charter Found., Inc., 857 So. 2d 202, 204 (Fla. 3d DCA 2003)).

29 Nat'l Advert. Co. v. Broward Cnty., 491 So. 2d 1262, 1263 (Fla. 4th DCA 1986).

30 Pollard v. Palm Beach Cnty., 560 So. 2d 1358, 1360 (Fla. 4th DCA 1990); *Katherine's Bay, LLC*, 52 So. 3d at 30.

31 Broward Cnty. v. G.B.V. Int'l, Ltd., 787 So. 2d 838, 846 (Fla. 2001).

32 261 So. 2d 832 (Fla. 1972).

33 Renard v. Dade Cnty., 261 So. 2d 832, 835 (Fla. 1972) (citation omitted) (quoting *Boucher v. Novotny*, 102 So. 2d 132, 135 (Fla. 1958)).

34 City of Fort Myers v. Splitt, 988 So. 2d 28, 32 (Fla 2d DCA 2008).

35 City of St. Petersburg v. Marelli, 728 So. 2d 1197, 1198 (Fla. 2d DCA 1999).

36 Elwyn v. City of Miami, 113 So. 2d 849, 854 (Fla. 1959).

37 Wingrove Ests. Homeowners Ass'n v. Paul Curtis Realty, Inc., 744 So. 2d 1242, 1243 (Fla. 5th DCA 1999).

38 State *ex rel.* Gardner v. Sailboat Key, Inc., 306 So. 2d 616, 617–18 (Fla. 3d DCA 1974).

39 Kagan v. West, 677 So. 2d 905, 908 (Fla 4th DCA 1996).

40 DiPietro v. Coletta, 512 So. 2d 1048, 1050 (Fla. 3d DCA 1987).

41 Educ. Dev. Ctr., Inc. v. City of W. Palm Beach, 541 So. 2d 106, 108 (Fla. 1989) (citing Bell v. City of Sarasota, 371 So. 2d 525 (Fla. 2d DCA 1979)).

42 Metro. Dade Cnty. v. Mingo, 339 So. 2d 302, 304 (Fla. 3d DCA 1976) (internal citations omitted).

43 Broward Cnty. v. G.B.V. Int'l, Ltd., 787 So. 2d 838, 846 n.25 (Fla. 2001); *see*, e.g., *Educ. Dev. Ctr., Inc.*, 541 So. 2d at 107–8 (Clarifying that the question for the circuit court is "not whether, upon review of the evidence in the record, there exists substantial competent evidence to support a position *contrary* to that reached by the agency").

44 Evergreen Tree Treasurers of Charlotte Cnty., Inc. v. Charlotte Cnty., 810 So. 2d 526, 531 (Fla. 2d DCA 2002).

45 *See* Baez v. Padron, 715 So. 2d 1128, 1128 (Fla. 3d DCA 1998) (per curiam) (stating the principle that the "appellant has the affirmative duty to present the appellate court with an adequate record for appellate review").

46 Dragomirecky v. Town of Ponce Inlet, 917 So. 2d 410, 412 (Fla. 5th DCA 2006).

47 City of Fort Myers v. Splitt, 988 So. 2d 28, 32 (Fla. 2d DCA 2008) (citing Dade Cnty. v. Marca, S.A., 326 So. 2d 183, 184 (Fla. 1976)).

48 Battaglia Fruit Co. v. City of Maitland, 530 So. 2d 940, 943 (Fla. 5th DCA 1988); *see also* Alger v. United States, 300 So. 3d 274, 277 n.3 (Fla. 3d DCA 2019) (citing Krivanek v. Take Back Tampa Pol. Comm., 625 So. 2d 840, 842 (Fla. 1993), for the proposition that failure to raise standing generally results in waiver).

49 Fla. R. App. P. 9.030(b)(2); Haines City Cmty. Dev. v. Heggs, 658 So. 2d 523, 530 (Fla. 1995).

50 Educ. Dev. Ctr., Inc. v. City of W. Palm Beach, 541 So. 2d 106, 108 (Fla. 1989). Thus,

> [a]s a case moves up the appellate ladder, each level of review does not become broader ... . [C]ommon sense dictates that no one enjoys three full repetitive reviews to, 1. a civil service board 2. a circuit court 3. a district court of appeal.
>
> City of Deerfield Beach v. Vaillant, 419 So. 2d 624, 626 (Fla. 1982) (citing City of Deerfield Beach v. Vaillant, 399 So. 2d 1045, 1047 (Fla. 4th DCA 1981), *aff'd*, 419 So. 2d 624 (Fla. 1982))

51 Custer Med. Ctr. v. United Auto. Ins. Co., 62 So. 3d 1086, 1092 (Fla. 2010) (citing *Heggs*, 658 So. 2d at 530).

52 Broward Cnty. v. G.B.V. Int'l, Ltd., 787 So. 2d 838, 844 (Fla. 2001) (citing Tamiami Trail Tours v. R.R. Comm'n, 174 So. 451, 454 (Fla. 1937)).

53 *Id.*

54 988 So. 2d 28 (Fla. 2d DCA 2008), *appeal dismissed*, 6 So. 3d 52 (Fla. 2009) (unpublished table decision).

# 12 Consistency challenge

The cause of action for challenging land use decisions on the ground that they are not consistent with the applicable comprehensive plan is the consistency challenge. The legislative authorization for the consistency challenge makes it the sole means to challenge whether a development order is consistent with the local government's comprehensive plan.[1] Because Florida Statutes section 163.3215 provides for the consistency challenge, some practitioners call it a 3215 challenge.

Florida statutes explain consistency:

> A development order or land development regulation shall be consistent with the comprehensive plan if the land uses, densities or intensities, and other aspects of development permitted by such order or regulation are compatible with and further the objectives, policies, land uses, and densities or intensities in the comprehensive plan and if it meets all other criteria enumerated by the local government.[2]

Statutes further define the term "development order" broadly as "any order granting, denying, or granting with conditions an application for a development permit."[3] A "development permit," in turn, "includes any building permit, zoning permit, subdivision approval, rezoning, certification, special exception, variance, or any other official action of local government having the effect of permitting the development of land."[4] The statutory authorization for the consistency challenge is found in Florida Statutes section 163.3215. That section also describes who has standing to bring a consistency challenge.

> **Standing to enforce local comprehensive plans through development orders.**
>
> (1) Subsections (3) and (4) provide the exclusive methods for an aggrieved or adversely affected party to appeal and challenge the consistency of a development order with a comprehensive plan adopted under this part The local government that issues the development order is to be named as a respondent in all proceedings under this section … .
>
> (2) As used in this section, the term "aggrieved or adversely affected party" means any person or local government that will suffer an adverse effect to an interest protected or furthered by the local government comprehensive plan, including interests related to health and safety, police and fire protection service systems, densities or intensities of development, transportation facilities, health care facilities, equipment or services, and environmental or natural resources. The alleged adverse interest may be shared in common with other members of the community at large but must exceed in degree the general interest in community good shared by all persons. The term includes the owner, developer, or applicant for a development order.
>
> (3) Any aggrieved or adversely affected party may maintain a de novo action for declaratory, injunctive, or other relief against any local government to challenge any decision of such

> local government granting or denying an application for, or to prevent such local government from taking any action on, a development order, as defined in s. 163.3164, which materially alters the use or density or intensity of use on a particular piece of property which is not consistent with the comprehensive plan adopted under this part. The de novo action must be filed no later than 30 days following rendition of a development order or other written decision, or when all local administrative appeals, if any, are exhausted, whichever occurs later.[5]

In addition to the cause of action created in section 163.3215(3), section 163.3215(4) provides an alternative process by which parties may challenge the development orders of local governments which have established procedures for quasi-judicial hearings to be heard by special masters whose decisions are subsequently binding on the local government.[6] In such instances, parties may appeal the decision of the special master by filing a writ of certiorari in the appropriate circuit court.

The time to file a consistency challenge begins to toll with the rendition of the development order.[7] As with the writ of certiorari, "rendition" in the context of a consistency challenge has a definite meaning before the courts.[8] Specifically, the time to file a consistency challenge begins to toll when a signed, written order is filed with the clerk.[9] Courts have rejected the notion that a notice of approval sent to an applicant constitutes a development order under section 163.3215 because people who might file a consistency challenge had no notice of the approval.[10] Further, local governments have an obligation to provide notice "where a proposed project will affect the property of a party other than the one seeking a permit."[11]

## Remedy available in consistency challenge

As well as giving an engrossing history of Florida's growth management legislation, *Pinecrest Lakes, Inc. v. Shidel* addresses what remedy is available to a successful plaintiff in a consistency challenge.

## Florida Fourth District Court of Appeal

### *Pinecrest Lakes, Inc. v. Shidel*[12]

### 2001

FARMER, J.

The ultimate issue raised in this case is unprecedented in Florida. The question is whether a trial court has the authority to order the complete demolition and removal of several multistory buildings because the buildings are inconsistent with the County's comprehensive land use plan. We conclude that the court is so empowered and affirm the decision under review.

Some twenty years ago, a developer purchased a 500-acre parcel of land in Martin County and set out to develop it in phases. Development there is governed by the Martin County Comprehensive Plan (the Comprehensive Plan).[2] Phase One of the property was designated under the Comprehensive Plan as "Residential Estate," meaning single-family homes on individual lots with a maximum density of 2 units per acre (UPA). The Comprehensive Plan provides that "[w]here single family structures comprise the dominant structure type within

2 *See* § 163.3167(2), Fla. Stat. (2000):

> Each local government shall prepare a comprehensive plan of the type and in the manner set out in this act or shall prepare amendments to its existing comprehensive plan to conform it to the requirements of this part in the manner set out in this part.

these areas, new development of undeveloped abutting lands *shall be required* to include compatible structure types of land immediately adjacent to existing single family development." [e.s.] Phases One through Nine were developed as single-family homes on individual lots in very low densities.

The subject of this litigation, Phase Ten, is a 21-acre parcel between Phase One and Jensen Beach Boulevard, a divided highway designated both as "major" and "arterial." Phase Ten was designated by the Comprehensive Plan as "Medium Density Residential" with a maximum of 8 UPA. The developer sought approval of three different site plans before finally erecting the buildings that are the subject of this litigation. In 1988, the developer first sought approval for an initial scheme of 3-story apartment buildings with a density of just under 8 UPA. Karen Shidel, since 1986 an owner of a single-family residence in the adjoining area of Phase One, along with other residents, opposed the project proposed by the developer. This initial site plan for Phase Ten was approved by the County but never acted upon.

Five years later the developer changed the proposed scheme to single family residences, and the County Commission approved a revised site plan for 29 single-family homes with a density of 1.37 UPA. Two years after that, however, the developer again changed its mind and returned to its original concept of multi-family structures. This time, the developer sought to develop 136 units in two-story buildings, with a density of 6.5 UPA. The County's growth management staff recommended that the County Commission approve this second revised site plan for Phase Ten. Following a hearing at which a number of people objected to the proposal, including Shidel, the County Commission approved the revision and issued a Development Order[3] for Phase Ten permitting the construction of 19 two-story buildings.

Claiming statutory authority, Shidel and another Phase One homeowner, one Charles Brooks, along with the Homeowners Associations for Phases One through Nine, then filed a verified complaint with the Martin County Commission challenging the consistency of the Development Order with the Comprehensive Plan, requesting rescission of the Development Order.[4] In response to the verified complaint, after a hearing the County Commission confirmed its previous decision to issue the Development Order.

Shidel and Brooks then filed a civil action in the Circuit Court against Martin County under the same statutory authority.[5] They alleged that the Development Order was inconsistent with the Comprehensive Plan. The developer intervened. Shidel and Brooks argued that their

3 *See* § 163.3164(7) and (8), Fla. Stat. (2000):

> "Development permit" includes any building permit, zoning permit, subdivision approval, rezoning, certification, special exception, variance, or any other official action of local government having the effect of permitting the development of land ... . "Development order" means any order granting, denying, or granting with conditions an application for a development permit.

4 *See* § 163.3215(4), Fla. Stat. (2000):

> As a condition precedent to the institution of an action pursuant to this section, the complaining party shall first file a verified complaint with the local government whose actions are complained of, setting forth the facts upon which the complaint is based and the relief sought by the complaining party. The verified complaint shall be filed no later than 30 days after the alleged inconsistent action has been taken. The local government receiving the complaint shall respond within 30 days after receipt of the complaint. Thereafter, the complaining party may institute the action authorized in this section. However, the action shall be instituted no later than 30 days after the expiration of the 30-day period which the local government has to take appropriate action.

5 *See* § 163.3215(1), Fla. Stat. (1995):

> Any aggrieved or adversely affected party may maintain an action for injunctive or other relief against any local government to prevent such local government from taking any action on a development order ... which materially alters the use or density or intensity of use on a particular piece of property that is not consistent with the comprehensive plan adopted under this part.

statutory challenge was a de novo proceeding in which the court should decide in the first instance whether the Development Order was consistent with the Comprehensive Plan. Martin County and the developer argued that the proceeding was in the nature of appellate review in which the County's determination was entitled to deference and the court should consider only whether there was substantial competent evidence supporting the Development Order. Basing its decision solely on a review of the record created before the County Commission, the trial court found that the Development Order was consistent with the Comprehensive Plan and entered final judgment in favor of the developer.

At that point, the developer took stock of its position. It had prevailed before the County Commission and—at least initially—in the trial court. Technically, however, its approval for the project was not final. Developer considered whether to proceed to construct the buildings or instead await appellate review of the trial court's decision. Ultimately the developer decided to commence construction, notwithstanding the pendency of an appeal. Accordingly, it applied for and received building permits for construction of Buildings 8, 9, 10, 11 and 12, and started on each of those buildings while the case was under consideration in court. When construction was just beginning, Shidel and Brooks sent written notice to the developer of their intention, should they prove successful in court, to seek demolition and removal of any construction undertaken while judicial consideration of the consistency issue was pending.

Appellate review did not produce the outcome for which the developer had hoped. In 1997 we reversed the trial court's decision that the County's consistency determination complied with the Comprehensive Plan. *Poulos v. Martin County*, 700 So. 2d 163 (Fla. 4th DCA 1997). Specifically, we concluded that section 163.3215 required de novo consideration in the trial court on the consistency issue. Our opinion explained:

> if section 163.3215 was intended to provide for the circuit court to conduct an appellate review by certiorari, then the statutory language permitting the filing of the action up to 90 days after the granting of the development order is in conflict with the 30 day deadline outlined under the Florida Rules of Appellate Procedure.

700 So. 2d at 165. We further adopted an analysis by Judge Wentworth as to the meaning of section 163.3215:

> the ... language in the statute ... provides only for a suit or action clearly contemplating an evidentiary hearing before the court to determine the consistency issue on its merits in the light of the proceedings below but not confined to the matters of record in such proceedings.

700 So. 2d at 166 (quoting from *Gregory v. City of Alachua*, 553 So. 2d 206, 211 (Fla. 1st DCA 1989) (Wentworth, J., dissenting)). We remanded the case for a trial de novo and for any appropriate relief.

On remand, the trial judge proceeded in two stages: the first stage involved a determination whether the Development Order was consistent with the Comprehensive Plan; and the second stage, which became necessary, addressed the remedy. While the case was pending on remand, developer continued with construction. The County conducted final inspections of Building 11 and 12, issuing certificates of occupancy (CO), and residents moved into the buildings. At the end of the consistency phase, the trial court entered a partial judgment finding that the Development Order was not consistent with the Comprehensive Plan. The trial de novo then proceeded to the remedy.

At the conclusion of the remedy phase, the trial court entered a Final Judgment. The court found that the Comprehensive Plan established a hierarchy of land uses, paying deference to lower density residential uses and providing protection to those areas. The "tiering policy" required that, for structures immediately adjacent to each other, any new structures to be added to the area must be both comparable and compatible to those already built and occupied.[8] The court then found significant differences between the northern tier of Phase One and the adjacent southern tier of Phase Ten. The structures in Phase One were single level, single family residences, while the structures in Phase Ten were two-story apartment buildings with eight residential units. Therefore, the court found, the 8-residential unit, two-story, apartment buildings in Phase Ten were not compatible or comparable types of dwelling units with the single family, single level residences in Phase One; nor were they of comparable density. Consequently, the court determined, the Development Order was inconsistent with the Comprehensive Plan.

As regards the remedy, the Final Judgment found no evidence indicating that either Brooks or the Homeowners Association were damaged by any diminution in value. The court found that the Homeowners Association was not a person within the meaning of section 163.3215(2) and therefore had no standing to seek relief under section 163.3215. Accordingly, only plaintiff Shidel was entitled to seek injunctive relief under section 163.3215.

In granting such relief, the court found that the developer had acted in bad faith. Specifically, the court found that the developer continued construction during the pendency of the prior appeal and continued to build and lease during the trial—even after losing on the consistency issue. The court found that the developer "acted at [its] own peril in doing precisely what this lawsuit sought to prevent and now [is] subject to the power of the court to compel restoration of the status prior to construction." The relief awarded was:

(1) the Court permanently enjoined Martin County from taking any further action on the subject Development Order for Phase Ten, other than to rescind it;
(2) the Court permanently enjoined developer and its successors in interest from any further development of Phase Ten under the subject Development Order; and
(3) the Court ordered developer to remove all apartment buildings from Phase Ten either through demolition or physical relocation by a date certain.

When the Final Judgment was entered, five of the eight-unit buildings had been constructed in Phase Ten (Buildings 8–12). Buildings 11 and 12 had already received their CO's, and fifteen of their sixteen units were actually occupied. Building 10 was fully completed and was awaiting final inspection as of the date the remedies stage of trial began. Buildings 8 and 9 were 50% and 66% completed, respectively, also as of that date.

Following the entry of Final Judgment, the developer filed this timely appeal and moved for a stay pending review. The trial court granted a stay only as to the demolition order, allowing lessees to continue in possession of those apartments in Buildings 9–12 under actual lease when the trial court entered final judgment, as well as to those leases in Building 8 in existence as of the date of filing of the notice of appeal. The developer was prohibited, however, from entering into any renewals of existing leases upon expiration of the original term or any new leases of any apartments. Upon review, we affirmed the stay order. We now explain our decision on the merits.

8

A project immediately adjacent to lands used or designated for lower intensity use should be given lesser density: (1) For that portion of said project abutting the existing development or area of lesser density, a density transition zone of *comparable density and compatible dwelling unit types shall be established* [e.s.] in the new project for a depth from the shared property line that is equivalent to the depth of the first tier of the adjoining development's lower density (i.e. the depth of the first block of single-family lots). Comprehensive Plan, § 4–5(A)(2)(b)

### *I. The Consistency Issue*

Initially the developer argues that the trial court erred in the consistency phase by failing to accord any deference to the County Commission's interpretation of its own Comprehensive Plan when the County approved the second revised site plan and its multi-story, multi-family buildings. Conceding that the proceedings are de novo and that the Development Order is subject to "strict scrutiny" under the Comprehensive Plan as to the consistency issue, the developer nevertheless argues that the courts must bow to the County's interpretation of its own Comprehensive Plan and the application of its many elements to the site plan. Developer argues that the statutes and cases accord such deference to a local government's interpretation of its own Comprehensive Plan and that it was reversible error for the trial court in this case to fail to do so. In particular, developer relies on *Sw. Ranches Homeowners Ass'n, Inc. v. Broward Cty.*, 502 So. 2d 931 (Fla. 4th DCA 1987), and *B.B. McCormick & Sons, Inc. v. City of Jacksonville*, 559 So. 2d 252 (Fla. 1st DCA 1990). According to developer, these cases authorize the use of the highly deferential "fairly debatable" standard of review—customary with zoning decisions—to land use determinations such as the issue of consistency in this case. We disagree.

As we have already seen in this dispute, the applicable statute provides that:

> [a]ny aggrieved or adversely affected party may maintain an action for injunctive or other relief against any local government to prevent such local government from taking any action on a development order ... which materially alters the use or density or intensity of use on a particular piece of property that is not consistent with the comprehensive plan ... .

§ 163.3215(1), Fla. Stat. (2000). This statute obviously creates an action for an injunction against the enforcement of a development order, rather than to carry out such an order. The statute is aimed at development orders—which, by their very nature, must have been approved by a local government—so it is clear that the Legislature did not mean that local governments or developers would be the parties seeking injunctive relief under this provision.

Moreover there is but one basis for issuing the injunction: that the development order is not consistent with the Comprehensive Plan to the detriment of adjoining property owners. Hence the issuance of an injunction under section 163.3215(1) necessarily requires the judge to determine in the first instance whether a development order is consistent with the Comprehensive Plan. When a statute authorizes a citizen to bring an action to enjoin official conduct that is made improper by the statute, and that same statute necessitates a determination by the judge in the action as to whether the official's conduct was improper under the statute, as a general matter the requirement for a determination of the propriety of the official action should not be understood as requiring the court to defer to the official whose conduct is being judged. While the Legislature could nevertheless possibly have some reason to require judges to require some deference to the officials whose conduct was thus put in issue, we would certainly expect to see such a requirement of deference spelled out in the statute with unmistakable clarity. Here it is not a question of any lack of clarity; the statute is utterly silent on the notion of deference. It is thus apparent that the structure and text of the statute do not impliedly involve any deference to the decision of the county officials. So we necessarily presume none was intended.[10]

10 To illustrate the point, we draw an analogy. The action by a county approving a development order could fairly and logically be compared to the actions of administrative agencies generally. Thus we might contrast section 163.3215(1) with comparable provisions of the Administrative Procedures Act. Section 120.68 generally grants parties in agency proceedings access to a court after the agency has finally

Section 163.3194 requires that all development conform to the approved Comprehensive Plan, and that development orders be consistent with that Plan.[11] The statute is framed as a rule, a command to cities and counties that they must comply with their own Comprehensive Plans after they have been approved by the State. The statute does not say that local governments shall have some discretion as to whether a proposed development should be consistent with the Comprehensive Plan. Consistency with a Comprehensive Plan is therefore not a discretionary matter. When the Legislature wants to give an agency discretion and then for the courts to defer to such discretion, it knows how to say that. Here it has not. We thus reject the developer's contention that the trial court erred in failing to defer to the County's interpretation of its own comprehensive plan.

Before we proceed to assess the trial court's determination on the consistency issue, we pause to consider the history of the land development statutes. The State of Florida did not assert meaningful formal control over the explosive and unplanned development of land in this state until the passage of the first growth management statute, the Local Government Comprehensive Planning Act of 1975. Chapters 75–257, Laws of Fla. (the 1975 Act). The 1975 Act forced counties and cities to adopt comprehensive plans, but they were left to interpret such plans for themselves, largely free from effective oversight by the state. *See, e.g., City of Jacksonville Beach v. Grubbs*, 461 So. 2d 160, 163 (Fla. 1st DCA 1984) (determination of when to conform more restrictive zoning ordinances with Comprehensive Plan is legislative judgment to be made by local governing body, subject only to limited judicial review for patent arbitrariness). The requirement of adopting a Comprehensive Plan was, therefore, only a small step. Moreover nothing in the legislation required local governments to comply with their own Comprehensive Plans or that all development be consistent with the Plan.

By the early 1980's it was widely recognized that the 1975 Act was proving ineffectual in regulating Florida's development. *See* Reid Ewing, *Florida's Growth Management Learning Curve*, 19 Va. Envt'l. L.J. 375 (2000). The lack of state control over interpretation of the Comprehensive Plan was often cited as a serious deficiency. As one such criticism described the situation:

> [f]rustration grew at the state level as well. Lacking the actual power to approve or disapprove local planning decisions, state and regional planners could not effectively coordinate and oversee local planning and regulation. Local governments changed their plans "willy-nilly virtually every time a city council or county commission met ... ."
>
> John M. DeGrove, *State and Regional Planning and Regulatory Activity: The Florida Experience and Lessons for Other Jurisdictions*, C390 ALI–ABA 397, 428 (1994)

acted. Section 120.68(4), however, limits review to the record in agency. There is no similar provision in section 163.3215. Moreover section 120.68(7) spells out in precise detail exactly what the reviewing court can do. Among its provisions is the following:

> The court shall remand a case to the agency for further proceedings consistent with the court's decision or set aside agency action, as appropriate, when it finds that ... (b) The agency's action depends on any finding of fact that is not supported by competent, substantial evidence in the record of a hearing conducted pursuant to ss. 120.569 and 120.57; however, the court shall not substitute its judgment for that of the agency as to the weight of the evidence on any disputed finding of fact ... (e) the agency's exercise of discretion was: 1. outside the range of discretion delegated to the agency by law; 2. inconsistent with agency rule; 3. inconsistent with officially stated agency policy or a prior agency practice, if deviation therefrom is not explained by the agency; or 4. otherwise in violation of a constitutional or statutory provision; *but the court shall not substitute its judgment for that of the agency on an issue of discretion.* [e.s.]

11 See § 163.3194(1)(a), Fla. Stat. (2000) ("After a comprehensive plan ... has been adopted in conformity with this act, all development undertaken by, and all actions taken in regard to development orders by, governmental agencies in regard to land covered by such plan or element shall be consistent with such plan or element as adopted."). [e.s.]

For another thing, the 1975 Act was criticized for failing to give affected property owners and citizen groups standing to challenge the land development decisions of local governments on the grounds that they were inconsistent with the Comprehensive Plan. The standing issue was considered in *Citizens Growth Mgmt. Coal. of W. Palm Beach Inc. v. City of W. Palm Beach*, 450 So. 2d 204 (Fla. 1984) (*CGMC*). *CGMC* involved a challenge by a citizens group to a local decision to allow the construction of a large scale residential and commercial complex. The court began by referring to *Renard v. Dade Cty.*, 261 So. 2d 832 (Fla. 1972), holding that standing to challenge local development decisions was limited to the highly deferential "fairly debatable" standard. Affected property owners in the vicinity of new development had no standing to seek enforcement of local comprehensive plans unless they could "prove special damages different in kind from that suffered by the community as a whole." 261 So. 2d at 834. The *CGMC* court determined that the 1975 Act did not change these rules on standing. 450 So. 2d at 208. The court reasoned that because the 1975 Act "did not specifically address the question" of standing, the statute was not meant to alter the common law standing requirements set forth in *Renard*, 450 So. 2d at 206–07.

Again, to return to the criticism, this limitation on standing to enforce local planning laws resulted in: "a failure to conform development decisions to the plan based upon the fact that citizens lacked standing to challenge development orders for lack of consistency with the comprehensive plan."

James C. Nicholas & Ruth L. Steiner, *Growth Management and Smart Growth in Florida*, 35 Wake Forest L. Rev. 645, 657 (2000) (quoting Daniel W. O'Connell, *Growth Management in Florida: Will State and Local Governments Get Their Acts Together?*, Florida Envt'l & Urban Issues, 1–5 (June 1984)). If affected property owners in the area of newly permitted development could not challenge a project on the grounds that it would be inconsistent with the Comprehensive Plan, that eliminated the only real check on local government compliance—a challenge by those most directly affected by a proposed development.

The growing pressure for a fundamental change in the growth management law is reflected in the following statement made just prior to the Legislature's adoption of the current law in 1985:

> In response to this lack of citizen standing, a citizen initiative began last year and thousands of signatures were collected around the state to bring the standing issue to a referendum vote. The petition specifically calls for a referendum on the issues of giving citizens a right in the state constitution to environmental health and welfare and providing them with legal standing to sue if government at the local, regional, or state level is not doing its job.
>
> That initiative fell just a few thousand signatures short of the required number for qualifying for a referendum in 1984. However, the initiative is continuing, and I feel confident that the issue will be brought to the voters of the state in 1985 unless the legislature addresses the issue more effectively than it did last year.

Kathleen Shea Abrams, *An Environmental Word*, 1 J. Land use Envt'l Law 155, 159 (1985). Clearly the pressure from a "civically militant electorate" was growing, and the elected representatives took notice of it. The result was the Growth Management Act of 1985. Chap. 85–55, Laws of Fla. This is essentially the statute we have today, parts of which have been cited in preceding paragraphs. Its most important provision for our purposes was section 163.3215, the provision used by Shidel to bring this action into court.

In *Southwest Ranches*, we observed that section 163.3215 had liberalized standing requirements and demonstrated "a clear legislative policy in favor of the enforcement of comprehensive plans by persons adversely affected by local action." 502 So. 2d at 935. In *Parker v.*

*Leon Cty.*, 627 So. 2d 476, 480 (Fla. 1993), the court held that "the legislature enacted section 163.3215 to ensure the standing for any person who 'will suffer an adverse effect to an interest protected ... by the ... comprehensive plan." 627 So. 2d at 479. The *Parker* court quoted with approval the above passage from *Southwest Ranches*, 627 So. 2d at 479. *See also Putnam Cty. Envt'l Council, Inc. v. Bd. of Cty. Comm'rs of Putnam Cty.*, 757 So. 2d 590, 593 (Fla. 5th DCA 2000) ("That standard changed, however, with the 1985 adoption of section 163.3215, which liberalized the standing requirements and 'demonstrat[ed] a clear legislative policy in favor of the enforcement of comprehensive plans by persons adversely affected by local action.'"). Thus, the criticism described above certainly was of great influence in the 1985 Legislature's formulation of the new standing provision. Affected citizens have been given a significantly enhanced standing to challenge the consistency of development decisions with the Comprehensive Plan.

The Growth Management Act of 1985 was discussed in what is now recognized as the most significant land use decision by the supreme court in the past decade, namely *Bd. of Cty. Comm'rs of Brevard Cty. v. Snyder*, 627 So. 2d 469 (Fla. 1993). *Snyder* involved a parcel then zoned only for single family homes and a proposed development of 5–6 units. The proposal also necessarily required a change of zoning. After substantial opposition, and in spite of a favorable staff recommendation, the County voted to deny the request without giving any reasons. Certiorari was denied in the circuit court, one judge dissenting. The Fifth District held that rezoning actions entailing the application of a general rule or policy to specific individuals, interests, or activities are quasi-judicial in nature and should be subjected to a stricter standard of judicial review. The court found that the proposed site plan was consistent with the Comprehensive Plan, that there was no evidence supporting the denial of any necessary rezoning, and that the denial of the request without giving any reasons was arbitrary and unreasonable.

After granting review, the supreme court was first concerned with the level of review given by the courts to such proceedings. The county took the position that it had been faced with primarily a legislative judgment because the landowner sought rezoning. As the court noted:

> Both federal and state courts adopted a highly deferential standard of judicial review early in the history of local zoning. In *Vill. of Euclid v. Ambler Realty Co.*, 272 U.S. 365 (1926), the United States Supreme Court held that "[i]f the validity of the legislative classification for zoning purposes be fairly debatable, the legislative judgment must be allowed to control." This Court expressly adopted the fairly debatable principle in *City of Miami Beach v. Ocean & Inland Co.*, 3 So. 2d 364 (1941).
>
> [c.o.]

627 So. 2d at 472. The court went on to note, however, that this tolerant form of judicial review had not proved satisfactory:

> Inhibited only by the loose judicial scrutiny afforded by the fairly debatable rule, local zoning systems developed in a markedly inconsistent manner. Many land use experts and practitioners have been critical of the local zoning system. Richard Babcock deplored the effect of "neighborhoodism" and rank political influence on the local decision-making process. Richard F. Babcock, *The Zoning Game* (1966). Mandelker and Tarlock recently stated that "zoning decisions are too often ad hoc, sloppy and self-serving decisions with well-defined adverse consequences without off-setting benefits." Daniel R. Mandelker and A. Dan Tarlock, *Shifting the Presumption of Constitutionality in Land-Use Law*, 24 Urb. L. 1, 2 (1992).

627 So. 2d at 472–73.

The court explained that in Florida the 1975 Act "was substantially strengthened by the Growth Management Act [of 1985]." 627 So. 2d at 473. After analyzing various provisions of the Growth Management Act of 1985, the court stated:

> We also agree with the court below that the review is subject to strict scrutiny. In practical effect, the review by strict scrutiny in zoning cases appears to be the same as that given in the review of other quasi-judicial decisions. *See Lee Cty. v. Sunbelt Equities, II, Ltd. P'ship*, 619 So. 2d 996 (Fla. 2d DCA 1993) (the term "strict scrutiny" arises from the necessity of strict compliance with comprehensive plan). This term as used in the review of land use decisions must be distinguished from the type of strict scrutiny review afforded in some constitutional cases. *Compare Snyder v. Bd. of Cty. Comm'rs*, 595 So. 2d 65, 75–76 (Fla. 5th DCA 1991) (land use), and *Machado v. Musgrove*, 519 So. 2d 629, 632 (Fla. 3d DCA 1987), *review denied*, 529 So. 2d 693 (Fla. 1988), *and review denied*, 529 So. 2d 694 (Fla. 1988) (land use), *with In re Estate of Greenberg*, 390 So. 2d 40, 42–43 (Fla. 1980) (general discussion of strict scrutiny review in context of fundamental rights), *appeal dismissed*, 450 U.S. 961 (1981), *Fla. High Sch. Activities Ass'n v. Thomas*, 434 So. 2d 306 (Fla. 1983) (equal protection), and *Dep't of Revenue v. Magazine Publishers of Am., Inc.*, 604 So. 2d 459 (Fla. 1992) (First Amendment).
> [e.s.]

627 So. 2d at 475.

In the foregoing quotation the supreme court drew a distinction between the use of strict scrutiny in land use cases and its use in other contexts. The court approved the analyses of the Fifth District in *Snyder* and the Third District in *Machado v. Musgrove*, 519 So. 2d 629, 632 (Fla. 3d DCA 1987), *review denied*, 529 So. 2d 693 (Fla. 1988), *review denied*, 529 So. 2d 694 (Fla. 1988), regarding land use decisions. These courts explained that strict scrutiny of local government development orders is necessary to insure that the local governments comply with the duty imposed by section 163.3194 to make decisions consistent with the Comprehensive Plan. In discussing the difference between a developer aggrieved by a land use decision of local government and an affected property owner in the vicinity aggrieved by a proposed new development, the *Snyder* court emphasized that section 163.3215 "provides a remedy for third parties to challenge the consistency of development orders." 627 So. 2d at 475.

As one pair of writers put it, "*Snyder* changed the rules of the game for local government land use approvals." John W. Howell & David J. Russ, *Planning v. Zoning: Snyder Decision Changes Rezoning Standards*, FLA. B.J., May 1994, at 16. And another pair noted:

> "The easygoing 'fairly debatable' test for site-specific rezonings was abandoned and the 'strict scrutiny' standard was adopted for the review of development orders under a county's comprehensive master plan."

Lucia A. Dougherty & Elliot H. Scherker, *Rights, Remedies, and Ratiocination: Toward a Cohesive Approach to Appellate Review of Land Use Orders After Board of County Commissioners v. Snyder*, 24 Stet. L. Rev. 311, 312 (1995). In light of this history, deferential review of the kind advocated by developer here is no longer the rule after *Snyder*.

Under section 163.3215 citizen enforcement is the primary tool for insuring consistency of development decisions with the Comprehensive Plan. Deference by the courts—especially of the kind argued by the developer in this case—would not only be inconsistent with the text and structure of the statute, but it would ignore the very reasons for adopting the legislation in the first place. When an affected property owner in the area of a newly allowed development brings a consistency challenge to a development order, a cause of action—as it were—for compliance with the Comprehensive Plan is presented to the court, in which the judge is required to pay deference only to the facts in the case and the applicable law. In light of the text of section 163.3215 and the foregoing history, we reject the developer's contention that the trial court erred in failing to defer to the County's interpretation of its own Comprehensive Plan.

Having thus decided that the trial court was correct in failing to accord any particular deference to the Martin County Commission in its interpretation of the Comprehensive Plan, we now proceed to consider the court's determination on the consistency issue. The trial court explained its decision as follows:

> The primary claim by [plaintiffs] is that the juxtaposition of multi-story, multi-family apartments in Phase 10 directly next to the single family homes in Phase 1 violates a number of provisions in the Comprehensive Plan. The provision of the Comprehensive Plan that is central to their argument is section 4–5(A)(2)(b), known as the "tiering policy." [*see* n. 6]
>
> The tiering policy was added to the Comprehensive Plan ... to address how development would be added to existing single-family residential communities. There was a concern ... over how existing single-family homes were being impacted by new, adjacent denser developments ... .
>
> The tiering policy required ... a transition zone along the southern portion of Phase 10 equal to "the depth of the first block of single-family lots" within the northern portion of Phase 1. The section requires that development in the first tier of Phase 10 be limited to construction "of comparable density and compatible dwelling unit types." The court finds that the appropriate measure is 225 feet, using the shortest average depth method of computation.
>
> No transition zone was established for Phase 10. The buildings along the first tier of Phase 10 are multi-family, multi-story, and have balconies. The southern tier of Phase 10 has a density of 6.6[UPA]. The overall density of Phase 10 is 6.5[UPA]. There is no meaningful difference in density across the entire western portion of Phase 10. The northern tier of Phase 1, on the other hand, is comprised entirely of single-family homes on 0.75 acre to 1.2 acre lots, with a density of 0.94[UPA].[13]
>
> There was no first tier transition zone established for Phase 10 as mandated by section 4–5(A)(2)(b). That section is not the only provision of the Comprehensive Plan that mandated compatible structures within the first tier of Phase 10. Section 4–4(M)(1)(e)(2) provided:
>
> > ... Where single family structures comprise the dominant structure type within [residential estate densities (RE–0.5A)], new development on undeveloped abutting lands shall be required to include compatible structure types of lands immediately adjacent to existing family development.
>
> ... Phase 1 is designated RE–0.5A.
>
> ... It is impossible ... to examine the photographs of the homes in the northern tier of Phase 1, and the apartment buildings in the southern tier of Phase 10, and find that they are either "compatible dwelling unit types" or "compatible structure types." The only residential structure that could be less compatible with the northern

13 At this point in the Final Judgment, the court went on to show in a comparative table that the change in density between the two tiers represented a 560% difference, the change in population a 492% difference, and the number of units a 418% difference.

> tier of Phase 1, would be a multi-story condominium building. There is no compatibility between the structures in the southern tier of Phase 10 and the northern tier of Phase 1. Further, an examination of the density of development in the two tiers at issue, precludes this court from finding that they are in any way comparable.
>
> ... [B]uffering does not grant relief to the [developer] under section 4–4(I)(5). That section deals with buffering between "incompatible land uses." The more specific Tiering Policy mandates compatibility. More importantly, even to the extent that the Comprehensive Plan might, in some instances, provide a builder with the ability to buffer changes in density, intensity or uses, the language of sections 4–4(M)(1)(e)(2) and 4–5(A)(2)(b) simply do not permit the type of development that is under construction in Phase 10.
>
> ... Based on the foregoing, the Court finds that the Development Order is inconsistent with the Comprehensive Plan. It is not compatible with, nor does it further the objective, policies, land uses, densities and intensities in the Comprehensive Plan. § 163.3194(3)(a). [e.o.]

We have carefully reviewed the record of the trial and the evidence presented. It is apparent that there is substantial competent evidence to support these findings. Developer argues that the court erred in its interpretation of the "tiering policy," in deeming it a mandatory requirement rather than a discretionary guide. We conclude that the trial court's construction is consistent with the plain meaning of the text of the Comprehensive Plan. *See* Comprehensive Plan, § 4–5(A)(2)(b) ("a density transition zone of comparable density and compatible dwelling unit types shall be established in the new project for a depth from the shared property line that is equivalent to the depth of the first tier of the adjoining development's lower density (i.e. the depth of the first block of single-family lots).") Moreover, given the evidence as to Martin County's adoption of the tiering policy, the record clearly supports the finding that the policy was intended to be applied in all instances of projects abutting single-family residential areas. We therefore affirm the finding of inconsistency and proceed to explain our decision on the remedy.

### *II. Remedy of Demolition*

Developer challenges what it terms the "enormity and extremity of the injunctive remedy imposed by the trial court." It argues that the trial court's order requiring the demolition of 5 multi-family residential buildings is the most radical remedy ever mandated by a Florida court because of an inconsistency with a Comprehensive Plan. Specifically, the contention is that the trial judge failed to balance the equities between the parties and thus ignored the evidence of a $3.3 million dollar loss the developer will suffer from the demolition of the buildings. The court failed to consider alternative remedies in damages, it argues, that would have adequately remedied any harm resulting from the construction of structures inconsistent with the Comprehensive Plan. Developer maintains that the trial court erroneously failed to give meaningful consideration to the traditional elements for the imposition of injunctive relief. It contends that the trial court proceeded on an erroneous conclusion that where an injunction is sought on the basis of a statutory violation, no proof is required as to the traditional elements for an injunction.

Traditionally, as the trial judge noted, it is true that injunctions are usually denied where the party seeking such relief fails to demonstrate a clear legal right, a particular harm for which there is no adequate remedy at law, and that considerations of the public interest would support the injunction. *See, e.g., St. Lucie Cty. v. St. Lucie Vill.*, 603 So. 2d 1289, 1292

(Fla. 4th DCA 1992). These are, of course, the necessary ingredients for equitable relief when we labor in the interplay of common law and equity, where ordinary legal remedies are unavailing.

Nonetheless, as between the State legislature and the several counties, the Legislature is the dominant creator of public duties and citizen rights. Recognizing that the Legislature has the sole power to create such public duties and citizen rights, it logically follows that the Legislature is necessarily endowed with the authority to specify precisely what remedies shall be used by judges to enforce a statutory duty—regardless of whether in general usage such a remedy usually requires additional factors before it is traditionally employed. When the Legislature creates a public duty and a corresponding right in its citizens to enforce the duty it has created, and provides explicitly that the remedy of vindication shall be an injunction, the Legislature has not thereby encroached on judicial powers ... .

In our view when the Legislature provides for an injunction in these circumstances, it has deliberately made the new public duty and its corresponding right of enforcement an integrated statutory prescription. By specifying that the public interest requires that a certain duty be vindicated in the courts and not primarily within other branches of government, the Legislature is well within its powers. Surely the Legislature's primary role in defining public policy under the constitution is broad enough to enable it to specify a legal remedy in an enactment, regardless of whether the traditional judicial restrictions on that remedy in other, non-statutory contexts would limit its usage. As the author of the primary duty, the Legislature alone shapes the form of its effectuating mechanism.

In section 163.3215, we think the Legislature has constructed such a statute. The statute leads off with a declaration that:

> Any aggrieved or adversely affected party may maintain an action for injunctive or other relief against any local government to prevent such local government from taking any action on a development order, as defined in s. 163.3164, which materially alters the use or density or intensity of use on a particular piece of property that is not consistent with the comprehensive plan adopted under this part.

From the plain and obvious meaning of this text we discern only two elements to the granting of an injunction against the enforcement of a development order: (a) the party is affected or aggrieved by (b) an approved project that is inconsistent with the Comprehensive Plan. In short, the existence of an affected neighbor is all that is necessary for the issuance of an injunction against a proposed land use that is inconsistent with the Comprehensive Plan ... . Here the statutory text makes the injunction the first and preferred remedy to alleviate the effects of an inconsistent land use. Hence, we read the statute to make the injunction the presumed remedy where the conditions prescribed are shown.

We disagree with the developer's contention that this statute was meant to create mere discretion in the court to issue an injunction. If injunctive relief is the specified, primary remedy to correct a violation of a public duty and to vindicate the right of a person affected by the violation of that duty, it can properly be deemed a rule that the Legislature has created, not a grant of discretion. Here the Legislature has devised an entire statutory scheme to insure that all counties have a Comprehensive Plan for the development of land within their respective jurisdictions. The scheme creates mandatory duties to have a plan, mandatory duties to have the plan approved by the state, and once approved mandatory duties to limit all developments so that they are consistent with the plan's requirements. At the end of all these mandatory duties—all these *shalls*—comes a new relaxation of the requirements on standing for citizen suits to enforce comprehensive land use plans and providing for the issuance of injunctions when an inconsistency affects another land owner. Judicial construction of that sole remedy as discretionary strikes us as remarkably inconsistent with not only the text of the statute itself but also with the purpose of the entire legislative scheme.

Developer lays great stress on the size of the monetary loss that it claims it will suffer from demolition, as opposed to the much smaller diminution in value that the affected property owner bringing this action may have suffered. It contends that a $3.3 million loss far outweighs the evidence of diminution in the value of Shidel's property, less than $26,000. Its primary contention here is that the trial judge erred in failing to weigh these equities in its favor and deny any remedy of demolition. Instead, as developer sees it, the court should have awarded money damages to eliminate the objector's diminution in value. Developer argued that it should be allowed instead of demolition it should also be allowed to build environmental barriers, green areas of trees and shrubbery, between the apartment buildings and the adjoining area of single family homes.

Developer emphasizes that we deal here with an expensive development: "a high quality, upscale project;" "forty units of high-quality garden apartments;" "five upscale multi-family dwellings, housing 40 garden apartments, at a value of approximately $3 million." Developer concedes that there is evidence showing that plaintiff Shidel's property is diminished by $26,000. It also concedes that the total diminution for all the homes bordering its project is just under $300,000. Developer contends, however, that the real countervailing harm to all these affected property owners in the vicinity is not any diminution in the value of their homes, but instead is merely "knowing that there is an upscale apartment building approximately a football field away, partially visible through some trees behind the house."

Section 163.3215 says nothing about weighing these specific equities before granting an injunction. If the Legislature had intended that injunctive enforcement of comprehensive plans in the courts be limited to cases where such imbalances of equities were not present, we assume that it would have said so. As important, such balancing if applied generally would lead to substantial non-compliance with comprehensive plans. We doubt that there will be many instances where the cost of the newly allowed construction will be less than any diminution resulting from an inconsistency. Entire projects of the kind permitted here will frequently far exceed the monetary harms caused to individual neighbors affected by the inconsistency. In other words, if balancing the equities—that is, weighing the loss suffered by the developer against the diminution in value of the objecting party—were required before demolition could be ordered, then demolition will never be ordered.

Moreover it is an argument that would allow those with financial resources to buy their way out of compliance with comprehensive plans. In all cases where the proposed use is for multiple acres and multiple buildings, the expenditures will be great. The greater will be its cost, and so will be a resulting loss from an after-the-fact demolition order. The more costly and elaborate the project, the greater will be the "imbalance in the equities." The more a developer is able to gild an inconsistency with nature's ornaments—trees, plants, flowers and their symbiotic fauna—the more certain under this argument will be the result that no court will enjoin an inconsistency and require its removal if already built.

In this case the alleged inequity could have been entirely avoided if developer had simply awaited the exhaustion of all legal remedies before undertaking construction. It is therefore difficult to perceive from the record any great inequity in requiring demolition. Shidel let the developer know when it was just beginning construction of the first building that she would seek demolition if the court found the project inconsistent. When developer decided to proceed with construction in spite of the absence of a final decision as to the merits of the challenge under section 163.3215, the developer was quite able to foresee that it might lose the action in court. It could not have had a reasonable expectation that its right to build what it had proposed was finally settled. It may have thought the decision to build before the consistency question was settled in court a reasonable "business decision," but that hardly makes it inequitable to enforce the rule as written.

It also seems quite inappropriate, if balancing of equities were truly required by this statute, to focus on the relatively small financial impacts suffered by those adjoining an inconsistent land use. The real countervailing equity to any monetary loss of the developer is in the flouting of the legal requirements of the Comprehensive Plan. Every citizen in the community is intangibly harmed by a failure to comply with the Comprehensive Plan, even those whose properties may not have been directly diminished in value.

We claim to be a society of laws, not of individual eccentricities in attempting to evade the rule of law. A society of law must respect law, not its evasion. If the rule of law requires land uses to meet specific standards, then allowing those who develop land to escape its requirements by spending a project out of compliance would make the standards of growth management of little real consequence. It would allow developers such as this one to build in defiance of the limits and then escape compliance by making the cost of correction too high. That would render section 163.3215 meaningless and ineffectual.

In this regard we are drawn to the views expressed in *Welton v. 40 Oak St. Bldg. Corp.*, 70 F.2d 377 (7th Cir. 1934), a case of strikingly analogous facts. There the developer applied for a permit to erect a building, and proceeded to build while its neighbor objected to the edifice and sought to show that the building plans did not comply with the zoning ordinances. When the agency approved the building he sought relief in the courts, finally being victorious in the state supreme court. Ownership of the building meanwhile passed to a federal receiver, and so the objecting neighbor sought to enforce his remedy by injunctive relief in the federal court. The trial judge denied an injunction. On appeal the Court of Appeals disagreed and ordered a mandatory injunction to "rebuild" the edifice in compliance with the zoning law, explaining:

> We have earnestly endeavored to place ourselves in a position to fully appreciate appellees' argument to the effect that enforcement of a right which arises out of an effort to give light and air to metropolitan areas is an equity that is outweighed by the dollars advanced by builders of twenty story buildings in defiance of zoning ordinances. We have also endeavored to obtain appellees' viewpoint when they propose a money judgment to one who suffers small financial loss as satisfaction for violation of important ordinances enacted for the benefit of the public. In the fight for better living conditions in large cities, in the contest for more light and air, more health and comfort, the scales are not well balanced if dividends to the individuals outweigh health and happiness to the community. Financial relief to appellants is not the only factor in weighing equities. There is involved that immeasurable but nevertheless vital element of respect for, and compliance with, the health ordinance of the city. The surest way to stop the erection of high buildings in defiance of zoning ordinances is to remove all possibility of gain to those who build illegally. Prevention will never be accomplished by compromise after the building is erected, or through payment of a small money judgment to some individual whose financial loss is an inconsequential item.

70 F.2d at 382–83

We agree with the Seventh Circuit that respect for law, in this case the Comprehensive Plan, trumps any "inequity" of financial loss arising from demolition.

Our understanding of section 163.3215 is thus different from equity's traditional use of its remedies. If, as we have shown, an injunction is the statutory remedy to insure consistency of development of property within the county, it does not seem to us that the kind of balancing advocated here would further that goal. In fact it would very likely lead to even more inconsistent development, particularly as to the kind of large scale project involved here with multiple buildings for multiple families. As we see it, the purpose of this statute is precisely against this kind of thinking. A clear rule is far more likely to erase the kind of legal unpredictability lamented by developer and amici.

The statute says that an affected or aggrieved party may bring an action to enjoin an inconsistent development allowed by the County under its Comprehensive Plan. The statutory rule is that if you build it, and in court it later proves inconsistent, it will have to come down. The court's injunction enforces the statutory scheme as written. The County has been ordered to comply with its own Comprehensive Plan and restrained from allowing inconsistent development; and the developer has been found to have built an inconsistent land use and has been ordered to remove it. The rule of law has prevailed.

We therefore affirm the final judgment of the trial court in all respects.

GUNTHER and GROSS, JJ., concur.

### *Discussion*

The Community Planning Act requires plaintiffs seeking to enforce local government comprehensive plans to subject themselves to substantial risk. The law provides for the prevailing party in a consistency challenge to be entitled to recover attorney fees and costs from the non-prevailing party. "The prevailing party in a challenge to a development order filed [as a consistency challenge] is entitled to recover reasonable attorney fees and costs incurred in challenging or defending the order, including reasonable appellate attorney fees and costs."[13] This award of attorney fees and costs counters the American Rule[14] and forces affected parties who seek to enforce comprehensive plans to also contend with financial jeopardy. The Florida Legislature added this barrier to citizen enforcement of comprehensive plans to the Community Planning Act in 2019.[15]

Note, however, that the award is only applicable to consistency challenges brought pursuant to section 163.3215(3).[16] In jurisdictions where a local government has established a process for a special master to conduct quasi-judicial hearings pursuant to section 163.3215(4), an affected party may appeal that decision on the ground that it is not in compliance using a writ of certiorari and without risking being subject to this punitive award of attorney fees.

## Standing in a consistency challenge

Prior to the legislature creating the consistency challenge, when someone sought to oppose a development action as in violation of a local government's land use laws, he or she had to meet the standing requirements established by common law. With the adoption of the Growth Management Act in 1985, however, a more liberalized standing requirement applied. Analysis of that standard is the subject of *Save the Homosassa River All., Inc. v. Citrus Cnty.*

## Florida Fifth District Court of Appeal

### *Save the Homosassa River Alliance, Inc. v. Citrus Cnty.*[17]

### 2009

GRIFFIN, J.

Save the Homosassa River Alliance, Inc., James Bitter, Rosemary Rendueles, and Priscilla Watkins [collectively "Plaintiffs"] appeal the trial court's order dismissing, with prejudice, their suit against Citrus County, Florida ["County"] and Homosassa River Resort, LLC ["Resort"] on the ground that they lack standing.

Resort owns property adjacent to the Homosassa River ["River"] in Old Homosassa, Florida. The Homosassa River is an Outstanding Florida Waterway and an essential manatee habitat.[1] There are two buildings on Resort's site, containing fifteen residential condominium units. Resort applied to the County for a land development code atlas amendment "to allow the development and redevelopment of 87 condominium dwelling units, retail space, amenities and parking" on this property. The project would result in the construction of four four-story residential structures. On July 11, 2006, Citrus County's Board of County Commissioners enacted Ordinance No. 2006–A13, which approved Resort's application and amended the County's land development code to reflect the approval.

Plaintiff Alliance is a not-for-profit corporation "committed to the preservation and conservation of environmentally sensitive lands and the wildlife in and around the Homosassa River and in Old Homosassa, Florida." Plaintiffs Bitter, Rendueles, and Watkins are individuals who own property in the area. On August 10, 2006, Plaintiffs filed this suit against the County, pursuant to section 163.3215, challenging the County's approval of Resort's application on the ground that it is inconsistent with the County's Comprehensive Land Use Plan, Citrus County Ordinance No. 89–04, as amended. On November 9, 2006, before the initial complaint was served on the County, Plaintiffs filed an Amended Complaint.

Resort was allowed to intervene in the dispute and the County filed a motion to dismiss, arguing that the Plaintiffs had failed to plead sufficient facts to establish standing. The trial court agreed and dismissed Plaintiffs' complaint, with twenty days to amend.

Plaintiffs filed their Second Amended Complaint against both the County and Resort, to which the County and Resort responded by filing a joint motion to dismiss. In their joint motion to dismiss, the County and Resort alleged that Plaintiffs had failed to establish standing because they had not sufficiently alleged (1) "any interest that exceeds in degree that of the general community," (2) "harm to such interests over and above that of their neighbors," or (3) "any nexus between the alleged comprehensive plan violations and the interests of the parties."[2]

The trial court heard arguments on the County and Resort's joint motion. At the hearing, Resort and the County essentially reiterated the points they had raised in their written motion and urged that the dismissal of the Second Amended Complaint be with prejudice. Plaintiffs argued that section 163.3215 gave affected citizens significantly enhanced standing to challenge the consistency of development decisions and that their allegations were sufficient to establish standing under this liberalized standard.

On about July 2, 2007, the trial court dismissed the Second Amended Complaint with prejudice, concluding that Plaintiffs had failed to sufficiently allege that their interests were adversely affected by the project in a way not experienced by the general population and because of insufficient "nexus" allegations. The trial court observed that

1 Resort's site is designated on the County's generalized future land use map ("GFLUM"), as CL, Low Intensity Coastal Lakes, which allows a maximum density of one (1) unit per 20 acres, is located in Flood Plain A–11, and is located in the Coastal High Hazard Zone.

2 Specifically, the County and Resort assert in their motion:

> There exists no allegations within the complaint that establish how the height of the building or the net increase in units will adversely impact the Alliance' [sic] educational purpose or interest in the manatee, Bitter's ability to fish in the river, Rendueles' ability to bicycle through Old Homosassa, or Watkins' ability to walk down the streets in Old Homosassa.

> [t]here are no allegations that the county-approved plan permits improper runoff into the river or that the proposed development will itself (other than by adding people to the mix) adversely affect the quality of water or access to the river.

Additionally, the trial court noted that "[t]here is no indication that residents living in this proposed project would add any more burden to the streets, storm drainage, river crowding, etc. than residents living elsewhere in the city."

Plaintiffs filed a motion for rehearing on July 11, 2007. In the motion for rehearing, Plaintiffs asserted that the trial court's analysis was not within the statute. They also objected that the trial court's dismissal "with prejudice" at that stage of the proceedings was premature and contrary to the existing case law. The trial court concluded that Plaintiffs had been given "ample opportunity to show standing if they could" and that they would not be helped by further delay. The trial court denied Plaintiffs' motion for rehearing.

### *The Second Amended Complaint*

Plaintiffs' Second Amended Complaint contains lengthy allegations in support of their standing to bring this suit. The complaint begins by introducing each of the plaintiffs (Alliance, Bitter, Rendueles, and Watkins). Alliance is a not-for-profit corporation committed to the preservation of the lands and the wildlife in and around the Homosassa River and Old Homosassa, Florida. The complaint explains that the group has "embarked on a specific and focused course" to protect the River from problems associated with improper and ineffective storm water management systems, overpopulation of the lands adjacent to the River, destruction of wetlands surrounding the River, degradation of the River's water quality, and excessive boat traffic upon the River. The group conducts seminars to educate the area's residents about the River and how to preserve it. One of the Alliance's main objectives has been "the orderly development and preservation of the character of Old Homosassa." Members of the group use the River for both educational and recreational purposes; have invested substantial effort and funds to protect and preserve the River and its endangered manatees; and have served on the Old Homosassa Area Redevelopment Plan steering committee.

The complaint alleges that Bitter is an active Alliance member who owns property about three miles from Resort's site. He is conscious of governmental actions that affect the health of the Homosassa River and participates actively in public conversations regarding development of the area. Bitter fishes in the River, frequently boats along it, and often visits its shores "to admire the beauty and wonder of the River and its wildlife." Additionally, Bitter receives potable water from the Homosassa Special Water District, fire protection from the County's fire department, police protection from the County's Sheriff's Department, and emergency services by Nature Coast EMS. Finally, it is alleged that in the event of a natural disaster or a threat of a natural disaster, Bitter would have to evacuate his property via West Fishbowl Drive, which is a two-lane road in Homosassa. "West Fishbowl Drive ... is along the evacuation route for [Resort's] property ... ."

Rendueles owns canal-front real property less than a mile from Resort's site. Rendueles worked on the County's Old Homosassa Overlay steering committee and actively participated during the County's public hearings on Resort's application. Additionally, it is alleged that Rendueles "enjoys the beauty of nature by traveling down the Homosassa River and walking and bicycling along the streets in Old Homosassa." She often visits the River's shores "to admire the beauty and wonder of the River and its wildlife." Rendueles receives potable water from the Homosassa Special Water District, fire protection from the County's fire department, police protection from the County's Sheriff's Department, and emergency services by Nature Coast EMS. In the event of a natural disaster or a threat of a natural disaster, Rendueles would evacuate her property via W. Yulee Drive, which is a two-lane road in Homosassa.

Watkins owns real property within Homosassa, Florida. She participates in Alliance's activities and actively participated during the County's public hearings on Resort's application. Watkins frequently kayaks on the River; bicycles along W. Halls River Road and W. Fishbowl Drive; and enjoys walking down Old Homosassa's uncrowded streets and roads. Watkins receives potable water from the Homosassa Special Water District, sewer services from Citrus County, fire protection from the County's fire department, police protection from the County's Sheriff's Department, and emergency services by Nature Coast EMS. In the event of a natural disaster or a threat of a natural disaster, Watkins would evacuate her property via W. Halls River Road, a two-lane road in Homosassa, which is along the evacuation route for Resort's property.

Plaintiffs allege that "[b]ecause of the County's adoption of a development order which is inconsistent with its adopted Comprehensive Plan[,] [Plaintiffs] will suffer an adverse effect to their interests furthered by the local government comprehensive plan ... ." In paragraph 27, Plaintiffs generally list protected interests that they claim will be adversely affected by the County's approval. Specifically, Plaintiffs allege:

> The Alliance and Property Owners, including the members of the corporation, will suffer adverse effects to interests protected or furthered by the adopted Plan, as amended, including but not limited to their property interests, their interest in protecting and maintaining the existing water quality of the Homosassa River, their interest in protecting the endangered Manatees, their interest in sufficient water and wastewater infrastructure, their interests in efficient and equitable distribution of land uses in the area, their interests in reasonable investment-backed expectations in their area, their interests in land use, their interests in preserving the character of Old Homosassa, their interests related to health and safety, including the safety and efficiency of recreation facilities and streets, police and fire protection, densities or intensities of development, including the compatibility of adjacent land uses, their interest in environmental or natural resources and their interest in wetland preservation.

In paragraphs 9 through 12, Plaintiffs allege how the harm they would each suffer "exceeds the harm caused to the public in general." With regard to Alliance, Plaintiffs allege:

> 12). Alliance will be harmed to a degree that exceeds the harm caused to the public in general because of the Alliance's investment of resources and volunteer activities to protect the health and welfare of the Homosassa River and to encourage environmentally sound development practices around the Homosassa River. Its tireless efforts to educate the public and to encourage clean and environmentally sound development will be for naught if the County continues to allow development that is inconsistent with the goals and objectives of its Comprehensive Plan.

With respect to each of the individual plaintiffs, Plaintiffs allege that Resort's proposed development activities would increase the number of people in the area and, accordingly, increase demands relating to public services, evacuation, traffic, and infrastructure. It is alleged that, given their proximity to "the project and given [their] use of the same water system, roadway system ... waterway system," and in the case of Watkins, sewer system, "[Plaintiffs] will suffer harm to a greater degree than that of the public in general." Plaintiffs additionally allege that Bitter would "be harmed to a degree that exceeds the harm caused to the public in general" because of his participation in the local government process and his volunteer efforts to preserve and protect the River; that Rendueles would "be harmed to a degree that exceeds the harm caused to the public in general" due to her proximity to the development, her location in the Coastal High Hazard Area, and her location within the Old Homosassa Redevelopment Area; and that Watkins would "be harmed to a degree that exceeds the harm caused to the public in general" because of her proximity to the development, her location within the Coastal High Hazard Area, her use of the River, and her active use of the roads and streets within Old Homosassa.

Finally, the complaint contains allegations concerning the interests the comprehensive plan is intended to protect and how Resort's proposed project is inconsistent with the plan. Plaintiffs allege that the plan's provisions are intended to:

a) Preserve, protect, and restore County's natural resources … .
b) Protect and maintain the water quality of the … Homosassa … [River] … .
c) Provide the GFLUM be recognized as the primary document used by County in land use regulation and in guiding future growth.
…
e) Provide that where County's LDC conflicts with or overlaps other regulations, whichever imposes the more stringent restrictions shall prevail.
f) Limit residential structures in the coastal high hazard area to two (2) stories.
g) Prohibit the expansion of R–2 occupancies in the coastal high hazard area.
h) Limit structures in the Old Homosassa Redevelopment Area to two (2) stories over the first living floor.
i) Require all structures constructed in the Old Homosassa Redevelopment Area to provide for a 10 foot step back of the second story over the first story.
j) Require all development in the Old Homosassa Redevelopment Area to further the character and vision provided for Old Homosassa and to be compatible with existing structures in the area.
k) Prohibit the development or expansion of general commercial uses within Old Homosassa.

The complaint then alleges that the proposed development is inconsistent with the Plan, because it:

a) Allows for the expansion of R–2 residential dwelling units in the coastal high hazard area.
b) Allows for the construction of three (3) story over parking residential structures in the coastal high hazard area.
c) Allows for the construction of structures that are not compatible with the character and vision of Old Homosassa.
d) Allows for the construction of four (4) residential structures which do not provide for a step back of stories.
e) Allows for increases in residential dwellings in the coastal high hazard area.
f) Allows for the expansion or development of new commercial uses within Old Homosassa.
g) Allows for the development of residential uses upon lands designated as GNC within Old Homosassa.

The trial court's order indicates that it dismissed Plaintiffs' Second Amended Complaint because it found that Plaintiffs had failed to sufficiently allege that their interests were adversely "affected by the project in a way not experienced by the general population."

Additionally, the trial court's order adopted the "nexus" argument of Resort and the County, ruling that "there must be some nexus between the alleged evil of the challenged action and the adverse [e]ffect claimed."

*Controlling Law*

"A local comprehensive land use plan is a statutorily mandated legislative plan to control and direct the use and development of property within a county or municipality. The plan is likened to a constitution for all future development within the governmental boundary." *Machado v. Musgrove*, 519 So. 2d 629, 631–32 (Fla. 3d DCA 1987) (citations omitted). *See also* § 163.3167, Fla. Stat. (2007) Once a comprehensive plan has been adopted pursuant to the Local Government Comprehensive Planning and Land Development Regulation Act, "all development undertaken by, and all actions taken in regard to development orders by, governmental agencies in regard to land covered by such plan" must be consistent with that plan. § 163.3194(1)(a), Fla. Stat. (2007); *see also* § 163.3164(7), Fla. Stat. (2007).

Prior to 1985, common law governed a third party's standing to intervene to challenge a development order as inconsistent with the governing comprehensive plan. *See Parker v. Leon Cty.*, 627 So. 2d 476, 479 (Fla. 1993), *Citizens Growth Mgmt. Coal., Inc. v. City of W. Palm Beach*, 450 So. 2d 204, 206–08 (Fla. 1984). The common law rule provided that, in order to have standing to challenge a land use decision, a party had to possess a legally recognized right that would be adversely affected by the decision or suffer special damages different in kind from that suffered by the community as a whole. *Putnam Cty. Envtl. Council, Inc. v. Bd. of Cty. Comm'rs*, 757 So. 2d 590, 592–93 (Fla. 5th DCA 2000); *Citizens Growth Mgmt. Coal., Inc.*, 450 So. 2d at 206. In 1985, the Florida Legislature reacted to the Supreme Court's 1984 decision in *Citizens Growth Management* that the common law rules of standing applied to the Growth Management Act by enacting section 163.3215, Florida Statutes.[6] Its stated purpose was "to ensure the standing for any person who 'will suffer an adverse effect to an interest protected ... by the ... comprehensive plan.'" *Parker*, 627 So. 2d at 479 (citing § 163.3215(2), Fla. Stat. (1985)); *see also Edu. Dev. Ctr., Inc. v. Palm Beach Cty.*, 751 So. 2d 621, 623 (Fla. 4th DCA 1999) (section 163.3215 is a remedial statute in that it "enlarged the class of persons with standing to challenge a development order as inconsistent with the comprehensive plan"). As a remedial statute, section 163.3215 is to "be liberally construed to advance the intended remedy ... ." *Edu. Dev. Ctr., Inc.*, 751 So. 2d at 623; *see also Dunlap v. Orange Cty.*, 971 So. 2d 171, 174 (Fla. 5th DCA 2007). There is no doubt that the purpose of the adoption of section 163.3215 was to liberalize standing in this context. *See City of Ft. Myers v. Splitt*, 988 So. 2d 28 (Fla. 2d DCA 2008).

In part, section 163.3215(3), Florida Statutes (2007), provides:

> Any aggrieved or adversely affected party may maintain a de novo action for declaratory, injunctive, or other relief against any local government to challenge any decision of such local government granting or denying an application for, or to prevent such local government from taking any action on, a development order, as defined in s. 163.3164,

6 The action underlying this appeal was brought pursuant to section 163.3215(3), Florida Statutes.

> which materially alters the use or density or intensity of use on a particular piece of property which is not consistent with the comprehensive plan adopted under this part.

Further, section 163.3215(2), Florida Statutes (2007), provides:

> As used in this section, the term "aggrieved or adversely affected party" means *any person*[7] or local government *that will suffer an adverse effect to an interest protected or furthered by the local government comprehensive plan*, including interests related to health and safety, police and fire protection service systems, densities or intensities of development, transportation facilities, health care facilities, equipment or services, and environmental or natural resources. *The alleged adverse interest* may be shared in common with other members of the community at large but *must exceed in degree the general interest in community good shared by all persons*. The term includes the owner, developer, or applicant for a development order.

[Emphasis added]. Thus, a person's standing to bring a challenge under section 163.3215(3) depends on (1) whether the interests the person alleges are "protected or furthered by the local government comprehensive plan"; if so, (2) whether those interests "exceed in degree the general interest in community good shared by all persons"; and (3) whether the interests will be adversely affected by the challenged decision. *See* § 163.3215(2), Fla. Stat. (2007); *see also Fla. Rock Props. v. Keyser*, 709 So. 2d 175, 177 (Fla. 5th DCA 1998).

There is nothing obscure about the statutory language requiring a person seeking standing to allege an interest that "[exceeds] in degree the general interest in community good shared by all persons" to establish standing. It simply means that a party must allege that they have an interest that is something more than "a general interest in community well being." *See Keyser*, 709 So. 2d at 177[8]; *see also Stranahan House, Inc. v. City of Fort Lauderdale*, 967 So. 2d 427, 434 (Fla. 4th DCA 2007).[9] The statute does not say that a party must be harmed to a greater degree than the general public. Not surprisingly, the case law assumes that an organization has an interest that is greater than "the general interest in community well being" when the organization's primary purpose includes protecting the particular interest that they allege will be adversely affected by the comprehensive plan violation. *See Stranahan House, Inc.*, 967 So. 2d at 434. The old common law test was so narrowly drawn

7 Section 163.3164(17), Florida Statutes (2007), provides that, as used in the Local Government Comprehensive Planning and Land Development Regulation Act, "[p]erson means an individual, corporation, governmental agency, business trust, estate, trust, partnership, association, two or more persons having a joint or common interest, or any other legal entity."

8 In *Florida Rock Properties*, 709 So. 2d at 177, this Court wrote:

> [K]eyser's standing to challenge the Board's zoning decision depends on (1) whether the personal and professional interests he alleged are 'protected or furthered by' Putnam County's comprehensive plan; if so, (2) *whether those interests are greater than the general interest in community well being*; and (3) whether the interests are or will be adversely affected by the challenged zoning decision.

[Emphasis added].

9 In *Stranahan House, Inc.*, 967 So. 2d at 434, the Fourth District wrote:

> Stranahan and Friends meet the test for standing outlined in *Florida Rock Properties v. Keyser*, 709 So. 2d 175, 177 (Fla. 5th DCA 1998). The interests alleged are protected by the City's comprehensive plan, *they are greater than the general interest in community well-being*, and the interests will be adversely affected by the development.

[Emphasis added].

that there often was no means of redress for a comprehensive plan violation. The expanded statutory test eliminates "gadfly" litigation, yet gives oversight to the segment of the public that is most likely to be knowledgeable about the interest at stake and committed to its protection. The statute expressly identifies by multiple examples the kinds of interests the legislature intended to protect:

> As used in this section, the term "aggrieved or adversely affected party" means any person or local government that will suffer an adverse effect to an interest protected or furthered by the local government comprehensive plan, *including interests related to health and safety, police and fire protection service systems, densities or intensities of development, transportation facilities, health care facilities, equipment or services, and environmental or natural resources.*

§ 163.3215(2), Fla. Stat. (2007) [emphasis added].

Application of the statutory test is illustrated by comparing two of the leading cases previously decided by this court. In *Keyser*, Timothy Keyser had filed a lawsuit challenging the decision of the Putnam County Commission to rezone a 509 acre parcel of Florida Rock Properties' land from agricultural to mining. This Court held that Keyser's allegation that the Commission's decision "would adversely affect his quality of life by its negative impact upon wildlife populations and habitats in Putnam County" was insufficient to establish standing. 709 So. 2d at 177. In explaining why the allegation was insufficient, this Court said, "Keyser never demonstrated any specific injury, only that the county would not be as bucolic as it once was. Keyser is a citizen with an interest in the environment and nothing more." *Id.*

In *Putnam Cty. Entl. Council, Inc.*, a company owned a piece of land adjacent to the Etoniah Creek State Forest, which was zoned for agricultural use. The company and the local school board "applied for a special exception to the county's comprehensive plan to allow the construction of a regional middle school complex on" the company's property. 757 So. 2d at 591. The application was approved, and the Putnam County Environmental Council ["PCEC"] subsequently filed a complaint, seeking to enforce Putnam County's comprehensive plan pursuant to Chapter 163. The trial court concluded that PCEC lacked standing to challenge the order under section 163.3215 and dismissed the action on that basis.

It [sic] its complaint, PCEC alleged that its "primary organizational purposes and activities include the study and protection of natural resources and the advocacy of sound land use and growth management policies affecting the environment"; that its officers and members had "initiated and facilitated the original public acquisition of the Etoniah Creek State Forest"; and that "[a] substantial number of [its] members, along with non-members who participate in PCEC-sponsored activities, use the Etoniah Creek State Forest for recreational and educational purposes." *Putnam Cty. Envtl. Council, Inc.*, 757 So. 2d at 592. Additionally, PCEC alleged:

> The use allowed under the special exception will adversely affect PCEC's use and its members' use of the adjacent Etoniah Creek State Forest as natural resource area. The use of the subject parcel for a school will adversely impact the ability of the Division of Forestry to use controlled burns to manage the adjacent state forest. Without controlled burns, habitat for a variety of species in the Etoniah Creek State Forest will be reduced or eliminated, thus adversely affecting the ability of PCEC, its members, and others who participate in PCEC-sponsored activities to observe or study those species. Also, without controlled burns, much of the forest will become overgrown with understory species, thus adversely affecting the ability of PCEC, its members, and others who participate in PCEC-sponsored activities to access and hike portions of Etoniah Creek State Forest. Furthermore, the physical presence of a school plant as well as the

> increased traffic and the activity, lights, and noise associated with a school facility, athletic fields, parking lots, and school bands are incompatible with Etoniah Creek State Forest's nature-based recreation and will discourage and interfere with the ability of wide-ranging species such as the black bear to reach or remain in the state forest. This will adversely affect the ability of PCEC, its members, and others who participate in PCEC-sponsored activities to observe or study those species ... .

*Id.*

In holding that PCEC had made sufficient allegations to establish standing, this Court said:

> [H]ere PCEC's complaint alleged specific injuries that PCEC would suffer if a middle school complex was constructed on Roberts' property, including the destruction of the habitat of species being studied by PCEC members and the elimination of PCEC members' access to the forest and the forest's creatures by the overgrowth of the forest. The diminution of species being studied by the group is a harm particular to PCEC, making PCEC more than just a group with amorphous "environmental concerns." Accordingly, the allegations set forth in PCEC's complaint are sufficient to demonstrate the requisite level of interest.
>
> PCEC's involvement in the original acquisition of the land for use as a state forest and its continued, active connection with that state forest further demonstrate an interest greater than that which all persons share in the community good.

*Id.* at 593–94.

On appeal, Plaintiffs begin with the premise that the trial court's dismissal order was based on the trial court's view that in order to have standing to mount a section 163.3215 challenge, the plaintiff must own real property adjacent to or very near the parcel at issue. It is true that there is much in the appealed order to suggest that was the court's view. We do not believe the court's analysis to be quite so narrow, however. It does appear that the trial court had difficulty envisioning how the "greater-in-degree" part of the statutory test for standing could be met if the plaintiff did not own adjacent real property. The "greater-in-degree" part of the test self-evidently would be met if the plaintiff is an adjacent property owner. Everyone else has to figure out how to surmount the tag-line test in *Keyser,*[10] i.e. how to be "something more" than just a "citizen with an interest in the environment."

The County contends that Plaintiffs' complaint lacks "facts sufficient to establish that the impact upon their educational efforts, enjoyment of the outdoors and use of government services is to a greater degree than others with the community," and that Plaintiffs have failed to establish precisely how the alleged comprehensive plan violations, which relate to increased height and density, would impact their interests (i.e. their educational efforts, enjoyment of the outdoors and use of government services) to any greater degree than the Old Homosassa community as a whole. In its separate Answer Brief, Resort similarly asserts that Plaintiffs failed to specifically identify an "adverse interest or impact that" they "could expect to occur due to [its] proposed hotel expansion" and failed to show that their "interests are adversely affected in a way not experienced by the general population."

Plaintiffs contend that the trial court's dismissal should be reversed because they have alleged concrete and specific adverse interests that exceed in degree the general interest in community good shared by all. Plaintiffs maintain that it is not necessary for them to show that they will suffer a unique harm and reject the appellees' position as being outside the

10 "Keyser is a citizen with an interest in the environment and nothing more." 709 So. 2d at 177.

express language and intent of the statute. We agree with Plaintiffs that the statutory test is directed to the quality of the interest of the person seeking standing; there is no requirement of a unique harm relative to the general population.

The allegations of the Second Amended Complaint amply demonstrate that each of the plaintiffs has an interest that is greater than "a general interest in community good shared by all persons." The allegations show that the Plaintiffs all have a direct and demonstrated concern for the protection of the interests furthered by the comprehensive plan that would be adversely affected by allowing a development that violates the plan. An interpretation of the statute that requires *harm* different in degree from other citizens would eviscerate the statute and ignore its remedial purpose. It drags the statute back to the common law test. The statute is designed to remedy the governmental entity's failure to comply with the established comprehensive plan, and, to that end, it creates a category of persons able to prosecute the claim. The statute is not designed to redress damage to particular plaintiffs. To engraft such a "unique harm" limitation onto the statute would make it impossible in most cases to establish standing and would leave counties free to ignore the plan because each violation of the plan in isolation usually does not uniquely harm the individual plaintiff. Rather, the statute simply requires a citizen/plaintiff to have a particularized *interest* of the kind contemplated by the statute, not a legally protectable right. [emphases added]

In sum, we conclude that the Second Amended Complaint adequately alleges Plaintiffs' standing to challenge the County's alleged failure to comply with its comprehensive plan in approving Resort's project. We accordingly reverse and remand for further proceedings.

REVERSED and REMANDED.

SAWAYA, J., concurs.

PLEUS, J., dissents, with opinion.

PLEUS, J., dissenting.

I dissent. The able and sage trial judge understood the case law and applied it properly. He correctly dismissed this case with prejudice for lack of standing because the plaintiffs repeatedly failed to allege any adverse effects, impact or harm they would suffer from the proposed development that was unique to them. Without it being unique to them, their interest cannot exceed in degree the general interest in the community good shared by all persons. The majority opinion eviscerates the "adverse effect" element of the standing requirement in subsection 163.3215(2), Florida Statutes, and stands in direct conflict with the case law interpreting that statute.

Subsection 163.3215(2) defines an "aggrieved or adversely affected party" as "any person or local government which *will suffer an adverse effect* to an interest furthered by the local government comprehensive plan ... ." (Emphasis added). It further states that "[t]he alleged adverse interest may be shared in common with other members of the community at large but *must exceed in degree the general interest in community good shared by all persons.*" (Emphasis added).

The cases discussing this section have uniformly interpreted it as requiring factual allegations that plaintiffs will suffer adverse effects and that those adverse effects will be greater than those suffered by the community at large. *See Dunlap v. Orange Cty.*, 971 So. 2d 171 (Fla. 5th DCA 2007); *Stranahan House, Inc. v. City of Fort Lauderdale*, 967 So. 2d 427 (Fla. 4th DCA 2007); *Payne v. City of Miami*, 927 So. 2d 904 (Fla. 3d DCA 2005); *Edgewater Beach Owners Ass'n, Inc. v. Walton Cty.*, 833 So. 2d 215 (Fla. 1st DCA 2002), *receded from on other grounds, Bay Point Club, Inc. v. Bay Cty.*, 890 So. 2d 256 (Fla. 1st DCA 2004); *Putnam Cty. Envtl. Council, Inc. v. Bd. of Cty. Comm'rs*, 757 So. 2d 590, 592–93 (Fla. 5th DCA 2000) *Fla. Rock Props. v. Keyser*, 709 So. 2d 175, 177 (Fla. 5th DCA 1998); *Pichette v. City of N. Miami*, 642 So. 2d 1165 (Fla. 3d DCA 1994); *Sw. Ranches Homeowners Ass'n, Inc. v. Broward Cty.*, 502 So. 2d 931 (Fla. 4th DCA 1987).

*Florida Rock*, in my view, is a correct analysis of the statute. It tells us two things. Owning real property in the vicinity of the rezoning, and being concerned about the effects of the rezoning, is not sufficient to confer jurisdiction. The rezoning must have a specific impact or involve some harm on or to the property owner or his property ... . [Judge Pleus' dissent continued by mentioning the types of injuries asserted by the plaintiffs in the cases he previously cited above, as well as two cases where the district courts of appeal affirmed that the plaintiffs had standing to sue.]

In the instant case, the plaintiffs failed to allege that they would suffer any adverse effect from the proposed development, much less any that would affect them to a greater degree than the community at large. The complaint alleges that the individual plaintiffs will suffer harm because the proposed development will increase demands on the potable water, sewer, traffic, evacuation, police and infrastructure systems. Simply alleging that development will increase demands on various resources does not equate to an adverse effect on an individual plaintiff. Instead, the complaint must allege ultimate facts showing how or why increased demands will result in adverse impacts to the plaintiffs. *See* Fla. R. Civ. P. 1.110(b) (requiring a "short and plain statement of ultimate facts showing pleader is entitled to relief"); *Williams v. Howard*, 329 So. 2d 277 (Fla. 1976) (noting that a "bare assertion" that one's legal rights will be affected, without alleging how or why, is not sufficient to establish standing to file a declaratory judgment action).

For example, will the increased numbers of people and demands arising from the proposed development degrade the plaintiffs' water quality? Will they reduce the plaintiffs' access to potable water? Will they increase the price plaintiffs pay for potable water? Will they reduce plaintiffs' access to fishing, boating and other activities in the Homosassa River? Will they cause increased response times from police and fire to plaintiffs' residences? Will they prevent plaintiffs from timely evacuating in an emergency? And, if so, how are any of these adverse effects suffered by the plaintiffs to a greater degree than the community at large? The complaint fails to allege any ultimate facts demonstrating that the plaintiffs will suffer adverse effects, much less adverse effects greater than the community at large. The complaint also alleges that the Alliance and the individual plaintiffs will be adversely affected because their "investment of resources and volunteer activities" to protect the river, educate the public and encourage responsible development will be "for naught" if the County continues to allow development that is inconsistent with the Comprehensive Plan. A similar argument was soundly rejected by the United States Supreme Court in *Sierra Club v. Morton*, 405 U.S. 727, 92 S.Ct. 1361, 31 L.Ed.2d 636 (1972), a case this Court followed in *Florida Rock* ... .

In this case, the majority concludes without any supporting analysis that the plaintiffs sufficiently allege that they will be "adversely affected by allowing a development that violates the plan." The majority's conclusion suffers from the same fatal flaw as the complaint itself—it is unsupported by any allegations of ultimate facts showing how or why the alleged violations will adversely affect the plaintiffs, and do so to a greater degree than the community at large.

More troubling is the majority's contradictory statement that a showing of harm is not required at all. It states:

> An interpretation of the statute that requires harm different in degree from other citizens would eviscerate the statute and ignore its remedial purpose. It drags the statute back to the common law test. The Statute is designed to remedy the governmental entity's failure to comply with the established comprehensive plan, and, to that end, it creates a category of persons able to prosecute the claim. The statute is not designed to redress damage to particular plaintiffs. To engraft such a "unique harm" limitation onto the statute would make it impossible in most cases to establish standing and would leave counties free to ignore the plan because each violation of the plan in isolation usually

> does not harm the individual plaintiff. Rather, the statute simply requires a citizen/plaintiff to have a particularized interest of the kind contemplated by the statute, not a legally protectable right.

This analysis is incorrect. By interpreting the statute as requiring only a particularized interest and not a particularized harm, it contravenes the plain language of the statute and conflicts with prior case law from this and other districts ... . Florida case law clearly requires more concrete injury than that alleged by the Plaintiffs. On this point the U.S. Supreme Court has previously recognized the requirement of an injury is specific—it requires a "concrete and particularized" injury in fact which "must affect the plaintiff in a personal and individual way," does not allow legal redress for any imaginable injury, and is not "an ingenious academic exercise in the conceivable." *Lujan v. Defenders of Wildlife*, 504 U.S. 555, 560, 112 S.Ct. 2130, 119 L.Ed.2d 351 (1992) ... . To demonstrate such an injury, the party seeking redress must state "specific facts" demonstrating "that one or more of respondents' members would thereby be directly affected" by the challenged action. *Id.* at 563, 112 S.Ct. 2130. This was not accomplished here. Plaintiffs' bare-bones allegations that the increases in density will affect their use of the river is, without more, "pure speculation and fantasy" and is insufficient to show the requisite actual, concrete injury ... .

I feel compelled to add the following observations from my experience in this area of the law.

No doubt the plaintiffs in this case are honest, sincere people who care deeply about the future of the Homosassa River. My remarks about certain so-called "environmentalists gadflies" should not be interpreted as a reference to them.

The opinion of Judge Griffin will be cited and used to open the floodgates to the environmental gadflies of the world. They will file spurious complaints which challenge rezoning on the basis that it violates the comprehensive plan. Local government will be hampered in doing what it is supposed to do. Property rights will be trampled by the delays. People who disagree with local decisions will find solace in the judicial branch by virtue of this Court's new-found authority which opens the courthouse door to attempts to overturn the decisions of local, duly elected officials. Every gadfly with some amorphous environmental agenda, and enough money to pay a filing fee, will be anointed with status simply because the gadfly wants to "protect the planet."

The environmental gadfly will win every time, not on the merits, but because, in the words of the trial judge, "[w]hen delay will prevent the construction of an approved but undesired development, then one may win by losing if the losing process is sufficiently long." For those who respect property rights, look out!

## Scope of consistency challenge

One Florida district court of appeal has limited availability of the consistency challenge to allegations that the development approval provided for *densities* or *intensities* which are not consistent with applicable laws. This case significantly narrows the scope of the consistency challenge and conflicts with other Florida district courts of appeal.

### Florida Second District Court of Appeal

### *Heine v. Lee Cnty.*[18]

### 2017

LaROSE, Judge.

Frederick and Barbara Heine appeal a final summary judgment entered in favor of Alico West Fund, LLC, and Lee County, in the Heines' lawsuit brought under section

163.3215(3), Florida Statutes (2015) (the Consistency Statute).[1] We have jurisdiction. *See* Fla. R. App. P. 9.030(b)(1)(A).

The Heines challenged a rezoning resolution approved by the Lee County Board of County Commissioners (the Board) that authorized rezoning of Alico's property. The Heines alleged that the resolution was inconsistent with various provisions of Lee County's comprehensive plan. The trial court found otherwise, ruling that the Heines' claims fell outside the purview of the Consistency Statute.

On appeal, the Heines raise several issues challenging summary judgment. After careful review of the record, and with the benefit of oral argument, we affirm in all respects. However, we write to explain why the trial court properly construed the Consistency Statute.

### Background

Alico owns over eight hundred acres of land in Lee County. North Lake is situated on the western portion of its property. The Heines live in a residential community south of the Alico property and the North Lake. Their residence faces the South Lake. The North Lake and South Lake are connected; the Heines enjoy a recreational easement for the use of the North Lake.

In 2010, Lee County amended its comprehensive plan. The amendment changed the land use designation for a portion of Alico's property to "University Community." The designation requires that "[a]ll development within the University Community must be designed to enhance and support [Florida Gulf Coast University]." The 2010 plan amendment significantly increased the potential development densities and intensities of Alico's property.

Following the 2010 plan amendment, Alico applied to rezone a portion of its property for a project called CenterPlace. Alico intended to develop CenterPlace to cater to the housing, commercial, and recreational needs of nearby University students, faculty, and staff. County zoning staff recommended approval of Alico's request. After several public hearings, a zoning hearing examiner, too, recommended approval. Subsequently, after another public hearing, the Board approved a resolution granting Alico's application.

The resolution rezoned Alico's property to "Compact Planned Development," and authorized an increase in development of up to 250 hotel rooms, 246,500 square feet of commercial/retail space, 100,000 square feet of office space, and 300,000 square feet of research and development space. The resolution also authorized up to 250 wet boat slips on the North Lake, 50 dry slips, installation of a boat ramp, and up to 20 trailer parking spaces.

Following Board approval, the Heines sued Lee County and Alico, alleging that the resolution was inconsistent with Lee County's comprehensive plan. The Heines challenged the resolution on numerous grounds: (1) failure to include enforcement conditions for the construction of a minimum square footage of commercial space and minimum residential density requirements; (2) failure to ensure the installation of plantings, buffers, and landscaping "using xeriscape principles"; (3) failure to "ensure that there will be a mix of housing types sufficient to meet the varying lifestyle of students, faculty, administration and support staff"; (4) failure to obtain prior approval by the University; (5) failure to give adequate consideration to noise, security, and visual impacts on the property; and, (6) failure to meet the 2010 plan amendment's safety requirements pertaining to the University. The trial court granted summary

1 The Heines also separately appealed the trial court's order dismissing their declaratory judgment action, and petitioned for issuance of a writ of certiorari, seeking second-tier review of the Board's resolution. These cases, along with the instant appeal, were consolidated to travel together.

judgment on Alico's and Lee County's joint motion, ruling that the Heines' challenges were not within the scope of the Consistency Statute because "they do not qualify as uses, densities, or intensities of uses."

### *Standard of Review*

We review the trial court's interpretation and construction of the Consistency Statute de novo. *See A.J.R. v. State*, 206 So. 3d 140, 142 (Fla. 2d DCA 2016) ("We also apply a de novo standard of review to a trial court's construction of a statute." (citing *State v. C.M.*, 154 So. 3d 1177, 1178 (Fla. 4th DCA 2015))). Further, because we are tasked with reviewing the trial court's award of summary judgment, we likewise employ de novo review. *Gator Boring & Trenching, Inc. v. Westra Constr. Corp.*, 210 So. 3d 175, 181 (Fla. 2d DCA 2016).

### *Analysis*

The Heines argue that the trial court erroneously limited the scope of claims allowed under the Consistency Statute. They insist that the trial court adopted a too narrow and restrictive reading of the Consistency Statute, thus thwarting its remedial purpose. They urge us to adopt an expansive reading of the statute so as to allow a broader variety of claims under the Consistency Statute. They maintain that reading the statute in pari materia with other statutory provisions compels reversal. *See State v. Fuchs*, 769 So. 2d 1006, 1009 (Fla. 2000) ("[S]tatutes which relate to the same or closely related subjects should be read in pari materia." (citing *State v. Ferrari*, 398 So. 2d 804, 807 (Fla. 1981))). We are not persuaded.

Florida law mandates consistency between a local government's comprehensive plan and its development orders. *See* § 163.3194(1)(a) ("After a comprehensive plan ... has been adopted in conformity with this act, all development undertaken by, and all actions taken in regard to development orders ... shall be consistent with such plan or element as adopted."). To ensure compliance with this obligation, the Florida Legislature permits "[a]ny aggrieved or adversely affected party [to] maintain a de novo action ... to challenge any decision of such local government granting ... a development order." § 163.3215(3); *see also Pinecrest Lakes, Inc. v. Shidel*, 795 So. 2d 191, 200 (Fla. 4th DCA 2001) ("[W]e observed that section 163.3215 had liberalized standing requirements and demonstrated 'a clear legislative policy in favor of the enforcement of comprehensive plans by persons adversely affected by local action.'" (quoting *Sw. Ranches Homeowners Ass'n v. Broward Cty.*, 502 So. 2d 931, 935 (Fla. 4th DCA 1987))).

But the type of claim allowed under the Consistency Statute is not unlimited. The statute authorizes an aggrieved party to bring an action to challenge a development order that "materially alters the use or density or intensity of use on a particular piece of property which is not consistent with the comprehensive plan." § 163.3215(3). A plain reading of this text compels us to conclude, as did the trial court, that the Heines' challenges to the rezoning resolution do not fall within the ken of these three areas.

"Legislative intent is the polestar that guides our analysis regarding the construction and application of the statute." *Diamond Aircraft Indus., Inc. v. Horowitch*, 107 So. 3d 362, 367 (Fla. 2013) (citing *Bautista v. State*, 863 So. 2d 1180, 1185 (Fla. 2003)). Accordingly, we "begin with the actual language used in the statute because legislative intent is determined first and foremost from the statute's text." *Raymond James Fin. Servs., Inc. v. Phillips*, 126 So. 3d 186, 190 (Fla. 2013) (quoting *Heart of Adoptions, Inc. v. J.A.*, 963 So. 2d 189, 198 (Fla. 2007)).

> When a statute is clear, courts will not look behind the statute's plain language for legislative intent or resort to rules of statutory construction to ascertain intent. Instead, the

> statute's plain and ordinary meaning must control, unless this leads to an unreasonable result or a result clearly contrary to legislative intent.

*State v. Burris*, 875 So. 2d 408, 410 (Fla. 2004) (citation omitted).

The pertinent language of the Consistency Statute is clear and unambiguous. The statute enunciates only three bases upon which a party may challenge a development order's purported inconsistency with a comprehensive plan. Therefore, we will not resort to rules of statutory construction to countenance the Heines' expansive view of the statute's scope. That task, if undertaken at all, is for the legislature. As our sister district observed, "there is no basis for us to look to 'polestars' when the ship of statutory interpretation is guided by clear text. That is to say, we look only to clear text for statutory meaning, not to the stars." *Brown v. State*, 848 So. 2d 361, 364 (Fla. 4th DCA 2003).

The Heines claim that the trial court should have construed the Consistency Statute in pari materia with section 163.3194(3)(a), which provides as follows:

> A development order or land development regulation shall be consistent with the comprehensive plan if the land uses, densities or intensities, *and other aspects of development permitted* by such order or regulation are compatible with and further the objectives, policies, land uses, and densities or intensities in the comprehensive plan and if it meets all other criteria enumerated by the local government.

[Emphasis added]. They argue that the language, "other aspects of development permitted," allows an attack upon the development order, apart from grounds of use, density, or intensity explicitly provided for in the Consistency Statute. However, once again, "the 'in pari materia' canon of statutory construction would be appropriate only if we found the statute ambiguous." *Brown*, 848 So. 2d at 364 [emphasis omitted]. We do not. We will not rewrite the Consistency Statute to include language omitted by the legislature. The Florida Supreme Court has observed:

> Even where a court is convinced that the Legislature really meant and intended something not expressed in the phraseology of the act, it will not deem itself authorized to depart from the plain meaning of the language which is free from ambiguity ... . If it has been passed improvidently the responsibility is with the Legislature and not the courts.

*Forsythe v. Longboat Key Beach Erosion Control Dist.*, 604 So. 2d 452, 454 (Fla. 1992) (quoting *Van Pelt v. Hilliard*, 78 So. 693, 694–95 (1918)); *see also Capeletti Bros., Inc v. Dep't of Transp.*, 499 So. 2d 855, 857 (Fla. 1st DCA 1986) ("The omission may be a legislative oversight; nevertheless, courts should not rewrite legislation to cure an omission by the legislature just because it seems to fit overall legislative policy.").

We have no basis to conclude that the absence of the "other aspects of development permitted" language in the Consistency Statute was a legislative oversight. *See, e.g., Aramark Unif. & Career Apparel, Inc. v. Easton*, 894 So. 2d 20, 24 (Fla. 2004) ("The absence of a causation requirement in the statute cannot be viewed as a legislative oversight."). The omission of such language is presumed to be deliberate, and is evidence that the Consistency Statute limits the scope of claims to use, density, and intensity challenges only. "This conclusion logically derives from a general principle of statutory construction, expressio unius est exclusio alterius, which means that 'express mention of one thing is the exclusion of another.'" *Citizens for Responsible Growth v. City of St. Pete Beach*, 940 So. 2d 1144, 1150 (Fla. 2d DCA 2006) (quoting *Inman v. State*, 916 So. 2d 59, 61 (Fla. 2d DCA 2005)).

The Heines argue that the Consistency Statute is remedial in nature; thus, it must be read liberally. *See Golf Channel v. Jenkins*, 752 So. 2d 561, 565–66 (Fla. 2000) ("[R]emedial statutes should be liberally construed in favor of granting access to the remedy provided by the Legislature." (citing *Arrow Air, Inc. v. Walsh*, 645 So. 2d 422, 424 (Fla. 1994))). In support of their position, they rely on *Educ. Dev. Ctr., Inc. v. Palm Beach Cty.*, 751 So. 2d 621, 623 (Fla. 4th DCA 1999). There, the Fourth District recognized that "[s]ection 163.3215 enlarged the class of persons with standing to challenge a development order as inconsistent with the comprehensive plan." *Id.* Our sister district stated that section 163.3215 "should be liberally construed to advance the intended remedy, *i.e., to ensure standing for any party with a protected interest under the comprehensive plan who will be adversely affected by the governmental entity's actions.*" *Id.* [emphasis added] (citing *Parker v. Leon Cty.*, 627 So. 2d 476, 479 (Fla. 1993)). The Heines, however, conflate the Consistency Statute's expansive conferral of standing with the scope of what a plaintiff with standing may challenge. *See Martin Cty. Conservation All. v. Martin Cty.*, 134 So. 3d 966, 967 (Fla. 1st DCA 2010) ("Section 163.3215 is a remedial statute designed to enlarge the class of persons with standing to challenge a local development order."). Because the Consistency Statute was intended to liberalize standing, not broaden the scope of what a party with standing may challenge beyond use, density, and intensity, the trial court did not err in construing the statute literally, rather than liberally.

## Conclusion

Because the trial court correctly construed the Consistency Statute as permitting only those challenges specifically authorized therein, and properly applied the statute to the facts of this case, we affirm.

Affirmed.

CRENSHAW and SLEET, JJ., Concur.

### *Discussion*

The *Heine* decision directly conflicts with numerous other published Florida district court opinions, as well as with the Florida Supreme Court holding in *Brevard Cnty. v. Snyder.*[19] Courts have repeatedly referred to the scope of the consistency challenge as including challenges alleging a development order to be inconsistent *with any aspect of a comprehensive plan*—from environmental protection to intergovernmental coordination. The following are specific statements from district courts on this subject:

- "[W]e reject the ... assertion that the land use element of its comprehensive plan alone should be considered in determining consistency ... . The other elements of the plan were adopted pursuant to the statutory mandate ... ."[20]
- "[D]evelopment challenged as contrary to master plans must be strictly construed and that the burden is on the developer to show by competent and substantial evidence that the development conforms strictly to the master plan, its elements, and objectives."[21]
- "It is well established that a development order shall be consistent with the governmental body's objectives, policies, land uses, etc., as provided in its comprehensive plan."[22]

Further, at least one other district court has interpreted the specific phrase in section 163.3215(3) "which materially alters the use or density or intensity of use on a particular piece of property" and ascribed to those words a meaning which is different from the meaning ascribed by the *Heine* court. Specifically, in *O'Neil v. Walton Cnty.*,[23] the First District Court of Appeal understood that clause as creating a threshold requirement for those development orders that are subject to a consistency challenge, and not as a limit on the scope of the consistency challenge itself.[24]

The *O'Neil* decision upheld dismissal of a consistency challenge on summary judgment because the subject development order from 2013 followed a previously approved development order from 2010 and "did not materially alter" the 2010 development order.[25] The court said:

> [B]ecause § 163.3215 is predicated upon showing a material alteration of property inconsistent with a Comp Plan, and here the County's 2010 order had already approved the placement and relative location of the things that Appellants challenge, this challenge to the 2013 order fails to meet the requirements of § 163.3215.[26]

The *O'Neil* court's understanding of § 163.3215 is, of course, not compatible with how the *Heine* court applied the provision.[27]

## Notes

1 Fla. Stat. § 163.3215(1); Bd. of Trs. of Internal Improvement Tr. Fund v. Seminole Cnty., 623 So. 2d 593, 596 (Fla. 5th DCA 1993).
2 Fla. Stat. § 163.3194(3)(a).
3 *Id.* § 163.3164(15).
4 *Id.* § 163.3164(16).
5 *Id.* §§ 163.3215(1)–(3).
6 *Id.* § 163.3215(4).
7 *Id.* § 163.3215(3).
8 5220 Biscayne Boulevard, LLC v. Stebbins, 937 So. 2d 1189, 1191 (Fla. 5th DCA 2006).
9 *Id.* at 1190.
10 Das v. Osceola Cnty., 685 So. 2d 990, 993 (Fla 5th DCA 1997), *appeal denied*, 715 So. 2d 1105 (Fla. 5th DCA 1998).
11 *Id.* at 994.
12 795 So. 2d 191 (Fla. 4th DCA), *appeal denied*, 802 So. 2d 486 (Fla. 4th DCA 2001).
13 Fla. Stat. § 163.3215(8)(c).
14 Under the "American Rule," attorney's fees in civil litigation are ordinarily borne by the party who incurs them, and a court cannot award the recovery of attorney's fees from an opposing litigant unless "authorized by statute or by agreement of the parties." Topalli v. Feliciano, 267 So. 3d 513, 518 (Fla. 2d DCA 2019) (citing Fla. Patient's Comp. Fund v. Rowe, 472 So. 2d 1145, 1148 (Fla. 1985)): *see* Pepper's Steel & Alloys, Inc. v. United States, 850 So. 2d 462, 465 (Fla. 2003) (mentioning that absent an authorization "by statute or by agreement of the parties," generally a litigant pays for his or her own fees in a lawsuit), *acq. in result* 348 F.3d 964 (11th Cir. 2003).
15 Ch. 2019-165, Laws of Fla. § 7.
16 Fla. Stat. § 163.3215(8)(c).
17 2 So. 3d 329 (Fla. 5th DCA 2008), *appeal denied*, 16 So. 3d 132 (Fla. 2009) (unpublished table decision).
18 221 So. 3d 1254 (Fla. 2d DCA 2017).
19 Brevard Cnty. v. Snyder, 627 So. 2d 469, 476 (Fla. 1993) (stating without qualification, "we hold that a landowner seeking to rezone property has the burden of proving that the proposal is consistent with the comprehensive plan").
20 Sw. Ranches Homeowners Ass'n, Inc. v. Broward Cnty., 502 So. 2d 931, 936 (Fla. 4th DCA 1987).
21 White v. Metro. Dade Cnty., 563 So. 2d 117, 128 (Fla. 3d DCA 1990) (citation omitted).
22 Dixon v. Jacksonville, 774 So. 2d 763, 764 (Fla. 1st DCA 2000).
23 149 So. 3d 699 (Fla. 1st DCA 2014).
24 *See* O'Neil v. Walton Cnty., 149 So. 3d 699, 703–5 (Fla. 1st DCA 2014).
25 *Id.* at 701.
26 *Id.*
27 *Compare* Heine v. Lee Cnty., 221 So. 3d 1254, 1258 (Fla. 2d DCA 2017), *with O'Neil*, 149 So. 3d at 701.

# 13 Declaratory judgment

In a land use context, the declaratory judgment action is generally appropriate for determining one's rights under legislative or administrative land use decisions. This text describes what constitutes a local government administrative land use decision below. Also, this general statement requires two caveats.

First, when the legislative decision to be challenged is adoption or amendment of a comprehensive plan and the basis of the challenge is whether the plan is *in compliance* with certain provisions described in section 163.3184(1)(b), Florida's Community Planning Act makes an appeal to DOAH the appropriate avenue for relief.[1]

Second, when an administrative decision is challenged on the grounds that it is not *consistent* as section 163.3194(3)(a) defines that term, then the appropriate cause of action is a consistency challenge pursuant to section 163.3215.[2]

Therefore, declaratory judgments are appropriate for just the subset of legislative land use decisions which are not appropriate for an appeal to DOAH and just the subset of administrative decisions which are not appropriate for a consistency challenge.

Land use decisions meeting these criteria include: comprehensive plan amendments which violate some rule not addressed in section 163.3184(1)(b); denials of proposed comprehensive plan amendments; and administrative decisions not challenged on consistency grounds.

Florida Statutes section 86.011 provides for declaratory judgments as original actions in the circuit court. A declaratory judgment is available to "[a]ny person claiming to be interested or who may be in doubt about his or her rights" under an ordinance.[3] However, Florida courts have subject-matter jurisdiction to hear a declaratory action only when a justiciable controversy as to a violation of the local government ordinance exists.[4] Florida courts have rejected suits for declaratory judgments in land use disputes by plaintiffs who lived too far from land subject to a land use action and who failed to allege "they would be affected by noise, traffic impact, land value diminution," or any other negative impact.[5]

In a declaratory judgment action, the court has jurisdiction to determine the plaintiff's rights under the law.[6] Plaintiffs can request additional supplemental relief, such as injunctive relief, which may be available.[7] The Florida Supreme Court has articulated the elements of a declaratory judgment action as follows.

> [T]here is a bona fide, actual, present practical need for the declaration; that the declaration should deal with a present, ascertained or ascertainable state of facts or present controversy as to a state of facts; that some immunity, power, privilege or right of the complaining party is dependent upon the facts or the law applicable to the facts; that there is some person or persons who have, or reasonably may have an actual, present, adverse and antagonistic interest in the subject matter, either in fact or law; that the antagonistic and adverse interest[s] are all before the court by proper process or class representation and that the

relief sought is not merely giving of legal advice by the courts or the answer to questions propounded from curiosity.[8]

## Identifying administrative decisions

Unlike state governments or the federal government, where a state constitution or the U.S. Constitution separates powers among several branches of government, local governments often mix legislative, judicial, and executive powers in a single body. In addition,

> on account of the inability of the three branches to respond to the demands of a changing social order, the Legislatures have created and the courts, both state and federal, have approved what the law-writers choose to call the fourth power in government, the administrative, which for practical purposes co-ordinates the other three departments and makes for a more flexible and efficient administration.[9]

Reviewing the common structures of local governments will help clarify how to identify administrative decisions.

Two forms of local government are typical in the United States: the mayor-council form and the council-manager form. Local governments with either of these two forms of government, however, are by no means uniform. In Florida, every city's charter establishes its structure, and each local government is unique.

In the *mayor-council form*, an elected body—called a council or a commission—is the local government's legislative body.[10] Voters directly elect a mayor who performs the executive, or administrative, functions.[11] The mayor-council government form is more common for large cities or counties.[12]

In the *council-manager form*, an elected legislative body hires a professional manager to handle administrative duties at the will of the legislative body.[13] The elected commission essentially serves both the legislative and—through its manager—the executive roles of local government.[14] The council-manager form is more common in medium-sized and small cities and counties.[15]

No city in Florida has a judicial branch.[16] The state fulfills the judicial role.[17] However, local governments often set up processes to adjudge rights and to ensure compliance with their own laws. Quasi-judicial land use decisions are an example of a judicial process managed by a local government. Another common subject matter for local government adjudicative action is code enforcement, such as nuisance abatement.

As we have learned with the distinction between legislative and quasi-judicial decisions, the character of a local government action impacts the due process rights of parties. The character of a local action also determines how someone pursues a judicial remedy. And local government actions are not just limited to being legislative or quasi-judicial. *City of St. Pete Beach v. Sowa* discusses administrative decisions and why the declaratory judgment is the appropriate cause of action for redressing administrative decisions.

### Florida Second District Court of Appeal

### *City of St. Pete Beach v. Sowa*[18]

### 2009

KELLY, Judge.

Ronald Holehouse and the City of St. Pete Beach seek certiorari review of a circuit court order that granted Walter Sowa, Jr.'s petition for writ of certiorari and quashed a building permit Mr. Holehouse obtained from the City. Because the issuance of the building permit was an executive decision that was not reviewable by certiorari, we grant the petition and quash the order of the circuit court.

A city official granted Mr. Holehouse a building permit to repair a four-unit apartment building damaged as a result of a hurricane. Mr. Sowa, a neighbor, challenged the permit by filing a petition for writ of certiorari in the circuit court. The circuit court granted the petition and quashed the permit after concluding that the City had violated its code in issuing the permit. This determination appears to have flowed from the court's finding that "[i]t is unclear from what authority this permit was issued." In reaching this conclusion, the circuit court relied on documents Mr. Sowa supplied in an appendix to his petition and which he argued demonstrated that the City should not have issued the permit.

The City and Mr. Holehouse contend that the circuit court did not have certiorari jurisdiction to review the City official's decision to issue the permit. We agree. "As a rule, only quasi-judicial actions [of local government agencies] are reviewable via certiorari." *Broward Cty. v. G.B.V. Int'l, Ltd.*, 787 So. 2d 838, 843 (Fla. 2001). A decision is judicial or quasi-judicial, as distinguished from executive, when notice and hearing are required and the judgment of the administrative agency is contingent on the showing made at the hearing. *DeGroot v. Sheffield*, 95 So. 2d 912, 915 (Fla. 1957). That is not the case here. A single city official made an executive decision to grant Mr. Holehouse's permit application; no hearing was conducted on the matter.

When an administrative official or agency acts in an executive or legislative capacity, the proper method of attack on the official's or agency's action "is a suit in circuit court for declaratory or injunctive relief on grounds that the action taken is arbitrary, capricious, confiscatory, or violative of constitutional guarantees." *Bd. of Cty. Comm'rs of Hillsborough Cty. v. Casa Dev. Ltd.*, 332 So. 2d 651, 654 (Fla. 2d DCA 1976). Certiorari review of a legislative or executive decision of an agency is inappropriate because, "[a]s a practical matter, when an executive makes a decision without conducting a hearing, there is nothing for the circuit court to review." *Pleasures II Adult Video, Inc. v. City of Sarasota*, 833 So. 2d 185, 189 (Fla. 2d DCA 2002). Here, because no hearing was conducted, the circuit court had no record to review. Instead, it relied on documents supplied by Mr. Sowa in an attempt to construct a record upon which it could review the City official's decision to issue the permit. By proceeding in this fashion when it lacked jurisdiction to do so, the circuit court departed from the essential requirements of the law. Accordingly, we grant the petition and quash the circuit court's order.

Petition granted.

### *Discussion*

Therefore, along with acting in a legislative or quasi-judicial capacity, a local government might act in an administrative (i.e. executive) capacity. When it does, one cannot appeal that decision using a writ of certiorari.[19] Nonetheless, a local government cannot always convert what should be a quasi-judicial decision—subject to review by a writ of certiorari—into an administrative decision—subject to challenge through a declaratory action—by making the decision at a staff level. When local government employees make a decision in a committee, Florida law requires that decision to occur in a public hearing and courts have found the nature of the decision to be quasi-judicial, rather than administrative.

The following language is an analysis on this point from the Second District Court of Appeal reviewing a land use decision made by a group of staff in Charlotte County meeting as a committee called the Development Review Committee (DRC).

> The Sunshine Law [(i.e. Florida's law requiring public meetings)] was enacted to "protect the public from closed door politics and, as such, the law must be broadly construed to

> effect its remedial and protective purpose." The Sunshine Law has historically been subject to two exceptions, the "staff exception" and the exception for "remoteness from the decision-making process." The circuit court applied the staff exception in the present case and concluded that the petitioners had no right to participate in the DRC meeting because DRC members were merely carrying out normal staff functions, which are not subject to the Sunshine Law. However, when, as here, public officials delegate their fact-finding duties and decision-making authority to a committee of staff members, those individuals no longer function as staff members but "stand in shoes of such public officials insofar as application of Government in Sunshine Law is concerned." Because the authority of final project approval has been delegated to the DRC by Charlotte County ordinance, county staff members who serve on the DRC function as public officials.[20]

Following this analysis, the district court over-ruled the circuit court's finding that the DRC's decision had been "quasi-executive" in nature and instead characterized it as quasi-judicial and subject to review by writ of certiorari.[21]

## Local governments must process some applications

Florida law requires local governments to process some applications to use land and provides deadlines for the review and final decision-making. These requirements prohibit a local government from too-slowly processing development applications or from rejecting a development proposal that requires an approval by simply not acting on it.

> Within 30 days after receiving an application for approval of a *development permit* or *development order*, a county must review the application for completeness and issue a letter indicating that all required information is submitted or specifying with particularity any areas that are deficient. If the application is deficient, the applicant has 30 days to address the deficiencies by submitting the required additional information. Within 120 days after the county has deemed the application complete, or 180 days for applications that require final action through a quasi-judicial hearing or a public hearing, the county must approve, approve with conditions, or deny the application for a development

**Timeline by which local governments must process some applications**

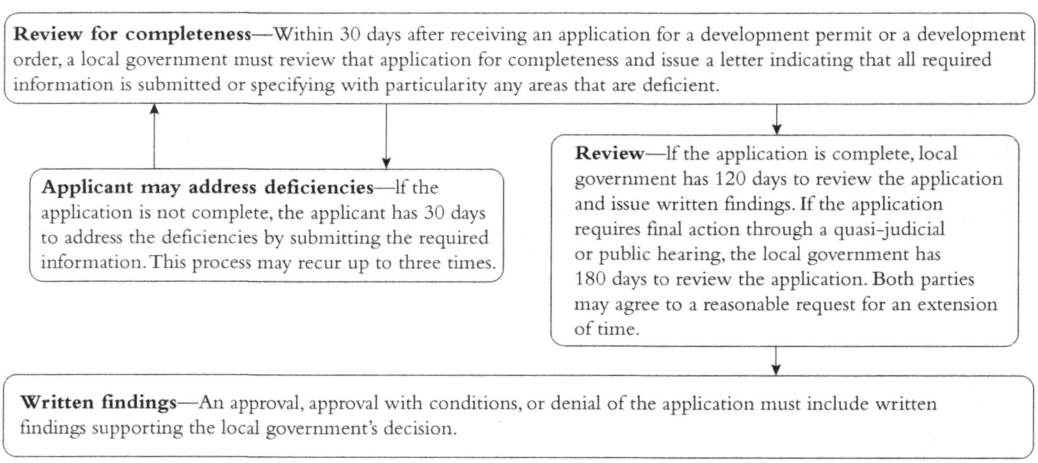


*Figure 13.1* Flow chart describing the timeline by which local governments must process some applications to use land

Note: *see* Fla. Stat. §§125.022(1) and 166.033

*Table 13.1* Key characteristics of four causes of action available to challenge local government land use decisions

| | *Decision to challenge* | *Jurisdiction* | *Evidentiary record* | *Standing* | *Scope of review* |
|---|---|---|---|---|---|
| Petition for hearing by DOAH | Comprehensive plan adoption or amendment on grounds decision was not consistent with requirements of law explicitly provided in statute; land use regulation as inconsistent with the applicable comprehensive plan. | Fla. Stat. § 163.3184(5); Fla. Stat. § 163.3213(1) | Hearing de novo | Any affected person who submitted comments during transmittal or adoption hearings and meets further requirements of F.S. § 163.3184(1)(a). Note lower bar for standing in initial administrative hearing than in subsequent judicial appeal. *See* Martin Cnty. Conservation Alliance v. Martin Cnty., 73 So. 3d 856 (Fla. 1st DCA 2011). | Whether plan is in compliance with certain provisions of state law as described in Fla. Stat. § 163.3184(1)(b). |
| Writ of certiorari | Quasi-judicial decision challenged on grounds other than consistency with comprehensive plan (e.g. violation of common law rules on variances or spot zoning). | Fla. R. App. P. 9.100(c)(2) | Record below | Plaintiff must allege "special damages peculiar to himself differing in kind as distinguished from damages differing in degree suffered by the community as a whole." Renard v. Dade Cnty., 261 So. 2d 831, 835 (Fla. 1972). | Whether (1) procedural due process was accorded, (2) essential requirements of law have been observed, and (3) findings are supported by competent substantial evidence. City of Deerfield Beach v. Vaillant, 419 So. 2d 624 (Fla. 1982). |
| Consistency challenge | Quasi-judicial decision alleged to be not consistent with comprehensive plan. | Fla. Stat. § 163.3215(3) | Hearing de novo | Aggrieved or adversely affected parties as defined in Fla. Stat. § 163.3215(2). However, standing is granted more broadly due to remedial nature of legislation. *See* Save the Homosassa River All., Inc. v. Citrus Cnty., Fla., 2 So. 3d 329 (Fla. 5th DCA, 2008). | Whether a development order is "consistent" with comprehensive plan, meaning: "the land uses, densities or intensities, and other aspects of development permitted ... are compatible with and further the objectives, policies, land uses, and densities or intensities in the comprehensive plan and [the development order] meets all other criteria ... ." Fla. Stat. § 163.3194(3)(a). |
| Declaratory judgment | Legislative or administrative except those legislative decisions for which petition for hearing by DOAH is appropriate cause of action. | Fla. Stat. § 86.011 | Hearing de novo | Any person claiming to be interested. *See* Fla. Stat. § 86.021. However, plaintiff must plead "actual, present, adverse and antagonistic interest in the subject matter." Coal. for Adequacy & Fairness in Sch. Funding, Inc. v. Chiles, 680 So. 2d 400, 404 (Fla. 1996). | Determination of rights under local government ordinance. See Fla. Stat. §§ 86.011 and 86.021. |

> permit or development order. Both parties may agree to a reasonable request for an extension of time, particularly in the event of a force majeure or other extraordinary circumstance. An approval, approval with conditions, or denial of the application for a development permit or development order must include written findings supporting the county's decision.[22]

While section 125.022 applies only to counties, Florida Statutes provide a more or less identical provision at section 166.033 that is applicable to municipalities.[23]

As used in this provision, a development permit is a "zoning permit, subdivision approval, rezoning, certification, special exception, variance, or any other official action of local government having the effect of permitting the development of land."[24] A development order is "any order granting, denying, or granting with conditions an application for a development permit."[25]

Note that the definitions of development permit and development order do not generally include legislative land use decisions and specifically do not include comprehensive plan amendments. Also, sections 125.022 and 166.033 do not apply to building permits. However, the Legislature has provided a similar standard that does require local governments to expeditiously process building permit applications.[26]

Florida statutes do not provide any consequences for local governments that fail to meet these prescribed deadlines. However, applicants could enforce either section 125.022 or 166.033 through a declaratory judgment action.

## Notes

1 Fla. Stat. §§ 163.3184(5)(a)–(e).
2 *Id.* § 163.3125(3).
3 *Id.* § 86.021.
4 *See* El Faison Dorado, Inc. v. Hillsborough Cnty., 483 So. 2d 518, 519 (Fla. 2d DCA 1986) (citing Askew v. City of Ocala, 348 So. 2d 308 (Fla. 1977)).
5 Pichette v. City of North Miami, 642 So. 2d 1165, 1166 (Fla 3d DCA 1994).
6 Fla. Stat. § 86.011.
7 *Id.* §§ 86.011(2), 86.061.
8 Coal. for Adequacy & Fairness in Sch. Funding, Inc. v. Chiles, 680 So. 2d 400, 404 (Fla. 1996) (citation omitted).
9 Clarke v. Morgan, 327 So. 2d 769, 773 (Fla. 1975) (quoting State *ex rel.* Taylor v. City of Jacksonville, 113 So. 2d 114, 115 (Fla. 1931)).
10 James E. Pate, *Mayor and Council Government*, in *Local Government and Administration* 181–82 (Am. Book Co. 1954).
11 *Id.* at 182–84.
12 *Id.*
13 James E. Pate, *Commission and Council–Manager Government*, in *Local Government and Administration* 206–8 (Am. Book Co. 1954).
14 *Id.* at 208–15.
15 *Id.* at 206–7.
16 *See* Fla Const. art. V, § 1 (declaring: "The judicial power shall be vested in a supreme court, district courts of appeal, circuit courts and county courts. No other courts may be established by the state, any political subdivision or any municipality"); *see also* Fla Const. art. V, §§ 4(a), 5(a), 6(a).
17 Florida counties are a part of Florida's state government and therefore act both as local governments and arms of the state. Counties have courts which function as a component of state government. However, in making land use decisions, Florida's counties are generally indistinguishable from municipalities.
18 4 So. 3d 1245 (Fla. 2d DCA 2009).
19 *See* Braden Woods Homeowners Ass'n, Inc. v. Mavard Trading, Ltd., 277 So. 3d 664, 672 (Fla. 2d DCA 2019) (commenting that if the action complained of "arises from an executive decision made by a County official without a hearing, there [is] no quasi-judicial action to review ... and certiorari review [is] not appropriate") (citation omitted).

20 Evergreen Tree Treasurers of Charlotte Cnty., Inc. v. Charlotte Cnty. Bd. of Cnty. Comm'rs, 810 So. 2d 526, 531–32 (Fla. 2d DCA 2002) (citations omitted).
21 *See id.* n.6.
22 Fla. Stat. § 125.022(1) (emphasis added).
23 *See id.* § 166.033(1).
24 *See id.* §§ 163.3164(16), 125.022(4).
25 *Id.* § 163.3164(15).
26 *See id.* § 553.792(1).

# Part III

# Property rights

# 14 Eminent domain

To this point, this text has identified the source of local government authority to regulate the use of land and has explained processes by which local governments wield that authority. This part shifts the focus to a force that limits local government authority to regulate the use of land: property rights protections in the U.S. Constitution and in Florida law.

The Takings Clause is a part of the Fifth Amendment to the U.S. Constitution. It states "nor shall private property be taken for public use, without just compensation."[1] This language is the foundation of three distinct concepts in land use law. This chapter includes two of these concepts: eminent domain and regulatory takings. A later chapter presents exactions, the third concept.

Eminent domain is the right of the state or federal government to purchase private property against an owner's will.[2] The Takings Clause places two limitations on its use: government may only take private property for public use and must pay just compensation.[3] The following case, *Kelo v. City of New London*, discusses what governmental purposes constitute public use.

### United States Supreme Court

### *Kelo v. City of New London*[4]

### 2005

Justice STEVENS delivered the opinion of the Court.

In 2000, the city of New London approved a development plan that, in the words of the Supreme Court of Connecticut, was "projected to create in excess of 1,000 jobs, to increase tax and other revenues, and to revitalize an economically distressed city, including its downtown and waterfront areas." 843 A.2d 500, 507 (2004). In assembling the land needed for this project, the city's development agent has purchased property from willing sellers and proposes to use the power of eminent domain to acquire the remainder of the property from unwilling owners in exchange for just compensation. The question presented is whether the city's proposed disposition of this property qualifies as a "public use" within the meaning of the Takings Clause of the Fifth Amendment to the Constitution.[1]

#### *I*

The city of New London (hereinafter City) sits at the junction of the Thames River and the Long Island Sound in southeastern Connecticut Decades of economic decline led a state agency in 1990 to designate the City a "distressed municipality." In 1996, the Federal

1 "[N]or shall private property be taken for public use, without just compensation." U.S. Const., Amdt. 5. That Clause is made applicable to the States by the Fourteenth Amendment. *See* Chicago, B. & Q.R. Co. v. Chicago, 166 U.S. 226 (1897).

Government closed the Naval Undersea Warfare Center, which had been located in the Fort Trumbull area of the City and had employed over 1,500 people. In 1998, the City's unemployment rate was nearly double that of the State, and its population of just under 24,000 residents was at its lowest since 1920.

These conditions prompted state and local officials to target New London, and particularly its Fort Trumbull area, for economic revitalization. To this end, respondent New London Development Corporation (NLDC), a private nonprofit entity established some years earlier to assist the City in planning economic development, was reactivated. In January 1998, the State authorized a $5.35 million bond issue to support the NLDC's planning activities and a $10 million bond issue toward the creation of a Fort Trumbull State Park. In February, the pharmaceutical company Pfizer Inc. announced that it would build a $300 million research facility on a site immediately adjacent to Fort Trumbull; local planners hoped that Pfizer would draw new business to the area, thereby serving as a catalyst to the area's rejuvenation. After receiving initial approval from the city council, the NLDC continued its planning activities and held a series of neighborhood meetings to educate the public about the process. In May, the city council authorized the NLDC to formally submit its plans to the relevant state agencies for review. Upon obtaining state-level approval, the NLDC finalized an integrated development plan focused on 90 acres of the Fort Trumbull area.

The Fort Trumbull area is situated on a peninsula that juts into the Thames River. The area comprises approximately 115 privately owned properties, as well as the 32 acres of land formerly occupied by the naval facility (Trumbull State Park now occupies 18 of those 32 acres). The development plan encompasses seven parcels. Parcel 1 is designated for a waterfront conference hotel at the center of a "small urban village" that will include restaurants and shopping. This parcel will also have marinas for both recreational and commercial uses. A pedestrian "riverwalk" will originate here and continue down the coast, connecting the waterfront areas of the development. Parcel 2 will be the site of approximately 80 new residences organized into an urban neighborhood and linked by public walkway to the remainder of the development, including the state park. This parcel also includes space reserved for a new U.S. Coast Guard Museum. Parcel 3, which is located immediately north of the Pfizer facility, will contain at least 90,000 square feet of research and development office space. Parcel 4A is a 2.4-acre site that will be used either to support the adjacent state park, by providing parking or retail services for visitors, or to support the nearby marina. Parcel 4B will include a renovated marina, as well as the final stretch of the riverwalk. Parcels 5, 6, and 7 will provide land for office and retail space, parking, and water-dependent commercial uses. App. 109–113.

The NLDC intended the development plan to capitalize on the arrival of the Pfizer facility and the new commerce it was expected to attract. In addition to creating jobs, generating tax revenue, and helping to "build momentum for the revitalization of downtown New London," *id*., at 92, the plan was also designed to make the City more attractive and to create leisure and recreational opportunities on the waterfront and in the park.

The city council approved the plan in January 2000, and designated the NLDC as its development agent in charge of implementation. *See* Conn. Gen. Stat. § 8–188 (2005). The city council also authorized the NLDC to purchase property or to acquire property by exercising eminent domain in the City's name. § 8–193. The NLDC successfully negotiated the purchase of most of the real estate in the 90-acre area, but its negotiations with petitioners failed. As a consequence, in November 2000, the NLDC initiated the condemnation proceedings that gave rise to this case.

## *II*

Petitioner Susette Kelo has lived in the Fort Trumbull area since 1997. She has made extensive improvements to her house, which she prizes for its water view. Petitioner Wilhelmina

Dery was born in her Fort Trumbull house in 1918 and has lived there her entire life. Her husband Charles (also a petitioner) has lived in the house since they married some 60 years ago. In all, the nine petitioners own 15 properties in Fort Trumbull—4 in parcel 3 of the development plan and 11 in parcel 4A. Ten of the parcels are occupied by the owner or a family member; the other five are held as investment properties. There is no allegation that any of these properties is blighted or otherwise in poor condition; rather, they were condemned only because they happen to be located in the development area.

In December 2000, petitioners brought this action in the New London Superior Court. They claimed, among other things, that the taking of their properties would violate the "public use" restriction in the Fifth Amendment. After a seven-day bench trial, the Superior Court granted a permanent restraining order prohibiting the taking of the properties located in parcel 4A (park or marina support). It, however, denied petitioners relief as to the properties located in parcel 3 (office space). App. to Pet. for Cert. 343–350.4.

After the Superior Court ruled, both sides took appeals to the Supreme Court of Connecticut. That court held, over a dissent, that all of the City's proposed takings were valid … . [R]elying on cases such as *Hawaii Housing Authority v. Midkiff*, 467 U.S. 229 (1984), and *Berman v. Parker*, 348 U.S. 26 (1954), the court held that such economic development qualified as a valid public use under both the Federal and State Constitutions. 843 A.2d at 527 … .

We granted certiorari to determine whether a city's decision to take property for the purpose of economic development satisfies the "public use" requirement of the Fifth Amendment. 542 U.S. 965 (2004).

### *III*

Two polar propositions are perfectly clear. On the one hand, it has long been accepted that the sovereign may not take the property of A for the sole purpose of transferring it to another private party B, even though A is paid just compensation. On the other hand, it is equally clear that a State may transfer property from one private party to another if future "use by the public" is the purpose of the taking; the condemnation of land for a railroad with common-carrier duties is a familiar example. Neither of these propositions, however, determines the disposition of this case.

As for the first proposition, the City would no doubt be forbidden from taking petitioners' land for the purpose of conferring a private benefit on a particular private party. *See Midkiff*, 467 U.S. at 245 ("A purely private taking could not withstand the scrutiny of the public use requirement; it would serve no legitimate purpose of government and would thus be void"); *Mo. Pac. Ry. Co. v. Nebraska*, 164 U.S. 403 (1896). Nor would the City be allowed to take property under the mere pretext of a public purpose, when its actual purpose was to bestow a private benefit. The takings before us, however, would be executed pursuant to a "carefully considered" development plan. 843 A.2d at 536. The trial judge and all the members of the Supreme Court of Connecticut agreed that there was no evidence of an illegitimate purpose in this case. Therefore, as was true of the statute challenged in *Midkiff*, 467 U.S. at 245, the City's development plan was not adopted "to benefit a particular class of identifiable individuals."

On the other hand, this is not a case in which the City is planning to open the condemned land—at least not in its entirety—to use by the general public. Nor will the private lessees of the land in any sense be required to operate like common carriers, making their services available to all comers. But although such a projected use would be sufficient to satisfy the public use requirement, this "Court long ago rejected any literal requirement that condemned property be put into use for the general public." *Id.* at 244. Indeed, while many state courts in the mid-nineteenth century endorsed "use by the public" as the proper definition of public use, that narrow view steadily eroded over time. Not only was the "use by the public" test difficult to administer (e.g., what proportion of the public need have access to the property? at what price?), but it proved to be impractical given the diverse and always evolving needs of society. Accordingly, when this Court began applying the Fifth Amendment to the States at the close of the nineteenth century, it embraced the broader and more natural interpretation of public use as "public purpose." *See, e.g., Fallbrook Irrigation Dist. v. Bradley*, 164 U.S. 112, 158–64 (1896). Thus, in a case upholding a mining company's use of an aerial bucket line to transport ore over property it did not own, Justice Holmes' opinion for the Court stressed "the inadequacy of use by the general public as a universal test." *Strickley v. Highland Boy Gold Mining Co.*, 200 U.S. 527, 531 (1906). We have repeatedly and consistently rejected that narrow test ever since.

The disposition of this case therefore turns on the question whether the City's development plan serves a "public purpose." Without exception, our cases have defined that concept broadly, reflecting our longstanding policy of deference to legislative judgments in this field.

In *Berman v. Parker*, 348 U.S. 26 (1954), this Court upheld a redevelopment plan targeting a blighted area of Washington, D. C., in which most of the housing for the area's 5,000 inhabitants was beyond repair. Under the plan, the area would be condemned and part of it utilized for the construction of streets, schools, and other public facilities. The remainder of the land would be leased or sold to private parties for the purpose of redevelopment, including the construction of low-cost housing.

The owner of a department store located in the area challenged the condemnation, pointing out that his store was not itself blighted and arguing that the creation of a "better balanced, more attractive community" was not a valid public use. *Id.* at 31. Writing for a unanimous Court, Justice Douglas refused to evaluate this claim in isolation, deferring instead to the legislative and agency judgment that the area "must be planned as a whole" for the plan to be successful. *Id.* at 34. The Court explained that "community redevelopment programs need not, by force of the Constitution, be on a piecemeal basis—lot by lot, building by building." *Id.* at 35. The public use underlying the taking was unequivocally affirmed:

> We do not sit to determine whether a particular housing project is or is not desirable. The concept of the public welfare is broad and inclusive ... . The values it represents are spiritual as well as physical, aesthetic as well as monetary. It is within the power of the legislature to determine that the community should be beautiful as well as healthy, spacious as well as clean, well-balanced as well as carefully patrolled. In the present case, the Congress and its authorized agencies have made determinations that take into account a wide variety of values. It is not for us to reappraise them. If those who govern the District of Columbia decide that the Nation's Capital should be beautiful as well as sanitary, there is nothing in the Fifth Amendment that stands in the way. *Id.*, at 33.

In *Hawaii Hous. Auth. v. Midkiff*, 467 U.S. 229 (1984), the Court considered a Hawaii statute whereby fee title was taken from lessors and transferred to lessees (for just compensation) in order to reduce the concentration of land ownership. We unanimously upheld the statute and rejected the Ninth Circuit's view that it was "a naked attempt on the part of the state of Hawaii to take the property of A and transfer it to B solely for B's private use and benefit." *Id.* at 235 (internal quotation marks omitted). Reaffirming *Berman*'s deferential approach to legislative judgments in this field, we concluded that the State's purpose of eliminating the "social and economic evils of a land oligopoly" qualified as a valid public use. 467 U.S. at 241–42. Our opinion also rejected the contention that the mere fact that the State immediately transferred the properties to private individuals upon condemnation somehow diminished the public character of the taking. "[I]t is only the taking's purpose, and not its mechanics," we explained, that matters in determining public use. *Id.* at 244 ... .

Viewed as a whole, our jurisprudence has recognized that the needs of society have varied between different parts of the Nation, just as they have evolved over time in response to changed circumstances. Our earliest cases in particular embodied a strong theme of federalism, emphasizing the "great respect" that we owe to state legislatures and state courts in discerning local public needs. *See Hairston v. Danville & W. Ry. Co.*, 208 U.S. 598, 606–07 (1908) (noting that these needs were likely to vary depending on a State's "resources, the capacity of the soil, the relative importance of industries to the general public welfare, and the long-established methods and habits of the people"). For more than a century, our public use jurisprudence has wisely eschewed rigid formulas and intrusive scrutiny in favor of affording legislatures broad latitude in determining what public needs justify the use of the takings power.

## *IV*

Those who govern the City were not confronted with the need to remove blight in the Fort Trumbull area, but their determination that the area was sufficiently distressed to justify a program of economic rejuvenation is entitled to our deference. The City has carefully formulated an economic development plan that it believes will provide appreciable benefits to the community, including—but by no means limited to—new jobs and increased tax revenue. As with other exercises in urban planning and development, the City is endeavoring to coordinate a variety of commercial, residential, and recreational uses of land, with the hope that they will form a whole greater than the sum of its parts. To effectuate this plan, the City has invoked a state statute that specifically authorizes the use of eminent domain to promote economic development. Given the comprehensive character of the plan, the thorough deliberation that preceded its adoption, and the limited scope of our review, it is appropriate for us, as it was in *Berman*, to resolve the challenges of the individual owners, not on a piecemeal basis, but rather in light of the entire plan. Because that plan unquestionably serves a public purpose, the takings challenged here satisfy the public use requirement of the Fifth Amendment.

To avoid this result, petitioners urge us to adopt a new bright-line rule that economic development does not qualify as a public use. Putting aside the unpersuasive suggestion that the City's plan will provide only purely economic benefits, neither precedent nor logic supports petitioners' proposal. Promoting economic development is a traditional and long-accepted function of government. There is, moreover, no principled way of distinguishing economic development from the other public purposes that we have recognized. In our cases upholding takings that facilitated agriculture and mining, for example, we emphasized the importance of those industries to the welfare of the States in question, *see, e.g., Strickley*, 200 U.S. 527; in *Berman*, we endorsed the purpose of transforming a blighted area into a "well-balanced" community through redevelopment, 348 U.S. at 33 [and] in *Midkiff*, we upheld the interest in breaking up a land oligopoly that "created artificial deterrents to the normal functioning of the State's residential land market," 467 U.S. at 242 ... . It would be incongruous to hold that the City's interest in the economic benefits to be derived from the development of the Fort Trumbull area has less of a public character than any of those other interests. Clearly, there is no basis for exempting economic development from our traditionally broad understanding of public purpose.

Petitioners contend that using eminent domain for economic development impermissibly blurs the boundary between public and private takings. Again, our cases foreclose this objection. Quite simply, the government's pursuit of a public purpose will often benefit individual private parties. For example, in *Midkiff*, the forced transfer of property conferred a direct and significant benefit on those lessees who were previously unable to purchase their homes ... . The owner of the department store in *Berman* objected to "taking from one businessman for the benefit of another businessman," 348 U.S. at 33, referring to the fact that under the redevelopment plan land would be leased or sold to private developers for redevelopment. Our rejection of that contention has particular relevance to the instant case: "The public end may be as well or better served through an agency of private enterprise than through a department of government—or so the Congress might conclude. We cannot say that public ownership is the sole method of promoting the public purposes of community redevelopment projects." *Id.* at 33–34[16]. It is further argued that without a bright-line rule nothing would stop a city from transferring citizen A's property to citizen B for the sole reason that citizen B will put the property to a more productive use and thus pay more taxes. Such a one-to-one transfer of property, executed outside the confines of an integrated development plan, is not presented in this case. While such an unusual exercise of government power would certainly raise a suspicion that a private purpose was afoot, the hypothetical cases posited by petitioners can be confronted if and when they arise. They do not warrant the crafting of an artificial restriction on the concept of public use.[19]

Alternatively, petitioners maintain that for takings of this kind we should require a "reasonable certainty" that the expected public benefits will actually accrue. Such a rule, however, would represent an even greater departure from our precedent. "When the legislature's purpose is legitimate and its means are not irrational, our cases make clear that empirical debates over the wisdom of takings—no less than debates over the wisdom of other kinds of socioeconomic legislation—are not to be carried out in the federal

16 Nor do our cases support Justice O'CONNOR's novel theory that the government may only take property and transfer it to private parties when the initial taking eliminates some "harmful property use." *Post*, at 2675 (dissenting opinion). There was nothing "harmful" about the nonblighted department store at issue in *Berman*, 348 U.S. 26; *see also* n. 13, *supra*; nothing "harmful" about the lands at issue in the mining and agriculture cases, *see, e.g., Strickley*, 200 U.S. 527; *see also* nn. 9, 11, *supra*; ... . In each case, the public purpose we upheld depended on a private party's future use of the concededly nonharmful property that was taken. By focusing on a property's future use, as opposed to its past use, our cases are faithful to the text of the Takings Clause. *See* U.S. Const., Amdt. 5 ("[N]or shall private property be taken for public use, without just compensation"). Justice O'CONNOR's intimation that a "public purpose" may not be achieved by the action of private parties, *see post*, at 2675, confuses the purpose of a taking with its mechanics, a mistake we warned of in *Midkiff*, 467 U.S., at 244. *See also Berman*, 348 U.S., at 33–34 ("The public end may be as well or better served through an agency of private enterprise than through a department of government").

19 A parade of horribles is especially unpersuasive in this context, since the Takings Clause largely "operates as a conditional limitation, permitting the government to do what it wants so long as it pays the charge." Eastern Enterprises v. Apfel, 524 U.S. 498, 545 (1998) (KENNEDY, J., concurring in judgment and dissenting in part). Speaking of the takings power, Justice Iredell observed that "[i]t is not sufficient to urge, that the power may be abused, for, such is the nature of all power,—such is the tendency of every human institution: and, it might as fairly be said, that the power of taxation, which is only circumscribed by the discretion of the Body, in which it is vested, ought not to be granted, because the Legislature, disregarding its true objects, might, for visionary and useless projects, impose a tax to the amount of

courts." *Midkiff*, 467 U.S. at 242–43.[20] ... The disadvantages of a heightened form of review are especially pronounced in this type of case. Orderly implementation of a comprehensive redevelopment plan obviously requires that the legal rights of all interested parties be established before new construction can be commenced. A constitutional rule that required postponement of the judicial approval of every condemnation until the likelihood of success of the plan had been assured would unquestionably impose a significant impediment to the successful consummation of many such plans.

Just as we decline to second-guess the City's considered judgments about the efficacy of its development plan, we also decline to second-guess the City's determinations as to what lands it needs to acquire in order to effectuate the project: "It is not for the courts to oversee the choice of the boundary line nor to sit in review on the size of a particular project area. Once the question of the public purpose has been decided, the amount and character of land to be taken for the project and the need for a particular tract to complete the integrated plan rests in the discretion of the legislative branch." *Berman*, 348 U.S. at 35–36.

In affirming the City's authority to take petitioners' properties, we do not minimize the hardship that condemnations may entail, notwithstanding the payment of just compensation. We emphasize that nothing in our opinion precludes any State from placing further restrictions on its exercise of the takings power. Indeed, many States already impose "public use" requirements that are stricter than the federal baseline. Some of these requirements have been established as a matter of state constitutional law, while others are expressed in state eminent domain statutes that carefully limit the grounds upon which takings may be exercised. As the submissions of the parties and their amici make clear, the necessity and wisdom of using eminent domain to promote economic development are certainly matters of legitimate public debate. This Court's authority, however, extends only to determining whether the City's proposed condemnations are for a "public use" within the meaning of the Fifth Amendment to the Federal Constitution. Because over a century of our case law interpreting that provision dictates an affirmative answer to that question, we may not grant petitioners the relief that they seek.

The judgment of the Supreme Court of Connecticut is affirmed.

It is so ordered.

Justice KENNEDY, concurring ...

I join in the opinion of the Court ...

Justice O'CONNOR, with whom THE CHIEF JUSTICE, Justice SCALIA, and Justice THOMAS join, dissenting.

Today the Court abandons this long-held ... limitation on government power [that a law that takes property from A and gives it to B is not a rightful exercise of legislative authority]. Under the banner of economic development, all private property is now vulnerable to

nineteen shillings in the pound. We must be content to limit power where we can, and where we cannot, consistently with its use, we must be content to repose a salutory confidence." *Calder*, 3 Dall., at 400 (opinion concurring in result)

20 *See also Boston & Maine Corp.*, 503 U.S. at 422–23 ("[W]e need not make a specific factual determination whether the condemnation will accomplish its objectives"); *Monsanto*, 467 U.S. at 1015 n. 18: ("... economic arguments are better directed to Congress. The proper inquiry before this Court is not whether the provisions in fact will accomplish their stated objectives. Our review is limited to determining that the purpose is legitimate and that Congress rationally could have believed that the provisions would promote that objective.")

being taken and transferred to another private owner, so long as it might be upgraded—i.e., given to an owner who will use it in a way that the legislature deems more beneficial to the public—in the process. To reason, as the Court does, that the incidental public benefits resulting from the subsequent ordinary use of private property render economic development takings "for public use" is to wash out any distinction between private and public use of property—and thereby effectively to delete the words "for public use" from the Takings Clause of the Fifth Amendment. Accordingly I respectfully dissent ... [and ask] Where is the line between "public" and "private" property use? We give considerable deference to legislatures' determinations about what governmental activities will advantage the public. But were the political branches the sole arbiters of the public–private distinction, the Public Use Clause would amount to little more than hortatory fluff. An external, judicial check on how the public use requirement is interpreted, however limited, is necessary if this constraint on government power is to retain any meaning ... .

Our cases have generally identified three categories of takings that comply with the public use requirement, though it is in the nature of things that the boundaries between these categories are not always firm. Two are relatively straightforward and uncontroversial. First, the sovereign may transfer private property to public ownership—such as for a road, a hospital, or a military base. *See, e.g., Old Dominion Land Co. v. United States*, 269 U.S. 55 (1925); *Rindge Co. v. Cty. of L.A.*, 262 U.S. 700 (1923). Second, the sovereign may transfer private property to private parties, often common carriers, who make the property available for the public's use—such as with a railroad, a public utility, or a stadium. *See, e.g., Nat'l R.R. Passenger Corp. v. Bos. & Me. Corp.*, 503 U.S. 407 (1992); *Mt. Vernon–Woodberry Cotton Duck Co. v. Ala. Interstate Power Co.*, 240 U.S. 30 (1916). But "public ownership" and "use-by-the-public" are sometimes too constricting and impractical ways to define the scope of the Public Use Clause. Thus we have allowed that, in certain circumstances and to meet certain exigencies, takings that serve a public purpose also satisfy the Constitution even if the property is destined for subsequent private use. *See, e.g., Berman v. Parker*, 348 U.S. 26 (1954); *Haw. Hous. Auth. v. Midkiff*, 467 U.S. 229 (1984).

This case returns us for the first time in over 20 years to the hard question of when a purportedly "public purpose" taking meets the public use requirement. It presents an issue of first impression: Are economic development takings constitutional? I would hold that they are not. We are guided by two precedents about the taking of real property by eminent domain. In *Berman*, we upheld takings within a blighted neighborhood of Washington, D.C. The neighborhood had so deteriorated that, for example, 64.3% of its dwellings were beyond repair. 348 U.S. at 30. It had become burdened with "overcrowding of dwellings," "lack of adequate streets and alleys," and "lack of light and air." *Id.* at 34. Congress had determined that the neighborhood had become "injurious to the public health, safety, morals, and welfare" and that it was necessary to "eliminat[e] all such injurious conditions by employing all means necessary and appropriate for the purpose," including eminent domain. *Id.* at 28 (internal quotation marks omitted). Mr. Berman's department store was not itself blighted. Having approved of Congress' decision to eliminate the harm to the public emanating from the blighted neighborhood, however, we did not second-guess its decision to treat the neighborhood as a whole rather than lot-by-lot. *Id.* at 34–35; *see also Midkiff*, 467 U.S. at 244 ("[I]t is only the taking's purpose, and not its mechanics, that must pass scrutiny").

In *Midkiff*, we upheld a land condemnation scheme in Hawaii whereby title in real property was taken from lessors and transferred to lessees. At that time, the State and Federal Governments owned nearly 49% of the State's land, and another 47% was in the hands of only 72 private landowners. Concentration of land ownership was so dramatic that on the State's most urbanized island, Oahu, 22 landowners owned 72.5% of the fee simple titles. *Id.* at 232. The Hawaii Legislature had concluded that the oligopoly in land ownership was "skewing the

State's residential fee simple market, inflating land prices, and injuring the public tranquility and welfare," and therefore enacted a condemnation scheme for redistributing title. *Ibid.*

In those decisions, we emphasized the importance of deferring to legislative judgments about public purpose. Because courts are ill equipped to evaluate the efficacy of proposed legislative initiatives, we rejected as unworkable the idea of courts' "deciding on what is and is not a governmental function and ... invalidating legislation on the basis of their view on that question at the moment of decision, a practice which has proved impracticable in other fields." *Id.* at 240–41 (quoting *United States ex rel. TVA v. Welch*, 327 U.S. 546, 552 (1946)); *see Berman, supra*, at 32 ("[T]he legislature, not the judiciary, is the main guardian of the public needs to be served by social legislation"); *see also Lingle v. Chevron U.S.A. Inc.*, 544 U.S. 528 (2005). Likewise, we recognized our inability to evaluate whether, in a given case, eminent domain is a necessary means by which to pursue the legislature's ends. *Midkiff, supra*, at 242; *Berman, supra*, at 33.

Yet for all the emphasis on deference, *Berman* and *Midkiff* hewed to a bedrock principle without which our public use jurisprudence would collapse: "A purely private taking could not withstand the scrutiny of the public use requirement; it would serve no legitimate purpose of government and would thus be void." *Midkiff*, 467 U.S. at 245; *id.* at 241 ("[T]he Court's cases have repeatedly stated that 'one person's property may not be taken for the benefit of another private person without a justifying public purpose, even though compensation be paid'" (quoting *Thompson v. Consol. Gas Util. Corp.*, 300 U.S. 55, 80 (1937))); *see also Mo. Pac. Ry. Co. v. Nebraska*, 164 U.S. 403, 417 (1896). To protect that principle, those decisions reserved "a role for courts to play in reviewing a legislature's judgment of what constitutes a public use ... [though] the Court in *Berman* made clear that it is 'an extremely narrow' one." *Midkiff, supra*, at 240 (quoting *Berman, supra*, at 32).

The Court's holdings in *Berman* and *Midkiff* were true to the principle underlying the Public Use Clause. In both those cases, the extraordinary, precondemnation use of the targeted property inflicted affirmative harm on society—in *Berman* through blight resulting from extreme poverty and in *Midkiff* through oligopoly resulting from extreme wealth. And in both cases, the relevant legislative body had found that eliminating the existing property use was necessary to remedy the harm. *Berman, supra*, at 28–29; *Midkiff, supra*, at 232. Thus a public purpose was realized when the harmful use was eliminated. Because each taking directly achieved a public benefit, it did not matter that the property was turned over to private use. Here, in contrast, New London does not claim that Susette Kelo's and Wilhelmina Dery's well-maintained homes are the source of any social harm. Indeed, it could not so claim without adopting the absurd argument that any single-family home that might be razed to make way for an apartment building, or any church that might be replaced with a retail store, or any small business that might be more lucrative if it were instead part of a national franchise, is inherently harmful to society and thus within the government's power to condemn ... .

I would hold that the takings in both Parcel 3 and Parcel 4A are unconstitutional, reverse the judgment of the Supreme Court of Connecticut, and remand for further proceedings.

Justice THOMAS, dissenting.

Though one component of the protection provided by the Takings Clause is that the government can take private property only if it provides "just compensation" for the taking, the Takings Clause also prohibits the government from taking property except "for public use."... The Public Use Clause, like the Just Compensation Clause, is therefore an express limit on the government's power of eminent domain. The most natural reading of the Clause is that it allows the government to take property only if the government owns, or the public has a legal right to use, the property, as opposed to taking it for any public purpose or necessity whatsoever ... . Our current Public Use Clause jurisprudence, as the Court notes, has rejected this natural reading of the Clause ... . I would revisit our Public Use Clause cases and consider returning to the original meaning of the Public Use Clause: that the government may take property only if it actually uses or gives the public a legal right to use the property ... . The consequences of today's decision are not difficult to predict, and promise to be harmful. So-called "urban renewal" programs provide some compensation for the properties they take, but no compensation is possible for the subjective value of these lands to the individuals displaced and the indignity inflicted by uprooting them from their homes. Allowing the government to take property solely for public purposes is bad enough, but extending the concept of public purpose to encompass any economically beneficial goal guarantees that these losses will fall disproportionately on poor communities. Those communities are not only systematically less likely to put their lands to the highest and best social use, but are also the least politically powerful. If ever there were justification for intrusive judicial review of constitutional provisions that protect "discrete and insular minorities," *United States v. Carolene Prods. Co.*, 304 U.S. 144, 152, n. 4 (1938), surely that principle would apply with great force to the powerless groups and individuals the Public Use Clause protects. The deferential standard this Court has adopted for the Public Use Clause is therefore deeply perverse. It encourages "those citizens with disproportionate influence and power in the political process, including large corporations and development firms," to victimize the weak. *Ante*, at 2677 (O'CONNOR, J., dissenting) ... . When faced with a clash of constitutional principle and a line of unreasoned cases wholly divorced from the text, history, and structure of our founding document, we should not hesitate to resolve the tension in favor of the Constitution's original meaning. For the reasons I have given ... I would reverse the judgment of the Connecticut Supreme Court.

### *Discussion*

In addition to the restrictions on eminent domain in the U.S. Constitution, Florida's state constitution includes the following limitation on the practice: "No private property shall be taken except for a public purpose and with full compensation therefor paid to each owner or secured by deposit in the registry of the court and available to the owner."[5]

In addition to that general limit on eminent domain, the Florida Constitution includes the following protection against transferring property acquired by eminent domain to private parties. Florida voters added the following language to the state constitution in 2006:

> Private property taken by eminent domain pursuant to a petition to initiate condemnation proceedings filed on or after January 2, 2007, may not be conveyed to a natural person or private entity except as provided by general law passed by a three-fifths vote of the membership of each house of the Legislature.[6]

Popular response to the holding in *Kelo* certainly motivated the addition of this limitation to the Florida Constitution.

Also, shortly after the Supreme Court decided *Kelo*, the Florida Legislature made eminent domain unavailable to address slum and blight:

> [T]he prevention or elimination of a slum area or blighted area as defined in this part and the preservation or enhancement of the tax base are not public uses or purposes for which private property may be taken by eminent domain and do not satisfy the public purpose requirement of s. 6(a), Art. X of the State Constitution.[7]

Florida was not alone in responding to *Kelo* by restricting availability of eminent domain through state law. Many other states took similar steps. Because of these responses, the *Kelo* decision had the practical effect of narrowing the usefulness of eminent domain, notwithstanding its holding.

## Box 14.1 Practice problem: Green Electric Co.

Green Electric Company is the private electric service provider in Collegeborough. In order to sell electricity to all of the residents of Collegeborough, Green Electric Company has built and maintains an extensive network of wires throughout the town. This network of wires connects every home and business in Collegeborough and occupies land on which Green Electric Company owns the right to maintain utility wires. In some instances, that is because Green Electric Company owns the land outright. In some instances, that is because Green Electric Company owns an easement giving it the right to have and maintain utility wires.

Data Deluge, Inc. is a private company in the business of selling high-speed internet services. Like selling electricity, selling high-speed internet services requires a network of wires. In the case of high-speed internet, those wires are fiber optic cables that transmit information using light. Because selling high-speed internet services is a relatively new business, Data Deluge, Inc.'s network of wires does not reach every home and business in Collegeborough.

Data Deluge, Inc. would like to grow quickly. However, the corporation knows that acquiring the land and easements it needs to connect all of the homes and businesses in Collegeborough would take decades. Data Deluge, Inc. approaches the city of Collegeborough with an offer to expand its network of fiber optic cables to every home and business in the city if Collegeborough gives Data Deluge, Inc. access to Green Electric Company's land and easements.

The city of Collegeborough hires an appraiser to determine the fair value of the right to use Green Electric Company's land and easements. Then, the city collects that amount of money from Data Deluge, Inc., gives it to Green Electric Company, and declares that Data Deluge, Inc. now owns the right to use Green Electric Company's network of land and easements for the installation of a network of fiber optic cables. The city conditions this whole arrangement on a promise Data Deluge, Inc. makes to connect all of the houses and businesses in Collegeborough with fiber optic cables and to grant any person who wants internet services access to these fiber optic cables to transmit information, so long as that person pays Data Deluge, Inc. a monthly fee for the service.

Green Electric Company doesn't like this arrangement because the electric service provider wanted to get into the business of selling high-speed internet services itself. To block this plan, and to keep Data Deluge, Inc.'s wires off of the land and easements it assembled, Green Electric Company sues Collegeborough, alleging that the plan is an exercise of eminent domain that violates the Takings Clause of the U.S. Constitution.

Evaluate Green Electric Company's claim.

## Notes

1 U.S. Const. amend. V.
2 Tahoe-Sierra Pres. Council, Inc. v. Tahoe Reg'l Plan. Agency, 535 U.S. 302, 321–22, 325–26 nn.23–6 (2002).
3 Ark. Game & Fish Comm'n v. United States, 568 U.S. 23, 31 (2012).
4 545 U.S. 469 (2005).
5 Fla Const. art. X, § 6(a).
6 *Id.* art. X, § 6(c).
7 Fla. Stat. § 163.335(7).

# 15 Per se regulatory takings

Although regulatory takings and eminent domain are both products of the Takings Clause, the two concepts are entirely distinct. In a circumstance of eminent domain, government openly seeks to take ownership of property.

A regulatory taking, on the other hand, is a circumstance in which government regulates property to such an extent that just compensation is owed although the government does not purport to own the property. But the *practical effect* is as if an ownership interest has transferred to government.

Three tests for regulatory takings exist. The first two tests are bright-line instances of regulatory takings and are called per se regulatory takings. This text calls these tests "just compensation owed if right to exclude is lost" and "just compensation is owed if all value is lost." The third test is the ad hoc balancing test for regulatory takings.

Note that this text presents these three tests in the order described above. This presentation puts the most conceptually simple test first and the most conceptually complex test last. That order will allow you to progress through regulatory takings concepts in order from the easiest to the most difficult. As a result, however, the several regulatory takings cases included in this text are not printed in the order in which the U.S. Supreme Court decided them.

Presenting the cases out of chronological order creates pedagogical challenges. Namely, some discussion of regulatory takings in cases you read first will not make full sense until you read other cases that come later in the book. Nonetheless, I have intentionally selected this order of cases to provide the most direct explanation of a difficult topic.

## Property is a "bundle of sticks"

Understanding regulatory takings requires a general understanding of the legal conception of property. A person without legal training would probably describe property by its physical characteristics. A building might be a "shack," with a "tin roof" that is "rusted."

The legal conception of property is different. Instead of describing property by its physical characteristics, the law conceptualizes property as a collection of the rights people have in relation to that property. Legal commenters sometimes analogize this collection of the rights people have in property as a bundle of sticks. "A common idiom describes property as a 'bundle of sticks'—a collection of individual rights which, in certain combinations, constitute property."[1] That analogy is helpful because, like a bundle of sticks, the bundle of rights that constitutes property can be split and divided.[2]

So, a *legal* description of a building might include the rights to live in it, to raze it, or to dig a well and draw water from the ground beneath it. The owner of a house could live in it while transferring the right to draw water to someone else. Ownership is divided, even though the property has not changed physically.

The rights in this "bundle" are not all of equal value. Some rights are more valuable than others. This statement is not just true when referring to market value. Courts assign different rights in property varying legal significance as well. For example, courts recognize the right to use property to the exclusion of others as an exceptionally high value.

> "Property" is more than just the physical thing—the land, the bricks, the mortar—it is also the sum of all the rights and powers incident to ownership of the physical thing. It is the tangible and the intangible. Property is composed of constituent elements and of these elements the right to *use* the physical thing to the exclusion of others is the most essential and beneficial.[3]

In contrast, courts assign the right to use property in a way that constitutes a nuisance a relatively low value.

## Just compensation owed if right to exclude is lost

The first per se rule, presented here in *Loretto v. Teleprompter Manhattan CATV Corp.*, is that governmental rules which obligate a property owner to suffer a physical invasion of his or her property (i.e. the property owner loses the right to exclude others) are permissible only when the government pays just compensation.

## United States Supreme Court

### *Loretto v. Teleprompter Manhattan CATV Corp.*[4]

### 1982

Justice MARSHALL delivered the opinion of the Court.

This case presents the question whether a minor but permanent physical occupation of an owner's property authorized by government constitutes a "taking" of property for which just compensation is due under the Fifth and Fourteenth Amendments of the Constitution. New York law provides that a landlord must permit a cable television company to install its cable facilities upon his property. N.Y. Exec. Law § 828(1) (McKinney Supp. 1981–1982). In this case, the cable installation occupied portions of appellant's roof and the side of her building. The New York Court of Appeals ruled that this appropriation does not amount to a taking. 423 N.E.2d 320 (1981). Because we conclude that such a physical occupation of property is a taking, we reverse.

### *I*

Appellant Jean Loretto purchased a five-story apartment building located at 303 West 105th Street, New York City, in 1971. The previous owner had granted appellees Teleprompter Corp. and Teleprompter Manhattan CATV (collectively Teleprompter) permission to install a cable on the building and the exclusive privilege of furnishing cable television (CATV) services to the tenants. The New York Court of Appeals described the installation as follows:

> On June 1, 1970 TelePrompter installed a cable slightly less than one-half inch in diameter and of approximately 30 feet in length along the length of the building about 18 inches above the roof top, and directional taps, approximately 4 inches by 4 inches by 4 inches, on the front and rear of the roof. By June 8, 1970 the cable had been extended another 4 to 6 feet and cable had been run from the directional taps to the adjoining building at 305 West 105th Street. *Id.* at 135.

Initially, Teleprompter's roof cables did not service appellant's building ... . Crucial to such a [cable] network is the use of so-called "crossovers"—cable lines extending from one building to another in order to reach a new group of tenants. Two years after appellant purchased the building, Teleprompter connected a "noncrossover" line—i.e., one that provided CATV service to appellant's own tenants—by dropping a line to the first floor down the front of appellant's building.

Prior to 1973, Teleprompter routinely obtained authorization for its installations from property owners along the cable's route, compensating the owners at the standard rate of 5% of the gross revenues that Teleprompter realized from the particular property. To facilitate tenant access to CATV, the State of New York enacted § 828 of the Executive Law, effective January 1, 1973. Section 828 provides that a landlord may not "interfere with the installation of cable television facilities upon his property or premises," and may not demand payment from any tenant for permitting CATV, or demand payment from any CATV company "in excess of any amount which the [State Commission on Cable Television] shall, by regulation, determine to be reasonable."... Pursuant to § 828(1)(b), the State Commission has ruled that a one-time $1 payment is the normal fee to which a landlord is entitled. *In the Matter of Implementation of Section 828 of the Executive Law*, No. 90004, Statement of General Policy (New York State Commission on Cable Television, Jan. 15, 1976)... .

Appellant did not discover the existence of the cable until after she had purchased the building. She brought a class action against Teleprompter in 1976 on behalf of all owners of real property in the State on which Teleprompter has placed CATV components, alleging that Teleprompter's installation was a trespass and, insofar as it relied on § 828, a taking without just compensation. She requested damages and injunctive relief. Appellee City of New York, which has granted Teleprompter an exclusive franchise to provide CATV within certain areas of Manhattan, intervened. The [New York] Supreme Court ... granted summary judgment to Teleprompter and the city, upholding the constitutionality of § 828... .

[T]he Court of Appeals, over dissent, upheld the statute. 423 N.E.2d 320 (1981). [It ruled that the law served a legitimate police purpose. The court held that § 828 did not "work a taking of appellant's property" and rejected the argument that a physical occupation authorized by the government was necessarily a taking.]... .

In light of its holding, the Court of Appeals had no occasion to determine whether the $1 fee ordinarily awarded ... was adequate compensation for the taking... .

### *II*

The Court of Appeals determined that § 828 serves the legitimate public purpose of "rapid development of and maximum penetration by a means of communication which has important educational and community aspects," 423 N.E.2d, at 329, and thus is within the State's police power. We have no reason to question that determination. It is a separate question, however, whether an otherwise valid regulation so frustrates property rights that compensation must be paid. *See Penn Cent. Transp. Co. v. New York City*, 438 U.S. 104, 127–28 (1978); *Del., L. & W. R. Co. v. Morristown*, 276 U.S. 182, 193 (1928). We conclude that a permanent physical occupation authorized by government is a taking... . Our constitutional history confirms the rule, recent cases do not question it, and the purposes of the Takings Clause compel its retention... .

#### *A*

[W]e have long considered a physical intrusion by government to be a property restriction of an unusually serious character for purposes of the Takings Clause. Our cases further establish that when the physical intrusion reaches the extreme form of a permanent physical occupation, a taking has occurred. In such a case, "the character of the government action" not only is an important factor in resolving whether the action works a taking but also is determinative. When faced with a constitutional challenge to a permanent physical occupation of real property, this Court has invariably found a taking. As early as 1872, in *Pumpelly v. Green Bay Co.*, 13 Wall. (80 U.S.) 166, this Court held that the defendant's construction, pursuant to state authority, of a dam which permanently flooded plaintiff's property constituted a taking. A unanimous Court stated, without qualification, that

> where real estate is actually invaded by superinduced additions of water, earth, sand, or other material, or by having any artificial structure placed on it, so as to effectually destroy or impair its usefulness, it is a taking, within the meaning of the Constitution. *Id.* at 181 ...

More recent cases confirm the distinction between a permanent physical occupation, a physical invasion short of an occupation, and a regulation that merely restricts the use of property... . Although this Court's most recent cases have not addressed the precise issue before us, they have emphasized that physical *invasion* cases are special and have not repudiated the rule that any permanent physical *occupation* is a taking. The cases state or imply that a physical invasion is subject to a balancing process, but they do not suggest that a permanent physical occupation would ever be exempt from the Takings Clause... . [Thus, if] the invasion was temporary and limited in nature, and [if] the owner had not exhibited an interest in excluding all persons from his property, "the fact that [the individuals] may have 'physically invaded' [the owners'] property cannot be viewed as determinative." ... [emphases in the original]

In short, when the "character of the governmental action," *Penn Cent.*, 438 U.S. at 124, is a permanent physical occupation of property, our cases uniformly have found a taking to the extent of the occupation, without regard to whether the action achieves an important public benefit or has only minimal economic impact on the owner.

*B*

The historical rule that a permanent physical occupation of another's property is a taking has more than tradition to commend it. Such an appropriation is perhaps the most serious form of invasion of an owner's property interests. To borrow a metaphor, *cf. Andrus v. Allard*, 444 U.S. 51, 65–66 (1979), the government does not simply take a single "strand" from the "bundle" of property rights: it chops through the bundle, taking a slice of every strand.

Property rights in a physical thing have been described as the rights "to possess, use and dispose of it." *United States v. Gen. Motors Corp.*, 323 U.S. 373, 378 (1945). To the extent that the government permanently occupies physical property, it effectively destroys each of these rights. First, the owner has no right to possess the occupied space himself, and also has no power to exclude the occupier from possession and use of the space. The power to exclude has traditionally been considered one of the most treasured strands in an owner's bundle of property rights. See *Kaiser Aetna*, 444 U.S. at 179–180; *see also* Restatement (First) of Property § 7 (1936). Second, the permanent physical occupation of property forever denies the owner any power to control the use of the property; he not only cannot exclude others, but can make no nonpossessory use of the property. Although deprivation of the right to use and obtain a profit from property is not, in every case, independently sufficient to establish a taking, see *Andrus v. Allard*, *supra*, at 66, it is clearly relevant. Finally, even though the owner may retain the bare legal right to dispose of the occupied space by transfer or sale, the permanent occupation of that space by a stranger will ordinarily empty the right of any value, since the purchaser will also be unable to make any use of the property.

Moreover, an owner suffers a special kind of injury when a *stranger* directly invades and occupies the owner's property… . [P]roperty law has long protected an owner's expectation that he will be relatively undisturbed at least in the possession of his property. To require, as well, that the owner permit another to exercise complete dominion literally adds insult to injury. See Frank I. Michelman, *Property, Utility, and Fairness: Comments on the Ethical Foundations of "Just Compensation" Law,* 80 Harv. L. Rev. 1165, 1228, & n. 110 (1967). Furthermore, such an occupation is qualitatively more severe than a regulation of the *use* of property, even a regulation that imposes affirmative duties on the owner, since the owner may have no control over the timing, extent, or nature of the invasion. See n. 19, *infra.*

The traditional rule also avoids otherwise difficult line-drawing problems. Few would disagree that if the State required landlords to permit third parties to install swimming pools on the landlords' rooftops for the convenience of the tenants, the requirement would be a taking. If the cable installation here occupied as much space, again, few would disagree that the occupation would be a taking. But constitutional protection for the rights of private property cannot be made to depend on the size of the area permanently occupied. Indeed, it is possible that in the future, additional cable installations that more significantly restrict a landlord's use of the roof of his building will be made. Section 828 requires a landlord to permit such multiple installations.

Finally, whether a permanent physical occupation has occurred presents relatively few problems of proof. The placement of a fixed structure on land or real property is an obvious fact that will rarely be subject to dispute. Once the fact of occupation is shown, of course, a court should consider the extent of the occupation as one relevant factor in determining the compensation due. For that reason, moreover, there is less need to consider the extent of the occupation in determining whether there is a taking in the first instance.

### *C*

Teleprompter's cable installation on appellant's building constitutes a taking under the traditional test. The installation involved a direct physical attachment of plates, boxes, wires, bolts, and screws to the building, completely occupying space immediately above and upon the roof and along the building's exterior wall… .

## *III*

Our holding today is very narrow. We affirm the traditional rule that a permanent physical occupation of property is a taking. In such a case, the property owner entertains a historically rooted expectation of compensation, and the character of the invasion is qualitatively more intrusive than perhaps any other category of property regulation. We do not, however, question the equally substantial authority upholding a State's broad power to impose appropriate restrictions upon an owner's use of his property.

Furthermore, our conclusion that § 828 works a taking of a portion of appellant's property does not presuppose that the fee which many landlords had obtained from Teleprompter prior to the law's enactment is a proper measure of the value of the property taken. The issue of the amount of compensation that is due, on which we express no opinion, is a matter for the state courts to consider on remand.

The judgment of the New York Court of Appeals is reversed, and the case is remanded for further proceedings not inconsistent with this opinion.

It is so ordered.

## Just compensation owed if all value lost

The second per se regulatory takings rule is that regulations which take all economic value require payment of just compensation. This rule has its roots in the case *Pa. Coal Co. v. Mahon*,[5] which found that a Pennsylvania law prohibiting the extraction of coal warranted payment of compensation. The Court said:

> Government hardly could go on if to some extent values incident to property could not be diminished without paying for every such change in the general law. As long recognized some values are enjoyed under an implied limitation and must yield to the police power. But obviously the implied limitation must have its limits or the contract and due process clauses are gone. One fact for consideration in determining such limits is the extent of the diminution. When it reaches a certain magnitude, in most if not in all cases there must be an exercise of eminent domain and compensation to sustain the act. So the question depends upon the particular facts.
>
> The general rule at least is that while property may be regulated to a certain extent, if regulation goes too far it will be recognized as a taking... . We are in danger of forgetting that a strong public desire to improve the public condition is not enough to warrant achieving the desire by a shorter cut than the constitutional way of paying for the change. As we already have said this is a question of degree—and therefore cannot be disposed of by general propositions... .[6]

Following the *Pa. Coal* decision, courts have applied the "too far" rule to mean that a regulation which deprives a property owner of *all value* constitutes a regulatory taking for which the regulating government must pay just compensation.[7]

The following case, *Lucas v. South Carolina Coastal Council*, applies the "too far" rule and presents an important exception to it. That is, government may regulate away rights a property owner did not have under common law without paying just compensation—even if doing so results in a complete diminution of value for the owner.[8] In this case, the specific right the Court contemplates the government regulating away is the property owner's right to constitute a nuisance.[9]

The property that was the subject of the litigation comprised two lots located on a barrier island in South Carolina, to the north of Charleston. In his dissent to the majority opinion, Justice Blackmun describes the property as follows:

> The area is notoriously unstable. In roughly half of the last 40 years, all or part of petitioner's property was part of the beach or flooded twice daily by the ebb and flow of the tide. Between 1957 and 1963, petitioner's property was under water. Between 1963 and 1973 the shoreline was 100 to 150 feet onto petitioner's property. In 1973 the first line of stable vegetation was about halfway through the property. Between 1981 and 1983, the Isle of Palms issued 12 emergency orders for sandbagging to protect property in the Wild Dune development. Determining that local habitable structures were in imminent danger of collapse, the Council issued permits for two rock revetments to protect condominium developments near petitioner's property from erosion; one of the revetments extends more than halfway onto one of his lots.[10]

Because of this instability, South Carolina prohibited construction of homes on the lots. That limitation is the alleged regulatory taking.

## United States Supreme Court

### *Lucas v. South Carolina Coastal Council*[11]

### 1992

Justice SCALIA delivered the opinion of the Court.

In 1986, petitioner David H. Lucas paid $975,000 for two residential lots on the Isle of Palms in Charleston County, South Carolina, on which he intended to build single-family homes. In 1988, however, the South Carolina Legislature enacted the Beachfront Management Act, S.C. Code Ann. § 48–39–250 et seq. (Supp. 1990), which had the direct effect of barring petitioner from erecting any permanent habitable structures on his two parcels. See § 48–39–290(A). A state trial court found that this prohibition rendered Lucas's parcels "valueless." App. to Pet. for Cert. 37. This case requires us to decide whether the Act's dramatic effect on the economic value of Lucas's lots accomplished a taking of private property under the Fifth and Fourteenth Amendments requiring the payment of "just compensation." U.S. Const., Amdt. 5.

### *I*

#### *A*

South Carolina's expressed interest in intensively managing development activities in the so-called "coastal zone" dates from 1977 when, in the aftermath of Congress's passage of the federal Coastal Zone Management Act of 1972, 86 Stat. 1280, as amended, 16 U.S.C. § 1451 et seq., the legislature enacted a Coastal Zone Management Act of its own. See S.C. Code Ann. § 48–39–10 et seq. (1987). In its original form, the South Carolina Act required owners of coastal zone land that qualified as a "critical area" (defined in the legislation to include beaches and immediately adjacent sand dunes, § 48–39–10(J)) to obtain a permit from the newly created South Carolina Coastal Council (Council) (respondent here) prior to committing the land to a "use other than the use the critical area was devoted to on [September 28, 1977]." § 48–39–130(A).

In the late 1970's, Lucas and others began extensive residential development of the Isle of Palms, a barrier island situated eastward of the city of Charleston. Toward the close of the development cycle for one residential subdivision known as "Beachwood East," Lucas in 1986 purchased the two lots at issue in this litigation for his own account. No portion of the lots, which were located approximately 300 feet from the beach, qualified as a "critical area" under the 1977 Act; accordingly, at the time Lucas acquired these parcels, he was not legally obliged to obtain a permit from the Council in advance of any development activity. His intention with respect to the lots was to do what the owners of the immediately adjacent parcels had already done: erect single-family residences. He commissioned architectural drawings for this purpose.

The Beachfront Management Act brought Lucas's plans to an abrupt end. Under that 1988 legislation, the Council was directed to establish a "baseline" connecting the landward-most "point[s] of erosion ... during the past forty years" in the region of the Isle of Palms that includes Lucas's lots. S.C. Code Ann. § 48–39–280(A)(2) (Supp. 1988). In action not challenged here, the Council fixed this baseline landward of Lucas's parcels. That was significant, for under the Act construction of occupiable improvements was flatly prohibited seaward of a line drawn 20 feet landward of, and parallel to, the baseline. § 48–39–290(A). The Act provided no exceptions.

*B*

Lucas promptly filed suit in the South Carolina Court of Common Pleas, contending that the Beachfront Management Act's construction bar effected a taking of his property without just compensation. Lucas did not take issue with the validity of the Act as a lawful exercise of South Carolina's police power, but contended that the Act's complete extinguishment of his property's value entitled him to compensation regardless of whether the legislature had acted in furtherance of legitimate police power objectives. Following a bench trial, the court agreed. Among its factual determinations was the finding that

> at the time Lucas purchased the two lots, both were zoned for single-family residential construction and ... there were no restrictions imposed upon such use of the property by either the State of South Carolina, the County of Charleston, or the Town of the Isle of Palms.

App. to Pet. for Cert. 36. The trial court further found that the Beachfront Management Act decreed a permanent ban on construction insofar as Lucas's lots were concerned, and that this prohibition "deprive[d] Lucas of any reasonable economic use of the lots,... eliminated the unrestricted right of use, and render[ed] them valueless." *Id.*, at 37. The court thus concluded that Lucas's properties had been "taken" by operation of the Act, and it ordered respondent to pay "just compensation" in the amount of $1,232,387.50. *Id.* at 40. [The Carolina Supreme Court reversed based on what it described as Lucas' concession that the Act was "properly and validly designed to ... preserve South Carolina's beaches"... . That court viewed Lucas' failure to attack the validity of the statute as dispositive, leaving the court no choice but to rule that "when a regulation respecting the use of property is designed 'to prevent serious public harm,' ... no compensation is owing under the Takings Clause regardless of the regulation's effect on the property's value.]... .

***III***

*A*

Prior to Justice Holmes's exposition in *Pennsylvania Coal Co. v. Mahon*, 260 U.S. 393 (1922), it was generally thought that the Takings Clause reached only a "direct appropriation" of property, *Legal Tender Cases*, 12 Wall. 457, 551, 20 L.Ed. 287 (1871), or the functional equivalent of a "practical ouster of [the owner's] possession," *Transp. Co. v. Chicago*, 99 U.S. 635, 642 (1879). See also *Gibson v. United States*. 166 U.S. 269, 275–76 (1897). Justice Holmes recognized in *Mahon*, however, that if the protection against physical appropriations of private property was to be meaningfully enforced, the government's power to redefine the range of interests included in the ownership of property was necessarily constrained by constitutional limits. 260 U.S. at 414–15. If, instead, the uses of private property were subject to unbridled, uncompensated qualification under the police power, "the natural tendency of human nature [would be] to extend the qualification more and more until at last private property disappear[ed]." *Id.* at 415. These considerations gave birth in that case to the oft-cited maxim that, "while property may be regulated to a certain extent, if regulation goes too far it will be recognized as a taking." *Ibid.*

Nevertheless, our decision in *Mahon* offered little insight into when, and under what circumstances, a given regulation would be seen as going "too far" for purposes of the Fifth

Amendment. In 70-odd years of succeeding "regulatory takings" jurisprudence, we have generally eschewed any "set formula" for determining how far is too far, preferring to "engag[e] in ... essentially ad hoc, factual inquiries." *Penn Central Transportation Co. v. New York City*, 438 U.S. 104, 124 (1978) (quoting *Goldblatt v. Hempstead*, 369 U.S. 590, 594 (1962)). See Richard A. Epstein, *Takings: Descent and Resurrection*, 1987 Sup. Ct. Rev. 1, 4 (1987). We have, however, described at least two discrete categories of regulatory action as compensable without case-specific inquiry... . The first encompasses regulations that compel the property owner to suffer a physical "invasion" of his property. In general (at least with regard to permanent invasions), no matter how minute the intrusion, and no matter how weighty the public purpose behind it, we have required compensation. For example, in *Loretto v. Teleprompter Manhattan CATV Corp.*, 458 U.S. 419 (1982), we determined that New York's law requiring landlords to allow television cable companies to emplace cable facilities in their apartment buildings constituted a taking, *id.* at 435–40, even though the facilities occupied at most only 1 ½ cubic feet of the landlords' property, see *id.* at 438 n.16. *See also United States v. Causby*, 328 U.S. 256, 265, and n.10 (1946) (physical invasions of airspace); *cf. Kaiser Aetna v. United States*, 444 U.S. 164 (1979) (imposition of navigational servitude upon private marina).

The second situation in which we have found categorical treatment appropriate is where regulation denies all economically beneficial or productive use of land. *See Agins*, 447 U.S. at 260; *see also Nollan v. Cal. Coastal Comm'n*, 483 U.S. 825, 834 (1987); *Keystone Bituminous Coal Ass'n. v. DeBenedictis*, 480 U.S. 470, 495 (1987); *Hodel v. Va. Surface Mining & Reclamation Ass'n., Inc.*, 452 U.S. 264, 295–96 (1981)... .

*B*

The trial court found Lucas's two beachfront lots to have been rendered valueless by respondent's enforcement of the coastal-zone construction ban. Under Lucas's theory of the case, which rested upon our "no economically viable use" statements, that finding entitled him to compensation ... [M]any of our prior opinions have suggested that "harmful or noxious uses" of property may be proscribed by government regulation without the requirement of compensation ... [W]e think he South Carolina Supreme Court was too quick to conclude that that principle decides the present case. The "harmful or noxious uses" principle was the Court's early attempt to describe in theoretical terms why government may, consistent with the Takings Clause, affect property values by regulation without incurring an obligation to compensate... .

[N]oxious-use logic cannot serve as a touchstone to distinguish regulatory "takings"—which require compensation—from regulatory deprivations that do not require compensation. *A fortiori* the legislature's recitation of a noxious-use justification cannot be the basis for departing from our categorical rule that total regulatory takings must be compensated. If it were, departure would virtually always be allowed. [This] approach would essentially nullify *Mahon*'s affirmation of limits to the noncompensable exercise of the police power. Our cases provide no support for this: None of them that employed the logic of "harmful use" prevention to sustain a regulation involved an allegation that the regulation wholly eliminated the value of the claimant's land... .

Where the State seeks to sustain regulation that deprives land of all economically beneficial use, we think it may resist compensation only if the logically antecedent inquiry into the nature of the owner's estate shows that the proscribed use interests were not part of his title to begin with. This accords, we think, with our "takings" jurisprudence, which has traditionally been guided by the understandings of our citizens regarding the content of, and the State's power over, the "bundle of rights" that they acquire when they obtain title to property... .

Where "permanent physical occupation" of land is concerned, we have refused to allow the government to decree it anew (without compensation), no matter how weighty the asserted "public interests" involved, *Loretto v. Teleprompter Manhattan CATV Corp.*, 458 U.S., at 426... . We believe similar treatment must be accorded confiscatory regulations, i.e., regulations that prohibit all economically beneficial use of land: Any limitation so severe cannot be newly legislated or decreed (without compensation), but must inhere in the title itself, in the restrictions that background principles of the State's law of property and nuisance already place upon land ownership. A law or decree with such an effect must, in other words, do no more than duplicate the result that could have been achieved in the courts—by adjacent landowners (or other uniquely affected persons) under the State's law of private nuisance, or by the State under its complementary power to abate nuisances that affect the public generally, or otherwise.

On this analysis, the owner of a lake-bed, for example, would not be entitled to compensation when he is denied the requisite permit to engage in a landfilling operation that would have the effect of flooding others' land. Nor the corporate owner of a nuclear generating plant, when it is directed to remove all improvements from its land upon discovery that the plant sits astride an earthquake fault. Such regulatory action may well have the effect of eliminating the land's only economically productive use, but it does not proscribe a productive use that was previously permissible under relevant property and nuisance principles. The use of these properties for what are now expressly prohibited purposes was always unlawful, and (subject to other constitutional limitations) it was open to the State at any point to make the implication of those background principles of nuisance and property law explicit. *See* Frank I. Michelman, *Property, Utility, and Fairness, Comments on the Ethical Foundations of "Just Compensation" Law*, 80 Harv. L. Rev. 1165, 1239–41 (1967). In light of our traditional resort to "existing rules or understandings that stem from an independent source such as state law" to define the range of interests that qualify for protection as "property" under the Fifth and Fourteenth Amendments, *Bd. of Regents of State Colleges v. Roth*, 408 U.S. 564, 577 (1972); *see, e.g.*, *Ruckelshaus v. Monsanto Co.*, 467 U.S. 986, 1011–12 (1984); *Hughes v. Washington*, 389 U.S. 290, 295 (1967) (Stewart, J., concurring), this recognition that the Takings Clause does not require compensation when an owner is barred from putting land to a use that is proscribed by those "existing rules or understandings" is surely unexceptional. When, however, a regulation that declares "off-limits" all economically productive or beneficial uses of land goes beyond what the relevant background principles would dictate, compensation must be paid to sustain it.

The "total taking" inquiry we require today will ordinarily entail (as the application of state nuisance law ordinarily entails) analysis of, among other things, the degree of harm to public lands and resources, or adjacent private property, posed by the claimant's proposed activities, *see, e.g.*, Restatement (Second) of Torts §§ 826, 827 (1979), the social value of the claimant's activities and their suitability to the locality in question, *see, e.g.*, *id.* §§ 828(a) and (b), 831, and the relative ease with which the alleged harm can be avoided through measures taken by the claimant and the government (or adjacent private landowners) alike, *see, e.g.*, *id.* §§ 827(e), 828(c), 830. The fact that a particular use has long been engaged in by similarly situated owners ordinarily imports a lack of any common-law prohibition (though changed circumstances or new knowledge may make what was previously permissible no longer so, see *id.* § 827, Cmt. g). So also does the fact that other landowners, similarly situated, are permitted to continue the use denied to the claimant.

[T]o win its case... . South Carolina must identify background principles of nuisance and property law that prohibit the uses [Lucas] now intends in the circumstances in which the property is presently found. Only on this showing can the State fairly claim that, in proscribing all such beneficial uses, the Beachfront Management Act is taking nothing.

The judgment is reversed, and the case is remanded for proceedings not inconsistent with this opinion.

So ordered.

### *Discussion*

The *Lucas* decision identifies common law nuisance as a background principle of law that limits the rights to property protected by the Takings Clause. But nuisance is not the only existing concept in law that might limit what constitutes property for the purposes of a regulatory takings analysis. In *Stop the Beach Renourishment, Inc. v. Fla. Dep't of Envt'l. Prot.*, the Court analyzed Florida real property laws regarding the deposition or erosion of sediments to or from waterfront land.[12] The Court applied this analysis to an alleged regulatory taking and found that no taking existed because "[t]he Takings Clause only protects property rights as they are established under state law, not as they might have been established or ought to have been established."[13] The decision is worth reading for its discussion of waterfront landowners' property rights and for insight into the politics of Florida's beach renourishment projects.

### Box 15.1 Practice problem: University View sidewalks

The Collegeborough neighborhood University View was subdivided in the 1970s. At that time, local regulations did not require that new roads in subdivisions include sidewalks. Also, because the University View land developer did not see a market demand for sidewalks, it did not include sidewalks in the development. As a result, folks walking in University View walk in the road.

The Collegeborough city council is concerned that the community's children are dying as a result of automobile crashes. The largest cause of death for Collegeborough residents under the age of 18 is injury and the largest cause of injury is automobile crashes. The council believes that building sidewalks in University View is one way to stop drivers from crashing cars into walking children.

The council funded money in its budget for the city public works department to build new sidewalks in University View. Because the city only owned the paved portion of the streets in University View, part of the funding was designated to go toward purchasing additional land alongside the roadway. Unfortunately, the city of Collegeborough did not allocate enough money to buy all of the property on which it intended to build sidewalks.

The city planners and the city attorney worked together to come up with the following plan, which the city has implemented. First, where a front yard was less than 50 feet deep, the city of Collegeborough bought the land on which it built sidewalks. Second, where a front yard was more than 50 feet deep (i.e. the house was more than 50 feet from the road), Collegeborough adopted an ordinance that allowed the city to build sidewalks and allowed people to use those sidewalks in University View, even though these sidewalks are built on property the city does not actually own.

Robert Lynn owns a home in University View that is more than 50 feet from the road. Since Collegeborough built a sidewalk along the road in front of Mr. Lynn's home, people sometimes walk there, about 75 feet from his house. Mr. Lynn does not like this. He has called the police several times on neighborhood children walking on the sidewalk in front of his home to reach a nearby school bus stop.

Recently, an officer responding to Mr. Lynn's call told Mr. Lynn he should stop calling the police to complain about people walking. "As long as people are on the sidewalk, they have a right to be there," the officer said, citing the city ordinance.

Mr. Lynn cannot take this affront anymore. He sues the city of Collegeborough, alleging that its ordinance is a violation of his rights to property under the Takings Clause of the U.S. Constitution.

Evaluate Mr. Lynn's claim.

## Notes

1 United States v. Craft, 535 U.S. 274, 278 (2002) (citations omitted).

2 Thus, where "an owner possesses a full 'bundle' of property rights, the destruction of one 'strand' of the bundle is not a taking." Tahoe-Sierra Pres. Council, Inc. v. Tahoe Reg'l Plan. Agency, 535 U.S. 302, 327 (2002) (quoting Andrus v. Allard, 444 U.S. 51, 65–6 (1979)).

3 Dickman v. Comm'r of Internal Revenue, 465 U.S. 330, 336 (1984) (citations omitted).

4 458 U.S. 419 (1982).

5 260 U.S. 393 (1922).

6 Pa. Coal Co. v. Mahon, 260 U.S. 393, 413–16 (1922).

7 E.g. Palazzolo v. Rhode Island, 533 U.S. 606, 617 (2001); Kavanau v. Santa Monica Rent Control Bd., 941 P.2d 851, 859 (Cal. 1997); Kafka v. Mont. Dep't of Fish, Wildlife, & Parks, 201 P.3d 8, 26–9 (Mont. 2008); Sheerr v. Twp. of Evesham, 445 A.2d 46, 48, 52–6 (N.J. Super. Ct. Law Div. 1982).

8 Lucas v. S.C. Coastal Council, 505 U.S. 1003, 1027–29 (1992).

9 *Lucas*, 505 U.S. at 1029–30.

10 *Lucas*, 505 U.S. at 1038–39 (1992) (Blackmun, J., dissenting) (citations omitted).

11 505 U.S. 1003 (1992).

12 Stop the Beach Renourishment, Inc. v. Fla. Dep't of Envt'L Prot., 560 U.S. 702, 708 (2010).

13 *Id.* at 732.

# 16 Ad hoc balancing test for regulatory takings

In *Penn Central Transportation Co. v. New York City,*[1] the U.S. Supreme Court conceded that it "quite simply, has been unable to develop any 'set formula' for determining when 'justice and fairness' require that economic injuries caused by public action be compensated by the government, rather than remain disproportionately concentrated on a few persons."[2]

Unfortunately, the Court's *Penn Central* decision does not provide perfect clarity. In this landmark case, and in the decades since, the courts have not adopted a takings test which is clearer than the two bright-line rules already discussed in this text.

Nonetheless, the *Penn Central* opinion does focus on three ideas to which the Court has returned in future cases. These concepts are: (1) the extent to which the governmental action inflicts economic losses on the owner; (2) the extent to which the governmental action interferes with the owner's reasonable investment-backed expectations; and (3) the character of the governmental action.[3] Together, these ideas are a third regulatory taking rule that may require local governments to pay compensation for some regulations even when the facts do not constitute a per se regulatory taking.

## *Penn Central* dispute

In addition to its significance to land use law, *Penn Central* is a keystone case for urban planning because of its impact on historic preservation. The issue in the case is whether the City of New York's Landmark Preservation Law constituted a regulatory taking of Grand Central Terminal, a building owned by the Penn Central Transportation Company. Understanding the context of this dispute requires knowing the fate of Pennsylvania Station, another New York City train station.

The Pennsylvania Railroad built Pennsylvania Station in 1910. Architects McKim, Mead & White designed the building in the Beaux-Arts style. Charles McKim said the station "celebrated entrance to one of the great metropolitan cities of the world." However, by 1963, travel by rail had declined and the costs of maintaining the building were not affordable. Pennsylvania Railroad demolished the building to make way for constructing Madison Square Garden in its place.

Destroying the building led to public outrage and the event catalyzed the historic preservation movement in the United States. New York City responded to the outcry by adopting its Landmarks Preservation Law in 1965. The destruction of Pennsylvania Station was on the city's mind when the Penn Central Transportation Company proposed changes to the Grand Central Terminal.

## *Penn Central* test

### *Economic losses on the property owner*

The extent to which the regulation inflicts economic losses on the property owner is an appropriate consideration in a takings analysis. Determining whether the economic impact of a regulation is to take all value requires considering the amount of value lost against the property itself. This inherently proportional analysis, therefore, requires deciding what is the whole property. And what exactly constitutes the whole property is not always clear.

This conundrum has been called the denominator problem and is exemplified in the dissenting opinion to *Penn Coal*. There, Justice Brandeis wrote:

> values are relative. If we are to consider the value of the coal kept in place by the restriction, we should compare it with the value of all other parts of the land. That is, with the value not of the coal alone, but with the value of the whole property.[4]

In *Penn Central*, the Court addressed this idea by saying that

> "[t]aking" jurisprudence does not divide a single parcel into discrete segments and attempt to determine whether rights in a particular segment have been entirely abrogated. In deciding whether a particular governmental action has effected a taking, this Court focuses rather both on the character of the action on the nature and extent of the interference with rights in the parcel as a whole—here, the city tax block designated as the "landmark site."[5]

Despite the Court's definite assertion that takings analysis compares value lost to the value of the whole, what constitutes the whole property is often the subject of disagreement. The case *Murr v. Wisconsin*,[6] which this text presents after *Penn Central*, addresses the denominator problem directly and provides a three-part test for determining what constitutes a whole property for the purposes of regulatory takings analysis.

### *Investment-backed expectations*

The *Penn Central* decision says a rule "may so frustrate distinct investment-backed expectations as to amount to a 'taking.'"[7] Unlike the economic loss analysis, considering a change in reasonable investment-backed expectations requires consideration of economic impact in light of the owner's past actions.

If a property owner purchased a property at a certain price in order to make a certain use of it as part of a business plan, an ordinance limiting that use—and therefore rendering the business plan valueless—may constitute a regulatory taking.[8] If the same property owner had instead inherited that property, and therefore had no investment-backed expectation of earning money from it, he or she would be less able to establish a regulatory taking. That said, the U.S. Supreme Court has "never held that a takings claim is defeated simply on account of the lack of a personal financial investment by a postenactment acquirer of property, such as a donee, heir, or devisee."[9]

In addition, the foreseeability of government regulation is relevant to evaluating a rule's impact on investment-backed expectations. A property owner could have anticipated a foreseeable regulation when deciding whether to purchase a property and deciding how much to pay for it. Like all other considerations in the ad hoc balancing test, however, this consideration is not dispositive. The court has rejected the notion that a property owner who has notice of a regulation, but who purchases a property anyway, is barred from claiming the lost value is a regulatory taking.[10]

### *Character of governmental action*

Finally, the character of the governmental action is an appropriate consideration in a regulatory takings analysis. This concept includes two ideas. First, the U.S. Supreme Court determined that "government actions that may be characterized as acquisitions of resources to permit or facilitate uniquely public functions have often been held to constitute 'takings.'"[11] The essence of this idea is the distribution of the burden of the taking. Has one property owner been singled out to suffer a burden which rightfully ought to be borne by the community as a whole?[12]

Courts look to reciprocity of advantage as one way to consider whether a regulation puts a property to a purely public purpose. If the claimant benefits from a regulation—even if other members of the public share in that benefit—then the regulation is less likely to constitute a taking because of the reciprocal benefit to the property owner.

Second, the U.S. Supreme Court acknowledged that governmental actions may constitutionally diminish some rights to use property to promote the "healthy, safety, morals, or general welfare"; zoning laws are "the classic example."[13] Restrictions on the use of property are likely to be constitutional when those interests in real estate which those rules diminish are not "sufficiently bound up with the reasonable expectation of the claimant to constitute 'property' for Fifth Amendment purposes."[14] The Court recognizes that some property interests are objectively less valuable than others.

An example of a less valuable right is one that would constitute a private nuisance—the loss of which can never constitute a taking, even when it results in a total diminution of value.[15] An example of a more valuable right is the right to exclude—the loss of which constitutes a per se regulatory taking.[16] When considering whether other rights are so essential to the concept of ownership that regulations which restrict them require compensation, consider how typical it would be for a local government regulation to limit those rights.

## United States Supreme Court

## *Penn Central Transp. Co. v. City of New York*[17]

## 1978

Mr. Justice BRENNAN delivered the opinion of the Court.

The question presented is whether a city may, as part of a comprehensive program to preserve historic landmarks and historic districts, place restrictions on the development of individual historic landmarks—in addition to those imposed by applicable zoning ordinances—without effecting a "taking" requiring the payment of "just compensation." Specifically, we must decide whether the application of New York City's Landmarks Preservation Law to the parcel of land occupied by Grand Central Terminal has "taken" its owners' property in violation of the Fifth and Fourteenth Amendments.

### I

### *A*

Over the past 50 years, all 50 States and over 500 municipalities have enacted laws to encourage or require the preservation of buildings and areas with historic or aesthetic importance.

These nationwide legislative efforts have been precipitated by two concerns. The first is recognition that, in recent years, large numbers of historic structures, landmarks, and areas have been destroyed without adequate consideration of either the values represented therein or the possibility of preserving the destroyed properties for use in economically productive ways. The second is a widely shared belief that structures with special historic, cultural, or architectural significance enhance the quality of life for all. Not only do these buildings and their workmanship represent the lessons of the past and embody precious features of our heritage, they serve as examples of quality for today. "[H]istoric conservation is but one aspect of the much larger problem, basically an environmental one, of enhancing—or perhaps developing for the first time—the quality of life for people."

New York City, responding to similar concerns and acting pursuant to a New York State enabling Act, adopted its Landmarks Preservation Law in 1965. *See* N.Y.C. Admin. Code, ch. 8–A, § 205–1.0 et seq. (1976). The city acted from the conviction that "the standing of [New York City] as a world-wide tourist center and world capital of business, culture and government" would be threatened if legislation were not enacted to protect historic landmarks and neighborhoods from precipitate decisions to destroy or fundamentally alter their character. § 205–1.0(a). The city believed that comprehensive measures to safeguard desirable features of the existing urban fabric would benefit its citizens in a variety of ways: e. g., fostering "civic pride in the beauty and noble accomplishments of the past"; protecting and enhancing "the city's attractions to tourists and visitors"; "support[ing] and stimul[ating] business and industry"; "strengthen[ing] the economy of the city"; and promoting "the use of historic districts, landmarks, interior landmarks and scenic landmarks for the education, pleasure and welfare of the people of the city." § 205–1.0(b).

The New York City law is typical of many urban landmark laws in that its primary method of achieving its goals is not by acquisitions of historic properties, but rather by involving public entities in land-use decisions affecting these properties and providing services, standards, controls, and incentives that will encourage preservation by private owners and users. While the law does place special restrictions on landmark properties as a necessary feature to the attainment of its larger objectives, the major theme of the law is to ensure the owners of any such properties both a "reasonable return" on their investments and maximum latitude to use their parcels for purposes not inconsistent with the preservation goals.

The operation of the law can be briefly summarized. The primary responsibility for administering the law is vested in the Landmarks Preservation Commission (Commission), a broad based, 11-member agency assisted by a technical staff. The Commission first performs the function, critical to any landmark preservation effort, of identifying properties and areas that have "a special character or special historical or aesthetic interest or value as part of the development, heritage or cultural characteristics of the city, state or nation." § 207–1.0(n); *see* § 207–1.0(h). If the Commission determines, after giving all interested parties an opportunity to be heard, that a building or area satisfies the ordinance's criteria, it will designate a building to be a "landmark," § 207–1.0(n), situated on a particular "landmark site," § 207–1.0(o), or will designate an area to be a "historic district," § 207–1.0(h).11 After the Commission makes a designation, New York City's Board of Estimate, after considering the relationship of the designated property "to the master plan, the zoning resolution, projected public improvements and any plans for the renewal of the area involved," § 207–2.0(g)(1), may modify or disapprove the designation, and the owner may seek judicial review of the final designation decision. Thus far, 31 historic districts and over 400 individual landmarks have been finally designated, and the process is a continuing one.

Final designation as a landmark results in restrictions upon the property owner's options concerning use of the landmark site. First, the law imposes a duty upon the owner to keep the exterior features of the building "in good repair" to assure that the law's objectives not be defeated by the landmark's falling into a state of irremediable disrepair.

See § 207–10.0(a). Second, the Commission must approve in advance any proposal to alter the exterior architectural features of the landmark or to construct any exterior improvement on the landmark site, thus ensuring that decisions concerning construction on the landmark site are made with due consideration of both the public interest in the maintenance of the structure and the landowner's interest in use of the property. *See* §§ 207–4.0 to 207–9.0.

In the event an owner wishes to alter a landmark site, three separate procedures are available through which administrative approval may be obtained. First, the owner may apply to the Commission for a "certificate of no effect on protected architectural features": that is, for an order approving the improvement or alteration on the ground that it will not change or affect any architectural feature of the landmark and will be in harmony therewith. *See* § 207–5.0. Denial of the certificate is subject to judicial review.

Second, the owner may apply to the Commission for a certificate of "appropriateness." *See* § 207–6.0. Such certificates will be granted if the Commission concludes—focusing upon aesthetic, historical, and architectural values—that the proposed construction on the landmark site would not unduly hinder the protection, enhancement, perpetuation, and use of the landmark. Again, denial of the certificate is subject to judicial review. Moreover, the owner who is denied either a certificate of no exterior effect or a certificate of appropriateness may submit an alternative or modified plan for approval. The final procedure—seeking a certificate of appropriateness on the ground of "insufficient return," see § 207–8.0—provides special mechanisms, which vary depending on whether or not the landmark enjoys a tax exemption, to ensure that designation does not cause economic hardship.

Although the designation of a landmark and landmark site restricts the owner's control over the parcel, designation also enhances the economic position of the landmark owner in one significant respect. Under New York City's zoning laws, owners of real property who have not developed their property to the full extent permitted by the applicable zoning laws are allowed to transfer development rights to contiguous parcels on the same city block. *See* New York City, Zoning Resolution Art. I, ch. 2, § 12–10 (1978) (definition of "zoning lot"). A 1968 ordinance gave the owners of landmark sites additional opportunities to transfer development rights to other parcels. Subject to a restriction that the floor area of the transferee lot may not be increased by more than 20% above its authorized level, the ordinance permitted transfers from a landmark parcel to property across the street or across a street intersection. In 1969, the law governing the conditions under which transfers from landmark parcels could occur was liberalized, see New York City Zoning Resolutions 74–79 to 74–793, apparently to ensure that the Landmarks Law would not unduly restrict the development options of the owners of Grand Central Terminal. *See* Marcus, *Air Rights Transfers in New York City*, 36 Law & Contemp. Prob. 372, 375 (1971). The class of recipient lots was expanded to include lots "across a street and opposite to another lot or lots which except for the intervention of streets or street intersections f[or]m a series extending to the lot occupied by the landmark building [, provided that] all lots [are] in the same ownership." New York City Zoning Resolution 74–79 [emphasis deleted]. In addition, the 1969 amendment permits, in highly commercialized areas like midtown Manhattan, the transfer of all unused development rights to a single parcel. *Ibid*.

### B

This case involves the application of New York City's Landmarks Preservation Law to Grand Central Terminal (Terminal). The Terminal, which is owned by the Penn Central Transportation Co. and its affiliates (Penn Central), is one of New York City's most famous buildings.

Opened in 1913, it is regarded not only as providing an ingenious engineering solution to the problems presented by urban railroad stations, but also as a magnificent example of the French beaux-arts style.

The Terminal is located in midtown Manhattan. Its south facade faces 42d Street and that street's intersection with Park Avenue. At street level, the Terminal is bounded on the west by Vanderbilt Avenue, on the east by the Commodore Hotel, and on the north by the Pan-American Building. Although a 20-story office tower, to have been located above the Terminal, was part of the original design, the planned tower was never constructed. The Terminal itself is an eight-story structure which Penn Central uses as a railroad station and in which it rents space not needed for railroad purposes to a variety of commercial interests. The Terminal is one of a number of properties owned by appellant Penn Central in this area of midtown Manhattan. The others include the Barclay, Biltmore, Commodore, Roosevelt, and Waldorf-Astoria Hotels, the Pan-American Building and other office buildings along Park Avenue, and the Yale Club. At least eight of these are eligible to be recipients of development rights afforded the Terminal by virtue of landmark designation.

On August 2, 1967, following a public hearing, the Commission designated the Terminal a "landmark" and designated the "city tax block" it occupies a "landmark site." The Board of Estimate confirmed this action on September 21, 1967. Although appellant Penn Central had opposed the designation before the Commission, it did not seek judicial review of the final designation decision.

On January 22, 1968, appellant Penn Central, to increase its income, entered into a renewable 50-year lease and sublease agreement with appellant UGP Properties, Inc. (UGP), a wholly owned subsidiary of Union General Properties, Ltd., a United Kingdom corporation. Under the terms of the agreement, UGP was to construct a multistory office building above the Terminal. UGP promised to pay Penn Central $1 million annually during construction and at least $3 million annually thereafter. The rentals would be offset in part by a loss of some $700,000 to $1 million in net rentals presently received from concessionaires displaced by the new building.

Appellants UGP and Penn Central then applied to the Commission for permission to construct an office building atop the Terminal. Two separate plans, both designed by architect Marcel Breuer and both apparently satisfying the terms of the applicable zoning ordinance, were submitted to the Commission for approval. The first, Breuer I, provided for the construction of a 55-story office building, to be cantilevered above the existing facade and to rest on the roof of the Terminal. The second, Breuer II Revised, called for tearing down a portion of the Terminal that included the 42d Street facade, stripping off some of the remaining features of the Terminal's facade, and constructing a 53-story office building. The Commission denied a certificate of no exterior effect on September 20, 1968. Appellants then applied for a certificate of "appropriateness" as to both proposals. After four days of hearings at which over 80 witnesses testified, the Commission denied this application as to both proposals.

The Commission's reasons for rejecting certificates respecting Breuer II Revised are summarized in the following statement: "To protect a Landmark, one does not tear it down. To perpetuate its architectural features, one does not strip them off." Record 2255. Breuer I, which would have preserved the existing vertical facades of the present structure, received more sympathetic consideration. The Commission first focused on the effect that the proposed tower would have on one desirable feature created by the present structure and its surroundings: the dramatic view of the Terminal from Park Avenue South. Although appellants had contended that the Pan-American Building had already destroyed the silhouette of the south facade and that one additional tower could do no further damage and might even provide a better background for the facade, the Commission disagreed, stating that it found the majestic approach from the south to be still unique in the city and that a 55-story tower atop the Terminal would be far more detrimental to its south facade than the Pan-American Building 375 feet away. Moreover, the Commission found that from closer vantage points the Pan Am Building and the other towers were largely cut off from view, which would not be the case of the mass on top of the Terminal planned under Breuer I. In conclusion, the Commission stated:

> [We have] no fixed rule against making additions to designated buildings—it all depends on how they are done ... . But to balance a 55-story office tower above a flamboyant Beaux-Arts facade seems nothing more than an aesthetic joke. Quite simply, the tower would overwhelm the Terminal by its sheer mass. The "addition" would be four times as high as the existing structure and would reduce the Landmark itself to the status of a curiosity.
>
> Landmarks cannot be divorced from their settings—particularly when the setting is a dramatic and integral part of the original concept. The Terminal, in its setting, is a great example of urban design. Such examples are not so plentiful in New York City that we can afford to lose any of the few we have. And we must preserve them in a meaningful way—with alterations and additions of such character, scale, materials and mass as will protect, enhance and perpetuate the original design rather than overwhelm it. *Id.* at 2251.

Appellants did not seek judicial review of the denial of either certificate. Because the Terminal site enjoyed a tax exemption, remained suitable for its present and future uses, and was not the subject of a contract of sale, there were no further administrative remedies available to appellants as to the Breuer I and Breuer II Revised plans. *See* n.13, *supra*. Further, appellants did not avail themselves of the opportunity to develop and submit other plans for the Commission's consideration and approval. Instead, appellants filed suit in New York Supreme Court, Trial Term, claiming, *inter alia*, that the application of the Landmarks Preservation Law had "taken" their property without just compensation in violation of the Fifth and Fourteenth Amendments ... . Appellants sought a declaratory judgment, injunctive relief barring the city from using the Landmarks Law to impede the construction of any structure that might otherwise lawfully be constructed on the Terminal site, and damages ... . The trial court granted the injunctive and declaratory relief, but severed the question of damages for a "temporary taking." Appellees appealed, and the New York Supreme Court, Appellate Division, reversed. The Appellate Division held that the restrictions on the development of the Terminal site were necessary to promote the legitimate public purpose of protecting landmarks and therefore that appellants could sustain their constitutional claims only by proof that the regulation deprived them of all reasonable beneficial use of the property ... . The New York Court of Appeals affirmed ... . That court summarily rejected any claim that the Landmarks Law had "taken" property without "just compensation,"... indicating that there could be no "taking" since the law had not transferred control of the property to the city, but only restricted appellants' exploitation of it ... . Appellants ... [then] filed a notice of appeal in this Court.

### *II*

The issue[] presented by appellants [is] whether the restrictions imposed by New York City's law upon appellants' exploitation of the Terminal site effect a "taking" of appellants' property for a public use within the meaning of the Fifth Amendment, which of course is made applicable to the States through the Fourteenth Amendment, *see Chi., B. & Q.R. Co. v. Chicago*, 166 U.S. 226 (1897) ... .

*A*

Before considering appellants' specific contentions, it will be useful to review the factors that have shaped the jurisprudence of the Fifth Amendment injunction "nor shall private property be taken for public use, without just compensation." The question of what constitutes a "taking" for purposes of the Fifth Amendment has proved to be a problem of considerable difficulty. While this Court has recognized that the "Fifth Amendment's guarantee ... [is] designed to bar Government from forcing some people alone to bear public burdens which, in all fairness and justice, should be borne by the public as a whole," *Armstrong v. United States*, 364 U.S. 40, 49 (1960), this Court, quite simply, has been unable to develop any "set formula" for determining when "justice and fairness" require that economic injuries caused by public action be compensated by the government, rather than remain disproportionately concentrated on a few persons. *See Goldblatt v. Hempstead*, 369 U.S. 590, 594 (1962). Indeed, we have frequently observed that whether a particular restriction will be rendered invalid by the government's failure to pay for any losses proximately caused by it depends largely "upon the particular circumstances [in that] case." *United States v. Cent. Eureka Mining Co.*, 357 U.S. 155, 168 (1958); *see United States v. Caltex, Inc.*, 344 U.S. 149, 156 (1952).

In engaging in these essentially ad hoc, factual inquiries, the Court's decisions have identified several factors that have particular significance. The economic impact of the regulation on the claimant and, particularly, the extent to which the regulation has interfered with distinct investment-backed expectations are, of course, relevant considerations. *See Goldblatt v. Hempstead, supra*, 369 U.S. at 594. So, too, is the character of the governmental action. A "taking" may more readily be found when the interference with property can be characterized as a physical invasion by government, see, e. g., *United States v. Causby*, 328 U.S. 256 (1946), than when interference arises from some public program adjusting the benefits and burdens of economic life to promote the common good.

"Government hardly could go on if to some extent values incident to property could not be diminished without paying for every such change in the general law," *Pa. Coal Co. v. Mahon*, 260 U.S. 393, 413 (1922), and this Court has accordingly recognized, in a wide variety of contexts, that government may execute laws or programs that adversely affect recognized economic values. Exercises of the taxing power are one obvious example. A second are the decisions in which this Court has dismissed "taking" challenges on the ground that, while the challenged government action caused economic harm, it did not interfere with interests that were sufficiently bound up with the reasonable expectations of the claimant to constitute "property" for Fifth Amendment purposes. *See*, e. g., *United States v. Willow River Power Co.*, 324 U.S. 499 (1945) (interest in high-water level of river for runoff for tailwaters to maintain power head is not property); *United States v. Chandler-Dunbar Water Power Co.*, 229 U.S. 53 (1913) (no property interest can exist in navigable waters); *see also Demorest v. City Bank Co.*, 321 U.S. 36 (1944); *Muhlker v. N.Y. & Harlem R.R. Co.*, 197 U.S. 544 (1905); Joseph L. Sax, *Takings and the Police Power*, 74 Yale L.J. 36, 61–62 (1964). More importantly for the present case, in instances in which a state tribunal reasonably concluded that "the health, safety, morals, or general welfare" would be promoted by prohibiting particular contemplated uses of land, this Court has upheld land-use regulations that destroyed or adversely affected recognized real property interests ... . Zoning laws are, of course, the classic example ... [of] permissible governmental action even when prohibiting the most beneficial use of the property ... .

Zoning laws generally do not affect existing uses of real property, but "taking" challenges have also been held to be without merit in a wide variety of situations when the challenged governmental actions prohibited a beneficial use to which individual parcels had previously been devoted and thus caused substantial individualized harm. *Miller v. Schoene*, 276 U.S. 272 (1928), is illustrative. In that case, a state entomologist, acting pursuant to a state statute, ordered the claimants to cut down a large number of ornamental red cedar trees because they produced cedar rust fatal to apple trees cultivated nearby. Although the statute provided for recovery of any expense incurred in removing the cedars, and permitted claimants to use the felled trees, it did not provide compensation for the value of the standing trees or for the resulting decrease in market value of the properties as a whole. A unanimous Court held that this latter omission did not render the statute invalid. The Court held that the State might properly make "a choice between the preservation of one class of property and that of the other" and since the apple industry was important in the State involved, concluded that the State had not exceeded "its constitutional powers by deciding upon the destruction of one class of property [without compensation] in order to save another which, in the judgment of the legislature, is of greater value to the public." *Id.* at 279.

Again, *Hadacheck v. Sebastian*, 239 U.S. 394 (1915), upheld a law prohibiting the claimant from continuing his otherwise lawful business of operating a brickyard in a particular physical community on the ground that the legislature had reasonably concluded that the presence of the brickyard was inconsistent with neighboring uses. *See also United States v. Cent. Eureka Mining Co., supra* (Government order closing gold mines so that skilled miners would be available for other mining work held not a taking); *Atchison, T. & S. F. R. Co. v. Pub. Utils. Comm'n*, 346 U.S. 346 (1953) (railroad may be required to share cost of constructing railroad grade improvement); *Walls v. Midland Carbon Co.*, 254 U.S. 300 (1920) (law prohibiting manufacture of carbon black upheld); *Reinman v. Little Rock*, 237 U.S. 171 (1915) (law prohibiting livery stable upheld); *Mugler v. Kansas*, 123 U.S. 623 (1887) (law prohibiting liquor business upheld).

*Goldblatt v. Hempstead, supra*, is a recent example. There, a 1958 city safety ordinance banned any excavations below the water table and effectively prohibited the claimant from continuing a sand and gravel mining business that had been operated on the particular parcel since 1927. The Court upheld the ordinance against a "taking" challenge, although the ordinance prohibited the present and presumably most beneficial use of the property and had, like the regulations in *Miller* and *Hadacheck*, severely affected a particular owner … . Because the restriction served a substantial public purpose, the Court thus held no taking had occurred. It is, of course, implicit in *Goldblatt* that a use restriction on real property may constitute a "taking" if not reasonably necessary to the effectuation of a substantial public purpose … or perhaps if it has an unduly harsh impact upon the owner's use of the property.

*Pennsylvania Coal Co. v. Mahon*, 260 U.S. 393 (1922), is the leading case for the proposition that a state statute … may so frustrate distinct investment-backed expectations as to amount to a "taking." There the claimant had sold the surface rights to particular parcels of property, but expressly reserved the right to remove the coal thereunder. A Pennsylvania statute, enacted after the transactions, forbade any mining of coal that caused the subsidence of any house, unless the house was the property of the owner of the underlying coal and was more than 150 feet from the improved property of another. Because the statute made it commercially impracticable to mine the coal, *id.* at 414, and thus had nearly the same effect as the complete destruction of rights claimant had reserved from the owners of the surface land, see *id.* at 414–15, the Court held that the statute was invalid as effecting a "taking" without just compensation. *See also Armstrong v. United States*, 364 U.S. 40 (1960) (Government's complete destruction of a materialman's lien in certain property held a "taking"); *Hudson Water Co. v. McCarter*, 209 U.S. 349, 355 (1908) (if height restriction makes property wholly useless "the rights of property … prevail over the other public interest" and compensation is required). *See generally* Frank I. Michelman, *Property, Utility, and Fairness: Comments on the Ethical Foundations of "Just Compensation" Law*, 80 Harv. L. Rev. 1165, 1229–34 (1967).

Finally, government actions that may be characterized as acquisitions of resources to permit or facilitate uniquely public functions have often been held to constitute "takings." *United States v. Causby*, 328 U.S. 256 (1946), is illustrative. In holding that direct overflights above the claimant's land, that destroyed the present use of the land as a chicken farm, constituted a "taking," *Causby* emphasized that Government had not "merely destroyed property [but was] using a part of it for the flight of its planes." *Id.* 328 U.S. at 262–63, n.7. *See also Griggs v. Allegheny Cty.*, 369 U.S. 84 (1962) (overflights held a taking); *Portsmouth Co. v. United States*, 260 U.S. 327 (1922) (United States military installations' repeated firing of guns over claimant's land is a taking); *United States v. Cress*, 243 U.S. 316 (1917) (repeated floodings of land caused by water project is taking); *but see YMCA v. United States*, 395 U.S. 85 (1969) (damage caused to building when federal officers who were seeking to protect building were attacked by rioters held not a taking). *See generally Michelman, supra*, at 1226–29; Joseph L. Sax, *Takings and the Police Power*, 74 Yale L.J. 36 (1964).

### *B*

In contending that the New York City law has "taken" their property in violation of the Fifth and Fourteenth Amendments, appellants make a series of arguments, which, while tailored to the facts of this case, essentially urge that any substantial restriction imposed pursuant to a landmark law must be accompanied by just compensation if it is to be constitutional. Before considering these, we emphasize what is not in dispute. Because this Court has recognized, in a number of settings, that States and cities may enact land-use restrictions or controls to enhance the quality of life by preserving the character and desirable aesthetic features of a city, see *New Orleans v. Dukes*, 427 U.S. 297 (1976); *Young v. Am. Mini Theatres, Inc.*, 427 U.S. 50 (1976); *Vill. of Belle Terre v. Boraas*, 416 U.S. 1, 9–10 (1974); *Berman v. Parker*, 348 U.S. 26, 33 (1954); *Welch v. Swasey*, 214 U.S. at 108, appellants do not contest that New York City's objective of preserving structures and areas with special historic, architectural, or cultural significance is an entirely permissible governmental goal. They also do not dispute that the restrictions imposed on its parcel are appropriate means of securing the purposes of the New York City law. Finally, appellants do not challenge any of the specific factual premises of the decision below. They accept for present purposes both that the parcel of land occupied by Grand Central Terminal must, in its present state, be regarded as capable of earning a reasonable return, and that the transferable development rights afforded appellants by virtue of the Terminal's designation as a landmark are valuable, even if not as valuable as the rights to construct above the Terminal. In appellants' view none of these factors derogate from their claim that New York City's law has effected a "taking."

They first observe that the airspace above the Terminal is a valuable property interest, citing *United States v. Causby, supra*. They urge that the Landmarks Law has deprived them of any gainful use of their "air rights" above the Terminal and that, irrespective of the value of the remainder of their parcel, the city has "taken" their right to this superadjacent airspace, thus entitling them to "just compensation" measured by the fair market value of these air rights.

Apart from our own disagreement with appellants' characterization of the effect of the New York City law, see *infra*, at 2665, the submission that appellants may establish a "taking" simply by showing that they have been denied the ability to exploit a property interest that they heretofore had believed was available for development is quite simply untenable. Were this the rule, this Court would have erred not only in upholding laws restricting the development of air rights, see *Welch v. Swasey, supra*, but also in approving those prohibiting both the subjacent, see *Goldblatt v. Hempstead*, 369 U.S. 590 (1962), and the lateral, see

*Gorieb v. Fox*, 274 U.S. 603 (1927), development of particular parcels. "Taking" jurisprudence does not divide a single parcel into discrete segments and attempt to determine whether rights in a particular segment have been entirely abrogated. In deciding whether a particular governmental action has effected a taking, this Court focuses rather both on the character of the action and on the nature and extent of the interference with rights in the parcel as a whole—here, the city tax block designated as the "landmark site."

Secondly, appellants, focusing on the character and impact of the New York City law, argue that it effects a "taking" because its operation has significantly diminished the value of the Terminal site. Appellants concede that the decisions sustaining other land-use regulations, which, like the New York City law, are reasonably related to the promotion of the general welfare, uniformly reject the proposition that diminution in property value, standing alone, can establish a "taking," see *Euclid v. Ambler Realty Co.*, 272 U.S. 365 (1926) (75% diminution in value caused by zoning law); *Hadacheck v. Sebastian*, 239 U.S. 394 (1915) (87 1/2% diminution in value); *cf. Eastlake v. Forest City Enters., Inc.*, 426 U.S. at 674 n.8, and that the "taking" issue in these contexts is resolved by focusing on the uses the regulations permit. *See also Goldblatt v. Hempstead, supra.* Appellants, moreover, also do not dispute that a showing of diminution in property value would not establish a taking if the restriction had been imposed as a result of historic-district legislation, *see generally Maher v. New Orleans*, 516 F.2d 1051 (5th Cir. 1975), but appellants argue that New York City's regulation of individual landmarks is fundamentally different from zoning or from historic-district legislation because the controls imposed by New York City's law apply only to individuals who own selected properties.

Stated baldly, appellants' position appears to be that the only means of ensuring that selected owners are not singled out to endure financial hardship for no reason is to hold that any restriction imposed on individual landmarks pursuant to the New York City scheme is a "taking" requiring the payment of "just compensation." Agreement with this argument would, of course, invalidate not just New York City's law, but all comparable landmark legislation in the Nation. We find no merit in it.

It is true, as appellants emphasize, that both historic-district legislation and zoning laws regulate all properties within given physical communities whereas landmark laws apply only to selected parcels. But, contrary to appellants' suggestions, landmark laws are not like discriminatory, or "reverse spot," zoning: that is, a land-use decision which arbitrarily singles out a particular parcel for different, less favorable treatment than the neighboring ones. *See* 2 A. Rathkopf, *The Law of Zoning and Planning* 26–4, & n.6 (4th ed. 1978). In contrast to discriminatory zoning, which is the antithesis of land-use control as part of some comprehensive plan, the New York City law embodies a comprehensive plan to preserve structures of historic or aesthetic interest wherever they might be found in the city, and as noted, over 400 landmarks and 31 historic districts have been designated pursuant to this plan ... .

Next, appellants observe that New York City's law differs from zoning laws and historic-district ordinances in that the Landmarks Law does not impose identical or similar restrictions on all structures located in particular physical communities. It follows, they argue, that New York City's law is inherently incapable of producing the fair and equitable distribution of benefits and burdens of governmental action which is characteristic of zoning laws and historic-district legislation and which they maintain is a constitutional requirement if "just compensation" is not to be afforded. It is, of course, true that the Landmarks Law has a more severe impact on some landowners than on others, but that in itself does not mean that the law effects a "taking." Legislation designed to promote the general welfare commonly burdens some more than others. The owners of the brickyard in *Hadacheck*, of the cedar trees in *Miller v. Schoene*, and of the gravel and sand mine in *Goldblatt v. Hempstead*, were uniquely burdened by the legislation sustained in those cases. Similarly, zoning laws often affect some property owners more severely than others but have not been held to be invalid on that account. For example, the property owner in *Euclid* who wished to use its property for industrial purposes was affected far more severely by the ordinance than its neighbors who wished to use their land for residences.

In any event, appellants' repeated suggestions that they are solely burdened and unbenefited is factually inaccurate. This contention overlooks the fact that the New York City law applies to vast numbers of structures in the city in addition to the Terminal—all the structures contained in the 31 historic districts and over 400 individual landmarks, many of which are close to the Terminal. Unless we are to reject the judgment of the New York City Council that the preservation of landmarks benefits all New York citizens and all structures, both economically and by improving the quality of life in the city as a whole—which we are unwilling to do—we cannot conclude that the owners of the Terminal have in no sense been benefited by the Landmarks Law. Doubtless appellants believe they are more burdened than benefited by the law, but that must have been true, too, of the property owners in *Miller*, *Hadacheck*, *Euclid*, and *Goldblatt*.

Appellants' final broad-based attack would have us treat the law as an instance, like that in *United States v. Causby*, in which government, acting in an enterprise capacity, has appropriated part of their property for some strictly governmental purpose. Apart from the fact that *Causby* was a case of invasion of airspace that destroyed the use of the farm beneath and this New York City law has in nowise impaired the present use of the Terminal, the Landmarks Law neither exploits appellants' parcel for city purposes nor facilitates nor arises from any entrepreneurial operations of the city. The situation is not remotely like that in *Causby* where the airspace above the property was in the flight pattern for military aircraft. The Landmarks Law's effect is simply to prohibit appellants or anyone else from occupying portions of the airspace above the Terminal, while permitting appellants to use the remainder of the parcel in a gainful fashion. This is no more an appropriation of property by government for its own uses than is a zoning law prohibiting, for "aesthetic" reasons, two or more adult theaters within a specified area, see *Young v. Am. Mini Theatres, Inc.*, 427 U.S. 50 (1976), or a safety regulation prohibiting excavations below a certain level. *See Goldblatt v. Hempstead*.

### *C*

Rejection of appellants' broad arguments is not, however, the end of our inquiry, for all we thus far have established is that the New York City law is not rendered invalid by its failure to provide "just compensation" whenever a landmark owner is restricted in the exploitation of property interests, such as air rights, to a greater extent than provided for under applicable zoning laws. We now must consider whether the interference with appellants' property is of such a magnitude that "there must be an exercise of eminent domain and compensation to sustain [it]." *Pa. Coal Co. v. Mahon*, 260 U.S. at 413. That inquiry may be narrowed to the question of the severity of the impact of the law on appellants' parcel, and its resolution in turn requires a careful assessment of the impact of the regulation on the Terminal site.

Unlike the governmental acts in *Goldblatt*, *Miller*, *Causby*, *Griggs*, and *Hadacheck*, the New York City law does not interfere in any way with the present uses of the Terminal. Its designation as a landmark not only permits but contemplates that appellants may continue to use the property precisely as it has been used for the past 65 years: as a railroad terminal containing office space and concessions. So the law does not interfere with what must be regarded as Penn Central's primary expectation concerning the use of the parcel. More importantly, on this record, we must regard the New York City law as permitting Penn Central not only to profit from the Terminal but also to obtain a "reasonable return" on its investment.

Appellants, moreover, exaggerate the effect of the law on their ability to make use of the air rights above the Terminal in two respects. First, it simply cannot be maintained, on this record, that appellants have been prohibited from occupying any portion of the airspace above the Terminal. While the Commission's actions in denying applications to construct an office building in excess of 50 stories above the Terminal may indicate that it will refuse to issue a certificate of appropriateness for any comparably sized structure, nothing the Commission has said or done suggests an intention to prohibit any construction above the Terminal. The Commission's report emphasized that whether any construction would be allowed depended upon whether the proposed addition "would harmonize in scale, material and character with [the Terminal]." Record 2251. Since appellants have not sought approval for the construction of a smaller structure, we do not know that appellants will be denied any use of any portion of the airspace above the Terminal.

Second, to the extent appellants have been denied the right to build above the Terminal, it is not literally accurate to say that they have been denied all use of even those pre-existing air rights. Their ability to use these rights has not been abrogated; they are made transferable to at least eight parcels in the vicinity of the Terminal, one or two of which have been found suitable for the construction of new office buildings. Although appellants and others have argued that New York City's transferable development-rights program is far from ideal, the New York courts here supportably found that, at least in the case of the Terminal, the rights afforded are valuable. While these rights may well not have constituted "just compensation" if a "taking" had occurred, the rights nevertheless undoubtedly mitigate whatever financial burdens the law has imposed on appellants and, for that reason, are to be taken into account in considering the impact of regulation. *Cf. Goldblatt v. Hempstead*, 369 U.S. at 594 n.3.

On this record, we conclude that the application of New York City's Landmarks Law has not effected a "taking" of appellants' property. The restrictions ... not only permit reasonable beneficial use of the landmark site but also afford appellants opportunities further to enhance not only the Terminal site proper but also other properties.

Affirmed.

Mr. Justice REHNQUIST, with whom THE CHIEF JUSTICE and Mr. Justice STEVENS join, dissenting.

Of the over one million buildings and structures in the city of New York, appellees have singled out 400 for designation as official landmarks. The owner of a building might initially be pleased that his property has been chosen by a distinguished committee of architects, historians, and city planners for such a singular distinction. But he may well discover, as appellant Penn Central Transportation Co. did here, that the landmark designation imposes upon him a substantial cost, with little or no offsetting benefit except for the honor of the designation. The question in this case is whether the cost associated with the city of New York's desire to preserve a limited number of "landmarks" within its borders must be borne by all of its taxpayers or whether it can instead be imposed entirely on the owners of the individual properties.

Only in the most superficial sense of the word can this case be said to involve "zoning." Typical zoning restrictions may, it is true, so limit the prospective uses of a piece of property as to diminish the value of that property in the abstract because it may not be used for the forbidden purposes. But any such abstract decrease in value will more than likely be at least partially offset by an increase in value which flows from similar restrictions as to use on neighboring properties. All property owners in a designated area are placed under the same restrictions, not only for the benefit of the municipality as a whole but also for the common benefit of one another. In the words of Mr. Justice Holmes, speaking for the Court in *Pa. Coal Co. v. Mahon*, 260 U.S. 393, 415 (1922), there is "an average reciprocity of advantage."

Where a relatively few individual buildings, all separated from one another, are singled out and treated differently from surrounding buildings, no such reciprocity exists. The cost to the property owner which results from the imposition of restrictions applicable only to his property and not that of his neighbors may be substantial—in this case, several million dollars—with no comparable reciprocal benefits ... . Under the historic-landmark preservation scheme adopted by New York, the property owner is under an affirmative duty to *preserve* his property *as a landmark* at his own expense ... . In August 1967, Grand Central Terminal was designated a landmark over the objections of its owner Penn Central. Immediately upon this designation, Penn Central, like all owners of a landmark site, was placed under an affirmative duty, backed by criminal fines and penalties, to keep "exterior portions" of the landmark "in good repair" ... [emphasis in the original].

The Fifth Amendment provides in part: "nor shal private property be taken for public use, without just compensation." In a very literal sense, the actions of appellees violated this constitutional prohibition. Before the city of New York declared Grand Central Terminal to be a landmark, Penn Central could have used its "air rights" over the Terminal to build a multistory office building, at an apparent value of several million dollars per year. Today, the Terminal cannot be modified in any form, including the erection of additional stories, without the permission of the Landmark Preservation Commission, a permission which appellants, despite good-faith attempts, have so far been unable to obtain ... .

Appellees do not dispute that valuable property rights have been destroyed. And the Court has frequently emphasized that the term "property" as used in the Taking Clause includes the entire "group of rights inhering in the citizen's [ownership]." *United States v. Gen. Motors Corp.*, 323 U.S. 373 (1945). The term is not used in the

> vulgar and untechnical sense of the physical thing with respect to which the citizen exercises rights recognized by law. [Instead, it] ... denote[s] the group of rights inhering in the citizen's relation to the physical THING, AS THE RIGHT TO POSSESS, USE AND DISPOSE OF IT ... . the constitutional provision is addressed to every sort of interest the citizen may possess. *Id.* at 377–78 [emphasis added].

While neighboring landowners are free to use their land and "air rights" in any way consistent with the broad boundaries of New York zoning, Penn Central, absent the permission of appellees, must forever maintain its property in its present state. The property has been thus subjected to a nonconsensual servitude not borne by any neighboring or similar properties.

Appellees have thus destroyed—in a literal sense, "taken"—substantial property rights of Penn Central ... . As Mr. Justice Holmes pointed out in *Pa. Coal Co. v. Mahon*, "the question at bottom" in an eminent domain case "is upon whom the loss of the changes desired should fall." 260 U.S. at 416. The benefits that appellees believe will flow from preservation of the Grand Central Terminal will accrue to all the citizens of New York City. There is no reason to believe that appellants will enjoy a substantially greater share of these benefits. If the cost of preserving Grand Central Terminal were spread evenly across the entire population of the city of New York, the burden per person would be in cents per year—a minor cost appellees would surely concede for the benefit accrued. Instead, however, appellees would impose the entire cost of several million dollars per year on Penn Central. But it is precisely this sort of discrimination that the Fifth Amendment prohibits ... . The city of New York is in a precarious financial state, and some may believe that the costs of landmark preservation will be more easily borne by corporations such as Penn Central than the overburdened individual taxpayers of New York. But these concerns do not allow us to ignore past precedents construing the Eminent Domain Clause to the end that the desire

**to improve the public condition is, indeed, achieved by a shorter cut than the constitutional way of paying for the change.**

## Denominator problem

One tenacious difficulty in evaluating the extent to which a regulation causes economic losses to a property owner has been determining what actually constitutes the property. A property owner alleging that a government rule requires compensation has an interest in defining the regulated property as equal to the interest lost due to the government regulation. That conception of the "whole property" is the necessary path to concluding that the regulation has deprived the owner of all value. In contrast, the government has an interest in defining the property as something more than the interest lost.

In the case *Tahoe-Sierra Pres. Council v. Tahoe Reg'l Plan. Agency*,[18] the Court wrestles with a particularly interesting application of this difficulty: whether a time-limited restriction on the use of property can constitute a regulatory taking. Essentially, the Court is contemplating whether the whole property can be a portion of the property divided in time:

> Property interests may have many different dimensions. For example, the dimensions of a property interest may include a physical dimension (which describes the size and shape of the property in question), a functional dimension (which describes the extent to which an owner may use or dispose of the property in question), and a temporal dimension (which describes the duration of the property interest). At base, the plaintiffs' argument is that we should conceptually sever each plaintiff's fee interest into discrete segments in at least one of these dimensions—the temporal one—and treat each of those segments as separate and distinct property interests for purposes of takings analysis. Under this theory, they argue that there was a categorical taking of one of those temporal segments.[19]

If the concept of dividing property in time seems inconceivable, think of a lease agreement for real property. You may even have a lease that gives you the right to occupy your home, to the exclusion of your landlord, but only for a limited amount of time. The lease is a routine way that people divide property ownership in time.

While the facts in *Tahoe-Sierra* are an example of temporal severance—or dividing property in time—*Murr v. Wisconsin* provides an example of horizontal severance—or dividing property physically, along the ground. *Murr v. Wisconsin* moves the concept of regulatory takings forward by providing a test to determine what amount of property constitutes the whole property for the purposes of a regulatory takings analysis. Use the *Murr v. Wisconsin* test to determine what is the whole property when applying either the "just compensation owed if all value lost" per se regulatory taking test or the ad hoc balancing test for regulatory taking.

## United States Supreme Court

### *Murr v. Wisconsin*[20]

### 2017

**Justice KENNEDY delivered the opinion of the Court.**

**The classic example of a property taking by the government is when the property has been occupied or otherwise seized. In the case now before the Court, petitioners contend that governmental entities took their real property—an undeveloped residential lot—not by some physical occupation, but instead by enacting burdensome regulations that forbid**

its improvement or separate sale because it is classified as substandard in size. The relevant governmental entities are the respondents.

Against the background justifications for the challenged restrictions, respondents contend there is no regulatory taking because petitioners own an adjacent lot. The regulations, in effecting a merger of the property, permit the continued residential use of the property including for a single improvement to extend over both lots. This retained right of the landowner, respondents urge, is of sufficient offsetting value that the regulation is not severe enough to be a regulatory taking. To resolve the issue whether the landowners can insist on confining the analysis just to the lot in question, without regard to their ownership of the adjacent lot, it is necessary to discuss the background principles that define regulatory takings ... .

Petitioners are two sisters and two brothers in the Murr family. Petitioners' parents arranged for them to receive ownership of two lots the family used for recreation along the Lower St. Croix River in the town of Troy, Wisconsin. The lots are adjacent, but the parents purchased them separately, put the title of one in the name of the family business, and later arranged for transfer of the two lots, on different dates, to petitioners ... .

For the area where petitioners' property is located, the Wisconsin rules prevent the use of lots as separate building sites unless they have at least one acre of land suitable for development. Wis. Admin. Code §§ NR 118.04(4), 118.03(27), 118.06(1)(a)(2)(a), 118.06(1)(b) (2017) ... .

Petitioners' parents purchased Lot F in 1960 and built a small recreational cabin on it. In 1961, they transferred title to Lot F to the family plumbing company. In 1963, they purchased neighboring Lot E, which they held in their own names ... .

Though each lot is approximately 1.25 acres in size, because of the waterline and the steep bank they each have less than one acre of land suitable for development. Even when combined, the lots' buildable land area is only 0.98 acres due to the steep terrain.

The lots remained under separate ownership, with Lot F owned by the plumbing company and Lot E owned by petitioners' parents, until transfers to petitioners. Lot F was conveyed to them in 1994, and Lot E was conveyed to them in 1995. *Murr v. St. Croix Cty. Bd. of Adjustment*, 796 N.W.2d 837, 841, 844 (Wis. Ct. App. 2011); 859 N.W.2d 628 (Wis. Ct. App. 2015) (unpublished opinion), App. to Pet. for Cert. A–3, ¶¶ 4–5 (there are certain ambiguities in the record concerning whether the lots had merged earlier, but the parties and the courts below appear to have assumed the merger occurred upon transfer to petitioners).

A decade later, petitioners became interested in moving the cabin on Lot F to a different portion of the lot and selling Lot E to fund the project. The unification of the lots under common ownership, however, had implicated the state and local rules barring their separate sale or development. Petitioners then sought variances from the St. Croix County Board of Adjustment to enable their building and improvement plan, including a variance to allow the separate sale or use of the lots. The Board denied the requests, and the state courts affirmed in relevant part. In particular, the Wisconsin Court of Appeals agreed with the Board's interpretation that the local ordinance "effectively merged" Lots E and F, so petitioners "could only sell or build on the single larger lot." *Murr*, *supra*, at 184, 796 N.W.2d at 844.

Petitioners filed the present action in state court, alleging that the state and county regulations worked a regulatory taking by depriving them of "all, or practically all, of the use of Lot E because the lot cannot be sold or developed as a separate lot." App. 9 ... . The Circuit Court of St. Croix County granted summary judgment to the State, explaining that petitioners retained "several available options for the use and enjoyment of their property." For example, they could preserve the existing cabin, relocate the cabin, or eliminate the cabin and build a new residence on Lot E, on Lot F, or across both lots. The court also found petitioners had not been deprived of all economic value of their property … . The Wisconsin Court of Appeals affirmed … conclud[ing] the merger regulations did not effect a taking [when conducting the takings analysis "on the Murrs' property as a whole" because] petitioners could not reasonably have expected to use the lots separately because they were "charged with knowledge of the existing zoning laws" when they acquired the property … . The Supreme Court of Wisconsin denied discretionary review. This Court granted certiorari … .

The Takings Clause of the Fifth Amendment provides that private property shall not "be taken for public use, without just compensation." The Clause is made applicable to the States through the Fourteenth Amendment. *Chi., B. & Q. R. Co. v. Chicago*, 166 U.S. 226 (1897). As this Court has recognized, the plain language of the Takings Clause "requires the payment of compensation whenever the government acquires private property for a public purpose," see *Tahoe-Sierra Pres. Council, Inc. v. Tahoe Reg'l Planning Agency*, 535 U.S. 302, 321 (2002), but it does not address in specific terms the imposition of regulatory burdens on private property. Indeed, "[p]rior to Justice Holmes's exposition in *Pa. Coal Co. v. Mahon*, 260 U.S. 393 (1922), it was generally thought that the Takings Clause reached only a direct appropriation of property, or the functional equivalent of a practical ouster of the owner's possession," like the permanent flooding of property. *Lucas v. S.C. Coastal Council*, 505 U.S. 1003, 1014 (1992) (citation, brackets, and internal quotation marks omitted); *accord, Horne v. Dep't of Agric.*, 576 U.S. ___, ___ (2015) (slip op., at 7); *see also Loretto v. Teleprompter Manhattan CATV Corp.*, 458 U.S. 419, 427 (1982). *Mahon*, however, initiated this Court's regulatory takings jurisprudence, declaring that "while property may be regulated to a certain extent, if regulation goes too far it will be recognized as a taking." 260 U.S. at 415. A regulation, then, can be so burdensome as to become a taking, yet the *Mahon* Court did not formulate more detailed guidance for determining when this limit is reached.

In the near century since *Mahon*, the Court for the most part has refrained from elaborating this principle through definitive rules. This area of the law has been characterized by "ad hoc, factual inquiries, designed to allow careful examination and weighing of all the relevant circumstances." *Tahoe–Sierra, supra*, at 322 (citation and internal quotation marks omitted). The Court has, however, stated two guidelines relevant here for determining when government regulation is so onerous that it constitutes a taking. First, "with certain qualifications … a regulation which 'denies all economically beneficial or productive use of land' will require compensation under the Takings Clause." *Palazzolo v. Rhode Island*, 533 U.S. 606, 617 (2001) (quoting *Lucas, supra*, at 1015). Second, when a regulation impedes the use of property without depriving the owner of all economically beneficial use, a taking still may be found based on "a complex of factors," including (1) the economic impact of the regulation on the claimant; (2) the extent to which the regulation has interfered with distinct investment-backed expectations; and (3) the character of the governmental action. *Palazzolo, supra*, at 617 (citing *Penn Cent. Transp. Co. v. New York City*, 438 U.S. 104, 124 (1978)) … .

This case presents a question that is linked to the ultimate determination whether a regulatory taking has occurred: What is the proper unit of property against which to assess the effect of the challenged governmental action? Put another way, "[b]ecause our test for regulatory taking requires us to compare the value that has been taken from the property with the value that remains in the property, one of the critical questions is determining how to define the unit of property 'whose value is to furnish the denominator of the fraction.'"

*Keystone Bituminous Coal Ass'n v. DeBenedictis*, 480 U.S. 470, 497 (1987) (quoting Frank I. Michelman, *Property, Utility, and Fairness*, 80 Harv. L. Rev. 1165, 1992 (1967)

As commentators have noted, the answer to this question may be outcome determinative. See Steven J. Eagle, *The Four-Factor Penn Central Regulatory Takings Test*, 118 Penn St. L. Rev. 601, 631 (2014); *see also* Danaya C. Wright, *A New Time for Denominators*, 34 Envtl. L. 175, 180 (2004). This Court, too, has explained that the question is important to the regulatory takings inquiry. "To the extent that any portion of property is taken, that portion is always taken in its entirety; the relevant question, however, is whether the property taken is all, or only a portion of, the parcel in question." *Concrete Pipe & Prods. of Cal., Inc. v. Constr. Laborers Pension Tr. for S. Cal.*, 508 U.S. 602, 644 (1993).

Defining the property at the outset, however, should not necessarily preordain the outcome in every case. In some, though not all, cases the effect of the challenged regulation must be assessed and understood by the effect on the entire property held by the owner, rather than just some part of the property that, considered just on its own, has been diminished in value. This demonstrates the contrast between regulatory takings, where the goal is usually to determine how the challenged regulation affects the property's value to the owner, and physical takings, where the impact of physical appropriation or occupation of the property will be evident.

While the Court has not set forth specific guidance on how to identify the relevant parcel for the regulatory taking inquiry, there are two concepts which the Court has indicated can be unduly narrow.

First, the Court has declined to limit the parcel in an artificial manner to the portion of property targeted by the challenged regulation. In *Penn Central*, for example, the Court rejected a challenge to the denial of a permit to build an office tower above Grand Central Terminal. The Court refused to measure the effect of the denial only against the "air rights" above the terminal, cautioning that "'taking' jurisprudence does not divide a single parcel into discrete segments and attempt to determine whether rights in a particular segment have been entirely abrogated." 438 U.S. at 130.

In a similar way, in *Tahoe–Sierra*, the Court refused to "effectively sever" the 32 months during which petitioners' property was restricted by temporary moratoria on development "and then ask whether that segment ha[d] been taken in its entirety." 535 U.S. at 331. That was because "defining the property interest taken in terms of the very regulation being challenged is circular." *Ibid.* That approach would overstate the effect of regulation on property, turning "every delay" into a "total ban." *Ibid.*

The second concept about which the Court has expressed caution is the view that property rights under the Takings Clause should be coextensive with those under state law. Although property interests have their foundations in state law, the *Palazzolo* Court reversed a state-court decision that rejected a takings challenge to regulations that predated the landowner's acquisition of title. 533 U.S. at 626–627. The Court explained that States do not have the unfettered authority to "shape and define property rights and reasonable investment-backed expectations," leaving landowners without recourse against unreasonable regulations. *Id.* at 626.

By the same measure, defining the parcel by reference to state law could defeat a challenge even to a state enactment that alters permitted uses of property in ways inconsistent with reasonable investment-backed expectations. For example, a State might enact a law that consolidates nonadjacent property owned by a single person or entity in different parts of the State and then imposes development limits on the aggregate set. If a court defined the parcel according to the state law requiring consolidation, this improperly would fortify the state law against a takings claim, because the court would look to the retained value in the property as a whole rather than considering whether individual holdings had lost all value.

As the foregoing discussion makes clear, no single consideration can supply the exclusive test for determining the denominator. Instead, courts must consider a number of factors. These include the treatment of the land under state and local law; the physical characteristics of the land; and the prospective value of the regulated land. The endeavor should determine whether reasonable expectations about property ownership would lead a landowner to anticipate that his holdings would be treated as one parcel, or, instead, as separate tracts. The inquiry is objective, and the reasonable expectations at issue derive from background customs and the whole of our legal tradition. Cf. *Lucas*, 505 U.S. at 1035 (Kennedy, J., concurring) ("The expectations protected by the Constitution are based on objective rules and customs that can be understood as reasonable by all parties involved").

First, courts should give substantial weight to the treatment of the land, in particular how it is bounded or divided, under state and local law. The reasonable expectations of an acquirer of land must acknowledge legitimate restrictions affecting his or her subsequent use and dispensation of the property. *See Ballard v. Hunter*, 204 U.S. 241, 262 (1907) ("Of what concerns or may concern their real estate men usually keep informed, and on that probability the law may frame its proceedings"). A valid takings claim will not evaporate just because a purchaser took title after the law was enacted. *See Palazzolo*, 533 U.S. at 627 (some "enactments are unreasonable and do not become less so through passage of time or title"). A reasonable restriction that predates a landowner's acquisition, however, can be one of the objective factors that most landowners would reasonably consider in forming fair expectations about their property. *See ibid.* ("[A] prospective enactment, such as a new zoning ordinance, can limit the value of land without effecting a taking because it can be understood as reasonable by all concerned"). In a similar manner, a use restriction which is triggered only after, or because of, a change in ownership should also guide a court's assessment of reasonable private expectations.

Second, courts must look to the physical characteristics of the landowner's property. These include the physical relationship of any distinguishable tracts, the parcel's topography, and the surrounding human and ecological environment. In particular, it may be relevant that the property is located in an area that is subject to, or likely to become subject to, environmental or other regulation. *Cf. Lucas, supra*, at 1035 (Kennedy, J., concurring) ("Coastal property may present such unique concerns for a fragile land system that the State can go further in regulating its development and use than the common law of nuisance might otherwise permit").

Third, courts should assess the value of the property under the challenged regulation, with special attention to the effect of burdened land on the value of other holdings. Though a use restriction may decrease the market value of the property, the effect may be tempered if the regulated land adds value to the remaining property, such as by increasing privacy, expanding recreational space, or preserving surrounding natural beauty. A law that limits use of a landowner's small lot in one part of the city by reason of the landowner's nonadjacent holdings elsewhere may decrease the market value of the small lot in an unmitigated fashion. The absence of a special relationship between the holdings may counsel against consideration of all the holdings as a single parcel, making the restrictive law susceptible to a takings challenge. On the other hand, if the landowner's other property is adjacent to the small lot, the market value of the properties may well increase if their combination enables the expansion of a structure, or if development restraints for one part of the parcel protect the unobstructed skyline views of another part. That, in turn, may counsel in favor of treatment as a single parcel and may reveal the weakness of a regulatory takings challenge to the law.

State and federal courts have considerable experience in adjudicating regulatory takings claims that depart from these examples in various ways. The Court anticipates that in applying the test above they will continue to exercise care in this complex area ... .

Under the appropriate multifactor standard, it follows that for purposes of determining whether a regulatory taking has occurred here, petitioners' property should be evaluated as a single parcel consisting of Lots E and F together.

First, the treatment of the property under state and local law indicates petitioners' property should be treated as one when considering the effects of the restrictions. As the Wisconsin courts held, the state and local regulations merged Lots E and F … . Petitioners' land was subject to this regulatory burden, moreover, only because of voluntary conduct in bringing the lots under common ownership after the regulations were enacted. As a result, the valid merger of the lots under state law informs the reasonable expectation they will be treated as a single property.

Second, the physical characteristics of the property support its treatment as a unified parcel. The lots are contiguous along their longest edge. Their rough terrain and narrow shape make it reasonable to expect their range of potential uses might be limited. Cf. App. to Pet. for Cert. A–5, ¶ 8 ("[Petitioners] asserted Lot E could not be put to alternative uses like agriculture or commerce due to its size, location and steep terrain"). The land's location along the river is also significant. Petitioners could have anticipated public regulation might affect their enjoyment of their property, as the Lower St. Croix was a regulated area under federal, state, and local law long before petitioners possessed the land.

Third, the prospective value that Lot E brings to Lot F supports considering the two as one parcel for purposes of determining if there is a regulatory taking. Petitioners are prohibited from selling Lots E and F separately or from building separate residential structures on each. Yet this restriction is mitigated by the benefits of using the property as an integrated whole, allowing increased privacy and recreational space, plus the optimal location of any improvements. See Case No. 12–CV–258, App. to Pet. for Cert. B–9 ("They have an elevated level of privacy because they do not have close neighbors and are able to swim and play volleyball at the property").

The special relationship of the lots is further shown by their combined valuation. Were Lot E separately saleable but still subject to the development restriction, petitioners' appraiser would value the property at only $40,000. We express no opinion on the validity of this figure. We also note the number is not particularly helpful for understanding petitioners' retained value in the properties because Lot E, under the regulations, cannot be sold without Lot F. The point that is useful for these purposes is that the combined lots are valued at $698,300, which is far greater than the summed value of the separate regulated lots (Lot F with its cabin at $373,000, according to respondents' appraiser, and Lot E as an undevelopable plot at $40,000, according to petitioners' appraiser). The value added by the lots' combination shows their complementarity and supports their treatment as one parcel … .

Considering petitioners' property as a whole, the state court was correct to conclude that petitioners cannot establish a compensable taking in these circumstances. Petitioners have not suffered a taking under *Lucas*, as they have not been deprived of all economically beneficial use of their property. *See* 505 U.S. at 1019. They can use the property for residential purposes, including an enhanced, larger residential improvement. *See Palazzolo*, 533 U.S. at 631 ("A regulation permitting a landowner to build a substantial residence … does not leave the property 'economically idle'"). The property has not lost all economic value, as its value has decreased by less than 10 percent. *See Lucas*, *supra*, at 1019, n.8 (suggesting that even a landowner with 95 percent loss may not recover).

Petitioners furthermore have not suffered a taking under the more general test of *Penn Central*. *See* 438 U.S. at 124. The expert appraisal relied upon by the state courts refutes any claim that the economic impact of the regulation is severe. Petitioners cannot claim that they reasonably expected to sell or develop their lots separately given the regulations which predated their acquisition of both lots. Finally, the governmental action was a reasonable land-use regulation, enacted as part of a coordinated federal, state, and local effort to preserve the river and surrounding land.

Like the ultimate question whether a regulation has gone too far, the question of the proper parcel in regulatory takings cases cannot be solved by any simple test. See *Ark. Game and Fish Comm'n v. United States*, 568 U.S. 23, 31 (2012). Courts must instead define the parcel in a manner that reflects reasonable expectations about the property. Courts must strive for consistency with the central purpose of the Takings Clause: to "bar Government from forcing some people alone to bear public burdens which, in all fairness and justice, should be borne by the public as a whole." *Armstrong*, 364 U.S. at 49. Treating the lot in question as a single parcel is legitimate for purposes of this takings inquiry, and this supports the conclusion that no regulatory taking occurred here.

The judgment of the Wisconsin Court of Appeals is affirmed.

It is so ordered.

Justice GORSUCH took no part in the consideration or decision of this case.

Chief Justice ROBERTS, with whom Justice THOMAS and Justice ALITO join, dissenting.

… . I would stick with our traditional approach: State law defines the boundaries of distinct parcels of land, and those boundaries should determine the "private property" at issue in regulatory takings cases. Whether a regulation effects a taking of that property is a separate question, one in which common ownership of adjacent property may be taken into account. Because the majority departs from these settled principles, I respectfully dissent … .

I respectfully dissent.

Justice THOMAS, dissenting.

I join THE CHIEF JUSTICE's dissent because it correctly applies this Court's regulatory takings precedents, which no party has asked us to reconsider. The Court, however, has never purported to ground those precedents in the Constitution as it was originally understood. In *Pa. Coal Co. v. Mahon*, 260 U.S. 393, 415 (1922), the Court announced a "general rule" that "if regulation goes too far it will be recognized as a taking." But we have since observed that, prior to *Mahon*, "it was generally thought that the Takings Clause reached only a 'direct appropriation' of property, *Legal Tender Cases*, 12 Wall. 457, 551, 20 L.Ed. 287 (1871), or the functional equivalent of a 'practical ouster of [the owner's] possession,' *Transp. Co. v. Chicago*, 99 U.S. 635, 642 (1879)."

*Lucas v. S.C. Coastal Council*, 505 U.S. 1003, 1014 (1992). In my view, it would be desirable for us to take a fresh look at our regulatory takings jurisprudence, to see whether it can be grounded in the original public meaning of the Takings Clause of the Fifth Amendment or the Privileges or Immunities Clause of the Fourteenth Amendment. *See generally* Michael B. Rappaport, *Originalism and Regulatory Takings: Why the Fifth Amendment May Not Protect Against Regulatory Takings, but the Fourteenth Amendment May*, 45 San Diego L. Rev. 729 (2008) (describing the debate among scholars over those questions).

**Box 16.1 Practice problem: Brett's timeshare**

Brett Colin owns a timeshare in sunny Bay County. That county is a popular destination for tourists who come for the year-round temperate climate and for the many recreational opportunities that the county's beautiful beaches offer.

A timeshare is an interest in real property that allows the owner to occupy the property only part-time. The ownership structure of Colin's timeshare is commonly called shared deed ownership. This means that Colin has one of many existing deeds to the property. Each deed entitles its owner to occupy the property for a portion of each year. In the case of Colin's timeshare, 24 deeds exist and the owner of each deed has the right to occupy the property for one-half of one month each year. Colin can select the dates he will occupy the property pursuant to a process his deed establishes.

Colin purchased this timeshare many years ago for $11,000 to use as a vacation destination for his family. Before purchasing the timeshare, Colin carefully compared the cost of the timeshare to hotels near the beach in Bay County. He found that, over time, he would save a substantial amount of money with the timeshare.

Interestingly, the state where Bay County is located has more than one-quarter of all timeshare units in the United States. To facilitate timeshares, the state has in effect a state law called the "Vacation Plan and Timesharing Act." One purpose of this law is to "create statutory recognition to real property timeshare plans" in the state.

The statute provides for deeds that, like Colin's, record ownership of a timeshare estate. A timeshare estate is "a right to occupy a timeshare unit, coupled with a freehold estate or an estate for years with a future interest in a timeshare property or a specified portion thereof, or coupled with an ownership interest in a condominium unit." The law also states that "a timeshare estate is a parcel of real property under the laws of this state."

Bay County has recently recognized that residents are having problems with vacation rentals. A "vacation rental" is any condominium unit, cooperative, single-family house, two-family house, three-family house, or four-family house that is transiently occupied by changing sets of people on a monthly or more frequent basis. App-based services that facilitate short-term rentals of real property have led to the rapid proliferation of vacation rentals in those Bay County neighborhoods that are closest to the beaches.

Residents of these near-beach neighborhoods have begun contacting elected officials to complain about unknown people walking in their neighborhoods; loud, weeknight parties held by vacation-rental customers; and poorly maintained, deteriorating vacation rentals.

In response to these constituent concerns, the Bay County Commission recently adopted an ordinance regulating vacation rentals. These are some of the more significant restrictions of the ordinance, which applies to all near-beach neighborhoods in the city, including the neighborhood where Colin's timeshare is located.

- Each vacation rental must provide at least one full-service bathroom for every four guests the vacation rental can accommodate.
- A vacation rental with three or more stories must stand for an annual inspection of all balconies, platforms, stairways, and railways to ensure they are safe, secure, and free of defects.
- And, vacation rental owners must report to the county office of business regulation the names of vacation rental occupants and those occupants may not reserve the property for a time period of less than one month.

At the hearing where the county adopted this ordinance, the Bay County planning director testified: "These short-term rental folks are usually partying. It quickly becomes a nuisance to those who are full-time residents here."

Before calling for a vote on the motion to approve the ordinance, the chair of the county commission said: "We must have separation between the full-time residents and short-term visitors. Putting these transient folks in our neighborhoods creates a huge conflict. It's all complaints about parking, noise and parties. The landlords are basically turning our single-family neighborhoods into commercial hotel districts. That's destroying the quality of our communities."

Once the Bay County vacation rental ordinance went into effect, it created a problem for the owners of all 24 deeds for Colin's timeshare property. Specifically, the ordinance's prohibition on occupants reserving a vacation rental for less than one month conflicts with their practice of occupying the timeshare property for half-month time periods. Under the county's vacation rental ordinance, Colin may not use his half-month timeshare.

Quickly, a real estate broker offered all owners of timeshares in Colin's property $8,000 each for their interests. Several timeshare owners sold. The real estate broker has now relisted the timeshares at a sale price of $34,000 for a pair of deeds that together give the owner the right to occupy the property for a full month. Colin is outraged because he has no use for a month-long timeshare. He simply cannot get the time off of work. Also, he and his family never partied or made loud noise.

To defend his family's tradition of vacationing in Bay County, Colin decides to sue the county alleging that its ordinance constitutes a regulatory taking. Evaluate Colin's claim using the three part regulatory takings rule from *Penn Central Transportation Co. v. New York City*. If necessary, determine what portion of the property constitutes the whole using the rule from *Murr v. Wisconsin*.

## Abandoned substantially advances test

While this text has addressed many regulatory takings tests, it has omitted one: the extinct substantially advances regulatory takings test. That test was a significant diversion in regulatory takings case law. Though it is no longer the law, several pre-2005 regulatory takings cases apply it. References to the substantially advances test are missing from the cases in this text only because I have edited them out to conserve length and to be clear.

The U.S. Supreme Court articulated the substantially advances regulatory takings test in *Agins v. City of Tiburon*, as "[t]he application of a general zoning law to particular property effects a taking if the ordinance does not *substantially advance* legitimate state interests."[21]

Courts subsequently relied on that pronouncement and developed the *Agins* "substantially advances" language into a full-blown regulatory takings test.

However, despite the existence of the substantially advances analysis for decades, the U.S. Supreme Court abandoned it in *Lingle v. Chevron U.S.A., Inc.*[22] The Court said:

> On occasion, a would-be doctrinal rule or test finds its way into our case law through simple repetition of a phrase—however fortuitously coined. A quarter century ago, in *Agins v. City of Tiburon*, the Court declared that government regulation of private property "effects a taking if [such regulation] does not substantially advance legitimate state interests ... ." Through reiteration in a half dozen or so decisions since *Agins*, this language has been ensconced in our Fifth Amendment takings jurisprudence.[23]

Despite its 25-year life span, the Court killed off the substantially advances test when it concluded "that this formula prescribes an inquiry in the nature of a due process, not a takings, test, and that it has no proper place in our takings jurisprudence."[24]

Further, the Court explained:

> The "substantially advances" formula suggests a means-ends test: It asks, in essence, whether a regulation of private property is *effective* in achieving some legitimate public purpose. An inquiry of this nature has some logic in the context of a due process challenge, for a regulation that fails to serve any legitimate governmental objective may be so arbitrary or irrational that it runs afoul of the Due Process Clause. But such a test is not a valid method of discerning whether private property has been "taken" for purposes of the Fifth Amendment.
>
> In stark contrast to the three regulatory takings tests [presented in *Loretto, Lucas* and *Penn Central*], the "substantially advances" inquiry reveals nothing about the *magnitude* or *character of the burden* a particular regulation imposes upon private property rights. Nor does it provide any information about how any regulatory burden is *distributed* among property owners. In consequence, this test does not help to identify those regulations whose effects are functionally comparable to government appropriation or invasion of private property; it is tethered neither to the text of the Takings Clause nor to the basic justification for allowing regulatory actions to be challenged under the Clause.[25]

With this language, the Court did more than abrogate its holding in *Agins*. It also further delineated what distinguishes a due process claim from a regulatory takings claim.

## Regulatory takings epilogue

Regulatory takings can be confusing. And the *Penn Central* ad hoc balancing test for regulatory takings is difficult to apply. The following quote from *First Eng. Evangelical Lutheran Church of Glendale v. L.A. Cnty.*,[26] a temporary regulatory takings case that preceded *Tahoe-Sierra*, is a fitting conclusion to any in-depth discussion of regulatory takings.

In this quote, Justice Stevens bemoans how the confusing state of regulatory takings jurisprudence challenges land use practitioners.

> It is no answer to say that "after all, if a policeman must know the Constitution, then why not a planner?" To begin with, the Court has repeatedly recognized that it itself cannot establish any objective rules to assess when a regulation becomes a taking. How then can it demand that land planners do any better? However confusing some of our criminal procedure cases may be, I do not believe they have been as open-ended and standardless as our regulatory takings cases are. As one commentator concluded: "The chaotic state of taking law makes it especially likely that availability of the damages remedy will induce land-use planning officials to stay well back of the invisible line that they dare not cross."[27]

Take this quote as an assurance. If you find regulatory takings confusing, you are in excellent company.

## Notes

1 438 U.S. 104, 124 (1978).
2 Penn Cent. Transp. Co. v. New York City, 438 U.S. 104, 124 (1978) (citation omitted).
3 *Id.*

4 Pa. Coal Co. v. Mahon, 260 U.S. 393, 419 (1922) (Brandeis, J., dissenting).
5 *Penn Cent.*, 438 U.S. 104, 130–31 (1978).
6 Murr v. Wisconsin, 137 S. Ct. 1933, 1945 (2017).
7 *Penn Cent.*, 438 U.S. at 127.
8 E.g. *Pa. Coal Co.*, 260 U.S. at 414–15.
9 Palazzolo v. Rhode Island, 533 U.S. 606, 635 (2001) (O'Connor, J., concurring) (citing Hodel v. Irving, 481 U.S. 704, 714–18 (1987)).
10 Palazzolo v. Rhode Island, 533 U.S. 606, 627 (2001).
11 Penn Cent. Transp. Co. v. New York City, 438 U.S. 104, 128 (1978).
12 *Id.* at 147 (Rehnquist, J., dissenting).
13 *Id.* at 125.
14 *Id.* (citations omitted).
15 Lucas v. S.C. Coastal Council, 505 U.S. 1003, 1022–26 (1992).
16 Kaiser Aetna v. United States, 444 U.S. 164 (1979).
17 438 U.S. 104 (1978).
18 535 U.S. 302 (2002).
19 Tahoe-Sierra Pres. Council, Inc. v. Tahoe Reg'l Plan. Agency, 535 U.S. 302, 318 (2002) (citing Tahoe-Sierra Pres. Council, Inc. v. Tahoe Reg'l Plan. Agency, 216 F.3d 764, 774 (9th Cir. 2000), *overruled by* Gonzalez v. Arizona, 677 F.3d 383 (9th Cir. 2012), *aff'd*, 570 U.S. 1 (2013)).
20 137 S. Ct. 1933 (2017).
21 Agins v. City of Tiburon, 447 U.S. 255, 260 (1980) (emphasis added) (citation omitted), *abrogated by* Lingle v. Chevron U.S.A., Inc., 544 U.S. 528 (2005).
22 544 U.S. 428 (2005).
23 *Lingle*, 544 U.S. 528, 531–32 (2005) (citations omitted).
24 *Id.* at 540.
25 *Id.* at 542 (citations omitted).
26 482 U.S. 304 (1987), *reh'g denied*, 258 Cal. Rptr. 893 (Cal. Dist. Ct. App. 1989), *and modified*, 258 Cal. Rptr. 893 (Cal. Dist. Ct. App. 1989).
27 First Eng. Evangelical Lutheran Church of Glendale v. L.A. Cnty., 482 U.S. 304, 340 n.17 (1987) (Stevens, J., dissenting) (citations omitted).

# 17 Florida law protections for property rights

In addition to the private property rights protections provided by the Takings Clause, private property rights protections have evolved through state common law and the Florida Legislature has created additional statutory protections.

## Florida Land Use and Environmental Dispute Resolution Act

In addition to the judicial causes of action discussed in Part II, citizens and landowners benefit from other statutory provisions that give them rights to interact with local governments regarding land development. The Florida Land Use and Environmental Dispute Resolution Act creates a resolution process that a property owner may instigate if he or she feels that a land use rule is unfair.

Specifically, a property owner may invoke the resolution process in response to any development order issued by any Florida government (e.g. the state, any regional governmental agency, or any local government) except for a comprehensive plan amendment.[1]

The broad definition of development order in this act includes most land use decisions and also includes environmental permits not generally addressed by this text. Because the resolution process is limited to property owners, however, a party affected by a development decision who does not have an interest in the regulated property (such as a neighbor) cannot invoke the resolution process.[2]

The resolution process entails a hearing, but is more akin to mediation than to a judicial process. A special magistrate agreed to by the parties oversees the resolution process.[3] This special magistrate does not need to be an attorney, but must be a mediator and must have knowledge of land use or environmental regulation.[4] The process includes an informal hearing which must be open to the public.[5]

The special magistrate's focus in the resolution process must be on the impact of the regulation on the property owner and on the benefit the public would derive from the government's action.[6] In considering this matter, the special magistrate should consider the history of the development and use of the property, the environmental and land use regulations affecting the property, and the reasonable expectations of the owner.[7]

As a result of the hearing process, the parties may mutually agree to an acceptable solution.[8] However, in the event the special magistrate cannot facilitate an amicable resolution, the resolution process will end with one of two outcomes.

First, the special magistrate can determine that the land use regulation is fair. In this case, that decision ends the resolution process and allows the property owner to pursue other remedies.[9]

Second,

> [i]f the special magistrate finds that the development order or enforcement action, or the development order or enforcement action in combination with the actions or regulations

> of other governmental entities, is unreasonable or unfairly burdens use of the owner's property, the special magistrate, with the owner's consent to proceed, may recommend one or more alternatives that protect the public interest served by the development order or enforcement action and regulations at issue but allow for reduced restraints on the use of the owner's real property … .[10]

Those "reduced restraints" on the property owner may include adjusting the land development or permit restrictions on the property, issuing the development order, or the government buying the property.[11]

The government may accept, modify, or reject the special magistrate's recommendation.[12] In any case, if the property owner is unhappy with the action taken by the government, the government must issue a written description of how the property owner may use his or her property.[13]

## Equitable estoppel

Common law equitable estoppel is a private property rights protection recognized by Florida courts. In a land use context, equitable estoppel acts to vest a property owner's rights to use property a certain way. This vesting arises when the owner has relied to his or her detriment on the local government regulating use of the property. The elements of equitable estoppel are:

(1) a property owner's good faith reliance;
(2) on some act or omission of the government; and
(3) a substantial change in position or the incurring of excessive obligations and expenses so that it would be highly inequitable and unjust to destroy the right he acquired.[14]

Like estoppel in other legal contexts, the essence of this private property rights protection is fairness.

> Stripped of the legal jargon which lawyers and judges have obfuscated it with, the theory of estoppel amounts to nothing more than an application of the rules of fair play. One party will not be permitted to invite another onto a welcome mat and then be permitted to snatch the mat away to the detriment of the party induced or permitted to stand thereon. A citizen is entitled to rely on the assurances or commitments of a zoning authority and if he does, the zoning authority is bound by its representations, whether they be in the form of words or deeds … .[15]

Equitable estoppel is also a component of the Florida statutory property rights protection law, the Harris Act.

## The Harris Act

The Bert J. Harris, Jr., Private Property Rights Protection Act (Harris Act)[16] grants monetary relief to property owners whose land government regulation inordinately burdens.[17] The Harris Act "provides a cause of action for governmental actions that may not rise to the level of a taking under the State Constitution or the United States Constitution."[18] While thinking of the Harris Act as "regulatory takings light" is tempting, the rule is distinct in character from the U.S. Constitutional protection against regulatory takings.

The essential protection of the Harris Act is against *inordinate burden*:

> When a *specific action* of a governmental entity has *inordinately burdened* an existing use of real property or a vested right to a specific use of real property, *the property owner of that real property* is entitled to relief, which may include compensation for the actual loss to the fair market value of the real property caused by the action of government … .[19]

The statutes define the key term here, inordinately burdened, as follows:

> The terms "inordinate burden" and "inordinately burdened":
>
> 1. Mean that an action of one or more governmental entities has directly restricted or limited the use of real property such that the property owner is permanently unable to attain the reasonable, investment-backed expectation for the existing use of the real property or a vested right to a specific use of the real property with respect to the real property as a whole, or that the property owner is left with existing or vested uses that are unreasonable such that the property owner bears permanently a disproportionate share of a burden imposed for the good of the public, which in fairness should be borne by the public at large.
> 2. Do not include temporary impacts to real property; impacts to real property occasioned by governmental abatement, prohibition, prevention, or remediation of a public nuisance at common law or a noxious use of private property … .[20]

These sections are the heart of the Harris Act and several aspects of them warrant consideration.

First, the limited availability of the Harris Act to recover for a *specific action* of a government means that property owners cannot invoke the Harris Act in facial challenges to regulations with broad applicability: rather, the Harris Act is available in as-applied challenges only.[21] Second, only the property owner of the real property that is subject to the inordinate burden has statutory standing to bring the Harris Act claim.[22] Leaseholders or other parties with a financial—but not an ownership—interest in the real estate do not have standing. Third, the Harris Act relates only to real property.[23] The statute does not protect rights to personal property. Recall that real property is fixed, like land and buildings.[24] Personal property is movable. Fourth, the Harris Act does not permit claims for temporary impacts to real property.[25] Finally, as with regulatory takings after *Lucas*, a local government may defend itself against a Harris Act claim by showing that the prohibited use constituted a nuisance.[26]

### *Understanding inordinate burden*

The definition of inordinate burden creates two independent instances in which a property owner may have a Harris Act claim. Paraphrased, they are that: (1) the owner cannot achieve his or her investment-backed expectation for an existing or for a vested use of the land; and (2) the owner unreasonably bears a disproportionate share of a burden imposed for the good of the public.[27]

Unfortunately, Florida courts have published a paucity of decisions discussing these two meanings of inordinate burden. Furthermore, what decisions do exist focus only on the first meaning related to achieving investment-backed expectations.[28] Just as with regulatory takings, therefore, when a regulation becomes "unreasonable such that the property owner bears permanently a disproportionate share of a burden imposed for the good of the public, which in fairness should be borne by the public at large"[29] is not clear.

### *Understanding existing use*

The Harris Act definition of inordinate burden includes the term "existing use."[30] In the law, the phrase "existing use" does not have its common, literal meaning (i.e. how someone is actually using land). Instead, existing use is:

1. An actual, present use or activity on the real property, including periods of inactivity which are normally associated with, or are incidental to, the nature or type of use; or
2. Activity or such reasonably foreseeable, nonspeculative land uses which are suitable for the subject real property and compatible with adjacent land uses and which have created an existing fair market value in the property greater than the fair market value of the actual, present use or activity on the real property.[31]

The following opinion, *Ocean Concrete, Inc. v. Indian River Cnty.*, applies this definition.

## Florida Fourth District Court of Appeal

## *Ocean Concrete, Inc. v. Indian River Cnty.*[32]

## 2018

DAMOORGIAN, J.

Appellants, Ocean Concrete, Inc. and its principal, George Maib, appeal a final judgment entered in favor of Indian River County (the "County") in Appellants' property rights related lawsuit against the County. The substance of this appeal is ... whether the court erred in its conclusion that Appellants failed to prove entitlement to relief under the Bert J. Harris, Jr. Property Rights Protection Act ... [W]e conclude that the trial court reversibly erred and remand for further proceedings.

### *Factual Background*

In 2002, Mr. Maib began formulating a plan to develop and run a concrete batch plant in the Treasure Coast area. A key element of the plan was acquiring a parcel of land with railway access which would allow him to keep costs down by importing raw material in bulk via freight train. With this is mind, Mr. Maib scouted the subject land, an 8.5+ acre parcel located near the city limits of the City of Sebastian in Indian River County. The parcel was zoned light industrial ("IL") under the County's zoning code which, at that time, provided that concrete batch plans were an allowed use in IL zoned districts. The lands surrounding the parcel, however, were primarily zoned for residential and limited commercial use. An aerial view of the parcel showed that the surrounding land was undeveloped.

In 2004, Mr. Maib entered into a contract to purchase the property for $575,000 with a 120 day inspection period. Mr. Maib retained an engineer to ascertain the feasibility of developing a concrete batch plant on the property. The engineer testified that after reviewing all relevant documents, he had no concerns about the feasibility of the project from either an engineering or development standpoint. The engineer drafted a conceptual, pre-application site plan for County review. Mr. Maib and his engineer attended a meeting with County planning staff where the staff represented that a concrete batch plant was a permitted use as a matter of right under the zoning code and provided feedback about the project. Mr. Maib and his engineer left the meeting believing that the development of the plant was feasible and that none of the feedback from the planning staff would prohibit the development. Based on the foregoing, Mr. Maib purchased the property.

In 2005, Mr. Maib filed a site plan application for review by the County's Technical Review Committee ("TRC"). The TRC responded to the application in writing by listing out several "discrepancies" which needed to be addressed before moving forward with the application. The TRC's discrepancy letter also noted that a concrete batch plant was a permissible use of the property as a matter of right, the discrepancies were not significant, and that no second TRC meeting would be required for reconsideration of the application. Mr. Maib then underwent efforts to remedy those discrepancies and also began improving the property. Specifically, Mr. Maib obtained permits to install storm water systems, installed wells, cleared and graded the property, planted a landscape buffer, and began to install a rail spur. He also formed Ocean Concrete, Inc., began developing a detailed business plan, and sought out financing for the project. During this process, Mr. Maib realized that it was going to take an additional two years to meet all of the technical requirements for approval of the site plan. Therefore, he let the site plan application expire in November of 2006 with the intent of filing a new site plan application and requesting a one year extension. Mr. Maib filed a new site plan application on December 6, 2006.

Thereafter, the TRC issued another discrepancy letter identifying the discrepancies in the site plan application which Mr. Maib was required to address, in writing, before proceeding. This discrepancy letter again noted that the "site is zoned IL, Light Industrial. Concrete batch plants are a use permitted by right in the IL district" and that "the discrepancies do not appear to be significant, therefore, no second TRC meeting will be required for reconsideration of the proposal." Mr. Maib continued to address the discrepancies but, as he did, the project began garnering public and governmental opposition.

The nearby City of Sebastian issued a resolution imploring the County to deny approval for the proposed Ocean Concrete project. Around this same time, a group of citizens formed an organization called "Stop Ocean Concrete." The leader of this organization appeared at a Board of County Commissioners ("BCC") meeting and asked the BCC to amend the zoning code to eliminate heavy process uses from the IL zoning district. The BCC then directed the planning staff to analyze the issue and shortly thereafter, the County's planning director issued a memo recommending that the BCC change the zoning code to "restrict industrial uses such as concrete plants and paper mills that process large quantities of materials, produce dust and noise, and have outdoor activities to the IG (General Industrial) district." At its next meeting, the BCC voted to have the staff change the zoning code as recommended.

Following the BCC's vote, County staff began the process of amending the zoning code. Inevitably, the impact of any changes on Mr. Maib's existing site plan application was a point of heavy discussion. A May 8, 2007 memo written by a senior planner noted:

> The Ocean Concrete project is opposed by many residents of Sebastian and the north county, as evidenced by petitions and letters of objection submitted to staff. That project's application will expire on December 6, 2007 if it is not approved by that date. Because that site plan application is active, changes to the IL district regulations will not affect that application unless special effective date provisions are added to the amendment ordinance. At this time, the County Attorney has not issued an opinion as to whether or not the county can legally apply the proposed amendment to an existing

application. The proposed changes will certainly affect applications to develop IL zoned sites submitted after the changes are adopted.

During this time and unbeknownst to Mr. Maib, the county attorney and the planning director were engaged in a discussion about whether the proposed change to the zoning code would apply to the Ocean Concrete project. After the attorney opined that the change would apply to the project, the Planning and Zoning Commission voted to recommend approval of the changes to the zoning code. Thereafter, the BCC unanimously voted to adopt the amendments to the zoning code "void of any exception or merit for grandfathering of vested rights."

Appellants filed a declaratory action in the circuit court seeking clarification of their rights to proceed under the site plan application. They also filed a request for a one year extension with the County on their pending application. The County denied the extension and based on the expiration of the application, denied Appellants' application. Appellants administratively appealed and amended their declaratory action complaint to add a cause of action for violation of the Harris Act. Appellants' administrative appeals were denied, causing Appellants to file a petition for writ of certiorari with the circuit court sitting in an appellate capacity. The circuit court determined that the County must either grant the extension, state a valid reason for denial, or deny the site plan on its merits. The BCC voted to grant Appellants a one year extension under the "old code" provisions.

Following the reinstatement of Appellants' application, the County staff approved the site plan application under the old zoning code conditioned on a finding by the Community Planning Director of a vested right of development under the old code. The Community Planning Director, found that there was no vested right and denied Appellants' site plan application under the new code. Mr. Maib appealed the denial to the Planning and Zoning Commission but, while his appeal was pending, lost the property to foreclosure. The Planning and Zoning Commission then dismissed Appellants' appeal as moot … .

The matter proceeded to a … trial … . At trial, Appellants presented expert testimony from a real property appraiser and construction business valuators. Appellant's experts valued the property with a completed concrete batch plant at $10 million. In turn, the County presented its own experts who opined that market value of the property before the zoning amendment was $1 million and that the change in the zoning amendment only reduced the property's value by 3.5%. The County also presented evidence to support its contention that operating a concrete batch plant on the property was not economically feasible.

At the conclusion of the trial, the … trial court found that Appellants did not prove that the County … violated the Harris Act … . Holding that the court erred in finding no violation of the Harris Act, we reverse and remand.

### *Analysis*

The Harris Act was enacted by the Florida Legislature in 1995 as a mechanism to protect and compensate any landowner whose property is affected by government action not rising to the level of a taking. § 70.001(1), Fla. Stat. (1995). To prevail under the Harris Act, the property owner must prove that "a specific action of a governmental entity has inordinately burdened an existing use of real property or a vested right to a specific use of real property." § 70.001(2), Fla. Stat. (2008). Accordingly, when a claim under the Harris Act is presented for judicial review, the court must first consider whether a claimed "existing use of the real property" or a claimed "vested right to a specific use of the real property" actually existed. If it finds either, it must next determine whether the government action inordinately burdened the property. § 70.001(6)(a), Fla. Stat. If the court also finds that that there was an inordinate burden, then it must impanel a jury to determine the total amount of compensation to the property owner for the loss caused by the inordinate burden to the property. § 70.001(6)(b), Fla. Stat. The party seeking relief under the Harris Act bears the burden of proof. *See Town of Ponce Inlet v. Pacetta, LLC*, 120 So. 3d 27, 29 (Fla. 5th DCA 2013).

In this case, the court found Appellants did not establish that the use of the property as a concrete batch plant was an existing use. Alternatively, it found that the County's actions did not inordinately burden the property. We review these determinations de novo. *City of Jacksonville v. Coffield*, 18 So. 3d 589, 594 (Fla. 1st DCA 2009).

*a) Existing Use*

The term "existing use" is defined by the Harris Act as:

> [1] an actual, present use or activity on the real property, including periods of inactivity which are normally associated with, or are incidental to, the nature or type of use or activity or
>
> [2] such reasonably foreseeable, nonspeculative land uses which are suitable for the subject real property and compatible with adjacent land uses and which have created an existing fair market value in the property greater than the fair market value of the actual, present use or activity on the real property.

§ 70.001(3)(b), Fla. Stat. (2008) [spacing and numbers added].

Because a concrete batch plant did not exist on the property, the court applied the second part of the "existing use" definition. Neither of the parties contend that this was improper. With this parameter in mind, the court then found that because a concrete batch plant was a permitted use as a matter of right under the County's old zoning code, it was a reasonably foreseeable use of Appellants' property. However, the court went on to find that a concrete batch plant was not a non-speculative use. This finding was rooted in economics, and more particularly, the court's determination that the project was not financially viable. The court also concluded that the use was not compatible with adjacent lands. For the reasons set forth below, we hold that the court's non-speculative use and compatibility analysis was legally incorrect.

I) REASONABLY FORESEEABLE, NONSPECULATIVE USE

Applying a plain language reading analysis to the statute leads us to conclude that the term relates to whether the actual *land use* is nonspeculative without concern to economics. The phrase "nonspeculative" appears in the definition of "existing use" as follows: [emphasis in the original]

> "reasonably foreseeable, nonspeculative land uses ..."

§ 70.001(3)(b), Fla. Stat. (2008).

The noun in the above phrase is "land uses." The terms "reasonably foreseeable" and "nonspeculative" are adjectives modifying the noun "land use." Thus, based on the grammatical structure, the key inquiry for the court is whether a concrete batch plant, as a *land use*, was foreseeable and nonspeculative at the time the County amended its zoning code [emphasis in the original].

Notably, at least one appellate judge has arrived at the same conclusion. In his dissent in *City of Jacksonville v. Smith*, 159 So. 3d 888, 913 (Fla. 1st DCA 2015), Judge Makar wrote:

> The point of subsection 2 [within the existing use definition] is not to preclude "speculation" in the financial sense; if that were the case, no privately-held real property would qualify because land ownership always involves an element of financial risk. Instead [the definition] is designed to limit possible future land uses to only those that are within reason, i.e., "reasonably foreseeable" and "nonspeculative." Stated differently, future uses that are merely theoretical or hypothetical do not qualify; they are speculative in the sense of these two terms.

The plain language of the Harris Act is clear: the term "nonspeculative" refers to the land use and, therefore, a "nonspeculative use" analysis really only comes into play when a party is arguing that it may have been able to use its land in the future for a purpose not expressly provided for by the zoning code at the time of the government action. Conversely, when the use was expressly provided for, as it was here, there is no need for a speculation analysis. Accordingly, based on the plain language of the Act, the court erred in concluding that a concrete batch plant was not a nonspeculative land use when making its "existing use" determination.[3]

#### II) COMPATIBLE WITH ADJACENT LAND USES

In addition to finding that Appellants did not meet the "nonspeculative land use" prong of the "existing use" definition under the Harris Act, the court also found that Appellants failed to establish that a concrete batch plant was compatible with adjacent land uses at the time the code was amended. The court's conclusion was based on the fact that the land west of the property and half of the land south of the property was zoned for residential use. Although much of that land remained vacant, the court concluded that based on east to west wind patterns, the residential areas would experience noise and dust pollution from the property if it was developed into a concrete batch plant. The court also gave weight to the County's determinations during the code amendment process that "heavy process uses such as concrete plants which involve outdoor storage and handling of large quantities of material that result in noise and dust impacts are more compatible with and appropriately located in IG [General Industrial] districts, removed from concentrations of residential areas and separated from commercial uses and light 'clean' industry."

3 *See* David L. Powell, Robert M. Rhodes, & Dan R. Stengle, *A Measured Step to Protect Private Property Rights*, 23 Fla. St. U. L. Rev. 255 (1995). Discussing the definition of the term "existing use" at play in the Harris Act the authors (who happened to work on the legislation), stated:

> As a legal concept for an existing land use, the alternative definition is well-grounded in the law of eminent domain. In a condemnation proceeding, valuation of the property is based upon the highest and best use. The highest and best use is not limited to those uses authorized under the existing land development regulations. If on the date of taking there is a reasonable probability of a land use change, that probability may be taken into account in determining valuation. An important factor in determining the highest and best use of property is whether the property is suitable for that proposed future use. However, such a future use may not be wholly speculative … .
>
> The proof necessary to establish that a future land use is reasonably foreseeable could come from such authorities as an adopted local comprehensive plan, local land development regulations, or a credible appraisal which relies at least in part on nonexisting but reasonably expected future uses.
>
> *Id.* at 267–68 (footnotes omitted)

It is axiomatic that if an area is zoned for a particular use, that use is deemed compatible with surrounding uses. *See Nostimo, Inc. v. City of Clearwater*, 594 So. 2d 779, 781 (Fla. 2d DCA 1992) (holding that use of property was compatible with surrounding or adjacent uses because it was a permitted use under the zoning code). Before the County amended the code, concrete batch plants were a permitted use on Appellants' property. Therefore, the use of the property as a concrete batch plant was *per se* compatible with the surrounding land uses. With this in mind, none of the County's evidence established that anything about the adjacent land uses changed between the time the old IL zoning description was created and the time it was amended. Accordingly, the court erred when it concluded that a concrete batch plant was not an "existing use" for the property because a concrete batch plant was not compatible with adjacent land uses at the time the code was amended.

*b) Inordinate Burden*

The Harris Act provides that the terms "inordinate burden" or "inordinately burdened" mean:

> [T]hat an action of one or more governmental entities has directly restricted or limited the use of real property such that the property owner is permanently unable to attain the reasonable, investment-backed expectation for the existing use of the real property or a vested right to a specific use of the real property with respect to the real property as a whole, or that the property owner is left with existing or vested uses that are unreasonable such that the property owner bears permanently a disproportionate share of a burden imposed for the good of the public, which in fairness should be borne by the public at large … .

§ 70.001(3)(e), Fla. Stat. (2008).

Here, although the court denied Appellants relief under the Harris Act based on its existing use analysis, it also cursorily addressed the inordinate burden prong of a claim under the Act, ruling that Appellants could not demonstrate a "reasonable, investment-backed expectation." The court's ruling on this point referenced its takings ruling, wherein the court found that Appellants did not establish that they had a reasonable, investment-backed expectation in developing a concrete batch plant because the "property contained site-specific conditions that entailed significant practical and financial impediments to its development as a concrete batch plant."

There are only two reported cases interpreting the phrase "reasonable, investment-backed expectations" in the specific context of the Harris Act. This Court's opinion in *Palm Beach Polo, Inc. v. Village of Wellington*, 918 So. 2d 988 (Fla. 4th DCA 2006), provides the most guidance. In that case, a developer made a Harris Act claim with respect to a wetland nature preserve which a local government required the developer to "restore, enhance, and preserve" as part of a Planned Unit Development. *Id.* at 990. On appeal, we held that the developer's claim under the Act was "frivolous" because, based on the physical characteristics and regulatory history of the preserve, there could be no reasonable expectation that the preserve would be used for anything other than conservation. *Id.* at 995. Citing our holding in *Palm Beach Polo, Inc.*, the First District later found that a landowner did not have a "reasonable, investment-backed expectation" of developing a parcel of land into a multi-family development after he learned that the only road leading to and from the property was being permanently closed. *Coffield*, 18 So. 3d at 595, 599. These cases establish that whether a landowner's expectations for development are "reasonable" and "investment-backed" depends on the physical and regulatory aspects of the property.

Despite the foregoing authority, the court relied on case law from the takings context when analyzing whether Appellants had a "reasonable, investment-backed expectation" of developing the property as a concrete batch plant. The court did so because the term "investment-backed expectations" is found in the test articulated by the United States Supreme Court for regulatory takings. *Penn Cent. Transp. Co. v. City of N.Y.*, 438 U.S. 104, 123 (1978). Although, based on the foregoing, it would seem reasonable to rely on takings cases, the Harris Act itself proclaims that it is "separate and distinct ... from the law of takings" and, to that end, also provides that "[t]his section may not necessarily be construed under the case law regarding takings if the governmental action does not rise to the level of a taking." §§ 70.001(1); 70.001(9), Fla. Stat. (2008). Thus, we hold that the court's reliance on federal takings cases as opposed to Florida law interpreting the Harris Act was misplaced.

Applying the applicable law, nothing about the physical or regulatory aspects of the property at the time of the government regulation made Appellants' expectations for the development of a concrete batch plant unreasonable. A concrete batch plant was a permitted use under the zoning code as a matter of right and throughout the site-plan approval process, Mr. Maib was led to believe that approval was inevitable. Further, Mr. Maib obtained the services of an expert engineer who told him that the development was feasible. Finally, the property abutted a railroad and Mr. Maib was able to install a spur to facilitate the importation and exportation of materials. That the overall undertaking may have been expensive and a significant task does not invalidate the fact that, based on the property itself, Appellants' investment-backed expectations were reasonable.

Based upon the foregoing, we reverse and remand this matter for a trial on damages suffered by Appellants under the Harris Act.

Affirmed in part, reversed in part and remanded.

TAYLOR AND MAY, JJ., concur.

### *Settlement may contravene law, but consider due process*

The Harris Act provides for a one-year statute of limitations on claims measured from the time the law or regulation is first applied to the real property.[33] But, before a property owner has a ripe Harris Act claim, he or she must engage in settlement discussions with the governmental entity.[34]

The only remedy available from the courts in a Harris Act claim is damages.[35] The law does not provide for equitable relief. In a settlement process, however, local governments can craft creative resolutions to a Harris Act claim.

These resolutions can even violate applicable land use regulations.[36] But, the circuit court must approve such a settlement agreement.

> When a governmental entity enters into a settlement agreement under this section which would have the effect of contravening the application of a statute as it would otherwise apply to the subject real property, the governmental entity and the property owner shall jointly file an action in the circuit court where the real property is located for approval of the settlement agreement by the court to ensure that the relief granted protects the public interest served by the statute at issue and is the appropriate relief necessary to prevent the governmental regulatory effort from inordinately burdening the real property.[37]

This framework gives local governments flexibility in resolving claims. But the Harris Act does not override state law and Constitutional procedural due process protections for affected parties such as public notice and a hearing.[38] Practitioners should be careful to afford due process even when permissibly contravening land use regulations as part of a Harris Act settlement.

### *Damages*

In the event a property owner and a government are not able to reach settlement, the property owner may file a claim in the circuit court.[39] With the claim, the property owner must file "a bona fide, valid appraisal" of the real property's value.[40] The issue before the circuit court is to be

> whether an existing use of the real property or a vested right to a specific use of the real property existed and, if so, whether, considering the settlement offer and statement of allowable uses, the governmental entity or entities have inordinately burdened the real property.[41]

If the court finds an inordinate burden, it must then pose the question of damages to a jury.

> [T]he court shall impanel a jury to determine the total amount of compensation to the property owner for the loss in value due to the inordinate burden to the real property. The award of compensation shall be determined by calculating the difference in the fair market value of the real property, as it existed at the time of the governmental action at issue, as though the owner had the ability to attain the reasonable investment-backed expectation or was not left with uses that are unreasonable, whichever the case may be, and the fair market value of the real property, as it existed at the time of the governmental action at issue, as inordinately burdened, considering the settlement offer together with the statement of allowable uses, of the governmental entity or entities. In determining the award of compensation, consideration may not be given to business damages relative to any development, activity, or use that the action of the governmental entity or entities, considering the settlement offer together with the statement of allowable uses has restricted, limited, or prohibited.[42]

Explaining the term "market value" and the exclusion of "business damages" from the amount of compensation available to Harris Act claimants requires a brief primer on real estate appraisal. Real estate appraisers employ three concepts of value, or appraisal approaches, when estimating the value of real estate: (1) the sales comparison approach; (2) the cost approach; and (3) the income capitalization approach.[43]

The sales comparison approach estimates value using the sale prices of comparable properties.[44] This approach is well suited for valuing single-family homes because sales data is routinely available for comparable properties and because financing terms (which influence sales price) are relatively standardized. This approach can be used to appraise other property types when data on comparable sales of property are available.

The cost approach estimates value by summing an estimated value of the underlying land and an estimated replacement cost for any improvements.[45] This approach is best suited to valuing new or almost new structures for two reasons. First, the estimated value of a new structure will not require adjustment for depreciation due to deterioration or obsolescence.[46] Second, replacing an older building might not be possible because of changing availability of construction materials, changes in construction practices, and changing skills in the labor market. Also, some historic structures derive value from their age.

The income capitalization approach estimates value by calculating a present value of the cash flow a property can generate.[47] This approach is best suited to valuing unique properties for which sales and cost data are not available. The income capitalization approach can develop an estimate of value for a generic purchaser of property; however, it is uniquely suited to estimating value for a particular owner of property.

Consider that, in the context of commercial property, different owners will be able to generate different amounts of profit from a given property because different owners have different business plans and different market advantages. For example, a drive-through restaurant might be valuable to McDonald's, but worthless to Google. Similarly, McDonald's might not be able to profit from a data center, while Google could. The income capitalization approach takes these differences into account.

Of the three appraisal approaches, the sales comparison approach best incorporates market data into an estimate of value. Therefore, it is the best for fulfilling the Harris Act's direction to measure damages equal to the loss in fair market value, excluding business damages.

When data on comparable sales are not available, an appraiser might be able to estimate market value using the cost approach. However, because the cost approach does not take into account allowed uses of the property, it is less suitable for measuring Harris Act damages than the sales comparison approach.

Because the income capitalization approach estimates value based on business earnings, and the Harris Act disallows business damages, the income capitalization approach would never be useful for measuring damages in a Harris Act claim.

## Further reading

Property rights protections can be conceptually difficult. And even instances which seem fundamentally unfair to property owners are not necessarily violations of property rights. Two cases worth reading for facts that may make you sympathetic to the property owner, yet which do not result in a holding in the property owner's favor, are *Town of Ponce Inlet v. Pacetta, LLC*[48] and *Citrus Cnty. v. Halls River Dev., Inc.*[49]

### Box 17.1 Practice problem: Kaliedoscopic phosphogypsum

Kaleidoscope, Inc. is a company that makes fertilizer. One ingredient in fertilizer is phosphorous. Kaleidoscope gets phosphorous from phosphate mines it owns which are concentrated at a few locations around the world. A large Kaleidoscope phosphate mine is in Central County, Florida, where phosphate rock is plentiful. The phosphate rocks are made of fossilized marine life that lived millions of years ago when Central County, Florida was under water.

In its Central County mine, Kaleidoscope scrapes sand and clay off of the ground to expose phosphate rock below. Then it excavates the phosphate rock, pumps water from the ground, and uses the water to separate the phosphate rock from the remaining sand and clay.

When it finishes processing the phosphate rock, Kaleidoscope has two materials: phosphorous and phosphogypsum. The phosphorous is a fertilizer ingredient. The phosphogypsum is a radioactive byproduct that Kaleidoscope stores in large waste piles called gypsum stacks.

Kaleidoscope has a problem. The combination of heavy gypsum stacks pressing down on the ground and the voids in the ground where the aquifer no longer holds groundwater caused the earth to collapse beneath gypsum stacks at the Kaleidoscope mine in Central County. Sink holes opened up and the radioactive phosphogypsum poured into the ground. To disarm environmental activists creating a public relations problem, Kaleidoscope needed to get rid of its remaining gypsum stacks, which were huge.

An executive at Kaleidoscope developed an innovative solution to this dilemma: manufacturing gypsum board, also called drywall. This building material overtook lath and plaster as the preferred construction method for walls during the mid-twentieth-century building boom that followed World War II. Drywall can be made by grinding phosphogypsum into a powder called stucco, mixing it with water to create a slurry, sandwiching that slurry between two sheets of thick paper, and then baking the slurry/paper sandwich until it is a hard board.

To effect this executive's plan, Kaleidoscope constructed a factory to manufacture the drywall at a cost of $30 million. This gypsum board factory has a unique design characteristic. The kiln in which the gypsum boards are baked is 75 yards long. The kiln contains a conveyor belt and dries the boards as they travel from the slurry vats to a staging area for shipping. The kiln itself is kept in a specially designed, long, skinny enclosure (like a hallway) that protrudes from the side of the factory. Because this unique building design can only be used to dry gypsum board, the factory cannot practically be used for any other purpose without extensive renovations costing an estimated $10 million. Ironically, therefore, even though the factory cost $30 million to build, its appraised market value is only $20 million.

About one year after Kaleidoscope's factory was up and running, the Central County Commission adopted an ordinance banning any manufacturing process in the county that used radioactive materials. The county adopted the ordinance specifically in response to resident concerns that grinding the radioactive phosphogypsum into stucco was causing some of that powder to become airborne. And inhaling radioactive dust is probably a cancer risk.

The ordinance meant that Kaleidoscope could no longer use its factory. The company hired an appraiser to produce two bona fide, valid appraisals. In the first appraisal, the appraiser determined that the factory has a value to Kaleidoscope for making drywall of $38,000,000. This number is higher than the construction cost of the factory because Central County is experiencing a construction boom and drywall is in demand. In the second appraisal, the appraiser estimates the value of Kaleidoscope's phosphogympsum to be $2,500,000, but only if it is used to make gypsum board on-site.

Kaleidoscope submits a claim to Central County for its losses and the county makes a settlement offer in compliance with Florida Statutes section 70.001(4). Kaleidoscope rejects that settlement offer and sues the county pursuant to Florida Statutes section 70.001(5)(b).

Evaluate both whether Kaleidoscope can recover its losses under the Bert Harris Act and, if it can, how much Central County is likely to have to pay to Kaleidoscope.

## Notes

1 *See* Fla. Stat. §§ 70.51(2)(a)–(b), (f), (3)–(4).
2 *See id.* §§ 70.51(d)–(e), (g), (3).
3 *Id.* § 70.51(c).
4 *Id.*
5 *Id.* § 70.51(17).

6 *Id.* §§ 70.51(18)(f).
7 Fla. Stat. §§ 70.51(18)(b)–(c), (e).
8 *Id.* § 70.51(17)(a).
9 *Id.* § 70.51(19)(a).
10 *Id.* § 70.51(19)(b).
11 *Id.* §§ 70.51(19)(b)(1), (9).
12 *Id.* §§ 70.51(21)(a)–(c).
13 Fla. Stat. § 70.51(22).
14 Franklin Cnty. v. Leisure Props., Ltd., 430 So. 2d 475, 479 (Fla. 1st DCA 1983) (citations omitted).
15 Town of Largo v. Imperial Homes Corp., 309 So. 2d 571, 573 (Fla. 2d DCA 1975) (citation omitted).
16 Fla. Stat. § 70.001(1).
17 *Id.*
18 *Id.* § 70.001(9).
19 *Id.* § 70.001(2) (emphases added).
20 *Id.* § 70.001(3)(e).
21 *See* M & H Profit, Inc. v. City of Pan. City, 28 So. 3d 71, 75–6 (Fla. 1st DCA 2009).
22 Fla. Stat. § 70.001(3)(f).
23 *Id.* § 70.006(3)(g).
24 22 Fla. Jur. 2d *Property* § 7 (2020).
25 Fla. Stat. § 70.001(3)(e)(2).
26 *Id.*
27 *See id.* § 70.001(3)(e)(1).
28 *See* City of Jacksonville v. Smith, 159 So. 3d 888, 907 n.24 (Fla. 1st DCA 2015) (Makar, J., dissenting) ("Reported cases under the Act are scarce, most involving the first statutory meaning of 'inordinate burden,' ..."), *appeal dismissed*, 220 So. 3d 1118 (Fla. 2017).
29 Fla. Stat. § 70.001(3)(e)(1).
30 *Id.*
31 *Id.* § 70.001(3)(b) (2019).
32 241 So. 3d 181 (Fla. 4th DCA), *reh'g denied*, No. SC18-729, 2018 WL 6506035, at *1 (Fla. 2018).
33 Fla. Stat. §§ 70.001(11)(a)(1)–(2).
34 *Id.* § 70.001(4)(c).
35 *Id.* §§ 70.001(6)(b), (6)(c)(1).
36 *Id.* § 70.001(4)(c)(1).
37 *Id.* § 70.001(4)(d)(2).
38 *Id.* §§ 70.001(4)(a)–(b), (11)(a)(1).
39 Fla. Stat. § 70.001(5)(b).
40 *Id.* § 70.001(4)(a).
41 *Id.* § 70.001(6)(a).
42 *Id.* § 70.001(6)(b).
43 *The Appraisal of Real Estate* 141 (Appraisal Inst, 13th edn 2008).
44 *Id.*
45 *Id.* at 142.
46 *Id.*
47 *Id.* at 143.
48 226 So. 3d 303 (Fla. 5th DCA 2017), *reh'g denied*, No. SC17-1897, 2018 WL 507415 (Fla. 2018) (unpublished table decision), *cert. denied*, 139 S. Ct. 181 (2018) (mem.).
49 8 So. 3d 413 (Fla. 5th DCA 2009), *reh'g denied* 23 So. 3d 712 (Fla. 2009) (unpublished table decision).

# Part IV

# Infrastructure

# 18 Exactions

As a product, real estate does not stand alone. Its value depends on the access and usefulness provided by public infrastructure.[1] Consider, a retail store isn't worth anything without roads allowing people to access it. And the value of a house reflects the quality of the public schools for which the house is zoned. Even rural land, which may be valuable for agriculture or mining, relies on the transportation service that roads, rails, or ports make possible. Because services require infrastructure, all land value reflects the availability and quality of infrastructure.[2]

An old adage in real estate is that the business is all about "location, location, location." And public services make some locations more valuable than others. As you read this part of the text, in addition to the principles of law discussed, consider the public services at issue. These cases relate to local government struggles to provide access to public parks, stormwater conveyances, water treatment areas, schools, and roads.

In every case, a government permitting development sought to also provide services to that development. Those public services required capital facilities. And those capital facilities cost money. How to pay that cost is a challenge for local governments. These cases help define the options local governments have to ensure public infrastructure exists.

## Municipal services are a big deal; just ask Hollywood

Public infrastructure and services are important to cities. We know this because Hollywood knows this. While planning and zoning may not be a part of the zeitgeist, public infrastructure is. The 1974 Oscar-winning film *Chinatown*[3] is an example of Hollywood making a film about the power of municipal service provision. A Los Angeles detective investigates a murder. Along the way, he uncovers a real-estate-development plot to deny water to the residents of the Valley (rural land near Los Angeles); then buy their parched land at a bargain; then annex the land into Los Angeles; and finally develop the Valley at higher densities the city water service would enable. The motive for murder was to keep a plot to change the value of real estate through urban service provision under wraps.

Perhaps the quintessential example is the 1988 movie *Who Framed Roger Rabbit?*[4] The plot was a murder mystery "whodunnit." Private detective Eddie Valiant searches for R.K. Maroon's killer. In the film's climax, we learn not only the identity of the murderer, but also his motivation. Judge Doom did it to get a hold of R.K. Maroon's estate. The deceased owned valuable land called Toon Town. Doom's plan included creating demand for this real estate by shutting down the Red Car—an affordable and convenient transit system—and replacing that transportation service with a freeway.

Here are the characters discussing Doom's vision:

> Eddie Valiant: So that's why you killed Acme and Maroon? For this freeway? I don't get it.
> Judge Doom: Of course not. You lack vision, but I see a place where people get on and off the freeway. On and off, off and on all day, all night. Soon, where Toon Town once stood will be a string of gas stations, inexpensive motels, restaurants that serve rapidly prepared food. Tire salons, automobile dealerships, and wonderful, wonderful billboards reaching as far as the eye can see. My God, it'll be beautiful.[5]

Judge Doom was crazy. But he also understood something important. The character of transportation infrastructure and services determines market demand for real estate, and not just market demand for real estate as in *whether* certain real estate is in demand. Transportation infrastructure determines *what kind of uses* and *what sort of urban design* the market will demand on certain land.[6]

When a freeway serves an area, people may want gas stations, motels, and drive-through restaurants. Where transit and walkable streets serve land, people may want a mixed-use neighborhood. The existence and the character of public infrastructure can define real estate value and create the market demands for development that make land use law relevant.

## Exactions from Takings Clause

The rule on exactions is the third concept—after eminent domain and regulatory takings—to come from the Takings Clause. However, exactions are completely different than either eminent domain or regulatory takings. An exaction is a permit condition that almost certainly would be a regulatory taking were it not required in conjunction with a permit.

In practice, two kinds of permit conditions are always exactions. First, a permit condition which requires a property owner to suffer a physical trespass is an exaction. That is the type of exaction present in both of the next two cases you will read, *Nollan* and *Dolan*. Second, a permit condition requiring a property owner to pay money is an exaction.

Not all exactions violate the Takings Clause. To be permissible, an exaction must meet two criteria. First, the ameliorating effect of the exaction must have an "essential nexus" with the harm caused by the development.[7] In other words, the benefit of the exaction must specifically address a harm caused by the development.

Second, the amount of benefit conferred by the exaction must be "roughly proportional" to the harm caused by the proposed development.[8] In making this determination, mathematical precision is not required.[9] But, the local government must make some "individualized determination" that the benefit of the permit condition is roughly proportional to the development's harm.[10]

### Essential nexus required

### United States Supreme Court

*Nollan v. California Coastal Comm'n*[11]

**1987**

Justice SCALIA delivered the opinion of the Court.

James and Marilyn Nollan appeal from a decision of the California Court of Appeal ruling that the California Coastal Commission could condition its grant of permission to rebuild their house on their transfer to the public of an easement across their beachfront property. 223 Cal. Rptr. 28 (Cal. Ct. App. 1986). The California court rejected their claim that imposition of that condition violates the Takings Clause of the Fifth Amendment, as incorporated against the States by the Fourteenth Amendment. *Ibid.* We noted probable jurisdiction. 479 U.S. 913 (1986).

## *I*

The Nollans own a beachfront lot in Ventura County, California. A quarter-mile north of their property is Faria County Park, an oceanside public park with a public beach and recreation area. Another public beach area, known locally as "the Cove," lies 1,800 feet south of their lot. A concrete seawall approximately eight feet high separates the beach portion of the Nollans' property from the rest of the lot. The historic mean high tide line determines the lot's oceanside boundary.

The Nollans originally leased their property with an option to buy. The building on the lot was a small bungalow, totaling 504 square feet, which for a time they rented to summer vacationers. After years of rental use, however, the building had fallen into disrepair, and could no longer be rented out.

The Nollans' option to purchase was conditioned on their promise to demolish the bungalow and replace it. In order to do so, under Cal. Pub. Res. Code Ann. §§ 30106, 30212, and 30600 (West 1986), they were required to obtain a coastal development permit from the California Coastal Commission. On February 25, 1982, they submitted a permit application to the Commission in which they proposed to demolish the existing structure and replace it with a three-bedroom house in keeping with the rest of the neighborhood.

The Nollans were informed that ... the Commission staff had recommended that the permit be granted subject to the condition that they allow the public an easement to pass across a portion of their property bounded by the mean high tide line on one side, and their seawall on the other side. This would make it easier for the public to get to Faria County Park and the Cove. The Nollans protested imposition of the condition, but the Commission overruled their objections and granted the permit subject to their recordation of a deed restriction granting the easement. App. 31, 34 ... [T]the Nollans [then] filed a petition for writ of administrative mandamus asking the Ventura County Superior Court to invalidate the access condition ... . The court agreed, and remanded the case to the Commission for a full evidentiary hearing on [the issue of whether the Nolan's proposed development would have a direct adverse impact on public access to the beach] ... .

[The Commission] found that the new house would increase blockage of the view of the ocean, thus contributing to the development of "a 'wall' of residential structures" that would prevent the public "psychologically ... from realizing a stretch of coastline exists nearby that they have every right to visit." *Id.* at 58. The new house would also increase private use of the shorefront. *Id.* at 59. These effects of construction of the house, along with other area development, would cumulatively "burden the public's ability to traverse to and along the shorefront." *Id.* at 65–66. Therefore the Commission could properly require the Nollans to offset that burden by providing additional lateral access to the public beaches in the form of an easement across their property. The Commission also noted that it had similarly conditioned 43 out of 60 coastal development permits along the same tract of land, and that of the 17 not so conditioned, 14 had been approved when the Commission did not have administrative regulations in place allowing imposition of the condition, and the remaining 3 had not involved shorefront property. *Id.* at 47–48.

The Nollans filed a supplemental petition for a writ of administrative mandamus with the Superior Court, in which they argued that imposition of the access condition violated the Takings Clause of the Fifth Amendment, as incorporated against the States by the Fourteenth Amendment. The Superior Court ruled in their favor on statutory grounds ... . The

Commission appealed to the California Court of Appeal. While that appeal was pending, the Nollans satisfied the condition on their option to purchase by tearing down the bungalow and building the new house, and bought the property. They did not notify the Commission that they were taking that action. The Court of Appeal reversed the Superior Court ... . Since, in the Court of Appeal's view, there was no statutory or constitutional obstacle to imposition of the access condition, the Superior Court erred in granting the writ of mandamus. The Nollans appealed to this Court, raising only the constitutional question.

### *II*

Had California simply required the Nollans to make an easement across their beachfront available to the public on a permanent basis in order to increase public access to the beach, rather than conditioning their permit to rebuild their house on their agreeing to do so, we have no doubt there would have been a taking. To say that the appropriation of a public easement across a landowner's premises does not constitute the taking of a property interest but rather (as Justice BRENNAN contends) "a mere restriction on its use," *post*, at 3154, n.3, is to use words in a manner that deprives them of all their ordinary meaning. Indeed, one of the principal uses of the eminent domain power is to assure that the government be able to require conveyance of just such interests, so long as it pays for them. Julius L. Sackman, 1 *Nichols on Eminent Domain* § 2.1[1] (rev. 3d ed. 1985), 2 *id.* § 5.01[5]; *see* 1 *id.* § 1.42 [9], 2 *id.* § 6.14. Perhaps because the point is so obvious, we have never been confronted with a controversy that required us to rule upon it, but our cases' analysis of the effect of other governmental action leads to the same conclusion. We have repeatedly held that, as to property reserved by its owner for private use, "the right to exclude [others is] 'one of the most essential sticks in the bundle of rights that are commonly characterized as property.'" *Loretto v. Teleprompter Manhattan CATV Corp.*, 458 U.S. 419, 433 (1982), quoting *Kaiser Aetna v. United States*, 444 U.S. 164, 176 (1979). In *Loretto* we observed that where governmental action results in "[a] permanent physical occupation" of the property, by the government itself or by others, see 458 U.S. at 432–33, n.9, "our cases uniformly have found a taking to the extent of the occupation, without regard to whether the action achieves an important public benefit or has only minimal economic impact on the owner," *id.* at 434–35. We think a "permanent physical occupation" has occurred, for purposes of that rule, where individuals are given a permanent and continuous right to pass to and fro, so that the real property may continuously be traversed, even though no particular individual is permitted to station himself permanently upon the premises ... .

Given, then, that requiring uncompensated conveyance of the easement outright would violate the Fourteenth Amendment, the question becomes whether requiring it to be conveyed as a condition for issuing a land-use permit alters the outcome. We have long recognized that land-use regulation does not effect a taking if it "substantially advance[s] legitimate state interests" and does not "den[y] an owner economically viable use of his land," (citations omitted) ... . [Our cases] have made clear, however, that a broad range of governmental purposes and regulations satisfies these requirements ... . The Commission argues that among these permissible purposes are protecting the public's ability to see the beach, assisting the public in overcoming the "psychological barrier" to using the beach created by a developed shorefront, and preventing congestion on the public beaches. We assume, without deciding, that this is so ... .

The Commission [also] argues that a permit condition that serves the same legitimate police-power purpose as a refusal to issue the permit should not be found to be a taking if the refusal to issue the permit would not constitute a taking. We agree. Thus, if the Commission attached to the permit some condition that would have protected the public's ability to see the beach notwithstanding construction of the new house-for example, a height limitation, a width restriction, or a ban on fences-so long as the Commission could have exercised its police power (as we have assumed it could) to forbid construction of the house altogether, imposition of the condition would also be constitutional. Moreover (and here we come closer to the facts of the present case), the condition would be constitutional even if it consisted of the requirement that the Nollans provide a viewing spot on their property for passersby with whose sighting of the ocean their new house would interfere. Although such a requirement, constituting a permanent grant of continuous access to the property, would have to be considered a taking if it were not attached to a development permit, the Commission's assumed power to forbid construction of the house in order to protect the public's view of the beach must surely include the power to condition construction upon some concession by the owner, even a concession of property rights, that serves the same end. If a prohibition designed to accomplish that purpose would be a legitimate exercise of the police power rather than a taking, it would be strange to conclude that providing the owner an alternative to that prohibition which accomplishes the same purpose is not.

The evident constitutional propriety disappears, however, if the condition substituted for the prohibition utterly fails to further the end advanced as the justification for the prohibition. When that essential nexus is eliminated, the situation becomes the same as if California law forbade shouting fire in a crowded theater, but granted dispensations to those willing to contribute $100 to the state treasury. While a ban on shouting fire can be a core exercise of the State's police power to protect the public safety, and can thus meet even our stringent standards for regulation of speech, adding the unrelated condition alters the purpose to one which, while it may be legitimate, is inadequate to sustain the ban. Therefore, even though, in a sense, requiring a $100 tax contribution in order to shout fire is a lesser restriction on speech than an outright ban, it would not pass constitutional muster. Similarly here, the lack of nexus between the condition and the original purpose of the building restriction converts that purpose to something other than what it was. The purpose then becomes, quite simply, the obtaining of an easement to serve some valid governmental purpose, but without payment of compensation. Whatever may be the outer limits of "legitimate state interests" in the takings and land-use context, this is not one of them. In short, unless the permit condition serves the same governmental purpose as the development ban, the building restriction is not a valid regulation of land use but "an out-and-out plan of extortion." *J.E.D. Assocs., Inc. v. Atkinson*, 432 A.2d 12, 14–15 (1981); see Brief for United States as *Amicus Curiae* 22 & n.20. See also *Loretto v. Teleprompter Manhattan CATV Corp.*, 458 U.S. at 439, n.17.

## *III*

The Commission claims that it concedes as much, and that we may sustain the condition at issue here by finding that it is reasonably related to the public need or burden that the Nollans' new house creates or to which it contributes. We can accept, for purposes of discussion, the Commission's proposed test as to how close a "fit" between the condition and the burden is required, because we find that this case does not meet even the most untailored standards. The Commission's principal contention to the contrary essentially turns on a play on the word "access." The Nollans' new house, the Commission found, will interfere with "visual access" to the beach. That in turn (along with other shorefront development) will interfere with the desire of people who drive past the Nollans' house to use the beach, thus creating a "psychological barrier" to "access." The Nollans' new house will also, by a process not altogether clear from the Commission's opinion but presumably potent enough to more than offset the effects of the psychological barrier, increase the use of the public beaches, thus creating the need for more "access." These burdens on "access" would be alleviated by a requirement that the Nollans provide "lateral access" to the beach.

Rewriting the argument to eliminate the play on words makes clear that there is nothing to it. It is quite impossible to understand how a requirement that people already on the public beaches be able to walk across the Nollans' property reduces any obstacles to viewing the beach created by the new house. It is also impossible to understand how it lowers any "psychological barrier" to using the public beaches, or how it helps to remedy any additional congestion on them caused by construction of the Nollans' new house. We therefore find that the Commission's imposition of the permit condition cannot be treated as an exercise of its land-use power for any of these purposes. Our conclusion on this point is consistent with the approach taken by every other court that has considered the question, with the exception of the California state courts ... .

We are left, then, with the Commission's justification for the access requirement unrelated to land-use regulation:

> Finally, the Commission notes that there are several existing provisions of pass and repass lateral access benefits already given by past Faria Beach Tract applicants as a result of prior coastal permit decisions. The access required as a condition of this permit is part of a comprehensive program to provide continuous public access along Faria Beach as the lots undergo development or redevelopment. App. 68.

That is simply an expression of the Commission's belief that the public interest will be served by a continuous strip of publicly accessible beach along the coast. The Commission may well be right that it is a good idea, but that does not establish that the Nollans (and other coastal residents) alone can be compelled to contribute to its realization. Rather, California is free to advance its "comprehensive program," if it wishes, by using its power of eminent domain for this "public purpose," *see* U.S. Const. amend. V; but if it wants an easement across the Nollans' property, it must pay for it.

Reversed.

## Rough proportionality required

### United States Supreme Court

### *Dolan v. City of Tigard*[12]

### 1994

Chief Justice REHNQUIST delivered the opinion of the Court.

Petitioner challenges the decision of the Oregon Supreme Court which held that the city of Tigard could condition the approval of her building permit on the dedication of a portion of her property for flood control and traffic improvements. 854 P.2d 437 (Or. 1993). We granted certiorari to resolve a question left open by our decision in *Nollan v. California Coastal Comm'n*, 483 U.S. 825 (1987), of what is the required degree of connection between the exactions imposed by the city and the projected impacts of the proposed development ...

#### *I*

[T]he city of Tigard, a community of some 30,000 residents on the southwest edge of Portland, developed a comprehensive plan and codified it in its Community Development Code

(CDC). The CDC requires property owners in the area zoned Central Business District to comply with a 15% open space and landscaping requirement, which limits total site coverage, including all structures and paved parking, to 85% of the parcel. CDC, ch. 18.66, App. to Pet. for Cert. G-16 to G-17. After the completion of a transportation study that identified congestion in the Central Business District as a particular problem, the city adopted a plan for a pedestrian/bicycle pathway intended to encourage alternatives to automobile transportation for short trips. The CDC requires that new development facilitate this plan by dedicating land for pedestrian pathways where provided for in the pedestrian/bicycle pathway plan.

The city also adopted a Master Drainage Plan (Drainage Plan). The Drainage Plan noted that flooding occurred in several areas along Fanno Creek, including areas near petitioner's property. Record, Doc. No. F, ch. 2, pp. 2–5 to 2–8; 4–2 to 4–6; Fig. 4–1. The Drainage Plan also established that the increase in impervious surfaces associated with continued urbanization would exacerbate these flooding problems. To combat these risks, the Drainage Plan suggested a series of improvements to the Fanno Creek Basin, including channel excavation in the area next to petitioner's property. App. to Pet. for Cert. G-13, G-38. Other recommendations included ensuring that the floodplain remains free of structures and that it be preserved as greenways to minimize flood damage to structures. Record, Doc. No. F, ch. 5, pp. 5–16 to 5–21. The Drainage Plan concluded that the cost of these improvements should be shared based on both direct and indirect benefits, with property owners along the waterways paying more due to the direct benefit that they would receive. *Id.* ch. 8, p. 8–11. CDC Chapters 18.84 and 18.86 and CDC § 18.164.100 and the Tigard Park Plan carry out these recommendations.

Petitioner Florence Dolan owns a plumbing and electric supply store located on Main Street in the Central Business District of the city. The store covers approximately 9,700 square feet on the eastern side of a 1.67-acre parcel, which includes a gravel parking lot. Fanno Creek flows through the southwestern corner of the lot and along its western boundary. The year-round flow of the creek renders the area within the creek's 100-year floodplain virtually unusable for commercial development. The city's comprehensive plan includes the Fanno Creek floodplain as part of the city's greenway system.

Petitioner applied to the city for a permit to redevelop the site. Her proposed plans called for nearly doubling the size of the store to 17,600 square feet and paving a 39-space parking lot. The existing store, located on the opposite side of the parcel, would be razed in sections as construction progressed on the new building. In the second phase of the project, petitioner proposed to build an additional structure on the northeast side of the site for complementary businesses and to provide more parking. The proposed expansion and intensified use are consistent with the city's zoning scheme in the Central Business District. CDC § 18.66.030, App. to Brief for Petitioner C-1 to C-3.

The City Planning Commission (Commission) granted petitioner's permit application subject to conditions imposed by the city's CDC. The CDC establishes the following standard for site development review approval:

> Where landfill and/or development is allowed within and adjacent to the 100-year floodplain, the City shall require the dedication of sufficient open land area for greenway adjoining and within the floodplain. This area shall include portions at a suitable elevation for the construction of a pedestrian/bicycle pathway within the floodplain in accordance with the adopted pedestrian/bicycle plan. CDC § 18.120.180.A.8, App. to Brief for Respondent B-45 to B-46.

Thus, the Commission required that petitioner dedicate[13] the portion of her property lying within the 100-year floodplain for improvement of a storm drainage system along Fanno

Creek and that she dedicate an additional 15-foot strip of land adjacent to the floodplain as a pedestrian/bicycle pathway. The dedication required by that condition encompasses approximately 7,000 square feet, or roughly 10% of the property. In accordance with city practice, petitioner could rely on the dedicated property to meet the 15% open space and landscaping requirement mandated by the city's zoning scheme. App. to Pet. for Cert. G-28 to G-29. The city would bear the cost of maintaining a landscaped buffer between the dedicated area and the new store. *Id.* at G-44 to G-45 ... .

The Commission made a series of findings concerning the relationship between the dedicated conditions and the projected impacts of petitioner's project. First, the Commission noted that "[i]t is reasonable to assume that customers and employees of the future uses of this site could utilize a pedestrian/bicycle pathway adjacent to this development for their transportation and recreational needs." City of Tigard Planning Commission Final Order No. 91-09 PC, App. to Pet. for Cert. G-24. The Commission noted that the site plan has provided for bicycle parking in a rack in front of the proposed building and "[i]t is reasonable to expect that some of the users of the bicycle parking provided for by the site plan will use the pathway adjacent to Fanno Creek if it is constructed." *Ibid.* In addition, the Commission found that creation of a convenient, safe pedestrian/bicycle pathway system as an alternative means of transportation "could offset some of the traffic demand on [nearby] streets and lessen the increase in traffic congestion." *Ibid.*

The Commission went on to note that the required floodplain dedication would be reasonably related to petitioner's request to intensify the use of the site given the increase in the impervious surface. The Commission stated that the "anticipated increased storm water flow from the subject property to an already strained creek and drainage basin can only add to the public need to manage the stream channel and floodplain for drainage purposes." *Id.* at G-37. Based on this anticipated increased storm water flow, the Commission concluded that "the requirement of dedication of the floodplain area on the site is related to the applicant's plan to intensify development on the site." *Ibid.* The Tigard City Council approved the Commission's final order, subject to one minor modification; the city council reassigned the responsibility for surveying and marking the floodplain area from petitioner to the city's engineering department. *Id.* at G-7. Petitioner appealed to the Land Use Board of Appeals (LUBA) on the ground that the city's dedication requirements were not related to the proposed development, and, therefore, those requirements constituted an uncompensated taking of her property under the Fifth Amendment ... .

[The Board] concluded that "there is a 'reasonable relationship' between the proposed development and the requirement to dedicate land along Fanno Creek for a greenway" ... [and] found a "reasonable relationship" between alleviating the impacts of increased traffic from the development and facilitating the provision of a pedestrian/bicycle pathway as an alternative means of transportation. The Oregon Court of Appeals affirmed ... . The Oregon Supreme Court [also] affirmed ... [and] decided that both the pedestrian/bicycle pathway condition and the storm drainage dedication had an essential nexus to the development of the proposed site. Therefore, the court found the conditions to be reasonably related to the impact of the expansion of petitioner's business. We granted certiorari ... .

### *II*

The Takings Clause of the Fifth Amendment of the United States Constitution, made applicable to the States through the Fourteenth Amendment, *Chi., B. & Q.R. Co. v. Chicago*, 166 U.S. 226, 239 (1897), provides: "[N]or shall private property be taken for public use, without just compensation." One of the principal purposes of the Takings Clause is "to bar Government from forcing some people alone to bear public burdens which, in all fairness and justice, should be borne by the public as a whole." *Armstrong v. United States*, 364 U.S. 40, 49 (1960). Without question, had the city simply required petitioner to dedicate a strip of land along Fanno Creek for public use, rather than conditioning the grant of her permit to redevelop her property on such a dedication, a taking would have occurred. *Nollan, supra*, 483 U.S. at 831. Such public access would deprive petitioner of the right to exclude others, "one of the most essential sticks in the bundle of rights that are commonly characterized as property." *Kaiser Aetna v. United States*, 444 U.S. 164, 176 (1979).

On the other side of the ledger, the authority of state and local governments to engage in land use planning has been sustained against constitutional challenge as long ago as our decision in *Village of Euclid v. Ambler Realty Co.*, 272 U.S. 365 (1926). "Government hardly could go on if to some extent values incident to property could not be diminished without paying for every such change in the general law." *Pa. Coal Co. v. Mahon*, 260 U.S. 393, 413 (1922) .... .

The sort of land use regulations discussed in the cases just cited, however, differ in two relevant particulars from the present case. First, they involved essentially legislative determinations classifying entire areas of the city, whereas here the city made an adjudicative decision to condition petitioner's application for a building permit on an individual parcel. Second, the conditions imposed were not simply a limitation on the use petitioner might make of her own parcel, but a requirement that she deed portions of the property to the city. In *Nollan, supra*, we held that governmental authority to exact such a condition was circumscribed by the Fifth and Fourteenth Amendments. Under the well-settled doctrine of "unconstitutional conditions," the government may not require a person to give up a constitutional right-here the right to receive just compensation when property is taken for a public use-in exchange for a discretionary benefit conferred by the government where the benefit sought has little or no relationship to the property. See *Perry v. Sindermann*, 408 U.S. 593 (1972); *Pickering v. Board of Ed. of Township High School Dist. 205, Will Cnty.*, 391 U.S. 563, 568 (1968).

Petitioner contends that the city has forced her to choose between the building permit and her right under the Fifth Amendment to just compensation for the public easements. Petitioner does not quarrel with the city's authority to exact some forms of dedication as a condition for the grant of a building permit, but challenges the showing made by the city to justify these exactions. She argues that the city has identified "no special benefits" conferred on her, and has not identified any "special quantifiable burdens" created by her new store that would justify the particular dedications required from her which are not required from the public at large.

### *III*

In evaluating petitioner's claim, we must first determine whether the "essential nexus" exists between the "legitimate state interest" and the permit condition exacted by the city. *Nollan*, 483 U.S. at 837. If we find that a nexus exists, we must then decide the required degree of connection between the exactions and the projected impact of the proposed development. We were not required to reach this question in *Nollan*, because we concluded that the connection did not meet even the loosest standard. *Id.* at 838. Here, however, we must decide this question.

### *A*

We addressed the essential nexus question in *Nollan*. The California Coastal Commission demanded a lateral public easement across the Nollans' beachfront lot in exchange for a permit to demolish an existing bungalow and replace it with a three-bedroom house. *Id.* at 828. The public easement was designed to connect two public beaches that were separated by the Nollan's property. The Coastal Commission had asserted that the public easement condition was imposed to promote the legitimate state interest of diminishing the "blockage of the view of the ocean" caused by construction of the larger house.

We agreed that the Coastal Commission's concern with protecting visual access to the ocean constituted a legitimate public interest. *Id.* at 835. We also agreed that the permit condition would have been constitutional "even if it consisted of the requirement that the Nollans provide a viewing spot on their property for passersby with whose sighting of the ocean their new house would interfere." *Id.* at 836. We resolved, however, that the Coastal Commission's regulatory authority was set completely adrift from its constitutional moorings when it claimed that a nexus existed between visual access to the ocean and a permit condition requiring lateral public access along the Nollans' beachfront lot. *Id.* at 837. How enhancing the public's ability to "traverse to and along the shorefront" served the same governmental purpose of "visual access to the ocean" from the roadway was beyond our ability to countenance. The absence of a nexus left the Coastal Commission in the position of simply trying to obtain an easement through gimmickry, which converted a valid regulation of land use into "an out-and-out plan of extortion" *Ibid.*, quoting *J.E.D. Assocs., Inc. v. Atkinson*, 432 A.2d 12, 14–15 (1981).

No such gimmicks are associated with the permit conditions imposed by the city in this case. Undoubtedly, the prevention of flooding along Fanno Creek and the reduction of traffic congestion in the Central Business District qualify as the type of legitimate public purposes we have upheld. *Agins*, 447 U.S. at 260–62. It seems equally obvious that a nexus exists between preventing flooding along Fanno Creek and limiting development within the creek's 100-year floodplain. Petitioner proposes to double the size of her retail store and to pave her now-gravel parking lot, thereby expanding the impervious surface on the property and increasing the amount of storm water runoff into Fanno Creek.

The same may be said for the city's attempt to reduce traffic congestion by providing for alternative means of transportation. In theory, a pedestrian/bicycle pathway provides a useful alternative means of transportation for workers and shoppers: "Pedestrians and bicyclists occupying dedicated spaces for walking and/or bicycling ... remove potential vehicles from streets, resulting in an overall improvement in total transportation system flow." A. Nelson, *Public Provision of Pedestrian and Bicycle Access Ways: Public Policy Rationale and the Nature of Private Benefits* 11, Center for Planning Development, Georgia Institute of Technology, Working Paper Series (Jan. 1994). *See also Intermodal Surface Transportation Efficiency Act of 1991*, Pub. L. 102–240, 105 Stat. 1914 (recognizing pedestrian and bicycle facilities as necessary components of any strategy to reduce traffic congestion).

### *B*

The second part of our analysis requires us to determine whether the degree of the exactions demanded by the city's permit conditions bears the required relationship to the projected impact of petitioner's proposed development. *Nollan, supra*, 483 U.S. at 834 ... . Here the Oregon Supreme Court deferred to what it termed the "city's unchallenged factual findings" supporting the dedication conditions and found them to be reasonably related to the impact of the expansion of petitioner's business.

The city required that petitioner dedicate "to the City as Greenway all portions of the site that fall within the existing 100-year floodplain [of Fanno Creek] ... and all property 15 feet above [the floodplain] boundary." *Id.*, at 113, n. 3, 854 P.2d at 439, n. 3. In addition, the city demanded that the retail store be designed so as not to intrude into the greenway area. The city relies on the Commission's rather tentative findings that increased storm water flow from petitioner's property "can only add to the public need to manage the [floodplain] for drainage purposes" to support its conclusion that the "requirement of dedication of the floodplain area on the site is related to the applicant's plan to intensify development on the site." City of Tigard Planning Commission Final Order No. 91-09 PC, App. to Pet. for Cert. G-37.

The city made the following specific findings relevant to the pedestrian/bicycle pathway:

> In addition, the proposed expanded use of this site is anticipated to generate additional vehicular traffic thereby increasing congestion on nearby collector and arterial streets. Creation of a convenient, safe pedestrian/bicycle pathway system as an alternative means of transportation could offset some of the traffic demand on these nearby streets and lessen the increase in traffic congestion.
>
> *Id.* at G-24

The question for us is whether these findings are constitutionally sufficient to justify the conditions imposed by the city on petitioner's building permit. Since state courts have been dealing with this question a good deal longer than we have, we turn to representative decisions made by them.

In some States, very generalized statements as to the necessary connection between the required dedication and the proposed development seem to suffice. *See, e.g., Billings Props., Inc. v. Yellowstone Cnty.*, 394 P.2d 182 (1964); *Jenad, Inc. v. Scarsdale*, 218 N.E.2d 673 (1966). We think this standard is too lax to adequately protect petitioner's right to just compensation if her property is taken for a public purpose.

Other state courts require a very exacting correspondence, described as the "specifi[c] and uniquely attributable" test. The Supreme Court of Illinois first developed this test in *Pioneer Trust & Savings Bank v. Mount Prospect*, 176 N.E.2d 799, 802 (1961). Under this standard, if the local government cannot demonstrate that its exaction is directly proportional to the specifically created need, the exaction becomes "a veiled exercise of the power of eminent domain and a confiscation of private property behind the defense of police regulations." 176 N.E.2d at 802. We do not think the Federal Constitution requires such exacting scrutiny, given the nature of the interests involved.

A number of state courts have taken an intermediate position, requiring the municipality to show a "reasonable relationship" between the required dedication and the impact of the proposed development. Typical is the Supreme Court of Nebraska's opinion in *Simpson v. N. Platte*, 206 292 N.W.2d 297, 301 (1980), where that court stated:

> The distinction, therefore, which must be made between an appropriate exercise of the police power and an improper exercise of eminent domain is whether the requirement has some reasonable relationship or nexus to the use to which the property is being made or is merely being used as an excuse for taking property simply because at that particular moment the landowner is asking the city for some license or permit.

Thus, the court held that a city may not require a property owner to dedicate private property for some future public use as a condition of obtaining a building permit when such future use is not "occasioned by the construction sought to be permitted." 292 N.W.2d at 302.

Some form of the reasonable relationship test has been adopted in many other jurisdictions. *See, e.g., Jordan v. Menomonee Falls*, 137 N.W.2d 442 (1965); *Collis v. Bloomington*, 246 N.W.2d 19 (1976) (requiring a showing of a reasonable relationship between the planned subdivision and the municipality's need for land); *College Station v. Turtle Rock Corp.*, 680 S.W.2d 802, 807 (Tex.1984); *Call v. W. Jordan*, 606 P.2d 217, 220 (Utah 1979) (affirming use of the reasonable relation test). Despite any semantical differences, general agreement exists among the courts "that the dedication should have some reasonable relationship to the needs created by the [development]." *Ibid. See generally* Nicholas V. Morosoff, Note, "'Take' My Beach Please!": *Nollan v. California Coastal Commission and a Rational-Nexus Constitutional Analysis of Development Exactions*, 69 Bos. U.L. Rev. 823 (1989); *see also Parks v. Watson*, 716 F.2d 646, 651–53 (9th Cir. 1983).

We think the "reasonable relationship" test adopted by a majority of the state courts is closer to the federal constitutional norm than either of those previously discussed. But we do not adopt it as such, partly because the term "reasonable relationship" seems confusingly similar to the term "rational basis" which describes the minimal level of scrutiny under the Equal Protection Clause of the Fourteenth Amendment. We think a term such as "rough proportionality" best encapsulates what we hold to be the requirement of the Fifth Amendment. No precise mathematical calculation is required, but the city must make some sort of individualized determination that the required dedication is related both in nature and extent to the impact of the proposed development ... .

We turn now to analysis of whether the findings relied upon by the city here, first with respect to the floodplain easement, and second with respect to the pedestrian/bicycle path, satisfied these requirements.

It is axiomatic that increasing the amount of impervious surface will increase the quantity and rate of storm water flow from petitioner's property. Record, Doc. No. F, ch. 4, p. 4–29. Therefore, keeping the floodplain open and free from development would likely confine the pressures on Fanno Creek created by petitioner's development. In fact, because petitioner's property lies within the Central Business District, the CDC already required that petitioner leave 15% of it as open space and the undeveloped floodplain would have nearly satisfied that requirement. App. to Pet. for Cert. G-16 to G-17. But the city demanded more—it not only wanted petitioner not to build in the floodplain, but it also wanted petitioner's property along Fanno Creek for its greenway system. The city has never said why a public greenway, as opposed to a private one, was required in the interest of flood control.

The difference to petitioner, of course, is the loss of her ability to exclude others. As we have noted, this right to exclude others is "one of the most essential sticks in the bundle of rights that are commonly characterized as property." *Kaiser Aetna*, 444 U.S. at 176. It is difficult to see why recreational visitors trampling along petitioner's floodplain easement are sufficiently related to the city's legitimate interest in reducing flooding problems along Fanno Creek, and the city has not attempted to make any individualized determination to support this part of its request.

The city contends that the recreational easement along the greenway is only ancillary to the city's chief purpose in controlling flood hazards. It further asserts that unlike the residential property at issue in *Nollan*, petitioner's property is commercial in character, and therefore, her right to exclude others is compromised. Brief for Respondent 41, quoting *United States v. Orito*, 413 U.S. 139, 142 (1973) ("The Constitution extends special safeguards to the privacy of the home"). The city maintains that "[t]here is nothing to suggest that preventing [petitioner] from prohibiting [the easements] will unreasonably impair the value of [her] property as a [retail store]." *PruneYard Shopping Ctr. v. Robins*, 447 U.S. 74, 83 (1980).

Admittedly, petitioner wants to build a bigger store to attract members of the public to her property. She also wants, however, to be able to control the time and manner in which they enter. The recreational easement on the greenway is different in character from the exercise of state-protected rights of free expression and petition that we permitted in *PruneYard*. In *PruneYard*, we held that a major private shopping center that attracted more than 25,000 daily patrons had to provide access to persons exercising their state constitutional rights to distribute pamphlets and ask passers-by to sign their petitions. *Id.* at 85. We based our decision, in part, on the fact that the shopping center "may restrict expressive activity by adopting time, place, and manner regulations that will minimize any interference with its commercial functions." *Id.* at 83. By contrast, the city wants to impose a permanent recreational easement upon petitioner's property that borders Fanno Creek. Petitioner would lose all rights to regulate the time in which the public entered onto the greenway, regardless of any interference it might pose with her retail store. Her right to exclude would not be regulated, it would be eviscerated.

If petitioner's proposed development had somehow encroached on existing greenway space in the city, it would have been reasonable to require petitioner to provide some alternative greenway space for the public either on her property or elsewhere. *See Nollan*, 483 U.S. at 836:

> Although such a requirement, constituting a permanent grant of continuous access to the property, would have to be considered a taking if it were not attached to a development permit, the Commission's assumed power to forbid construction of the house in order to protect the public's view of the beach must surely include the power to condition construction upon some concession by the owner, even a concession of property rights, that serves the same end.

But that is not the case here. We conclude that the findings upon which the city relies do not show the required reasonable relationship between the floodplain easement and the petitioner's proposed new building.

With respect to the pedestrian/bicycle pathway, we have no doubt that the city was correct in finding that the larger retail sales facility proposed by petitioner will increase traffic on the streets of the Central Business District. The city estimates that the proposed development would generate roughly 435 additional trips per day. Dedications for streets, sidewalks, and other public ways are generally reasonable exactions to avoid excessive congestion from a proposed property use. But on the record before us, the city has not met its burden of demonstrating that the additional number of vehicle and bicycle trips generated by petitioner's development reasonably relate to the city's requirement for a dedication of the pedestrian/bicycle pathway easement. The city simply found that the creation of the pathway "could offset some of the traffic demand ... and lessen the increase in traffic congestion."

As Justice Peterson of the Supreme Court of Oregon explained in his dissenting opinion, however, "[t]he findings of fact that the bicycle pathway system '*could* offset some of the traffic demand' is a far cry from a finding that the bicycle pathway system *will*, or is *likely to*, offset some of the traffic demand." 854 P.2d at 447 [emphasis in the original]. No precise mathematical calculation is required, but the city must make some effort to quantify its findings in support of the dedication for the pedestrian/bicycle pathway beyond the conclusory statement that it could offset some of the traffic demand generated.

### *IV*

Cities have long engaged in the commendable task of land use planning, made necessary by increasing urbanization, particularly in metropolitan areas such as Portland. The city's goals of reducing flooding hazards and traffic congestion, and providing for public greenways, are laudable, but there are outer limits to how this may be done. "A strong public desire to improve the public condition [will not] warrant achieving the desire by a shorter cut than the constitutional way of paying for the change." *Pa. Coal*, 260 U.S. at 416.

The judgment of the Supreme Court of Oregon is reversed, and the case is remanded for further proceedings not inconsistent with this opinion.

It is so ordered.

***Discussion***

A significant exactions decision coming after *Nollan* and *Dolan* is *Koontz v. St. Johns River Water Mgmt. Dist.*[14] In that case, which arose from a development dispute on the fringes of the Orlando metro area, the Court held "that the government's demand for property from a land-use permit applicant must satisfy the requirements of *Nollan* and *Dolan* even when the government denies the permit and even when its demand is for money."[15]

That two-part holding prevents two government actions from being successful strategies at avoiding exactions. First, government cannot avoid the rule on exactions by saying a permit is denied unless an applicant accedes to a certain demand for infrastructure.[16] Second, government cannot avoid the rule on exactions by giving an applicant the opportunity to pay a fee in lieu of giving up some right to real property.[17]

Florida courts have determined that the Florida Constitution's property rights protections protect property owners from exactions and that those protections have the same reach as the federal court rules on exactions.[18] A Florida state court case that clearly applies the rule on exactions to a dispute over permit conditions is *Highlands-in-the-Woods, L.L.C. v. Polk Cnty.*[19]

### Box 18.1 Practice problem: CHEAP apartments

Collegeborough has a traffic problem. For years, the city has permitted development without putting a plan in place to handle the traffic created by more houses and businesses. The people of Collegeborough are angry because of the time they must spend in traffic—particularly on congested University Avenue.

When people get angry, elected officials demand solutions from the planning department. The Collegeborough planners, therefore, create a plan for a dedicated busway on University Avenue that will solve all of the congestion on that street.

Collegeborough Housing Enrichment and Profit, Inc., or CHEAP, is a multi-family housing developer and property manager in Collegeborough. The company specializes in student housing and is the landlord for about half of the students studying at State University.

Because State University is expanding its undergraduate student population, CHEAP sees an opportunity in the marketplace to provide more apartments for students. The developer draws up plans for a new 500-unit apartment complex to be built on University Avenue and submits a development application to the planning department for the city of Collegeborough.

When reviewing CHEAP's application, the Collegeborough planners study the transportation impacts of the proposed development. They determine the apartment complex will create some new demand for transportation services on University Avenue. To address this problem, they approve CHEAP's application on the condition that CHEAP build all of the dedicated busway improvements outlined in their plan.

Collegeborough Housing Enrichment and Profit, Inc. thinks that this permit condition is an unlawful exaction and sues to have it removed from its permit requirements.

Evaluate CHEAP's claim.

## Notes

1 John M. Levy, *Contemporary Urban Planning*, 134–35 (11th edn 2017).
2 *Id.*
3 *Chinatown* (Long Road Productions 1974).
4 *Who Framed Roger Rabbit?* (Amblin Entertainment 1988).

5 *Id.*
6 Rachel MacCleery et al., *Active Transportation and Real Estate: The Next Frontier* 2–34 (Urb. Land Inst. 2016).
7 Highlands-in-the-Woods, L.L.C. v. Polk Cnty., 217 So. 3d 1175, 1179 (Fla. 2d DCA 2017) (quoting Dolan v. City of Tigard, 512 U.S. 374, 386 (1994)).
8 *Id.* at 1179 (quoting *Dolan*, 512 U.S. at 391).
9 *See Dolan*, 512 U.S. at 391.
10 *Id.*; City of Monterey v. Del Monte Dunes at Monterey, Ltd., 526 U.S. 687, 703 (1999).
11 483 U.S. 825 (1987).
12 512 U.S. 374 (1994).
13 In real property law, the term "dedicate" means to donate real property to government for a public purpose. Bonifay v. Dickson, 459 So. 2d 1089, 1093–94 (Fla. 1st DCA 1984); *see also* City of Miami Beach v. Miami Beach Improvement Co., 14 So. 2d 172, 175–76 (Fla. 1943). For example, when a local government approves a subdivision, the applicant for the subdivision often dedicates the land that will be the roads within the subdivision. Afterwards, the roads become government property, so that the public has the right to use them and the obligation to maintain them. *Bonifay*, 459 So. 2d at 1094–95.
14 570 U.S. 595 (2013).
15 Koontz v. St. Johns River Water Mgmt. Dist., 570 U.S. 595, 619 (2013).
16 *Id.* at 606.
17 *Id.* at 612.
18 St. Johns River Water Mgmt. Dist. v. Koontz, 77 So. 3d 1220, 1222 (Fla. 2011), *rev'd*, 570 U.S. 595 (2013).
19 Highlands-in-the-Woods, L.L.C. v. Polk Cnty., 217 So. 3d 1175 (Fla. 2d DCA 2017).

# 19 Taxes, assessments, and fees

This chapter distinguishes three different kinds of government charges: taxes, assessments, and fees. We are all generally familiar with the concept of taxation: the law compels people to pay money to government. But governments raise money through many different kinds of charges, not all of which are taxes. We care whether a charge is a tax, an assessment, or a fee because that distinction often tells us whether a charge is lawful.

Recall that Florida is a home rule state. The state has broadly delegated to local governments the power to carry on municipal government. However, Florida has not broadly delegated to its local governments the power to tax. The Florida Constitution provides: "No tax shall be levied except in pursuance of law."[1]

As a result, local governments in Florida may only levy those taxes that state law explicitly allows.[2] But, local governments in Florida can charge fees[3] within their power to carry on municipal government without legislative authorization.[4] An impact fee is a type of fee that local governments charge developers to cover the cost of building the new capital infrastructure that the local government needs so it can provide services to new development.[5] Impact fees are one-time costs paid by developers of new real estate, not by the owners of existing real estate. Charging an impact fee is also within a local government's police power to carry out municipal government.[6]

Because of this framework, the validity of an impact fee in Florida depends on whether the charge is an ultra vires tax or a constitutionally allowed fee—permitted by the state constitution's delegation of home rule authority to local governments.[7] The Florida Supreme Court has described local government charges as falling into one of three categories:

- *Taxes* are compulsory charges paid into a government's general revenue.[8]
- *Assessments* are charges levied on a property to recover the cost of a government expenditure that benefits that specific property.[9] A classic example of an assessment is a charge to recover the cost of constructing a road that serves a discrete set of properties.[10]
- A *fee* is a voluntary charge paid in exchange for a government service where the amount of the charge relates to the cost of the service.[11]

And the Florida Supreme Court has said the following regarding its ability to tell these different charges from one another:

> We have previously recognized that user fees and special assessments are similar. We have defined user fees as
>
> > charges based upon the proprietary right of the governing body permitting the use of the instrumentality involved. Such fees share common traits that distinguish them from taxes: they are charged in exchange for a particular governmental service which benefits

the party paying the fee in a manner not shared by other members of society, and they are paid by choice, in that the party paying the fee has the option of not utilizing the governmental service and thereby avoiding the charge.

Similarly, special assessments are "charge[s] assessed against [the] property of some particular locality because that property derives some special benefit [from] the expenditure of [the] money."[12]

Florida's highest court has further distinguished between taxes and assessments:

> [A] legally imposed special assessment is not a tax. Taxes and special assessments are distinguishable in that, while both are mandatory, there is no requirement that taxes provide any specific benefit to the property; instead, they may be levied throughout the particular taxing unit for the general benefit of residents and property. *On the other hand, special assessments must confer a specific benefit upon the land burdened by the assessment.*[13]

Common purposes for special assessments include benefitting specific properties by constructing or improving streets, constructing or improving seawalls, protecting the properties from fire, or constructing water utilities.[14]

As discussed previously, the distinctions between these different types of charges are not just semantic. Whether a charge is a tax, an assessment, or a fee determines whether a local government has the authority to levy it. In *Contractors and Builders Ass'n of Pinellas Cnty. v. City of Dunedin*, an impact fee case decided in 1976, the Florida Supreme Court framed the arguments of the parties thusly:

> Plaintiffs in the trial court, petitioners here, are building contractors, an incorporated association of contractors, and owners of land situated within the city limits of Dunedin. They do not complain of all the fees Dunedin requires to be collected upon issuance of building permits, but contend that monies which the city collects and earmarks for "capital improvements to the (water and sewerage) system as a whole" constitute taxes, which a municipality is forbidden to impose, in the absence of enabling legislation. It is agreed on all sides that "a municipality cannot impose a tax, other than ad valorem taxes, unless authorized by general law," and that no general law gives such authorization here. Respondent contends that these fees are not taxes, but user charges analogous to fees collected by privately owned utilities for services rendered.[15]

Ultimately, the court found the impact fees to be constitutionally permissible fees.[16] And it established the *dual rational nexus test* as the means to determine whether a charge is a lawful impact fee.[17]

## Community development districts

While collecting charges for public services at a local level is generally the purview of cities and counties, Florida law sometimes provides for other entities to levy taxes and fees. In the context of land use, the community development district (CDD) is an important funding tool available to developers of major real estate projects. The Uniform Community Development District Act of 1980, codified as Chapter 190 Florida Statutes, provides for the creation and management of CDDs.[18] A CDD is an independent, special-purpose government with the ability to: issue debt; develop, own, and maintain infrastructure; and collect taxes and fees.[19] Developers create CDDs so they may borrow money, spend that money on capital infrastructure to serve real estate development, and then repay the debt from CDD revenue rather than from revenue earned by selling or leasing the served real estate product.[20]

Depending on the size of a CDD, a developer may apply to create it by application to either a county or to the state.[21] Once a CDD is created, it will have an initial board of supervisors comprising five persons designated by the applicant.[22] Subsequently, the CDD must hold elections to select the members of its board of supervisors.[23] This board of supervisors then controls the CDD. Eventually, its members must be residents of the CDD and be registered voters.[24]

### Assessments

The case *City of Winter Springs v. State* analyzes the special benefits requirement of assessments, as well as a requirement that an assessment be fairly apportioned.

## Florida Supreme Court

## *City of Winter Springs v. State*[25]

## 2001

HARDING, J.

We have on appeal the final judgment of the trial court refusing to validate special assessment bonds. We have jurisdiction. Art. V, § 3(b)(2), Fla. Const. For the reasons expressed, we reverse the trial court's judgment and remand the cause for further bond validation proceedings.

Appellant, the City of Winter Springs, Florida (City), filed a complaint for validation of special assessment bonds for the financing of local improvements in a discrete portion of the City known as the Tuscawilla Lighting and Beautification District (District).[1] Proposed improvements include enhanced landscaping, signage, and lighting at various locations within the District. Appellees, the State of Florida and Intervenors on behalf of the Property Owners and Citizens of the City of Winter Springs (Validation Opponents), filed an answer opposing validation of the bonds. After a bench trial, the trial court denied the City's complaint to validate the bonds, holding that the special assessment was not in compliance with the law. The City timely filed this direct appeal.

This Court's scope of review in bond validation cases is limited to the following issues: (1) whether the public body has the authority to issue bonds; (2) whether the purpose of the obligation is legal; and (3) whether the bond issuance complies with the requirements of the law. *See State v. Inland Protection Fin. Corp.*, 699 So. 2d 1352 (Fla. 1997); *Poe v. Hillsborough Cnty.*, 695 So. 2d 672 (Fla. 1997); *N. Palm Beach Cnty. Water Control Dist. v. State*, 604 So. 2d 440 (Fla. 1992); *Taylor v. Lee Cnty.*, 498 So. 2d 424 (Fla. 1986). To comply with the requirements of the law, a special assessment funding a bond issuance must satisfy the following two-prong test: (1) the property burdened by the assessment must derive a special benefit from the service provided by the assessment; and (2) the assessment for the services must be properly apportioned among the properties receiving the benefit. *See Lake Cnty. v. Water*

1 Tuscawilla is a Planned Unit Development located within the City, consisting of a number of different independent developments with approximately four thousand homes, a county club and golf course, and several commercial properties. In the early 1990's, a group of Tuscawilla homeowners approached the City requesting authority to form a taxing district for the maintenance and improvement of certain common areas within Tuscawilla no longer being maintained by the developer.

*Oak Mgmt. Corp.*, 695 So. 2d 667, 668 (Fla. 1997) (citing *City of Boca Raton v. State*, 595 So. 2d 25, 30 (Fla. 1992)). "[T]he standard [of review] is the same for both prongs; that is, the legislative determination as to the existence of special benefits and as to the apportionment of the costs of those benefits should be upheld unless the determination is arbitrary." *Sarasota Cnty. v. Sarasota Church of Christ*, 667 So. 2d 180, 184 (Fla. 1995).

In this case, however, the City's legislative finding that the special assessment confers a special benefit upon the land burdened by the assessment was not arbitrary and, therefore, was entitled to a presumption of correctness by the trial court. By substituting its own judgment for that of the locally elected officials, and thus failing to attach a presumption of correctness to the legislative determination, the trial court erred as a matter of law.

Validation Opponents argue there is no evidence to support the City's conclusion that the improvements will provide a special benefit to all tax parcels located within the District. Section 1.03(E) of City Resolution 99–884, however, provides the City's specific findings regarding the "special benefits" derived from the improvements:

> The Tuscawilla Improvements will provide a special benefit to all Tax Parcels located within the Tuscawilla Improvement Area ... by *improving and enhancing the exterior subdivision boundaries, the interior subdivision areas, the subdivision identity, and the subdivision aesthetics and safety, thus enhancing the value, use and enjoyment of such property.*

City of Winter Springs, Fla., Resol. No. 99–884 (July 12, 1999) [emphasis added]. Moreover, the City did employ the services of an outside consultant and appraiser to specifically "analyze whether or not such improvements would have a beneficial impact on home values in the general area." Letter from Appraiser to City of Winter Springs (April 10, 1998). After evaluating the nature, and area, of the proposed improvements, the property appraiser concluded that there would be a beneficial impact on overall property values in the area:

> [W]e reviewed numerous subdivisions and PUDS ... [and] had discussions with residential appraisers, developers, and Realtors regarding beautification projects, either in place or proposed, so that we might have an insight into market opinion on this issue. From this analysis, it was concluded that having improvements, such as those proposed for the Tuscawilla PUD and described to us, in place enhances the market perception of the area and, ultimately, the surrounding property values within the development ... . There appears to be a positive and certain influence on the market value for properties in areas where such improvements are made.

*Id.* In addition, during the validation hearing, the appraiser provided uncontroverted testimony regarding the special benefit conferred upon properties in the District:

> Q. [City Counsel] Now, Mr. Robbins, what did you, based on your investigation and your work in this project, what was your opinion in terms of what these improvements would have on the value of property, beneficial value of this property in the assessment area.
> A. [Appraiser] I concluded that there would be a positive, general overall benefit to the surrounding properties.
> Q. [City Counsel] Could you tell the Court basically why you felt that.
> A. [Appraiser] It was from my discussions with the developers, residential appraisers, and realtors, and engaging them in a discussion about what the impact of these types of improvements generally have on, or what their perception of those impacts are. And to

see every person that I discussed this matter they conveyed to me for various reasons it would have a positive overall impact on those surrounding homes.

Validation opponents also argue that because other people outside of the District may benefit from the improvements, the improvements do not confer a "special" benefit upon property owners in the District. This argument fails, however, because the mere fact that the opponents presented testimony that non-neighborhood residents drive through the District on their way to other parts of the City, and *en route* will incidentally benefit from improvements in the District such as new signs, landscaping and street lighting, does not invalidate the special assessment. *See Charlotte Cnty. v. Fiske*, 350 So. 2d 578, 581 (Fla. 2d DCA 1977) (holding that a special benefit is not lost merely because other properties incidentally benefit); *see also Lake Cnty.*, 695 So. 2d at 670 (holding that a special benefit can only be conferred to the real property itself, i.e., not to mere passersby).

This Court has held that "if reasonable persons may differ as to whether the land assessed was benefitted by the local improvement, the findings of the city officials must be sustained." *City of Boca Raton v. State*, 595 So. 2d 25, 30 (Fla. 1992). Accordingly, the trial court failed to give appropriate deference to the legislative findings of the City and to the record evidence that provided support for those findings. The specific findings of the City Commission declare that the assessment for the District would improve exterior subdivision boundaries, interior subdivision areas, subdivision identity and subdivision aesthetics, and would enhance the safety, value, and the use and enjoyment of all properties within the District. These findings are supported by the analysis and testimony of the City's appraiser, who was specifically employed to address the benefit question. Moreover, Validation Opponents adduced no evidence to counter these legislative findings. Without any evidence or rational basis to overcome the presumption of correctness which attends the City's legislative findings, there can be no invalidation of the bonds.[4]

The second prong of the special assessment test established in City of Boca Raton requires that the assessment be fairly and reasonably apportioned among the properties that receive the special benefit. *See City of Boca Raton*, 595 So. 2d at 29. And though a court may recognize valid alternative methods of apportionment, so long as the legislative determination by the City is not arbitrary, a court should not substitute its judgment for that of the local legislative body. *See Sarasota Church of Christ, Inc.*, 667 So. 2d at 184; *see also Harris v. Wilson*, 693 So. 2d 945, 947 (Fla. 1997); *State v. Sarasota Cnty.*, 693 So. 2d 546, 548 (Fla. 1997).

The City's method for apportioning the costs of the proposed improvements was thoughtfully selected to assure equitable treatment to every land owner in the District. Through its Resolution 99–884, the City provided the framework for apportionment of the beautification assessment to be "substantially proportional to the area of Buildings located [within the District]." City of Winter Springs, Fla., Resol. 99–884 § 1.03(F) (July 12, 1999). Inasmuch as the District contains single-family homes, multifamily buildings, and a few commercial properties, the City first sought to determine whether all three property uses would benefit from the proposed improvements on the same basis. It determined they would not, as its consultant testified at the trial: "[W]e know for a fact from analysis that single-family [residences]

4 Further, this Court has stated that, "[i]n evaluating whether a special benefit is conferred to property ... the test is whether there is a 'logical relationship' between the services provided and the benefit to real property." Lake County v. Water Oak Mgt. Corp., 695 So. 2d 667, 669 (Fla. 1997) (citing Whisnant v. Stringfellow, 50 So. 2d 885 (Fla. 1951), and Crowder v. Phillips, 146 Fla. 440, 1 So. 2d 629 (1941) (on rehearing)). Here, it is not unreasonable to conclude that there is a "logical relationship" between the proposed beautification and lighting enhancements within the District and the special benefit of enhancing the values of individual properties situated therein.

produce [ ] a different impact on the road system and the community as more than say multi-family condos or apartments, that there's a different benefit realized."

The City then analyzed the mix of properties within the District to find an appropriate basis for assessing the different property uses equitably. It determined that the average square footage of each single-family dwelling unit in the District—the vastly predominant form of property use—was 2200 square feet. It then created a formula that assigned each single-family home an "equivalent residential unit" value of 1, and it extrapolated the ERU value to the multifamily dwelling units and to the commercial properties in the District based on square footage. It then determined that vacant parcels would pay the same as a single-family dwelling unit, and that commercial property would in no event be assessed less than a single-family home. This method, the City Commission found, had the effect of "fairly and reasonably allocating the cost to specially benefitted property, based upon the number of ERUs attributable to each benefitted property in the manner hereinafter described." City Resol. 99–884 § 1.03(G).

Moreover, there was testimony by the City Manager at the validation hearing that nearly all property owners in the District use the Winter Springs Boulevard entry for access to their property: "The majority of people and to some degree I would say every individual that lives in the district is going to use that road."

The City also brought forward expert witness testimony that the location of any particular properties in relation to the improvements was not an appropriate factor for allocation, because

> the main benefit of the improvements ... was to provide an enhanced identity to the community, safety, and landscaping. All of those are the types of benefits that in our professional opinion spread equally throughout the entire community.

This testimony was bolstered by the expert's observation on cross-examination that "[t]he other enhancements, such as street lights, which enhance[ ] the safety of the community ... are equally enjoyed also by everybody in that community."

Though a court, like Validation Opponents, might envision alternative apportionment schemes (e.g. based upon square footage of each particular home, or the proximity of a property in relation to each of the proposed improvements, or even based in some part upon studied usage of various roadways), the choice of apportioning assessments by one or another methodology is not for this Court—or even Validation Opponents.[6] Rather, it is a City responsibility in the first instance which must be upheld if not arbitrary. *See Sarasota Church of Christ*, 667 So. 2d at 184.

6 It should be noted, however, that in Rushfeldt v. Metropolitan Dade County, 630 So. 2d 643 (Fla. 3d DCA 1994), the court addressed a contention from property owners that fair apportionment required a different assessment for residents close to and remote from guard gate improvements and guard services in a gated neighborhood. The court categorically rejected that contention, holding there is no requirement for "tiered assessments based on a property's proximity to the entrance," and that distinction being suggested between residents in the neighborhood "could make it impossible to ever create a special taxing district." *Rushfeldt*, 630 So. 2d at 645 (quoting trial court's judgment). The *Rushfeldt* decision is particularly pertinent here, because the court there sustained the very same improvements which are at issue here—streetlights, landscaped green areas, and better roads. *Id.* To the same effect is Northern Palm Beach County Water Control District v. State, 604 So. 2d 440 (Fla. 1992), which also upheld special assessments for signs, landscaping, irrigation, and street lighting in a mixed-use community with more than 2000 residential properties.

Moreover, a mere disagreement of experts as to the choice of methodology is legally inconsequential. *See Rosche v. City of Hollywood*, 55 So. 2d 909, 913 (Fla. 1952) ("If the evidence as to benefits is conflicting and depends upon the judgment of witnesses, the findings of the City Commission will not be disturbed."). In fact, the validation opponents' expert witness recognized that his opinion on methodology did not invalidate the one selected by the City:

> Q. [City Counsel] Are you saying that these assessments are invalid?
> A. [Opponents Expert] No. I'm not saying that any assessment is invalid. It happens all the time. I'm just saying that this particular assessment with four thousand plus homes was not treated properly, in my opinion. I concluded that there would be a positive, general overall benefit to the surrounding properties.

As this Court noted in *City of Fort Myers v. State*, 117 So. 97, 104 (Fla. 1928), however, "[n]o system of appraising benefits or assessing costs has yet been devised that is not open to some criticism." Rather, a host of elements enter into the proration of benefits, including:

> [P]hysical condition, nearness to or remoteness from residential and business districts, desirability for residential or commercial purposes, and many other peculiar to the locality where the lands improved are located.

*Meyer v. City of Oakland Park*, 219 So. 2d 417, 419–20 (Fla. 1969). The "Equivalent Residential Unit" ("ERU") method of apportioning based upon average building square footage of single family and multi-family residences was reasonable. There is no requirement to "tier" assessments based on proximity to the improvement, nor is there any requirement to value the benefit on each individual property within the District.

Even an unpopular decision, when made correctly, must be upheld. A review of the record in this case yields competent, substantial evidence to support the City's determination of apportionment and, therefore, the City's findings regarding apportionment cannot be said to be "arbitrary." Rather, in this instance, the City's findings are entitled to a presumption of correctness, and the trial court erred as a matter of law in substituting its judgment for that of the locally elected officials.

Therefore, the judgment of the trial court appealed from is reversed, and the cause remanded for further bond validation proceedings consistent with this opinion.

It is so ordered.

WELLS, C.J., and SHAW, ANSTEAD, PARIENTE, LEWIS and QUINCE, JJ., concur.

## Impact fees

Both case law recognizing the dual rational nexus text and the Florida Impact Fee Act[26] govern the levy of impact fees in the state of Florida. The following case, *St. Johns Cnty. v. Ne. Fla. Builders Ass'n.*, applies the dual rational nexus test.

### Florida Supreme Court

***St. Johns Cnty. v. Ne. Fla. Builders Ass'n, Inc.***[27]

**1991**

GRIMES, Justice.

We review *St. Johns County v. Northeast Florida Builders Association*, 559 So. 2d 363 (Fla. 5th DCA 1990), in which the district court of appeal certified as a question of great public importance the question of whether St. Johns County could impose an impact fee on new residential construction to be used for new school facilities ... .

In 1986, St. Johns County initiated a comprehensive study of whether to impose impact fees to finance additional infrastructure required to serve new growth and development. At the request of the St. Johns County School Board, the county included educational facilities impact fees within the scope of the study. In August of 1987, the county's consultant, Dr. James Nicholas, submitted a methodology report setting forth what action the county could take to maintain an acceptable level of service for public facilities. The report calculated the cost of educational facilities needed to provide sufficient school capacity to serve the estimated new growth and development and suggested a method of allocating that cost to each unit of new residential development. As a consequence, on October 20, 1987, the county enacted the St. Johns County Educational Facilities Impact Fee Ordinance.

The ordinance specifies that no new building permits will be issued except upon the payment of an impact fee. The fees are to be placed in a trust fund to be spent by the school board solely to "acquire, construct, expand and equip the educational sites and educational capital facilities necessitated by new development." St. Johns Cnty., Fla., Ordinance 87–60, § 10(B) (Oct. 20, 1987). Any funds not expended within six years, together with interest, will be returned to the current landowner upon application. The ordinance also provides credits to feepayers for land dedications and construction of educational facilities. The ordinance recites that it is applicable in both unincorporated and incorporated areas of the county, except that it is not effective within the boundaries of any municipality until the municipality enters into an interlocal agreement with the county to collect the impact fees.

The Northeast Florida Builders Association together with a private developer (builders) filed suit against the county and its county administrator (county) seeking a declaratory judgment that the ordinance was unconstitutional ... . The trial court entered summary judgment for the builders, declaring the ordinance to be unconstitutional on a variety of grounds. In a split decision, the district court of appeal affirmed, holding that the ordinance violated the constitutional mandate for a uniform system of free public schools.

This Court upheld the imposition of impact fees to pay for the expansion of water and sewer facilities in *Contractors & Builders Ass'n v. City of Dunedin*, 329 So. 2d 314 (Fla. 1976). We stated:

> Raising expansion capital by setting connection charges, which do not exceed a pro rata share of reasonably anticipated costs of expansion, is permissible where expansion is reasonably required, if use of the money collected is limited to meeting the costs of expansion.

*Id.* at 320. In essence, we approved the imposition of impact fees that meet the requirements of the dual rational nexus test adopted by other courts in evaluating impact fees. *See* Julian Conrad Juergensmeyer & Robert Mason Blake, *Impact fees: An Answer to Local Governments' Capital Funding Dilemma*, 9 Fla. St. U.L. Rev. 415 (1981). This test was explained in *Hollywood, Inc. v. Broward Cnty.*, 431 So. 2d 606, 611–12 (Fla. 4th DCA), *review denied*, 440 So. 2d 352 (Fla. 1983), as follows:

> In order to satisfy these requirements, the local government must demonstrate a reasonable connection, or rational nexus, between the need for additional capital facilities and the growth in population generated by the subdivision. In addition, the government must show a reasonable connection, or rational nexus, between the expenditures of

> the funds collected and the benefits accruing to the subdivision. In order to satisfy this latter requirement, the ordinance must specifically earmark the funds collected for use in acquiring capital facilities to benefit the new residents.

The use of impact fees has become an accepted method of paying for public improvements that must be constructed to serve new growth. See *Home Builders & Contractors Ass'n v. Bd. of Cnty. Comm'rs*, 446 So. 2d 140 (Fla. 4th DCA 1983) (road impact fees upheld), *review denied*, 451 So. 2d 848 (Fla.), *appeal dismissed*, 469 U.S. 976 (1984); *Hollywood, Inc. v. Broward Cnty.*, 431 So. 2d at 606 (park impact fees upheld). However, the propriety of imposing impact fees to finance new schools is an issue of first impression in Florida.

Turning to the first prong of the dual rational nexus test, we must decide whether St. Johns County demonstrated that there is a reasonable connection between the need for additional schools and the growth in population that will accompany new development. In the ordinance, the county commissioners made a legislative finding that the county "must expand its educational facilities in order to maintain current levels of service if new development is to be accommodated without decreasing current levels of service." St. Johns Cnty., Fla., Ordinance 87–60, § 1(C) (Oct. 20, 1987). No one quarrels with this proposition. However, an impact fee to be used to fund new schools is different from one required to build water and sewer facilities or even roads. Many of the new residents who will bear the burden of the fee will not have children who will benefit from the new schools. Thus, Dr. Nicholas determined that on average there are 0.44 public school children per single-family home in St. Johns County. Applying the single-family home ratio to a per-student cost calculation, he concluded that it required $2,899 per new single-family home to build the school space anticipated to be needed to serve the children who would live in the new homes. Finding that existing taxes and revenue sources would produce $2,451 per single-family home, Dr. Nicholas concluded that for each new single-family home there was an average net cost of $448 for building new schools that would not be covered by existing revenue mechanisms. He made similar calculations based upon his determination of the number of public school children residing in multiple family units of construction.

The builders argue that because many of the new residences will have no impact on the public school system, the impact fee is nothing more than a tax insofar as those residences are concerned. We reject this contention as too simplistic. The same argument could be made with respect to many other facilities that governmental entities are expected to provide. Not all of the new residents will use the parks or call for fire protection, yet the county will have to provide additional facilities so as to be in a position to serve each dwelling unit. During the useful life of the new dwelling units, school-age children will come and go. It may be that some of the units will never house children. However, the county has determined that for every one hundred units that are built, forty-four new students will require an education at a public school. The St. Johns County impact fee is designed to provide the capacity to serve the educational needs of all one hundred dwelling units. We conclude that the ordinance meets the first prong of the rational nexus test.

The question of whether the ordinance meets the requirements of the second prong of the test is more troublesome. As indicated, we see no requirement that every new unit of development benefit from the impact fee in the sense that there must be a child residing in that unit who will attend public school. It is enough that new public schools are available to serve that unit of development. Thus, if this were a countywide impact fee designed to fund construction of new schools as needed throughout the county, we could easily conclude that the second prong of the test had been met.

However, the St. Johns County impact fee is not effective within the boundaries of a municipality unless the municipality enters into an interlocal agreement with the county to collect the fee. The ordinance provides that the funds shall be spent solely for school construction necessitated by new development. However, there is nothing to keep impact fees from being spent to build schools to accommodate new development within a municipality that has not entered into the interlocal agreement. Therefore, as in the ordinance first considered in *Contractors & Builders Ass'n v. City of Dunedin*, there is no restriction on the use of the funds to ensure that they will be spent to benefit those who have paid the fees. As a consequence, we hold that no impact fee may be collected under the ordinance until such time as substantially all of the population of St. Johns County is subject to the ordinance … .

We quash the decision below and uphold the validity of the ordinance … . However, no impact fee may be collected under the ordinance until the second prong of the dual rational nexus test has been met.

It is so ordered.

SHAW, C.J., and OVERTON, McDONALD, BARKETT, KOGAN and HARDING, JJ., concur.

### *Discussion*

After the analysis in *Koontz*, impact fees—which are monetary payments paid to comply with a permit condition—are clearly exactions. In practice, therefore, an impact fee must meet the dual rational nexus test, to comply with Florida state law requirements, and the *Nollan* and *Dolan* tests, to comply with the U.S. Constitution.

In addition to the judicially derived rule on impact fees, the Florida Legislature has adopted the Florida Impact Fee Act,[28] which provides standards local governments must meet when charging impact fees. That law recognizes that local governments may charge impact fees pursuant to their home rule powers.[29] It then sets many standards for impact fees should a local government charge one. For example, a local government may not require an applicant to pay impact fees "earlier than the date of issuance of a building permit."[30] Also, the act establishes the preponderance of the evidence standard as the standard of review a local government must meet to defend its impact fee from judicial challenge.[31]

### *Fees and affordable housing*

The Florida Impact Fee Act allows local governments to waive impact fees for housing that meets a statutory definition of affordability.[32] This express permission for local governments to exempt certain developments from the requirement of paying impact fees does not comply with the dual rational nexus test. Therefore, this statutory allowance makes an impact fee less like a fee—charged under a local government's home rule powers and subject to the dual rational nexus test—and more like a tax charged without relation to any government services provided under the express authorization of Florida law.

Florida Statutes also place more stringent requirements on local government authority to charge impact fees for affordable housing than they place on impact fees for other infrastructure. *Inclusionary zoning* is the practice of conditioning permission to develop housing on a requirement that some portion of the built housing be affordable.[33] Florida Statutes allow local governments to implement inclusionary zoning programs, and to allow developers to opt out of providing the mandatory housing by paying a fee instead.[34] *Linkage fees* are impact fees a local government collects to provide affordable housing. Florida Statutes allow local governments to levy linkage fees.[35] However, if a Florida local government implements an inclusionary zoning program or a linkage fee, that local government "must provide incentives to fully offset all costs to the developer of its affordable housing contribution or linkage fee."[36]

**Box 19.1 Practice problem: Epic One**

Epic Properties builds multi-family housing in Collegeborough's city center. The developer specializes in higher-end apartments for young professionals who want to live where they can walk or bike to downtown Collegeborough or to State University.

One of the most expensive parts of developing apartments in a walkable neighborhood is providing space to park cars. The parcels of property in central Collegeborough are large enough to fit nice buildings, but not large enough to also fit large parking lots. As a result, Epic Properties typically dedicates a floor of its buildings to parking so that tenants may drive their cars inside the building to store them. This "structured parking" ends up costing about $20,000 per parking space.

For its newest apartment building, called Epic One, Epic Properties has decided to not include any space for parking cars. Based on market research it has conducted, Epic Properties believes it can lease all of the units in Epic One to tenants who do not want to rent a parking space along with their housing. These potential tenants get around by walking, biking, or riding on the Collegeborough Transit System. By saving the great cost of providing space to store cars in Epic One, the apartment building will be very competitive on cost compared to other new apartments in central Collegeborough.

At development review, the Collegeborough city staff determine that Epic One meets all of the requirements of the Collegeborough development code. Staff approves the development proposal with one condition. Epic Properties must pay the "road access fee" prior to leasing any of the apartments in Epic One.

The road access fee is a charge that Collegeborough levies on all new development in the city. The government uses the proceeds from the fee to build new roads in the city which are listed on the Road Improvement Plan, or the RIP. The RIP is Collegeborough's long-term plan to handle increased traffic from new growth in population.

Collegeborough determined the amount of the fee by calculating how much it would cost to build all of the road improvements on the RIP and designating that amount $X. Then, the city transportation planner calculated how many automobile trips would be accommodated by the RIP and designated that amount Y. Therefore, $X/Y represented the cost of providing one new trip through the RIP. Finally, the city used generally accepted transportation planning estimates of the "trip generation rate" for new development and multiplied that rate by $X/Y to get the appropriate fee for any given development.

Epic Properties objects to paying the road access fee, saying that, as applied to Epic One, it is an unlawful impact fee. It argues that, because Epic One will have no parking, the city cannot make it pay the fee.

Evaluate Epic Properties' claim using the dual rational nexus test.

## Notes

1 Fla. Const. art. VII, § 1(a).

2 Although local governments in Florida are not required to levy taxes by law, they may levy taxes "in pursuance of law." W.J. Howey Co. v. Williams, 195 So. 181, 182 (Fla. 1940) (stating the general rule that "statutes are by the [Florida] constitution either required or authorized to provide for levying taxes"), *reh'g denied*, 196 So. 214 (Fla. 1940).

3 A "fee" is distinct from a tax because a fee is a charge in exchange for particular government services that benefit the individual (who is voluntarily paying the fee) in a manner not shared by other members of the public. Jasinski v. City of Miami, 269 F. Supp. 2d 1341, 1348 (S.D. Fla. 2003), *aff'd*, 99 F. App'x 887 (11th Cir. 2004) (unpublished table decision); City of Miami v. Haigley, 143 So. 3d 1025, 1029 (Fla. 3d DCA 2014) (citing State v. City of Port Orange, 650 So. 2d 1, 3 (Fla. 1993)).

4 12A Fla. Jur. 2d *Counties and Municipal Corporations* § 315 (2020).
5 Home Builders & Contractors Ass'n of Palm Beach Cnty., Inc. v. Palm Beach Cnty., 446 So. 2d 140, 143–44 (Fla. 4th DCA 1983), *appeal dismissed*, 469 U.S. 976 (1984); City of Key West v. R.L.J.S. Corp., 537 So. 2d 641, 643–44, 647–48 (Fla. 3d DCA), *reh'g denied*, 545 So. 2d 1367 (Fla. 1989) (unpublished table decision).
6 Fla. Stat. § 163.31801(2); 50 Fla. Jur. 2d *Taxation* § 11 (2020).
7 Fla. Stat. § 163.31801(2).
8 City of N. Lauderdale v. SMM Props., 825 So. 2d 343, 348 (Fla. 2002) (citing Collier Cnty. v. State, 733 So. 2d 1012, 1018 (Fla. 1999)).
9 Fla. Legislature Off. of Econ. & Demographic Rsch., 2016 Local Government Financial Information Handbook 15 (2016) [hereinafter 2016 Local Government Handbook].
10 *Id.*
11 Crist v. Ervin, 56 So. 3d 745, 748 (Fla. 2010) (citing State v. City of Port Orange, 650 So. 2d 1, 3 (Fla. 1994)).
12 City of Gainesville v. State, 863 So. 2d 138, 144 (Fla. 2003) (citations omitted).
13 Collier Cnty. v. State, 733 So. 2d 1012, 1017 (Fla. 1999) (quoting City of Boca Raton v. State, 595 So. 2d 25, 29 (Fla. 1992), *modified*, 733 So. 2d 1012 (Fla. 1999)).
14 2016 Local Government Handbook 15.
15 Contractors and Builders Ass'n of Pinellas Cnty. v. City of Dunedin, 329 So. 2d 314, 317 (Fla. 1976) (citations omitted).
16 *City of Dunedin*, 329 So. 2d at 318.
17 *Id.* at 320.
18 *See* Fla. Stat. ch. 190.
19 Fla. Stat. § 190.003(6).
20 12A Fla. Jur. 2d *Counties & Municipal Corporations* § 119 (2020).
21 Fla. Stat. §§ 190.005(1)(a), (1)(b).
22 *Id.* § 190.005(1)(a)3.
23 *Id.* §§ 190.006(2)(a), (2)(b).
24 *Id.*
25 776 So. 2d 255 (Fla. 2001).
26 Fla. Stat. § 163.31801(1).
27 583 So. 2d 635 (Fla. 1991).
28 Fla. Stat. § 163.31801(1).
29 *Id.* § 163.31801(2).
30 *Id.* § 163.31801(3)(e).
31 *Id.* § 163.31801(7).
32 *Id.* § 163.31801(8).
33 *See id.* §§ 125.01055(2), 166.04151(2).
34 Fla. Stat. §§ 125.01055(2) (applicable to counties), 166.04151(2) (applicable to cities).
35 *Id.* §§ 125.01055(3) (applicable to counties), 166.04151(2) (applicable to cities).
36 *Id.* § 125.01055(4) (applicable to counties); *see also id.* § 166.04151(4) (applicable to cities).

# 20 Tax increment financing

A traditionally substantial revenue source for local governments is ad valorem taxation. Ad valorem taxation is a periodically recurring tax on the value of real estate.[1] On an annual basis, a local government will require owners of real and personal property in its jurisdiction to pay a tax on the value of property they own.[2]

The Florida Constitution makes ad valorem taxation the principal means for funding local government. It provides "[c]ounties, school districts, and municipalities shall, and special districts may, be authorized by law to levy ad valorem taxes and may be authorized by general law to levy other taxes, for their respective purposes ... ."[3]

You are likely familiar with sales taxes for which rates are established by percentages which are hundredths of the value. For example, Florida levies a 6 percent sales tax,[4] meaning that for every dollar of goods purchased, a consumer pays six cents. The amount of taxes levied, measured by the percent, is a percentage rate.

Analogously, ad valorem tax rates are established by mils which are thousandths of the value.[5] For example, where a local government has an ad valorem tax rate of one mil, a property owner who owns a piece of real estate with a taxable value of $100,000 will pay $100. The amount of taxes levied, measured by the mil, is a millage rate.

This is a real-world example. For 2015, the Miami-Dade County Property Appraiser assigned a taxable value of $30,964,928,312 to all property in the city of Miami Beach, Florida. The city levies ad valorem taxes at a millage rate of 5.9123. Therefore, one can calculate the city's revenue from ad valorem taxation that year to be $183,073,945 as follows:

$$\$30,964,928,312 \times \frac{5.9123}{1000} = \$183,073,945$$

Tax increment financing (TIF) is a way for local governments to measure an amount of money to allocate toward certain expenditures based, in part, on these basic concepts related to ad valorem taxation.[6] Specifically, TIF is the amount of ad valorem revenue a local government derives from a property in a given year minus the ad valorem revenue the local government would have derived from that property if the property had the tax rate and valuation of some given base year.[7] The given base year is the year in which a local government borrows money to be repaid by tax increment or the year it begins allocating tax increment to a specified purpose.[8]

For example, if a property has a taxable value in 2020 of $1,000,000 and a local government taxes that property at a millage rate of 10, the property would yield $10,000 in revenue. If, by 2025, the taxable value of that property had appreciated to $1,500,000 and the local government had kept the same millage rate, that property would yield $15,000 in revenue. In this example, if the local government had established 2020 as the base year, the tax increment for that property in 2015 would be $15,000 less $10,000 or $5,000.

In the figure representing tax increment, the amount of the tax increment in a given year is the difference between the line representing the ad valorem revenue and the line representing the base year ad valorem revenue. As the figure suggests, as long as property values rise over time, the tax increment grows over time.

Tax increment financing is significant because local governments can borrow money using TIF-financed bonds without adhering to the referendum requirement of Article VII, Section 12 of the Florida Constitution.[9] That provision of the Florida Constitution reads:

> **Local bonds**.—Counties, school districts, municipalities, special districts and local governmental bodies with taxing powers *may issue bonds*, certificates of indebtedness or any form of tax anticipation certificates, *payable from ad valorem taxation and maturing more than twelve months after issuance only*:
>
> (a) to finance or refinance capital projects authorized by law and only *when approved by vote of the electors* who are owners of freeholds therein not wholly exempt from taxation; or
>
> (b) to refund outstanding bonds and interest and redemption premium thereon at a lower net average interest cost rate.[10]

Therefore, Florida local governments may generally only issue bonds which mature more than one year after issuance if voters approve the bond issue in a referendum. Despite this constitutional requirement, a local government may issue bonds to be repaid with ad valorem revenues without a referendum in two circumstances.

First, the Community Redevelopment Act,[11] which is codified as Part III, Chapter 163, Florida Statutes (2019), authorizes local governments to issue TIF bonds to pay for community redevelopment activities without a referendum. Second, the Florida Supreme Court has determined that when a local government uses TIF to budget for the repayment of debt, that local government may exercise its home rule powers to borrow money without holding a referendum.[12] This chapter discusses both of these circumstances in greater detail.

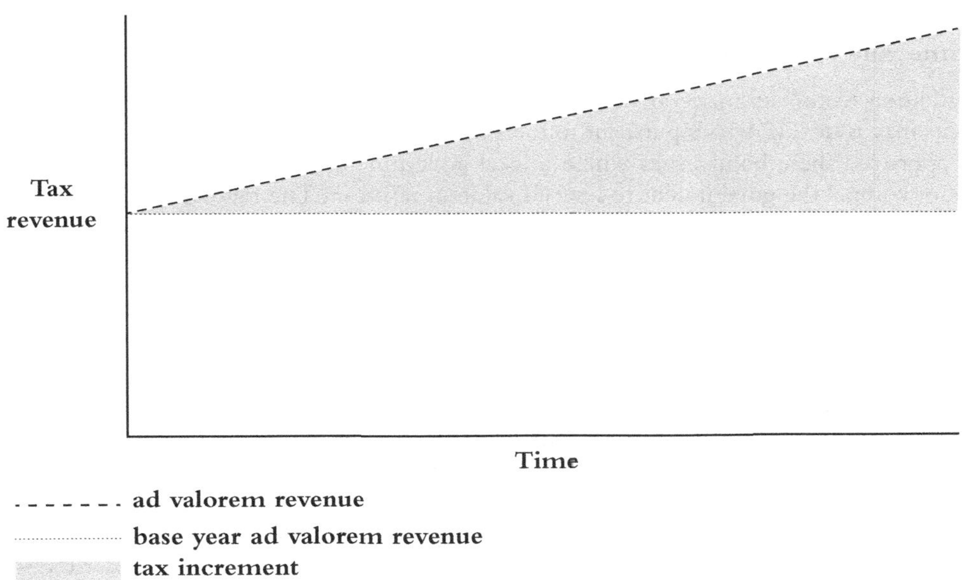


*Figure 20.1* Tax increment over time

## Community Redevelopment Act

Community Redevelopment Agencies (CRAs) are public agencies local governments may create pursuant to the Community Redevelopment Act.[13] Every CRA manages a redevelopment trust fund funded by the local government through tax increment.[14] CRAs may spend these funds on redevelopment projects to address blighted conditions in their areas.[15]

For a municipality, a powerful aspect of a CRA is that—once created—a CRA controls more ad valorem tax revenue from its geographic area than the municipality would alone. This is because the tax increment that the law allocates to a CRA trust fund is calculated using the city *and the county* millage rates.[16]

When determining the amount of money which goes into a redevelopment trust fund, Florida Statutes provide:

> The annual funding of the redevelopment trust fund shall be in an amount not less than that increment in the income, proceeds, revenues, and funds of *each taxing authority* derived from or held in connection with the undertaking and carrying out of community redevelopment under this part.[17]

Therefore, to calculate tax increment to determine redevelopment trust fund revenue, one uses not only the millage rate of the local government that created and controls the CRA, but also the millage rate of other taxing authorities. This allows a municipality creating a CRA to increase the total amount of money over which it has discretion.

The Florida Legislature requires—as a necessary precondition for creating a Community Redevelopment Agency—that a local government determine the geographic area proposed to be a Community Redevelopment Area is a slum or is blighted.[18] Establishing that slum or blight exist is a fact-intensive exercise appropriate for planning professionals. The task requires collecting data, analyzing data to show whether the area meets statutory definitions of slum and blight, and presenting the data and analysis in a format appropriate for local government decision-makers to easily draw conclusions. The work of professional planners can be a dispositive issue in evaluating the legality of CRAs and their financing tools.[19]

## Home rule authority to issue tax increment bonds

In addition to the authority granted by the Community Redevelopment Act, local governments may issue TIF bonds pursuant to their home rule powers. The Florida Supreme Court has approved these bond issues where a local government structures them so that creditors cannot compel the government to levy ad valorem taxation. The following discussion, originally from *State v. Miami Beach Redevelopment Agency*,[20] relates to a bond issue for a community redevelopment agency. But Florida's highest court has subsequently applied it to bonds issued independent of the Community Redevelopment Act.

> [T]here is nothing in the constitution to prevent a county or city from using ad valorem tax revenues where they are required to compute and set aside a prescribed amount, when available, for a discreet [sic] purpose. The purpose of the constitutional limitation is unaffected by the legal commitment; the taxing power of the governmental units is unimpaired. *What is critical to the constitutionality of the bonds is that, after the sale of bonds, a bondholder would have no right, if the redevelopment trust fund were insufficient to meet the bond obligations and the available resources of the county or city were insufficient to allow for the promised contributions, to compel by judicial action the levy of ad valorem taxation.* Under the statute authorizing this bond financing the governing bodies are not obliged nor can they be compelled to levy any ad valorem taxes in any year. The only obligation is to appropriate a sum equal to any tax increment generated in a particular year from the ordinary, general

levy of ad valorem taxes otherwise made in the city and county that year. Issuance of these bonds without approval of the voters of Dade County and the City of Miami Beach, consequently, does not transgress article VII, section 12.[21]

The Florida Supreme Court most recently considered this question in 2008 in its decision *Strand v. Escambia Cnty.*[22] The background story of *Strand* is a roller coaster of changing perceptions of the law that wreaked real havoc on local governments and the bondholders who finance their infrastructure projects. The Florida Supreme Court issued its first decision on *Strand* on September 6, 2007.[23] That unanimous decision not only struck down tax increment financing when not authorized by a referendum, it reversed the then 26-year-old *Miami Beach* precedent. The status of *billions of dollars* of outstanding bonds was in question and new TIF debt issuance stopped. Countless public infrastructure projects and joint-public-private development projects were in limbo.

In response to this literal chaos, the Florida Supreme Court accepted briefs in support of rehearing from the attorney general, the Florida League of Cities, the Florida Redevelopment Association, the Florida Association of Counties, and the Florida School Boards Association. The opinion that followed was a complete reversal of the prior *Strand* decision.[24] The final *Strand* opinion not only left *Miami Beach* intact, it allowed local governments to continue to issue TIF bonds under their home rule powers when they exercise caution to not actually pledge their ad valorem taxing authority.[25]

## Notes

1 Fla. Stat. § 192.001(1).
2 *Id.* § 192.001(2); 50 Fla. Jur. 2d *Taxation* § 5 (2020).
3 Fla. Const. art. VII, § 9(a).
4 Fla. Stat. § 212.05(1)(a).
5 *Id.* § 200.001(6) ("At the time millage rates are published for the purpose of giving notice, the rates shall be stated in terms of dollars and cents per thousand dollars of assessed property value").
6 42 Fla. Jur. 2d *Public Securities and Obligations* § 88 (2020).
7 Fla. Stat. §§ 163.387(1)(a)(1)–(2); *see also* Harry M. Hipler, *Tax Increment Financing in Florida: A Tool for Local Government Revitalization, Renewal, and Redevelopment*, 81 Fla. Bar J. 66, 69 (2007).
8 Hipler, *supra* note 7.
9 42 Fla. Jur. 2d *Public Securities and Obligations* § 88 (2020).
10 Fla. Const. art. VII, § 12 (emphases added).
11 E.g. Fla. Stat. § 163.330.
12 *See* State v. Miami Beach Redevelopment Agency, 392 So. 2d 975 (Fla. 1980).
13 Fla. Stat. §§ 163.356(1)–(2).
14 *Id.* §§ 163.353, 163.370(f)–(g), 163.370(l).
15 *Id.* §§ 163.358, 163.370(n).
16 *Id.* § 163.387(2)(a).
17 *Id.* § 163.387(1)(a) (emphasis added).
18 *Id.* §§ 163.355, 163.340(7)–(8), 163.340(8).
19 *See*, e.g., City of Parker v. State, 992 So. 2d 171 (Fla. 2008).
20 State v. Miami Beach Redevelopment Agency, 392 So. 2d 975 (Fla. 1980).
21 Strand v. Escambia Cnty., 992 So. 2d 150, 158 (Fla. 2008) (quoting State v. Miami Beach Redevelopment Agency, 392 So. 2d 875, 898–99 (Fla. 1980)).
22 992 So. 2d 150 (Fla. 2008).
23 Strand v. Escambia Cnty., 32 Fla. L. Weekly S550, 2007 WL 2492294 (Fla. 2007), *withdrawn*, 992 So. 2d 150 (Fla. 2008).
24 992 So. 2d at 152 (mentioning that "[u]pon consideration of appellee Escambia County's motion for rehearing, we withdraw our revised opinion, filed on September 28, 2007, and substitute the following opinion").
25 *Id.* at 158–61.

# 21 Concurrency

Florida Statutes section 163.3180 mandates that local governments implement concurrency, a growth management tool with significant impacts on land use.[1] At its essence, concurrency is the integration of land use planning and infrastructure provision. The requirement is beguiling. While theoretically simple and sound, concurrency is unexpectedly complex in application. The system has also, in some circumstances, had unexpected and undesirable consequences.

The fundamental requirement of concurrency is that public facilities be in place to provide public services to a development no later in time than when a local government finally permits that development. Florida Statutes provide:

> Consistent with public health and safety, sanitary sewer, solid waste, drainage, adequate water supplies, and potable water *facilities shall be in place and available to serve new development no later than the issuance by the local government of a certificate of occupancy* or its functional equivalent.[2]

A certificate of occupancy is the final permit given by a local government to a building.[3] This permit acknowledges that construction is complete and the building may be used for its intended purpose.[4] The significance of the term "concurrency" is that the public facility be available and that the development be complete concurrently, or at the same moment in time.

Concurrency is a powerful tool in the growth management toolbox because it literally blocks development when adequate public facilities are not available. If a developer wants permission to build, but the public facilities are not available to meet concurrency, the developer itself must pay for the needed infrastructure improvements as a precondition for permitting—even if the proposal otherwise meets all applicable land development regulations.[5]

This theoretically ensures local governments do not approve applications for development to which they cannot provide services. John DeGrove, former Florida Secretary of the Department of Community Affairs, called concurrency "the most powerful policy requirement built into the growth management system."[6]

The state *requires* local governments to implement concurrency for sewers, solid waste, drainage, water supply, and potable water.[7] Local governments *may* adopt concurrency for transportation and for schools if their rules meet additional criteria provided in Florida Statutes at section 163.3180(5) for transportation and section 163.3180(6) for schools.

## Address level of service through capital improvements element

Concurrency works in part by addressing the *level of service* for the infrastructure serving the development anticipated in a comprehensive plan's future land use element through the plan's *capital improvements element*.[8]

Florida Statutes define level of service as

> an indicator of the extent or degree of service provided by, or proposed to be provided by, a facility based on and related to the operational characteristics of the facility. Level of service shall indicate the capacity per unit of demand for each public facility.[9]

For example, a wastewater system might have a level of service measured in gallons per capita per day. Or, a road might have a level of service measured in vehicles per lane per hour. Grouping roadway capacities and lettering the resulting thresholds (like academic grades) is customary when discussing roadway level of service. Planners often refer to a congested roadway as having a level of service D or to a little-used roadway as having a level of service A. Because setting the level of service is a policy decision, a local government can use its discretion over level of service to decide that it wants to tolerate congestion.

The Community Planning Act requires every local government's comprehensive plan to include a capital improvements element "designed to consider the need for and the location of public facilities in order to encourage the efficient use of such facilities."[10] The element must provide "[s]tandards to ensure the availability of public facilities and the adequacy of those facilities to meet established acceptable levels of service."[11] To address future capacity demands, the element must have

> [a] schedule of capital improvements which includes any publicly funded projects of federal, state, or local government, and which may include privately funded projects for which the local government has no fiscal responsibility. Projects necessary to ensure that any adopted level-of-service standards are achieved and maintained for the 5-year period must be identified as either funded or unfunded and given a level of priority for funding.[12]

This schedule is generally the most prominent part of the capital improvements element. It often looks like a table of very generally described infrastructure projects along with estimated costs and sources of funding for that project. Amendments to a capital improvements element are not held to the same procedural standards as other comprehensive plan amendments.[13]

## Judicial consideration of concurrency

The leading judicial opinion evaluating a local government concurrency program is *In re Golden v. Planning Bd. of Town of Ramapo*.[14] In the opinion, the Court of Appeals of New York, the highest court in New York State, evaluated whether an ordinance of the Town of Ramapo exceeded the town's authority under New York's zoning enabling legislation and whether the ordinance violated the U.S Constitution.[15]

The Town of Ramapo called its ordinance one that provided for "timed growth," "sequential development," or "phased growth."[16] In practice, the town's rules were similar to concurrency programs under Florida law. The rule's purpose was to ensure that "[r]esidential development ... proceed[ed] according to the provision of adequate municipal facilities and services."[17]

The town required a special permit to authorize the subdivision of land for the purpose of developing houses.[18] Whether the Town of Ramapo would issue that permit depended on whether certain infrastructure and services were available.

> The standards for the issuance of special permits are framed in terms of the availability to the proposed subdivision plat of five essential facilities or services: specifically (1) public sanitary sewers or approved substitutes; (2) drainage facilities; (3) improved public parks or recreation facilities, including public schools; (4) State, county or town roads—major, secondary or collector; and, (5) firehouses.[19]

The Court of Appeals observed:

> The undisputed effect of these integrated efforts in land use planning and development is to provide an over-all program of orderly growth and adequate facilities through a sequential development policy commensurate with progressing availability and capacity of public facilities.[20]

This language summarizes the court's conclusion:

> Every restriction on the use of property entails hardships for some individual owners. Those difficulties are invariably the product of police regulation and the pecuniary profits of the individual must in the long run be subordinated to the needs of the community. The fact that the ordinance limits the use of, and may depreciate the value of the property will not render it unconstitutional, however, unless it can be shown that the measure is either unreasonable in terms of necessity or the diminution in value is such as to be tantamount to a confiscation ...
>
> Without a doubt restrictions upon the property in the present case are substantial in nature and duration. They are not, however, absolute ... [P]roperty owners under the terms of the amendments may elect to accelerate the date of development by installing, at their own expense, the necessary public services ...
>
> ⋆ ⋆ ⋆
>
> In sum, where it is clear that the existing physical and financial resources of the community are inadequate to furnish the essential services and facilities which a substantial increase in population requires, there is a rational basis for "phased growth" and hence, the challenged ordinance is not violative of the Federal and State Constitutions.[21]

No published opinion in Florida seriously considers the proposition that the U.S. Constitution does not allow concurrency as a tool to regulate land development.

## The special case of transportation concurrency

Transportation concurrency comes with a set of problems that concurrency mandates for other public services do not raise. When the Florida Legislature imposed the concurrency mandate, it required transportation concurrency, just as Florida Statutes require concurrency for other services.[22] By 2011, however, frustrations with transportation concurrency had grown so significant that the legislature repealed the mandate.[23]

Two planning concepts can help explain the failure of transportation concurrency. First, counterintuitively, increasing road capacity often worsens motor-vehicle congestion.[24] Planners call this phenomenon *induced travel*.[25] In the face of this reality, transportation concurrency's principal solution to traffic congestion was more road capacity.

Second, urban form significantly impacts transportation demand.

> [C]onventional suburban development is characterized by separation of land uses, a less connected system of roadways, low density, and a lack of facilities for transit, bicycles, and pedestrians. In contrast, traditional neighborhood development has a mix of land uses, an interconnected street network, high density of development, and pedestrian oriented features. This design, which is a major component of multimodal planning, has the potential to reduce the impact of development on the transportation system generally, and on the adjacent arterials particularly, through: (1) reduced automobile trip generation, (2) high rates of internal capture (i.e., more trips on the local street network and *not* on adjacent

arterials), (3) more trips by alternative modes of travel, (4) more trip chaining (an activity pattern that chains a series of trips together), and (5) reduced trip distance.[26]

Despite this relationship between land use and transportation, transportation concurrency actually discouraged infill development and traditional neighborhood development, while it encouraged conventional suburban development. Although well-intentioned, therefore, transportation concurrency did not abate traffic congestion.

### *Transportation planning after mandatory concurrency*

The futility of transportation concurrency led to a major change with the 2011 Community Planning Act.[27] That law made transportation concurrency optional and significantly revised Florida Statutes' direction to local governments for drafting the transportation elements of their comprehensive plans.[28] While these changes addressed concerns over transportation concurrency's failures and inequities, local government still needed policies to deal with traffic congestion and to promote desirable development patterns.

Florida law addresses transportation planning through a series of policies the Community Planning Act requires or encourages local governments to adopt in their transportation elements. Every comprehensive plan must include

> [a] transportation element addressing mobility issues in relationship to the size and character of the local government. The purpose of the transportation element shall be to plan for a multimodal transportation system that places emphasis on public transportation systems, where feasible. The element shall provide for a safe, convenient multimodal transportation system, coordinated with the future land use map or map series and designed to support all elements of the comprehensive plan.[29]

Further,

> [t]he element shall reflect the data, analysis, and associated principles and strategies relating to ... [t]he growth trends and travel patterns and interactions between land use and transportation ... [and] [t]he projected transportation system levels of service and system needs based upon the future land use map and the projected integrated transportation system.[30]

The Community Planning Act provisions above apply to a local government's comprehensive plan without regard to whether it implements transportation concurrency.[31] In addition, section 163.3180 provides the following:

> *If* a local government applies transportation concurrency in its jurisdiction, *it is encouraged* to develop policy guidelines and techniques to address potential negative impacts on future development ... [i]n urban infill and redevelopment, and urban service areas ... [and on] community desired types of development, such as redevelopment, or job creation projects.[32]

### *Proportionate share*

Florida statutes require local governments that implement transportation concurrency to provide opportunities for proportionate share.[33] In 2005, the Florida Legislature adopted the Growth Management Reform Act, which provided for proportionate share.[34] At that time,

Florida's real estate economy was booming. Numerous development projects were stymied by transportation concurrency requirements and Florida identified proportionate share as a transportation concurrency exemption that would allow development to go forward even when public facilities were inadequate to serve that development. Consequently, Florida statutes now provide the following:

> Local governments that continue to implement a transportation concurrency system ... *must* ... [a]llow an applicant ... to satisfy the transportation concurrency requirements of the local comprehensive plan ... if ... [t]he applicant in good faith offers to enter into a binding agreement to pay for or construct its *proportionate share* of required improvements ...[35]

And,

> [t]he proportionate-share contribution shall be calculated based upon the number of trips from the proposed development expected to reach roadways during the peak hour from the stage or phase being approved, divided by the change in the peak hour maximum service volume of roadways resulting from construction of an improvement necessary to maintain or achieve the adopted level of service, multiplied by the construction cost, at the time of development payment, of the improvement necessary to maintain or achieve the adopted level of service.[36]

Expressed algebraically, the above-described proportionate share equation is:

$$Proportionate\ share\ contribution = \frac{Number\ of\ trips}{Change\ in\ volume\ from\ improvement} \times Improvement\ cost$$

One consequence of proportionate share is that, when implemented, a local government's transportation concurrency program will no longer meet the central objective of concurrency.

> An applicant shall not be held responsible for the additional cost of reducing or eliminating deficiencies ... If any road is determined to be transportation deficient without the project traffic under review, the costs of correcting that deficiency shall be removed from the project's proportionate-share calculation *and the necessary transportation improvements to correct that deficiency shall be considered to be in place for purposes of the proportionate-share calculation*. The improvement necessary to correct the transportation deficiency is the funding responsibility of the entity that has maintenance responsibility for the facility. The development's proportionate share shall be calculated only for the needed transportation improvements that are greater than the identified deficiency.[37]

In a post-concurrency world, therefore, traffic congestion cannot be the basis of a local government's denial of an application to develop land. Finally, proportionate share often exists alongside other transportation funding mechanisms. When it does, an "applicant shall receive a credit on a dollar-for-dollar basis for impact fees, mobility fees, and other transportation concurrency mitigation requirements paid or payable in the future for the project."[38]

### *Mobility fees*

Mobility fees are another alternative to transportation concurrency. Unlike proportionate share—which is used in conjunction with transportation concurrency—mobility fees are a strategy for funding transportation that a local government might implement independent of whether it has a transportation concurrency program.[39]

The basic mobility fee methodology comprises several steps. First, a local government develops a multi-modal transportation plan and determines the total cost of implementing that plan.[40] Second, the local government determines how many new trips (or instances of people using transportation services) the transportation plan will accommodate.[41] Then, the local government divides the cost of the plan by the number of trips to get a cost per trip.[42] Once this amount is determined, a local government can charge new development a mobility fee based on the transportation demand for the project.[43]

Expressed algebraically, the described mobility fee equation is:

$$Mobility\ fee\ for\ project = \frac{Mobility\ plan\ cost}{Change\ in\ trips\ due\ to\ mobility\ plan} \times project\ trips$$

This methodology is similar to how local governments calculate impact fee amounts. And, in fact, mobility fees are a kind of impact fee. A "mobility fee-based funding system must comply with s.163.31801 [the dual rational nexus test] governing impact fees."[44]

Many local governments are adopting mobility fees because they offer policy advantages over road impact fees, transportation concurrency, and proportionate share. One advantage of mobility fees is that they can fund truly multi-modal transportation plans. This means local governments can use mobility fee revenue to accommodate people using transit, riding bicycles, and walking—as well as people driving cars. Another advantage of mobility fees is that—when supporting data exist—local governments can charge disparate rates to different developments to incentivize desirable development types. Common beneficiaries of these policy preferences are so-called traditional neighborhood developments or developments near transit infrastructure.

## Notes

1 Fla. Stat. §§ 163.3180(b)(1), (b)(4).
2 *Id.* § 163.3180(2) (emphasis added).
3 *Id.* § 553.79(1)(a).
4 *Id.* § 553.79(2).
5 *Id.* §§ 553.79(19), 163.3180(1)(a), (1)(b).
6 John M. DeGrove, *Florida's Greatest Challenge: Managing Massive Growth*, in *Implementation of the 1985 Growth Management Act: From Planning to Land Development Regulations* 5 (B. Brumback & M. J. Marvin eds, 1989).
7 Fla. Stat. § 163.3180(1).
8 *Id.* §§ 163.3180(1)(b), 163.3177(3).
9 *Id.* § 163.3164(28).
10 *Id.* § 163.3177(3)(a).
11 *Id.* § 163.3177(3)(a)3.
12 *Id.* §163.3177(3)(a)4.
13 Fla. Stat. § 163.3177(3)(b).
14 In re Golden v. Plan. Bd. of Ramapo, 285 N.E.2d 291 (N.Y.), *appeal dismissed*, 409 U.S. 1003 (1972).
15 *Id.* at 364–65.
16 *Id.* at 376, 378.
17 *Id.* at 367.
18 *Id.* at 367–68.
19 *Id.* at 368.
20 In re Golden v. Plan. Bd. of Ramapo, 285 N.E.2d 291, 369 (N.Y. 1972).
21 *Id.* at 381–83 (citations omitted).
22 Ch. 93-206, Laws of Fla. § 8.
23 Ch. 2011-139, Laws of Fla. §15.

24 Robert B. Noland & Lewison L. Lem, *A Review of the Evidence for Induced Travel and Changes in Transportation and Environmental Policy in the US and the UK*, 7 Transp. Rsch. 1, 4–5, 9–17 (2002).
25 *Id.* at 2–5.
26 Ruth L. Steiner, *Transportation Concurrency: An Idea Before its Time?*, in *Growth Management in Florida: Planning for Paradise* 217 (Timothy S. Chapin et al. eds, 2007).
27 Linda Loomis Shelley & Karen Brodeen, *Home Rule Redux: The Community Planning Act of 2011*, 85 Fla. Bar. J. 49, 50 (2011).
28 *Id.* at 50–1.
29 Fla. Stat. § 163.3177(6)(b).
30 *Id.* § 163.3177(6)(b)1.
31 *Id.* § 163.3180(4).
32 *Id.* § 163.3180(5)(e) (emphases added).
33 *Id.* § 163.3180(5)(h)1.c.
34 Ch. 2005-157, 2005-290, 2005-291, Laws of Fla.
35 Fla. Stat. § 163.3180(5)(h)1.c.(I) (emphases added).
36 *Id.* § 163.3180(5)(h)2.a.
37 *Id.* § 163.3180(5)(h)2., 2.b (emphasis added).
38 *Id.* § 163.3180(5)(h)2.e.
39 *Id.* § 163.3180(5)(f)2.
40 Karen E. Seggerman, et al., Ctr. for Urb. Transp. Affs. Univ. S. Fla., *Evaluation of the Mobility Fee Concept* 26 (2009).
41 *Id.* at 27.
42 *Id.*
43 *Id.* at 28.
44 Fla. Stat. § 163.3180(5)(i).

# 22 Development agreements

A development agreement is a contract between a local government and a real estate developer in which the local government vests a development project against regulatory changes and the real estate developer commits to funding public infrastructure or services.[1]

Florida statutes authorize the use of development agreements through the Florida Local Government Development Agreement Act, which is codified at sections 163.3220 through 163.3243. Among the legislative declarations in the law is the intent "to encourage a stronger commitment to comprehensive and capital facilities planning, ensure the provision of adequate public facilities for development, encourage the efficient use of resources, and reduce the economic cost of development."[2] A local government must record a development agreement for it to have effect.[3]

By entering into a development agreement, a local government subjects itself to the restriction that its "laws and policies governing the development of the land at the time of the execution of the development agreement shall govern the development of the land for the duration of the development agreement."[4] The local government may amend its land use regulations after it enters into the development agreement, but only after making certain findings related to the new regulations' impact on the development which is the subject of the agreement.[5]

In exchange for this protection against future changes in law, a developer may be bound to build infrastructure to serve the development.[6] The development agreement will include a description of the "public facilities that will service the development, including who shall provide such facilities; the date any new facilities, if needed, will be constructed" and a "schedule to assure public facilities are available concurrent with the impacts of the development," which must be included in the development agreement.[7] If the developer fails to live up to its end of the agreement, the local government may modify or abandon the agreement.[8]

## Contract zoning

Contract zoning is the local government practice of changing zoning or approving development for consideration.[9] Consideration is a legal term of art referring to a bargained-for benefit in a contract.[10] In other words, consideration is the thing that incentivizes parties to enter into an agreement.

In contract zoning, the consideration given by the local government is generally a relaxed land use regulation and the consideration given by the developer is some commitment designed to limit the negative impacts of the development.[11] While contract zoning can protect the public while liberalizing land use restrictions, many jurisdictions—including the state of Florida—prohibit the practice.[12] The following case, *Morgran Co., Inc. v. Orange Cnty.*, presents an important lesson: when a local government makes development decisions paired with commitments from a developer to provide infrastructure, that local government must be cautious to avoid contract zoning.

## Florida Fifth District Court of Appeals

## *Morgran Co., Inc., v. Orange Cnty.*[13]

## 2002

GRIFFIN, J.

Morgran Company, Inc. ["Morgran"] sued Orange County for breach of contract and promissory estoppel and appeals the dismissal of its complaint. Although we affirm, we write because Morgran contends the decision represents a misapplication of the law of contract zoning. This case may also serve as a cautionary tale for anyone who enters into a contract with Orange County.

Morgran is a developer of real estate. Its complaint against Orange County related to its attempt to develop 437 acres located in Orange County into a primarily residential, mixed-use land development. The complaint alleges that the property was originally zoned agricultural; that Morgran was required to apply for an amendment to the County's Comprehensive Policy Plan ["CPP"] in order to develop the property as desired; that the property also had to be rezoned to the Planned Development ["PD"] classification; that the amendment to the CPP was approved by Orange County's Board of County Commissioners in November of 1998; that following the amendment to the CPP, the County entered into a "Developer's Agreement" providing that the County would adopt an amendment to the CPP, and would "support and expeditiously process" Morgran's rezoning application in exchange for Morgran's agreement to donate 50 acres to the County for use as a park once the rezoning was accomplished; that Morgran submitted its application for rezoning on March 8, 2000, but the County breached its obligation to "support and expeditiously process" the request for rezoning by, instead, affirmatively advocating the denial of the application; and that their application for rezoning was ultimately denied by the County in a hearing before the Board of County Commissioners. Morgran seeks to recover damages, including the difference in the value of the property if zoned PD, delay damages, expenditures associated with the rezoning application and attorney's fees.

Apparently, the cause of Orange County's decision to renege on its agreement was a subsequent edict by then County Chairman, Mel Martinez, that the county reject any development requests for rezoning in areas where the Orange County School Board considered the schools to be overcrowded. When Morgran sought to have Orange County abide by its agreement, the county disavowed the contract as a void effort to engage in contract zoning.[1]

Contract zoning is, in essence, an agreement by a governmental body with a private landowner to rezone property for consideration. This practice has long been disapproved in Florida in cases such as *Hartnett v. Austin*, 93 So. 2d 86 (Fla. 1956) and *Chung v. Sarasota Cnty.*, 686 So. 2d 1358 (Fla. 2d DCA 1996). Orange County's position is that its agreement to "support and expeditiously process" Morgran's rezoning application is unambiguously

1 Orange County also contended that suit was precluded by virtue of the terms of paragraph 3(i) of the Developer's Agreement:

> Notwithstanding the County's agreement to support and expeditiously process the rezoning of the Property as set forth above, Developer understands that such rezoning process is subject to all County ordinances and regulations governing rezoning, including, but not limited to, review by the Development Review Committee ("DRC"), all applicable public hearings, and approval by the Board of County Commissioners. Further, Developer understands and concedes that the County will not and cannot by law waive the requirements governing the rezoning process.

void as a matter of law, since this agreement with Morgran requires the County to contract away its police powers ...

Relying on cases such as *Hartnett* and *Chung*, Orange County reasons that if the County cannot be bound to approve the rezoning application, it likewise cannot be bound to support that application. Morgran responds that there is a distinction between an obligation to support the request for rezoning and an obligation to approve the request. They urge that both parties, aware of the law of contract zoning, developed this carefully worded, highly negotiated contract language that "does not purport, either impliedly or expressly, to restrict or any way interfere with, the exercise of the Board of County Commissioner's police power as the final zoning authority in the County."

This argument, we fear, draws too fine a distinction. Morgran entered into its Developer's Agreement with "Orange County, a political subdivision of the State of Florida." The governing body of Orange County is the Board of County Commissioners. The agreement was executed by Mel Martinez, "Orange County Chairman," on behalf of the Board of County Commissioners. Orange County's zoning decisions are made by the Planning and Zoning Commission and the Board of Zoning Adjustment. *See* §§ 501 and 502 of the Orange County Code. However, review of these initial zoning decisions are taken to the Board of County Commissioners, which considers the issue *de novo* and which has final authority.

Development agreements are expressly permitted by the Florida Statutes. *See* Fla. Stat. §§ 163.3220–.3243 (1999). A development agreement has been defined as "a contract between a [local government] and a property owner/developer, which provides the developer with vested rights by freezing the existing zoning regulations applicable to a property in exchange for public benefits." Brad K. Schwartz, *Development Agreements: Contracting for Vested Rights*, 28 B.C. Env't Affs. L. Rev. 719 (2001). Florida law permits local governments to impose "conditions, terms and restrictions" as part of these agreements, where necessary for the public health, safety or welfare of its citizens. Fla. Stat. § 163.3227(1)(h) (1999). The problem in this case lies with Orange County's obligation to "support" Morgran's request for rezoning, as part of that development agreement. If the Board of County Commissioners has already contracted to "support" Morgran's request for rezoning, it has invalidly contracted away its discretionary legislative power as the final decisionmaking authority. The clause in the contract which provides that the "rezoning process is subject to all County ordinances and regulations governing rezoning," does not cure the problem. In *Chung*, in rejecting a similar argument, the court noted that any hearings regarding the issue of rezoning would "be a pro forma exercise since the County has already obligated itself to a decision." 686 So. 2d at 1360. The court rejected *Molina v. Tradewinds Dev. Corp.*, 526 So. 2d 695 (Fla. 4th DCA 1988) to the extent it implied that an obligation to comply with applicable zoning regulations precluded a finding of illegal contract zoning ...

Morgran urges that the contractual provision that binds the County to support rezoning means only County staff, not the Board. First, given the absence of language of such pivotal importance in the agreement, we decline to find a latent ambiguity. Second, we doubt it would matter. Morgran seemingly draws a distinction between the Board acting in its executive (governing) capacity and the Board acting in its quasi-judicial capacity in zoning cases. We find this distinction to be unworkable. Whichever hat it is wearing, the County is still the County.

Morgran next complains that the trial court erred in the dismissal with prejudice of its claim for promissory estoppel. The rule, however, is that estoppel cannot be applied against a governmental entity to accomplish an illegal result. *Branca v. City of Miramar*, 634 So. 2d 604 (Fla. 1994). It has been specifically held that estoppel cannot be used by a landowner to enforce a contract which constitutes "contract zoning." *P.C.B. P'ship v. City of Largo*, 549 So. 2d 738, 741–42 (Fla. 2d DCA 1989) ("A party entering into a contract with a municipality is bound to know the extent of the municipality's power to contract, and the municipality will not be estopped to assert the invalidity of a contract which it had no power to execute.")

Additionally, a party cannot reasonably rely upon a promise, the enforcement of which would be contrary to established public policy. *Brine v. Fertitta*, 537 So. 2d 113 (Fla. 2d DCA 1988) ...

AFFIRMED in part; REVERSED in part; and REMANDED.

SAWAYA and ORFINGER, R. B., JJ., concur.

## Box 22.1 Practice problem: Carson Towne Centre

Central County has transportation congestion problems. All of the county's arterial roadways have too much traffic. The commute on State Highway from Rural Community to State University in Collegeborough is awful. The new favorite mantra of the Collegeborough Chamber of Commerce is that the county's inaction on the transportation issue is costing Central County economic development.

The Central County Commission responds to the criticism by drafting this new rule for inclusion in the land development code: "The county may not issue a certificate of occupancy for new development unless transportation facilities sufficient to accommodate traffic are in place and available to serve that new development." Along with this rule, the commission proposes to adopt standards for the maximum amount of traffic it would tolerate on all arterial roadways in the county. The commission would adopt a table into the code that would present these standards listed as a number of car trips allowed per day on each one-quarter-mile segment of arterial roadway. And the commission would approve a methodology for determining how much new traffic a development would create.

While this new transportation rule is pending, Scott Carson submits a development plan application to the county proposing to build Carson Towne Centre, a lifestyle center (like an outdoor mall with big box anchor tenants). Carson has intentionally misspelled the words "towne" and "centre" in the name of his proposed development at the recommendation of a marketing firm in Bay Town, which is obnoxious.

Carson is wary of the pending adoption of the proposed county transportation rule. He has proposed Carson Towne Centre be located on land he owns adjacent to a particularly congested portion of State Highway. He knows that his development will also generate lots of new traffic. Carson expects the new rule would add tremendous costs to developing Carson Towne Centre.

To forestall the application of the proposed rule to his project, Carson goes to a Central County Commission meeting around the same time he submits his development plan application and presents the commission with a draft written contract that has the following terms.

- Scott Carson will pay to construct a new intersection with traffic signal and turn lanes on State Highway at the entrance to Carson Towne Centre. The draft contract includes dates by which Carson would complete this construction.

- Central County will expeditiously process the development plan application for Carson Towne Centre.
- And, Central County will exempt Carson Towne Centre from application of the proposed transportation rule even if it became law before the county issues Carson Towne Centre a certificate of occupancy.

At the meeting where Carson presents this draft agreement, he lobbies the commissioners forcefully. In a long speech, he tells them that if they don't take this deal, he won't build Carson Towne Centre. Community residents will never be able to shop at the retail stores or dine at the restaurants he plans to recruit as tenants. He emphasizes that everyone loves the hip chain-restaurant P.F. Macaroni Factory, but Central County won't get one unless the county commission accepts Carson's proposal. Also, Carson says his offer to build the new intersection is very generous and, if the elected officials really care about traffic congestion, they will take the improvement he is offering them for free.

Carson's haranguing works. The county commission accepts his terms. They vote to approve the contract and the chair signs the document on the spot. While Scott Carson is pleased with this outcome, the group Collegians for Wise Growth is not. This group is a team of citizen activists fighting for fiscally responsible growth management in Collegeborough and in Central County. Collegians for Wise Growth knows that the new intersection with traffic signal and turn lanes will cost Carson only a small fraction of his financial liability under the proposed—but not yet adopted—transportation rule. The group also knows Carson Towne Centre will make congestion much worse. Collegians for Wise Growth characterizes the contract between Carson and Central County as corporate welfare.

To have the contract nullified, Collegians for Wise Growth files a lawsuit alleging that the bargained-for exchange between Carson and Central County is illegal contract zoning.

Evaluate the organization's claim.

## Notes

1 7 Fla. Jur. 2d *Building, Zoning, and Land Controls* § 168 (2020).
2 Fla. Stat. § 163.3220(3).
3 *Id.* § 163.3239.
4 *Id.* § 163.3233(1).
5 *Id.* §§ 163.3233(2)(a)–(2)(e).
6 *Id.* §§ 163.3220(2)(b), 163.3239.
7 *Id.* § 163.3227(1)(d).
8 Fla. Stat. § 163.3235.
9 7 Fla. Jur. 2d *Building, Zoning, and Land Controls* § 188 (2020).
10 Restatement (Second) of Contracts § 71 (Am. Law Inst. 1981).
11 Chung v. Sarasota Cnty., 686 So. 2d 1358, 1359–60 (Fla. 2d DCA 1996).
12 Hartnett v. Austin, 93 So. 2d 86, 89 (Fla. 1956) (en banc).
13 818 So. 2d 640 (Fla. 5th DCA 2002).

# 23 Plats and restrictive covenants

## Subdivision

Subdivision is generally the process of splitting land into lots for conveyance and into land dedicated for access and public services such as roads and utilities. Governments effect subdivision by recording a drawing of subdivided land—called a plat—in the public records. Florida Statutes govern subdivision at Chapter 177. These rules focus primarily on how to draw and record plats.[1]

Historically, facilitating the sale of land was the reason for subdivision.[2] Describing land on a deed by reference to a recorded plat is easier and less prone to error than describing land with a metes and bounds description. By the early twentieth century, however, subdivision came to constitute, along with zoning, the foundation of land use law.[3]

Of all land use decisions, subdivision has the most lasting and significant effect on urban form. Subdivision decides the relationship between public and private space. And subdivision plats are more permanent than other land use decisions.

> Although the subdivision of land occurs early in the development process, its impact on the community is lasting because "[t]he pattern of subdivision becomes the pattern of a community, which in turn may influence the character of an entire city."[4]

Compare the existing form of your community's downtown to the recorded plat for that area. Even when a plat is hundreds of years old—practically ancient by Floridian terms—the relationship between public and private space today typically matches the plat.

Once a recorded plat exists, local government land use controls may relate to it. For example, street-side setbacks and build-to lines inherently refer to developable land's relationship to a street. In addition, local governments may allocate permission to develop land—most commonly as single-family residences—by the platted lot.[5] For a platted lot to have significance for later land development regulation, however, *a local government's laws must assign that significance.* Florida law does not inherently connect the platting process to other land development regulations.[6]

## Restrictive covenants

Restrictive covenants are a property law tool to limit the use of property. Also called negative easements or equitable servitudes, restrictive covenants are "not easements in the strict sense of the word but are more properly classified as rights arising out of contract" and recorded through a deed.[7]

Sometimes local governments incorporate restrictive covenants into land use approvals in order to create very specific limitations on the uses of property. The facts of *Metro. Dade Cnty. v. Fontainbleau Gas & Wash, Inc.* are an example of this practice.

> Trafalgar Developers filed an application with the county requesting a change in zoning from RU–5A Semi-professional Office to BU–1A Limited Business and a variance of zoning regulations pertaining to a wall requirement as to a parcel of land in Dade County. In the letter of intent accompanying the application, Trafalgar's lawyer indicated that the company would voluntarily offer a written covenant restricting use of the property to a bank or savings and loan. The county commission rezoned the subject property. A preamble to the zoning resolution clearly expressed that the county commission granted rezoning only for a bank or savings and loan and accepted the property owner's offer of a restrictive covenant and the county's option to enforce this restriction.[8]

In this context, the likely purpose of the restrictive covenant is to allay community concern that a change of zoning designation will allow a broad range of new uses that may not be compatible with surrounding land uses. A developer that intends to use property in a narrower way, to which the community would not object, might consent to a restrictive covenant because such a limitation could placate concerned neighbors.

Despite its usefulness, a restrictive covenant has at least three fundamental characteristics which make it unlike a land use restriction and an unreliable safeguard for those now-pacified neighbors. First, the local government has no obligation to enforce the terms of the restrictive covenant. As the beneficiary of a restrictive covenant, a local government would have the ability—but not the obligation—to exercise its enforcement rights.[9] In contrast, Florida Statutes require local governments to comply with their comprehensive plan and other land development regulations.[10]

Second, if a property owner fails to comply with a restrictive covenant and the local government chooses not to exercise its enforcement rights under the declaration, the parties who would have standing to enforce a violation of the local government's land use laws may not have standing to enforce the covenant. "The general theory behind the right to enforce restrictive covenants is that the covenants must have been made with or for the benfit [sic] of the one seeking to enforce them."[11]

Third, a party benefitting from a restrictive covenant can generally rescind that covenant unilaterally.[12] In contrast, restrictions which are based in land use law come with procedures that protect affected parties' constitutional due process rights.[13]

Despite these deficiencies, courts may consider declarations imposed as a result of a government approval process to be more than mere real estate restrictions. The decision *Save Calusa Tr. v. St. Andrews Holdings, Ltd.* holds that a "duly imposed restrictive covenant in this case is a governmental regulation, rather than an estate, interest, claim or charge affecting the marketability of the property's title."[14] Thus, a restrictive covenant arising from a permit to use land may sit in a unique location, between land use and real property law.

## Notes

1 *See* Fla. Stat. §§ 177.011–177.051.
2 Julian Conrad Juergensmeyer & Thomas E. Roberts, *Land Use Planning and Development Regulation Law* 255 (Thompson W. 2nd edn 2007).
3 *Id.* at 253.
4 *Id.* at 254 (citing R. Freilich and M. Schulz, *Model Subdivision Regulations Planning and Law* 1 (Am. Plan. Ass'n 1995)).
5 *See*, e.g., St. Petersburg City Code § 16.60.030.2.A (referring to platted lots as "lot[s] of record").
6 Outlaw v. Kinsey, 286 So. 2d 602, 602–3 (Fla. 1st DCA 1973).
7 Bd. of Pub. Instruction of Dade Cnty. v. Town of Bay Harbor Islands, 81 So. 2d 637, 640 (Fla. 1955); *see also* Osius v. Barton, 147 So. 862, 868 (Fla. 1933).
8 Metro. Dade Cnty. v. Fontainebleau Gas & Wash, Inc., 570 So. 2d 1006, 1006–07 (Fla. 3d DCA 1990).

9 *Osius*, 147 So. at 868.
10 Fla. Stat. § 163.3194(1)(a).
11 *Osius*, 147 So. at 865.
12 Johnson v. Three Bays Props. No. 2, Inc., 159 So. 2d 924, 925 & n.1 (Fla. 3d DCA 1964).
13 Jennings v. Dade Cnty., 589 So. 2d 1337, 1340 (Fla. 3d DCA 1991).
14 Save Calusa Tr. v. St. Andrews Holdings, Ltd., 193 So. 3d 910, 916 (Fla. 3d DCA), *reh'g denied*, No. SC16-1189, 2017 WL 7574142, at *1 (Fla. Dec. 29, 2016).

# Part V

# Additional U.S. Constitutional issues

# 24 Equal protection

This chapter is about protections in the U.S. Constitution against local government land use regulations based on unacceptable criteria, such as race. The Equal Protection Clause within the Fourteenth Amendment to the U.S. Constitution states: "No State shall ... deny to any person within its jurisdiction the equal protection of the laws."[1] Like the rest of the Fourteenth Amendment, the United States added the Equal Protection Clause to the Constitution following the Civil War in 1865 to protect the rights of formerly enslaved people, now free due to passage of the Thirteenth Amendment, from arbitrary state discrimination.[2]

The following case, *Buchanan v. Warley*, does not present the current law on equal protection. Still, the case is valuable because its facts are an example of a local government designing land use rules explicitly to segregate its community by race. Land use practitioners should know that racism in land use has been pervasive and that legally mandated segregation made extant marks on American communities.[3] Also note that *Buchanan* and *City of Cleburne v. Cleburne Living Center*, the second case in this chapter, use anachronistic and possibly offensive language to refer to Blacks and to people with mental disabilities respectively. These decisions reflect accepted wording for the time. That we now regard as offensive words previously considered acceptable to describe certain groups of people is evidence of the historical prejudice against these people.[4]

## United States Supreme Court

### *Buchanan v. Warley*[5]

### 1917

Mr. Justice DAY delivered the opinion of the Court.

Buchanan, plaintiff in error, brought an action in the chancery branch of Jefferson circuit court of Kentucky for the specific performance of a contract for the sale of certain real estate situated in the city of Louisville at the corner of Thirty-seventh street and Pflanz avenue. The offer in writing to purchase the property contained a proviso:

> It is understood that I am purchasing the above property for the purpose of having erected thereon a house which I propose to make my residence, and it is a distinct part of this agreement that I shall not be required to accept a deed to the above property or to pay for said property unless I have the right under the laws of the state of Kentucky and the city of Louisville to occupy said property as a residence.

This offer was accepted by the plaintiff.

To the action for specific performance the defendant by way of answer set up the condition above set forth, that he is a colored person, and that on the block of which the lot in controversy is a part, there are ten residences, eight of which at the time of the making of the contract were occupied by white people, and only two (those nearest the lot in question) were occupied by colored people, and that under and by virtue of the ordinance of the city of Louisville, approved May 11, 1914, he would not be allowed to occupy the lot as a place of residence.

In reply to this answer the plaintiff set up, among other things, that the ordinance was in conflict with the Fourteenth Amendment to the Constitution of the United States, and hence no defense to the action for specific performance of the contract.

In the court of original jurisdiction in Kentucky, and in the Court of Appeals of that state, the case was made to turn upon the constitutional validity of the ordinance. The Court of Appeals of Kentucky, 177 S.W. 472 (Ky. 1915), held the ordinance valid and of itself a complete defense to the action.

The title of the ordinance is:

> An ordinance to prevent conflict and ill-feeling between the white and colored races in the city of Louisville, and to preserve the public peace and promote the general welfare, by making reasonable provisions requiring, as far as practicable, the use of separate blocks, for residences, places of abode, and places of assembly by white and colored people respectively.

By the first section of the ordinance it is made unlawful for any colored person to move into and occupy as a residence, place of abode, or to establish and maintain as a place of public assembly any house upon any block upon which a greater number of houses are occupied as residences, places of abode, or places of public assembly by white people than are occupied as residences, places of abode, or places of public assembly by colored people ...

The ordinance contains other sections and a violation of its provisions is made an offense.

The assignments of error in this court attack the ordinance upon the ground that it violates the Fourteenth Amendment of the Constitution of the United States, in that it abridges the privileges and immunities of citizens of the United States to acquire and enjoy property, takes property without due process of law, and denies equal protection of the laws ... The property here involved was sold by the plaintiff ... a white man, on the terms stated, to a colored man; ... But for the ordinance the state courts would have enforced the contract, and the defendant would have been compelled to pay the purchase price and take a conveyance of the premises ...

We pass then to a consideration of the case upon its merits. This ordinance prevents the occupancy of a lot in the city of Louisville by a person of color in a block where the greater number of residences are occupied by white persons; where such a majority exists colored persons are excluded. This interdiction is based wholly upon color; simply that and nothing more. In effect, premises situated as are those in question in the so-called white block are effectively debarred from sale to persons of color, because if sold they cannot be occupied by the purchaser nor by him sold to another of the same color.

This drastic measure is sought to be justified under the authority of the state in the exercise of the police power. It is said such legislation tends to promote the public peace by preventing racial conflicts; that it tends to maintain racial purity; that it prevents the deterioration of property owned and occupied by white people, which deterioration, it is contended, is sure to follow the occupancy of adjacent premises by persons of color.

The authority of the state to pass laws in the exercise of the police power, having for their object the promotion of the public health, safety and welfare is very broad as has been affirmed in numerous and recent decisions of this court. Furthermore the exercise of this power, embracing nearly all legislation of a local character is not to be interfered with by the courts where it is within the scope of legislative authority and the means adopted reasonably tend to accomplish a lawful purpose. But it is equally well established that the police power, broad as it is, cannot justify the passage of a law or ordinance which runs counter to the limitations of the federal Constitution; that principle has been so frequently affirmed in this court that we need not stop to cite the cases.

The federal Constitution and laws passed within its authority are by the express terms of that instrument made the supreme law of the land. The Fourteenth Amendment protects life, liberty, and property from invasion by the states without due process of law. Property is more than the mere thing which a person owns. It is elementary that it includes the right to acquire, use, and dispose of it. The Constitution protects these essential attributes of property. *Holden v. Hardy*, 169 U.S. 366, 391 (1898). Property consists of the free use, enjoyment, and disposal of a person's acquisitions without control or diminution save by the law of the land. 1 *Blackstone's Commentaries* (Cooley's Edn) 127 ...

The concrete question here is: May the occupancy, and, necessarily, the purchase and sale of property of which occupancy is an incident, be inhibited by the states, or by one of its municipalities, solely because of the color of the proposed occupant of the premises? ... The question now presented makes it pertinent to inquire into the constitutional right of the white man to sell his property to a colored man, having in view the legal status of the purchaser and occupant.

Following the Civil War certain amendments to the federal Constitution were adopted, which have become an integral part of that instrument, equally binding upon all the states and fixing certain fundamental rights which all are bound to respect. The Thirteenth Amendment abolished slavery in the United States and in all places subject to their jurisdiction, and gave Congress power to enforce the amendment by appropriate legislation. The Fourteenth Amendment made all persons born or naturalized in the United States, citizens of the United States and of the states in which they reside, and provided that no state shall make or enforce any law which shall abridge the privileges or immunities of citizens of the United States, and that no state shall deprive any person of life, liberty, or property without due process of law, nor deny to any person the equal protection of the laws ... While a principal purpose of the latter amendment [the Fourteenth] was to protect persons of color, the broad language used was deemed sufficient to protect all persons, white or black, against discriminatory legislation by the states. This is now the settled law. In many of the cases since arising the question of color has not been involved and the cases have been decided upon alleged violations of civil or property rights irrespective of the race or color of the complainant ...

In *Strauder v. W. Virginia*, 100 U.S. 303 (1879), this court held that a colored person charged with an offense was denied due process of law by a statute which prevented colored men from sitting on the jury which tried him. Mr. Justice Strong, speaking for the court, again reviewed the history of the amendments, and among other things, in speaking of the Fourteenth Amendment, said:

> It [the Fourteenth Amendment] was designed to assure to the colored race the enjoyment of all the civil rights that under the law are enjoyed by white persons, and to give to that race the protection of the general government, in that enjoyment, whenever it should be denied by the states. It not only gave citizenship and the privileges of citizenship to persons of color, but it denied to any state the power to withhold from them the equal protection of the laws, and authorized Congress to enforce its provisions by appropriate legislation. * * * It ordains that no state shall make or enforce any laws which shall abridge the privileges or immunities of citizens of the United States. * * *

> It ordains that no state shall deprive any person of life, liberty, or property, without due process of law, or deny to any person within its jurisdiction the equal protection of the laws.
>
> What is this but declaring that the law in the states shall be the same for the black as for the white; that all persons, whether colored or white, shall stand equal before the laws of the states, and, in regard to the colored race, for whose protection the amendment was primarily designed that no discrimination shall be made against them by law because of their color? * * *
>
> The Fourteenth Amendment makes no attempt to enumerate the rights it designed to protect. It speaks in general terms, and those are as comprehensive as possible. Its language is prohibitory; but every prohibition implies the existence of rights and immunities, prominent among which is an immunity from inequality of legal protection, either for life, liberty, or property. Any state action that denies this immunity to a colored man is in conflict with the Constitution ...

Colored persons are citizens of the United States and have the right to purchase property and enjoy and use the same without laws discriminating against them solely on account of color. *Hall v. De Cuir*, 95 U.S. 485, 508 (1877) ... The Fourteenth Amendment and these statutes enacted in furtherance of its purpose operate to qualify and entitle a colored man to acquire property without state legislation discriminating against him solely because of color.

The defendant in error insists that *Plessy v. Ferguson*, 163 U.S. 537 (1896), is controlling in principle in favor of the judgment of the court below. In that case this court held that a provision of a statute of Louisiana requiring railway companies carrying passengers to provide in their coaches equal but separate accommodations for the white and colored races did not run counter to the provisions of the Fourteenth Amendment. It is to be observed that in that case there was no attempt to deprive persons of color of transportation in the coaches of the public carrier, and the express requirements were for equal though separate accommodations for the white and colored races. In *Plessy v. Ferguson*, classification of accommodations was permitted upon the basis of equality for both races ... That there exists a serious and difficult problem arising from a feeling of race hostility which the law is powerless to control, and to which it must give a measure of consideration, may be freely admitted. But its solution cannot be promoted by depriving citizens of their constitutional rights and privileges.

As we have seen, this court has held laws valid which separated the races on the basis of equal accommodations in public conveyances, and courts of high authority have held enactments lawful which provide for separation in the public schools of white and colored pupils where equal privileges are given. But in view of the rights secured by the Fourteenth Amendment to the federal Constitution such legislation must have its limitations, and cannot be sustained where the exercise of authority exceeds the restraints of the Constitution. We think these limitations are exceeded in laws and ordinances of the character now before us.

It is the purpose of such enactments, and, it is frankly avowed it will be their ultimate effect, to require by law, at least in residential districts, the compulsory separation of the races on account of color. Such action is said to be essential to the maintenance of the purity of the races, although it is to be noted in the ordinance under consideration that the employment of colored servants in white families is permitted, and nearby residences of colored persons not coming within the blocks, as defined in the ordinance, are not prohibited.

The case presented does not deal with an attempt to prohibit the amalgamation of the races. The right which the ordinance annulled was the civil right of a white man to dispose of his property if he saw fit to do so to a person of color and of a colored person to make such disposition to a white person.

It is urged that this proposed segregation will promote the public peace by preventing race conflicts. Desirable as this is, and important as is the preservation of the public peace, this aim cannot be accomplished by laws or ordinances which deny rights created or protected by the federal Constitution.

It is said that such acquisitions by colored persons depreciate property owned in the neighborhood by white persons. But property may be acquired by undesirable white neighbors or put to disagreeable though lawful uses with like results.

We think this attempt to prevent the alienation of the property in question to a person of color was not a legitimate exercise of the police power of the state, and is in direct violation of the fundamental law enacted in the Fourteenth Amendment of the Constitution preventing state interference with property rights except by due process of law. That being the case, the ordinance cannot stand. *Booth v. Illinois*, 184 U.S. 425, 429 (1902); *Otis v. Parker*, 187 U.S. 606, 609 (1903).

Reaching this conclusion it follows that the judgment of the Kentucky Court of Appeals must be reversed, and the cause remanded to that court for further proceedings not inconsistent with this opinion.

Reversed.

## Discussion

While *Buchanan v. Warley* represents a positive step toward equal treatment of all people, the Court's decree did not eradicate discriminatory zoning. Specifically in Florida, overtly racist ordinances survived the Court's prohibition for more than half a century.

> In Florida, a West Palm Beach racial zoning ordinance was adopted in 1929, a dozen years after *Buchanan*, and was maintained after 1960. The Orlando suburb of Apopka adopted an ordinance banning blacks from living on the north side of the railroad tracks and whites from living on the south side. It remained in effect until 1968.[6]

## Class-based discrimination

The Equal Protection Clause does not prohibit all discrimination. "Equal protection does not require that all persons be dealt with identically, but it does require that a distinction made have some relevance to the purpose for which the classification is made."[7] An example of obviously permissible government discrimination is deciding whether to issue a professional license based on a person's education.

The first step in evaluating whether governmental discrimination violates equal protection is to determine the basis of the discrimination. Courts ask, what characteristic is the government using to separate people into different groups for disparate treatment? Discrimination based on some characteristics—like race or religion—is practically never permissible. Discrimination based on other characteristics—such as age—is unlikely to violate the Equal Protection Clause.

Depending on the basis of discrimination, a court applies one of three standards of review to determine whether a law violates the U.S. Constitution. Those three standards are strict scrutiny, intermediate scrutiny, and rational basis review.[8] Like the fairly debatable standard, each of the equal protection standards of review has two parts. The first part characterizes the significance of the governmental interest the rule in question must serve. The second part characterizes the required connection between the governmental interest and the regulation.

Although the basis of discrimination determines the standard of review, courts have not adopted a test to determine which bases of discrimination match which standards of review. Instead, one must look to specific precedents to determine how classes are protected.

Finally, only *intentional* governmental discrimination violates the Equal Protection Clause.[9] Laws which have a disparate impact on a class of people—but which are not intentionally discriminatory—are not equal protection violations.[10]

### *Strict scrutiny*

Strict scrutiny[11] review applies to laws targeting a *suspect class*. Suspect "classifications are more likely than others to reflect deep-seated prejudice rather than legislative rationality in pursuit of some legitimate objective."[12] Suspect classifications include those based on race, religion, and national origin.[13] To defend a regulation against strict scrutiny, government must "demonstrate with clarity that its purpose or interest is both constitutionally permissible and *substantial*, and that its use of the classification is *necessary* ... to the accomplishment of its purpose."[14]

### *Intermediate scrutiny*

Intermediate scrutiny review applies to laws targeting quasi-suspect groups. Governmental classifications which are quasi-suspect include sex[15] and illegitimacy.[16] "To withstand intermediate scrutiny, a statutory classification must be *substantially* related to an *important* governmental objective."[17]

### *Rational basis*

All laws must meet rational basis review. In an equal protection context, rational basis review applies when neither strict scrutiny nor intermediate scrutiny applies (i.e. when the classification the government employs does not relate to a suspect class or to a quasi-suspect class). The U.S. Supreme Court has described rational basis review as a highly deferential standard.

> This inquiry employs a relatively relaxed standard reflecting the Court's awareness that the drawing of lines that create distinctions is peculiarly a legislative task and an unavoidable one. Perfection in making the necessary classifications is neither possible nor necessary. Such action by a legislature is *presumed to be valid*.[18]

To pass rational basis review, a government must show that its law "bear[s] some *rational* relationship to a *legitimate* state purpose."[19]

## Supreme Court of the United States

## *City of Cleburne v. Cleburne Living Center*[20]

## 1985

Justice WHITE delivered the opinion of the Court.

A Texas city denied a special use permit for the operation of a group home for the mentally retarded, acting pursuant to a municipal zoning ordinance requiring permits for such homes. The Court of Appeals for the Fifth Circuit held that mental retardation is a "quasi-suspect" classification and that the ordinance violated the Equal Protection Clause because it did not substantially further an important governmental purpose. We hold that a lesser standard of scrutiny is appropriate, but conclude that under that standard the ordinance is invalid as applied in this case.

### *I*

In July 1980, respondent Jan Hannah purchased a building at 201 Featherston Street in the city of Cleburne, Texas, with the intention of leasing it to Cleburne Living Center, Inc. (CLC), for the operation of a group home for the mentally retarded. It was anticipated that the home would house 13 retarded men and women, who would be under the constant supervision of CLC staff members. The house had four bedrooms and two baths, with a half bath to be added. CLC planned to comply with all applicable state and federal regulations.

The city informed CLC that a special use permit would be required for the operation of a group home at the site, and CLC accordingly submitted a permit application. In response to a subsequent inquiry from CLC, the city explained that under the zoning regulations applicable to the site, a special use permit, renewable annually, was required for the construction of "[h]ospitals for the insane or feeble-minded, or alcoholic [sic] or drug addicts, or penal or correctional institutions." The city had determined that the proposed group home should be classified as a "hospital for the feebleminded." After holding a public hearing on CLC's application, the City Council voted 3 to 1 to deny a special use permit.

CLC then filed suit in Federal District Court against the city and a number of its officials, alleging, inter alia, that the zoning ordinance was invalid on its face and as applied because it discriminated against the mentally retarded in violation of the equal protection rights of CLC and its potential residents. The District Court found that "[i]f the potential residents of the Featherston Street home were not mentally retarded, but the home was the same in all other respects, its use would be permitted under the city's zoning ordinance," and that the City Counsel's [sic] decision "was motivated primarily by the fact that the residents of the home would be persons who are mentally retarded." App. 93, 94. Even so, the District Court held the ordinance and its application constitutional. Concluding that no fundamental right was implicated and that mental retardation was neither a suspect nor a quasi-suspect classification, the court employed the minimum level of judicial scrutiny applicable to equal protection claims. The court deemed the ordinance, as written and applied, to be rationally related to the city's legitimate interests in "the legal responsibility of CLC and its residents ... the safety and fears of residents in the adjoining neighborhood," and the number of people to be housed in the home. *Id.* at 103.

The Court of Appeals for the Fifth Circuit reversed, determining that mental retardation was a quasi-suspect classification and that it should assess the validity of the ordinance under intermediate-level scrutiny. 726 F.2d 191 (5th Cir. 1984). Because mental retardation was in fact relevant to many legislative actions, strict scrutiny was not appropriate. But in light of the history of "unfair and often grotesque mistreatment" of the retarded, discrimination against them was "likely to reflect deep-seated prejudice." *Id.* at 197. In addition, the mentally retarded lacked political power, and their condition was immutable ... Applying the test that it considered appropriate, the court held that the ordinance was invalid on its face because it did not substantially further any important governmental interests. The Court of Appeals went on to hold that the ordinance was also invalid as applied ...

### *II*

The Equal Protection Clause of the Fourteenth Amendment commands that no State shall "deny to any person within its jurisdiction the equal protection of the laws," which is essentially a direction that all persons similarly situated should be treated alike. *Plyler v. Doe*, 457

U.S. 202, 216 (1982) ... The general rule is that legislation is presumed to be valid and will be sustained if the classification drawn by the statute is rationally related to a legitimate state interest. *Schweiker v. Wilson*, 450 U.S. 221, 230 (1981); *United States R.R. Ret. Bd. v. Fritz*, 449 U.S. 166, 174–75 (1980); *Vance v. Bradley*, 440 U.S. 93, 97 (1979); *New Orleans v. Dukes*, 427 U.S. 297, 303 (1976) ...

The general rule gives way, however, when a statute classifies by race, alienage, or national origin. These factors are so seldom relevant to the achievement of any legitimate state interest that laws grounded in such considerations are deemed to reflect prejudice and antipathy—a view that those in the burdened class are not as worthy or deserving as others. For these reasons and because such discrimination is unlikely to be soon rectified by legislative means, these laws are subjected to strict scrutiny and will be sustained only if they are suitably tailored to serve a compelling state interest. *McLaughlin v. Florida*, 379 U.S. 184, 192 (1964); *Graham v. Richardson*, 403 U.S. 365 (1971) ...

Legislative classifications based on gender also call for a heightened standard of review. That factor generally provides no sensible ground for differential treatment. "[W]hat differentiates sex from such nonsuspect statuses as intelligence or physical disability ... is that the sex characteristic frequently bears no relation to ability to perform or contribute to society." *Frontiero v. Richardson*, 411 U.S. 677, 686 (1973) (plurality opinion). Rather than resting on meaningful considerations, statutes distributing benefits and burdens between the sexes in different ways very likely reflect outmoded notions of the relative capabilities of men and women. A gender classification fails unless it is substantially related to a sufficiently important governmental interest. *Miss. Univ. for Women v. Hogan*, 458 U.S. 718 (1982); *Craig v. Boren*, 429 U.S. 190 (1976). Because illegitimacy is beyond the individual's control and bears "no relation to the individual's ability to participate in and contribute to society," *Mathews v. Lucas*, 427 U.S. 495, 505 (1976), official discriminations resting on that characteristic are also subject to somewhat heightened review. Those restrictions "will survive equal protection scrutiny to the extent they are substantially related to a legitimate state interest." *Mills v. Habluetzel*, 456 U.S. 91, 99 (1982).

We have declined, however, to extend heightened review to differential treatment based on age: "While the treatment of the aged in this Nation has not been wholly free of discrimination, such persons, unlike, say, those who have been discriminated against on the basis of race or national origin, have not experienced a "history of purposeful unequal treatment" or been subjected to unique disabilities on the basis of stereotyped characteristics not truly indicative of their abilities. *Mass. Bd. of Ret. v. Murgia*, 427 U.S. 307, 313 (1976)." The lesson of *Murgia* is that where individuals in the group affected by a law have distinguishing characteristics relevant to interests the State has the authority to implement, the courts have been very reluctant, as they should be in our federal system and with our respect for the separation of powers, to closely scrutinize legislative choices as to whether, how, and to what extent those interests should be pursued. In such cases, the Equal Protection Clause requires only a rational means to serve a legitimate end.

### *III*

Against this background, we conclude for several reasons that the Court of Appeals erred in holding mental retardation a quasi-suspect classification calling for a more exacting standard of judicial review than is normally accorded economic and social legislation. First, it is undeniable, and it is not argued otherwise here, that those who are mentally retarded have a reduced ability to cope with and function in the everyday world ... [A]s the testimony in this record indicates, they range from those whose disability is not immediately evident to those who must be constantly cared for. They are thus different, immutably so, in relevant respects, and the States' interest in dealing with and providing for them is plainly a legitimate one. How this large and diversified group is to be treated under the law is a difficult and often a technical matter, very much a task for legislators guided by qualified professionals and not by the perhaps ill-informed opinions of the judiciary ...

Fourth, if the large and amorphous class of the mentally retarded were deemed quasi-suspect for the reasons given by the Court of Appeals, it would be difficult to find a principled way to distinguish a variety of other groups who have perhaps immutable disabilities setting them off from others, who cannot themselves mandate the desired legislative responses, and who can claim some degree of prejudice from at least part of the public at large. One need mention in this respect only the aging, the disabled, the mentally ill, and the infirm. We are reluctant to set out on that course, and we decline to do so.

Doubtless, there have been and there will continue to be instances of discrimination against the retarded that are in fact invidious, and that are properly subject to judicial correction under constitutional norms. But the appropriate method of reaching such instances is not to create a new quasi-suspect classification and subject all governmental action based on that classification to more searching evaluation. Rather, we should look to the likelihood that governmental action premised on a particular classification is valid as a general matter, not merely to the specifics of the case before us. Because mental retardation is a characteristic that the government may legitimately take into account in a wide range of decisions, and because both State and Federal Governments have recently committed themselves to assisting the retarded, we will not presume that any given legislative action, even one that disadvantages retarded individuals, is rooted in considerations that the Constitution will not tolerate.

Our refusal to recognize the retarded as a quasi-suspect class does not leave them entirely unprotected from invidious discrimination. To withstand equal protection review, legislation that distinguishes between the mentally retarded and others must be rationally related to a legitimate governmental purpose. This standard, we believe, affords government the latitude necessary both to pursue policies designed to assist the retarded in realizing their full potential, and to freely and efficiently engage in activities that burden the retarded in what is essentially an incidental manner. The State may not rely on a classification whose relationship to an asserted goal is so attenuated as to render the distinction arbitrary or irrational. See *Zobel v. Williams*, 457 U.S. 55, 61–63 (1982); *United States Dept. of Agric. v. Moreno*, 413 U.S. 528, 535 (1973). Furthermore, some objectives—such as "a bare ... desire to harm a politically unpopular group," *id.* at 534—are not legitimate state interests ... Beyond that, the mentally retarded, like others, have and retain their substantive constitutional rights in addition to the right to be treated equally by the law.

### *IV*

We turn to the issue of the validity of the zoning ordinance insofar as it requires a special use permit for homes for the mentally retarded. We inquire first whether requiring a special use permit for the Featherston home in the circumstances here deprives respondents of the equal protection of the laws. If it does, there will be no occasion to decide whether the special use permit provision is facially invalid where the mentally retarded are involved, or to put it another way, whether the city may never insist on a special use permit for a home for the mentally retarded in an R-3 zone ...

The city does not require a special use permit in an R-3 zone for apartment houses, multiple dwellings, boarding and lodging houses, fraternity or sorority houses, dormitories, apartment hotels, hospitals, sanitariums, nursing homes for convalescents or the aged (other than for the insane or feebleminded or alcoholics or drug addicts), private clubs or fraternal orders, and other specified uses. It does, however, insist on a special permit for the Featherston home, and it does so, as the District Court found, because it would be a facility for the mentally retarded. May the city require the permit for this facility when other care and multiple-dwelling facilities are freely permitted?

It is true, as already pointed out, that the mentally retarded as a group are indeed different from others not sharing their misfortune, and in this respect they may be different from those who would occupy other facilities that would be permitted in an R-3 zone without a special permit. But this difference is largely irrelevant unless the Featherston home and those who would occupy it would threaten legitimate interests of the city in a way that other permitted uses such as boarding houses and hospitals would not. Because ... the record does not reveal any rational basis for believing that the Featherston home would pose any special threat to the city's legitimate interests, we affirm the judgment below insofar as it holds the ordinance invalid as applied in this case ...

[T]he Council was concerned with the negative attitude of the majority of property owners located within 200 feet of the Featherston facility, as well as with the fears of elderly residents of the neighborhood. But mere negative attitudes, or fear, unsubstantiated by factors which are properly cognizable in a zoning proceeding, are not permissible bases for treating a home for the mentally retarded differently from apartment houses, multiple dwellings, and the like ... "Private biases may be outside the reach of the law, but the law cannot, directly or indirectly, give them effect." ...

The short of it is that requiring the permit in this case appears to us to rest on an irrational prejudice against the mentally retarded ...

The judgment of the Court of Appeals is affirmed insofar as it invalidates the zoning ordinance as applied to the Featherston home ...

It is so ordered.

## Classes of one

In addition to the three equal protection standards of review discussed to this point, the Equal Protection Clause has produced a fourth test that is applied to *classes of one*. The class of one test determines whether an incident of discrimination against one or more people, but not based on any class membership of those persons, violates the Equal Protection Clause.[21]

Such discrimination is unconstitutional when (1) government intentionally treats someone differently from others who are similarly situated and (2) there is no rational basis for the difference in treatment.[22] The test does not require animus against the party receiving the differential treatment.[23]

### Box 24.1 Practice problem: Rick Stumbly

Lindsey Tea, age 17, died of alcohol poisoning during an off-campus Omicron Tau Rho fraternity social last fall. Tea, a senior at Collegeborough High School, had attended the social with friends who are freshmen at State University and who are undergoing initiation into Omicron Tau Rho. The state attorney has charged nine members of the fraternity with hazing, a crime. Upon Tea's death, State University President Janet Foxx immediately suspended all fraternities on the State University campus and began working with a variety of governmental agencies to prevent future hazing deaths.

Collegeborough residents quickly became engaged in the response to Tea's death. Because Tea was a minor who was not a student at State University, residents responded to Tea's death as a community crisis, not just as an on-campus problem. President Foxx and Collegeborough Mayor Tyler Chestnut issued this joint statement: "We pray that Lindsey's parents can find some comfort in knowing that we are working hard on this and that Lindsey's death can perhaps serve as a catalyst to change our campus and our city."

Several months later, after research and discussion, the State University Board of Governors and the Collegebrough City Commission held a joint meeting to adopt reforms intended to protect community safety. The meeting began with technical presentations by experts brought in to educate the governors and commissioners.

Professor James Beam presented results of his research showing that males who lived for at least one semester in a fraternity house had significantly higher rates of binge drinking during and after college up through age 35, compared to their peers in college not involved in fraternities. Among males at age 35, 65 percent of the residential fraternity members reported two or more alcohol use disorder symptoms, compared to 33 percent of non-residential fraternity members, and 22 percent of college students who were not involved in fraternities.

Dr. Paula Rindt, an expert in public health and land use, testified that fraternities tend to encourage dangerous drinking behaviors, and, at their worst, engage in highly offensive and sometimes criminal hazing rituals. Especially when fraternity houses are located off-campus, these activities conflict with community residents.

After these presentations, each of the bodies present—the governors and the commissioners—adopted changes in law or policy.

- The Board of Governors increased funding to staff more mental health counselors in the university office of student wellness.
- The Board of Governors adopted a medical amnesty program designed to encourage students to immediately seek medical help if a hazing ritual injured someone.
- The City Commission adopted a new ordinance disallowing off-campus fraternity houses.

These are the details of the new city ordinance. It works by creating an overlay zoning district in Collegeborough. This is essentially a mapped area including all of Collegeborough that is not part of the State University campus, but that is within three miles of State University campus. Then, within this area, a fraternity house is not a permitted use in any zoning category. The rule defines "fraternity house" as follows:

> A fraternity house is a building used as a residence for males which has only one dining facility and one kitchen. This term includes any building originally designed and constructed for such purposes or any structure converted to this use. This term does not include any building or structure which houses three or fewer people or which houses any number of people related by blood, adoption, or marriage.

Rick Stumbly, a member of Omicron Tau Rho fraternity, opposes the new ordinance. He considers himself and his fraternity brothers—who all live together in a house near

State University campus in Collegeborough—to be family, but they are not related by blood, adoption, or marriage. The new ordinance would require Stumbly to change his living situation.

Stumbly teams up with the Collegeborough Civil Liberties Foundation to file a lawsuit seeking to block the Collegeborough ordinance by claiming that the rule violates the Equal Protection Clause. Evaluate Stumbly's claim.

## Notes

1 U.S. Const. amend. XIV, § 1.
2 *The Slaughter-House Cases*, 83 U.S. 36, 68, 79–82 (1872).
3 *See generally* Richard Rothstein, *The Color of Law: A Forgotten History of How Our Government Segregated America* (Liveright Publ'g Corp. 2018).
4 In support of a determination that discrimination against people with mental disabilities has been rooted in "deep-seated prejudice," the U.S. Court of Appeals for the Fifth Circuit observed: "Once-technical terms for various degrees of retardation—e.g. 'idiots,' 'imbeciles,' 'morons'—have become popular terms of derision." Cleburne Living Ctr., Inc. v. City of Cleburne, 726 F.2d 191, 197 (5th Cir. 1984) (citations omitted).
5 245 U.S. 60 (1917).
6 Rothstein, *supra* note 3, at 47.
7 Baxstrom v. Herold, 383 U.S. 107, 111 (1966) (citation omitted).
8 Clark v. Jeter, 486 U.S. 456, 461 (1988).
9 Washington v. Davis, 426 U.S. 229, 240–41 (1976).
10 Vill. of Arlington Heights v. Metro. Hous. Dev. Corp., 429 U.S. 252, 265–68 (1977).
11 Recall that the standard of review that a court will use to determine whether a local government has correctly decided a quasi-judicial decision also has the name strict scrutiny. The term "strict scrutiny" in an equal protection context has a different meaning than the term "strict scrutiny" in a quasi-judicial decision-making context.
12 Plyler v. Doe, 457 U.S. 202, 216 n.14 (1982).
13 Loving v. Virginia, 388 U.S. 1, 11–12 (1967) (race); Brown v. Bd. of Educ., 347 U.S. 483, 493–95 (1954) (same), *amended by* 349 U.S. 294 (1955); City of New Orleans v. Dukes, 427 U.S. 297, 303 (1976) (race, religion, or alienage).
14 Fisher v. Univ. of Tex. at Austin, 136 S. Ct. 2198, 2207 (2016) (emphases added) (citations omitted).
15 Miss. Univ. for Women v. Hogan, 458 U.S. 718, 723–24 (1982).
16 Gomez v. Perez, 409 U.S. 535, 538 (1973).
17 Clark v. Jeter, 486 U.S. 456, 461 (1988) (emphases added).
18 Mass. Bd. of Ret. v. Murgia, 427 U.S. 307, 314 (1976) (emphasis added) (citations omitted).
19 Dallas v. Stanglin, 490 U.S. 19, 23 (1989) (emphases added) (quoting San Antonio Indep. Sch. Dist. v. Rodriguez, 411 U.S. 1, 44 (1973)).
20 473 U.S. 432 (1985).
21 Vill. of Willowbrook v. Olech, 528 U.S. 562, 564 (2000).
22 *Id.*
23 *Id.* at 565.

# 25 Speech

## Substantive due process

Chapter 4, "Substantive due process," taught you to use the fairly debatable standard to evaluate whether a legislative land use decision violates substantive due process rights. This chapter, "Speech," and the next chapter, "Religion," add to this explanation of substantive due process by providing additional standards of review and explaining when they apply.

While the fairly debatable standard is the default standard to evaluate whether a land use rule violates substantive due process, when a land use rule implicates a fundamental right, courts will subject that rule to a heightened standard of review.

> The substantive component of the Due Process Clause protects those rights that are "fundamental," that is, rights that are "implicit in the concept of ordered liberty." The Supreme Court has deemed that most—but not all—of the rights enumerated in the Bill of Rights are fundamental; certain unenumerated rights (for instance, the penumbral right of privacy) also merit protection. It is in this framework that fundamental rights are incorporated against the states. A finding that a right merits substantive due process protection means that the right is protected "against 'certain government actions regardless of the fairness of the procedures used to implement them.'"[1]

Additional unenumerated rights which are fundamental rights "are the rights to marry; to have children; to direct the education and upbringing of one's children; to martial privacy; to use contraception; to bodily integrity; and to abortion."[2]

## Sign regulations

The First Amendment to the U.S. Constitution says in part "Congress shall make no law ... abridging the freedom of speech."[3] The Florida Constitution says in its Declaration of Rights "[n]o law shall be passed to restrain or abridge the liberty of speech."[4] This right to free speech is a fundamental right.[5] Nonetheless, Florida Statutes require local governments to regulate signs, a form of speech.[6] And the U.S. Supreme Court has approved of such regulations.

> While signs are a form of expression protected by the Free Speech Clause, they pose distinctive problems that are subject to municipalities' police powers. Unlike oral speech, signs take up space and may obstruct views, distract motorists, displace alternative uses for land, and pose other problems that legitimately call for regulation. It is common ground that governments may regulate the physical characteristics of signs .. .[7]

To evaluate whether a sign regulation is permissible, a court will apply one of two standards of review: modified intermediate scrutiny or strict scrutiny.

### *Modified intermediate scrutiny*

Courts apply a modified form of intermediate scrutiny to evaluate regulations governing commercial speech[8] and content-neutral regulations restricting speech.[9]

#### *Commercial speech*

The Constitution "accords a lesser protection to commercial speech than to other constitutionally guaranteed expression."[10] Still, the First Amendment protects commercial speech and courts will evaluate sign regulations limiting commercial speech using the following test:

> In commercial speech cases, then, a four-part analysis has developed. At the outset, we must determine whether the expression is protected by the First Amendment. For commercial speech to come within that provision, it at least must concern lawful activity and not be misleading. Next, we ask whether the asserted governmental interest is substantial. If both inquiries yield positive answers, we must determine whether the regulation directly advances the governmental interest asserted, and whether it is not more extensive than is necessary to serve that interest.[11]

This test is similar to all three of the tests courts apply to equal protection claims in that it requires consideration of both the governmental interest in the regulation and of the extent to which the regulation furthers that governmental interest.

#### *Content-neutral regulations*

Content-neutral, or non-communicative, characteristics of signs include "size, building materials, lighting, moving parts, and portability."[12] Local government sign regulations often regulate many such aspects of signs such as area, height, brightness, placement on a property, or manner of construction. Courts also characterize these aspects as "time, place, and manner restrictions."[13]

This is the test applicable to such restrictions on signs:

> [G]overnment may impose reasonable restrictions on the time, place, or manner of protected speech, provided the restrictions "are justified without reference to the content of the regulated speech, that they are narrowly tailored to serve a significant governmental interest, and that they leave open ample alternative channels for communication of the information."[14]

The Court has found two common justifications for sign ordinances to be substantial government interests that satisfy modified intermediate scrutiny: traffic safety and aesthetics.[15] The Florida Constitution goes further with regard to aesthetics, saying: "It shall be the policy of the state to conserve and protect its natural resources *and scenic beauty*."[16]

No bright line rules exist to help evaluate whether a regulation has the requisite connection to the stated public purpose that modified intermediate scrutiny requires. But the Court has provided guidance:

> To satisfy this standard, a regulation need not be the least speech-restrictive means of advancing the Government's interests. "Rather, the requirement of narrow tailoring is

> satisfied 'so long as the ... regulation promotes a substantial government interest that would be achieved less effectively absent the regulation.'" Narrow tailoring in this context requires, in other words, that the means chosen do not "burden substantially more speech than is necessary to further the government's legitimate interests."[17]

Government must be careful, however, to not draft rules which are too restrained (i.e., that are too careful to avoid burdening more speech than is necessary). Exceptions to restrictions on signage that a local government adopts in good faith may actually undermine sign regulations. "[A]n exemption from an otherwise permissible regulation of speech may represent a governmental 'attempt to give one side of a debatable public question an advantage in expressing its views to the people.'"[18] And

> [e]xemptions from an otherwise legitimate regulation of a medium of speech may be noteworthy for a reason quite apart from the risks of viewpoint and content discrimination: They may diminish the credibility of the government's rationale for restricting speech in the first place.[19]

To read a decision with fun Florida facts that applies modified intermediate scrutiny, review *Solomon v. City of Gainesville.*[20] That case concerned the sign of Leonardo's Pizza, which depicts an adaptation of Leonardo da Vinci's *Vitruvian Man*. For nearly half a century, Leonardo's served pizza by the slice across the street from the University of Florida campus. But in the 1980s, the city of Gainesville sought to enforce an ordinance against the pizza parlor that prohibits signs of an "obscene, indecent or immoral nature."[21]

#### *Strict scrutiny*

The following case, *Reed v. Town of Gilbert*, states that "[c]ontent-based laws—those that target speech based on its communicative content—are presumptively unconstitutional and may be justified only if the government proves that they are narrowly tailored to serve compelling state interests."[22] That test is strict scrutiny, the same test courts will apply to evaluate government discrimination against suspect classifications. Strict scrutiny is a high bar for an ordinance to meet and courts are unlikely to uphold content-based sign regulations.[23] As a result, whether a regulation is content-based is practically dispositive of its constitutionality.

## United States Supreme Court

## *Reed v. Town of Gilbert*[24]

## 2015

Justice THOMAS delivered the opinion of the Court.

The town of Gilbert, Arizona (or Town), has adopted a comprehensive code governing the manner in which people may display outdoor signs. Gilbert, Ariz., Land Development Code (Sign Code or Code), ch. 1, § 4.402 (2005). The Sign Code identifies various categories of signs based on the type of information they convey, then subjects each category to different restrictions. One of the categories is "Temporary Directional Signs Relating to a Qualifying Event," loosely defined as signs directing the public to a meeting of a nonprofit group. § 4.402(P). The Code imposes more stringent restrictions on these signs than it does on signs conveying other messages. We hold that these provisions are content-based regulations of speech that cannot survive strict scrutiny.

*I*

*A*

The Sign Code prohibits the display of outdoor signs anywhere within the Town without a permit, but it then exempts 23 categories of signs from that requirement. These exemptions include everything from bazaar signs to flying banners. Three categories of exempt signs are particularly relevant here.

The first is "Ideological Sign[s]." This category includes any "sign communicating a message or ideas for noncommercial purposes that is not a Construction Sign, Directional Sign, Temporary Directional Sign Relating to a Qualifying Event, Political Sign, Garage Sale Sign, or a sign owned or required by a governmental agency." Sign Code, Glossary of General Terms (Glossary), p. 23 [emphasis deleted]. Of the three categories discussed here, the Code treats ideological signs most favorably, allowing them to be up to 20 square feet in area and to be placed in all "zoning districts" without time limits. § 4.402(J).

The second category is "Political Sign[s]." This includes any "temporary sign designed to influence the outcome of an election called by a public body." Glossary 23.2 The Code treats these signs less favorably than ideological signs. The Code allows the placement of political signs up to 16 square feet on residential property and up to 32 square feet on nonresidential property, undeveloped municipal property, and "rights-of-way." § 4.402(I).3 These signs may be displayed up to 60 days before a primary election and up to 15 days following a general election. *Ibid.*

The third category is "Temporary Directional Signs Relating to a Qualifying Event." This includes any "Temporary Sign intended to direct pedestrians, motorists, and other passersby to a 'qualifying event.'" Glossary 25 (emphasis deleted). A "qualifying event" is defined as any "assembly, gathering, activity, or meeting sponsored, arranged, or promoted by a religious, charitable, community service, educational, or other similar non-profit organization." *Ibid.* The Code treats temporary directional signs even less favorably than political signs. Temporary directional signs may be no larger than six square feet. § 4.402(P). They may be placed on private property or on a public right-of-way, but no more than four signs may be placed on a single property at any time. *Ibid.* And, they may be displayed no more than 12 hours before the "qualifying event" and no more than 1 hour afterward. *Ibid.*

*B*

Petitioners Good News Community Church (Church) and its pastor, Clyde Reed, wish to advertise the time and location of their Sunday church services. The Church is a small, cash-strapped entity that owns no building, so it holds its services at elementary schools or other locations in or near the Town. In order to inform the public about its services, which are held in a variety of different locations, the Church began placing 15 to 20 temporary signs around the Town, frequently in the public right-of-way abutting the street. The signs typically displayed the Church's name, along with the time and location of the upcoming service. Church members would post the signs early in the day on Saturday and then remove them around midday on Sunday. The display of these signs requires little money and manpower, and thus has proved to be an economical and effective way for the Church to let the community know where its services are being held each week.

This practice caught the attention of the Town's Sign Code compliance manager, who twice cited the Church for violating the Code. The first citation noted that the Church exceeded the time limits for displaying its temporary directional signs. The second citation referred to the same problem, along with the Church's failure to include the date of the event on the signs. Town officials even confiscated one of the Church's signs, which Reed had to retrieve from the municipal offices ...

## *II*

### *A*

The First Amendment, applicable to the States through the Fourteenth Amendment, prohibits the enactment of laws "abridging the freedom of speech." U.S. Const. amend. 1. Under that Clause, a government, including a municipal government vested with state authority, "has no power to restrict expression because of its message, its ideas, its subject matter, or its content." *Police Dep't of Chi. v. Mosley*, 408 U.S. 92, 95 (1972). Content-based laws—those that target speech based on its communicative content—are presumptively unconstitutional and may be justified only if the government proves that they are narrowly tailored to serve compelling state interests. *R.A.V. v. St. Paul*, 505 U.S. 377, 395 (1992); *Simon & Schuster, Inc. v. Members of N.Y. State Crime Victims Bd.*, 502 U.S. 105, 115, 118 (1991).

Government regulation of speech is content based if a law applies to particular speech because of the topic discussed or the idea or message expressed. *E.g., Sorrell v. IMS Health, Inc.*, 564 U.S. ——, —— – —— (2011); *Carey v. Brown*, 447 U.S. 455, 462 (1980); *Mosley, supra*, at 95. This commonsense meaning of the phrase "content based" requires a court to consider whether a regulation of speech "on its face" draws distinctions based on the message a speaker conveys. *Sorrell, supra*, at ——. Some facial distinctions based on a message are obvious, defining regulated speech by particular subject matter, and others are more subtle, defining regulated speech by its function or purpose. Both are distinctions drawn based on the message a speaker conveys, and, therefore, are subject to strict scrutiny.

Our precedents have also recognized a separate and additional category of laws that, though facially content neutral, will be considered content-based regulations of speech: laws that cannot be "justified without reference to the content of the regulated speech," or that were adopted by the government "because of disagreement with the message [the speech] conveys," *Ward v. Rock Against Racism*, 491 U.S. 781, 791 (1989). Those laws, like those that are content based on their face, must also satisfy strict scrutiny.

### *B*

The Town's Sign Code is content based on its face. It defines "Temporary Directional Signs" on the basis of whether a sign conveys the message of directing the public to church or some other "qualifying event." Glossary 25. It defines "Political Signs" on the basis of whether a sign's message is "designed to influence the outcome of an election." *Id.* at 24. And it defines "Ideological Signs" on the basis of whether a sign "communicat[es] a message or ideas" that do not fit within the Code's other categories. *Id.* at 23. It then subjects each of these categories to different restrictions.

The restrictions in the Sign Code that apply to any given sign thus depend entirely on the communicative content of the sign. If a sign informs its reader of the time and place a book club will discuss John Locke's Two Treatises of Government, that sign will be treated differently from a sign expressing the view that one should vote for one of Locke's followers in an upcoming election, and both signs will be treated differently from a sign expressing an ideological view rooted in Locke's theory of government. More to the point, the Church's signs inviting people to attend its worship services are treated differently from signs conveying other types of ideas. On its face, the Sign Code is a content-based regulation of speech. We thus have no need to consider the government's justifications or purposes for enacting the Code to determine whether it is subject to strict scrutiny ...

A law that is content based on its face is subject to strict scrutiny regardless of the government's benign motive, content-neutral justification, or lack of "animus toward the ideas contained" in the regulated speech ... We have thus made clear that "[i]llicit legislative intent is not the *sine qua non* of a violation of the First Amendment," and a party opposing the government "need adduce 'no evidence of an improper censorial motive.'" ... In other words, an innocuous justification cannot transform a facially content-based law into one that is content neutral ... Innocent motives do not eliminate the danger of censorship presented by a facially content-based statute, as future government officials may one day wield such statutes to suppress disfavored speech ...

The Town [reasons] that "content based" is a term of art that "should be applied flexibly" with the goal of protecting "viewpoints and ideas from government censorship or favoritism." Brief for Respondents 22. In the Town's view, a sign regulation that "does not censor or favor particular viewpoints or ideas" cannot be content based. *Ibid.* The Sign Code allegedly passes this test because its treatment of temporary directional signs does not raise any concerns that the government is "endorsing or suppressing 'ideas or viewpoints,'" *id.* at 27, and the provisions for political signs and ideological signs "are neutral as to particular ideas or viewpoints" within those categories. *Id.* at 37.

This analysis conflates two distinct but related limitations that the First Amendment places on government regulation of speech. Government discrimination among viewpoints—or the regulation of speech based on "the specific motivating ideology or the opinion or perspective of the speaker"—is a "more blatant" and "egregious form of content discrimination." *Rosenberger v. Rector and Visitors of Univ. of Va.*, 515 U.S. 819, 829 (1995). But it is well established that "[t]he First Amendment's hostility to content-based regulation extends not only to restrictions on particular viewpoints, but also to prohibition of public discussion of an entire topic." *Consol. Edison Co. of N.Y. v. Pub. Serv. Comm'n of N. Y.*, 447 U.S. 530, 537 (1980).

Thus, a speech regulation targeted at specific subject matter is content based even if it does not discriminate among viewpoints within that subject matter. *Ibid.* ...

Finally, the Court of Appeals characterized the Sign Code's distinctions as turning on "the content-neutral element[] of who is speaking through the sign ..." 707 F.3d at 1069 ... [T]he fact that a distinction is speaker based does not, as the Court of Appeals seemed to believe, automatically render the distinction content neutral. Because "[s]peech restrictions based on the identity of the speaker are all too often simply a means to control content," *Citizens United v. Fed. Election Comm'n*, 558 U.S. 310, 340 (2010), we have insisted that "laws favoring some speakers over others demand strict scrutiny when the legislature's speaker preference reflects a content preference," *Turner*, 512 U.S. at 658. Thus, a law limiting the content of newspapers, but only newspapers, could not evade strict scrutiny simply because it could be characterized as speaker based. Likewise, a content-based law that restricted the political speech of all corporations would not become content neutral just because it singled out corporations as a class of speakers. *See Citizens United, supra*, at 340–41 ... This type of ordinance may seem like a perfectly rational way to regulate signs, but a clear and firm rule governing content neutrality is an essential means of protecting the freedom of speech, even if laws that might seem "entirely reasonable" will sometimes be "struck down because of their content-based nature."

### *III*

Because the Town's Sign Code imposes content-based restrictions on speech, those provisions can stand only if they survive strict scrutiny, "which requires the Government to prove that the restriction furthers a compelling interest and is narrowly tailored to achieve that interest," *Ariz. Free Enter. Club's Freedom Club PAC v. Bennett*, 564 U.S. ——, —— (2011) (quoting *Citizens United*, 558 U.S. at 340). Thus, it is the Town's burden to demonstrate that the Code's differentiation between temporary directional signs and other types of signs, such as political signs and ideological signs, furthers a compelling governmental interest and is narrowly tailored to that end. *See ibid.*

The Town cannot do so. It has offered only two governmental interests in support of the distinctions the Sign Code draws: preserving the Town's aesthetic appeal and traffic safety. Assuming for the sake of argument that those are compelling governmental interests, the Code's distinctions fail as hopelessly underinclusive.

Starting with the preservation of aesthetics, temporary directional signs are "no greater an eyesore," *Discovery Network*, 507 U.S. at 425, than ideological or political ones. Yet the Code allows unlimited proliferation of larger ideological signs while strictly limiting the number, size, and duration of smaller directional ones. The Town cannot claim that placing strict limits on temporary directional signs is necessary to beautify the Town while at the same time allowing unlimited numbers of other types of signs that create the same problem.

The Town similarly has not shown that limiting temporary directional signs is necessary to eliminate threats to traffic safety, but that limiting other types of signs is not. The Town has offered no reason to believe that directional signs pose a greater threat to safety than do ideological or political signs. If anything, a sharply worded ideological sign seems more likely to distract a driver than a sign directing the public to a nearby church meeting.

In light of this underinclusiveness, the Town has not met its burden to prove that its Sign Code is narrowly tailored to further a compelling government interest. Because a "law cannot be regarded as protecting an interest of the highest order, and thus as justifying a restriction on truthful speech, when it leaves appreciable damage to that supposedly vital interest unprohibited," *Republican Party of Minn. v. White*, 536 U.S. 765, 780 (2002), the Sign Code fails strict scrutiny.

### *IV*

Our decision today will not prevent governments from enacting effective sign laws. The Town asserts that an "absolutist" content-neutrality rule would render "virtually all distinctions in sign laws ... subject to strict scrutiny," Brief for Respondents 34–35, but that is not the case. Not "all distinctions" are subject to strict scrutiny, only content-based ones are. Laws that are content neutral are instead subject to lesser scrutiny. *See Clark*, 468 U.S. at 295.

The Town has ample content-neutral options available to resolve problems with safety and aesthetics. For example, its current Code regulates many aspects of signs that have nothing to do with a sign's message: size, building materials, lighting, moving parts, and portability. *See, e.g.*, § 4.402(R). And on public property, the Town may go a long way toward entirely forbidding the posting of signs, so long as it does so in an evenhanded, content-neutral manner. *See Taxpayers for Vincent*, 466 U.S. at 817 (upholding content-neutral ban against posting signs on public property). Indeed, some lower courts have long held that similar content-based sign laws receive strict scrutiny, but there is no evidence that towns in those jurisdictions have suffered catastrophic effects. *See, e.g.*, *Solantic, LLC v. Neptune Beach*, 410 F.3d 1250, 1264–69 (11th Cir. 2005) (sign categories similar to the town of Gilbert's were content based and subject to strict scrutiny); *Matthews v. Needham*, 764 F.2d 58, 59–60 (1st Cir. 1985) (law banning political signs but not commercial signs was content based and subject to strict scrutiny).

We acknowledge that a city might reasonably view the general regulation of signs as necessary because signs "take up space and may obstruct views, distract motorists, displace alternative uses for land, and pose other problems that legitimately call for regulation." *City of*

*Ladue*, 512 U.S. at 48. At the same time, the presence of certain signs may be essential, both for vehicles and pedestrians, to guide traffic or to identify hazards and ensure safety. A sign ordinance narrowly tailored to the challenges of protecting the safety of pedestrians, drivers, and passengers—such as warning signs marking hazards on private property, signs directing traffic, or street numbers associated with private houses—well might survive strict scrutiny. The signs at issue in this case, including political and ideological signs and signs for events, are far removed from those purposes. As discussed above, they are facially content based and are neither justified by traditional safety concerns nor narrowly tailored.

We reverse the judgment of the Court of Appeals and remand the case for proceedings consistent with this opinion.

It is so ordered.

Justice ALITO, with whom Justice KENNEDY and Justice SOTOMAYOR join, concurring.

I join the opinion of the Court but add a few words of further explanation ...

As the Court shows, the regulations at issue in this case are replete with content-based distinctions, and as a result they must satisfy strict scrutiny. This does not mean, however, that municipalities are powerless to enact and enforce reasonable sign regulations. I will not attempt to provide anything like a comprehensive list, but here are some rules that would not be content based:

Rules regulating the size of signs. These rules may distinguish among signs based on any content-neutral criteria, including any relevant criteria listed below.

Rules regulating the locations in which signs may be placed. These rules may distinguish between free-standing signs and those attached to buildings.

Rules distinguishing between lighted and unlighted signs.

Rules distinguishing between signs with fixed messages and electronic signs with messages that change.

Rules that distinguish between the placement of signs on private and public property.

Rules distinguishing between the placement of signs on commercial and residential property.

Rules distinguishing between on-premises and off-premises signs.

Rules restricting the total number of signs allowed per mile of roadway.

Rules imposing time restrictions on signs advertising a one-time event. Rules of this nature do not discriminate based on topic or subject and are akin to rules restricting the times within which oral speech or music is allowed ...

Properly understood, today's decision will not prevent cities from regulating signs in a way that fully protects public safety and serves legitimate esthetic objectives.

## Corporate brand expression

In additional to constitutional limits on sign regulation, the Florida Legislature has pre-empted local governments from regulating corporate brand expression.

> A political subdivision of this state may not adopt or enforce any ordinance or impose any building permit or other development order requirement that: ... Contains any building, construction, or aesthetic requirement or condition that conflicts with or impairs corporate trademarks, service marks, trade dress, logos, color patterns, design scheme insignia, image standards, or other features of corporate branding identity on real property or improvements thereon ... .[25]

The statute does include an exemption allowing local governments to regulate corporate brand expression on development within historic preservation districts.[26]

### Box 25.1 Practice problem: NextGen Promotions

Collegeborough seeks to guarantee that people with disabilities have the same opportunities as everyone else to participate in the mainstream of life in Collegeborough. The Collegeborough City Council wants everyone to enjoy employment opportunities, to purchase goods and services, and to participate in Collegeborough government programs and services, without regard to whether any individual person has a disability.

In pursuit of these objectives, the city impanels a Collegian Disabilities Committee to review city ordinances, to hear testimony from residents in public hearings, and to make recommendations on changes in law that will improve access to public life by all Collegians (Collegian is the demonym of Collegeborough residents).

The Collegian Disabilities Committee spends many months on these tasks before authoring a final report to the City Council. A recommendation of the final report is that the city require all signage in Collegeborough to be legible to blind and visually impaired Collegians. The report recommends that the city amend its sign ordinance to provide the following:

> Signs which communicate a written message are expressly prohibited unless simultaneously presented in visually readable characters and a tactile writing system for blind or visually impaired persons such as Braille. This prohibition shall not apply to signs the Manual on Uniform Traffic Control Devices describes as necessary for traffic safety.

NextGen Promotions is a marketing and public relations firm in Collegeborough that specializes in technologically cutting-edge marketing strategies for businesses seeking to attract savvy consumers. This year, NextGen Promotions has rolled out "augmented reality advertisements" to promote events for its clients. Augmented reality advertisements provide smartphone users with a composite image on their device comprising a computer-generated image overlaid on a real-world picture their devices' cameras capture in real time. This sounds complicated, but NextGen Promotions outsources its application design work to a firm in India and can produce these revolutionary advertisements for a very low cost to clients.

NextGen Promotion's clients love this advertising method because they can present an advertising experience that reflects their brand identity in a powerful and authentic way. One client, the owner of Lou's Brew Through—a drive-through alcohol retail store—said, "no other form of advertising lets us express ourselves and our annual 20% off, direct-to-the-driver light beer sales event in such a personal and profound way."

NextGen Promotion has placed matrix barcodes around Collegeborough to indicate places where smartphone users may view their augmented reality advertisements. Matrix barcodes (sometimes called by the trademarked names "Quick Response Code" or "QR Code") are two-dimensional, machine-readable bar codes made up of black and white patterns arranged in a square. When a smartphone user sees a matrix barcode installed by NextGen Promotion, he or she can point his or her smartphone at the matrix barcode and see an augmented reality advertisement.

Collegeborough takes the advice of the Collegian Disabilities Committee and amends the city sign ordinance with the recommended language. Shortly after this rule change, a Collegeborough code enforcement officer determines that NextGen Promotions' matrix barcodes violate the city ordinance because they contain a written message, but are not provided either in "visually readable characters" or in "a tactile writing system for blind or visually impaired persons such as Braille." The officer believes the content of these advertisements—characters that only a computer can recognize—is illegal. She issues a citation to NextGen Promotions that will accrue fines until NextGen Promotions takes down the matrix barcodes.

NextGen Promotions believes the city ordinance violates its rights to free speech because it will have to end all of its augmented reality advertisement campaigns and because the city regulation is based on the content of NextGen Promotion's matrix barcodes. Collegeborough disagrees because the city believes it is not regulating what NextGen Promotions says, just the manner in which NextGen Promotions says it.

NextGen Promotions sues, alleging the First Amendment violation. Evaluate the company's claim.

## Notes

1 McKinney v. Pate, 20 F.3d 1550, 1556 (11th Cir. 1994) (citations omitted).
2 Washington v. Glucksberg, 117 S. Ct. 2258, 2267 (1997) (citations omitted).
3 U.S. Const. amend. I.
4 Fla. Const. art. I, § 4.
5 W. Va. State Bd. of Educ. v. Barnette, 319 U.S. 624, 638–39 (1943); Lucas v. Forty-Fourth Gen. Assembly of Colo., 377 U.S. 713, 736 (1964).
6 Fla. Stat. § 163.3202(2)(f).
7 City of Ladue v. Gilleo, 512 U.S. 43, 48 (1994).
8 Cent. Hudson Gas & Elec. Corp. v. Pub. Serv. Comm'n of N.Y., 447 U.S. 557 (1980).
9 Turner Broad. Sys., Inc. v. F.C.C., 512 U.S. 622, 662 (1994).
10 *Cent. Hudson*, 447 U.S. at 563.
11 *Id.* at 566.
12 Reed v. Town of Gilbert, 576 U.S. 155, 173 (2015).
13 *See* Va. State Bd. of Pharmacy v. Va. Citizens Consumer Council, Inc., 425 U.S. 748, 771 (1976).
14 Ward v. Rock Against Racism, 491 U.S. 781, 791 (1989) (citations omitted).
15 Metromedia, Inc. v. City of San Diego, 453 U.S. 490, 507 (1981).
16 Fla. Const. art II, § 7(a) (emphasis added).
17 Turner Broad. Sys., Inc. v. F.C.C., 512 U.S. 622, 662 (1994) (citations omitted).
18 City of Ladue v. Gilleo, 512 U.S. 43, 51 (1994).
19 *Id.* at 52.
20 Solomon v. City of Gainesville, 763 F.2d 1212 (11th Cir. 1985), *aff'd*, 796 F.2d 1464 (11th Cir. 1986)
21 *Id.* at 1213.
22 Reed v. Town of Gilbert, 576 U.S. 155, 163 (2015).
23 Susan L. Trevarthen & Adam M. Hapner, *The True Impact of Reed v. Town of Gilbert on Sign Regulation*, 49 Stetson L. Rev. 509, 512 (2020).
24 576 U.S. 155 (2015).
25 Fla. Stat. § 553.79(20)(a)1.
26 *Id.* at § 553.79(20)(d).

# 26 Religion

The First Amendment to the U.S. Constitution says in part, "Congress shall make no law respecting an establishment of religion, or prohibiting the free exercise thereof ..."[1] This language comprises the Establishment Clause—prohibiting the government from establishing religion—and the Free Exercise Clause—protecting the right to practice religion or not.

These two clauses provide distinct constraints on government behavior regarding religion:

> The purposes of the First Amendment guarantees relating to religion were twofold: to foreclose state interference with the practice of religious faiths, and to foreclose the establishment of a state religion familiar in other Eighteenth Century systems. Religion and government, each insulated from the other, could then coexist.[2]

Together, the Establishment Clause and the Free Exercise Clause make up what Thomas Jefferson referred to as a "wall" of separation between church and state.[3]

## Establishment

*Larkin v. Grendel's Den, Inc.* is a U.S. Supreme Court decision applying the Establishment Clause to a land use dispute.[4] A Massachusetts statute had allowed the Holy Cross Armenian Catholic Parish to veto a liquor license application by the nearby Grendel's Den Restaurant & Bar.[5] The court said it

> has consistently held that a statute must satisfy three criteria to pass muster under the Establishment Clause: First, the statute must have a secular legislative purpose; second, its principal or primary effect must be one that neither advances nor inhibits religion ... finally, the statute must not foster "an excessive government entanglement with religion."[6]

In reviewing the Massachusetts statute, the court observed that the "joint exercise of legislative authority by Church and State provides a significant symbolic benefit to religion."[7] The decision held that the law violated the second and third criteria of the Establishment Clause test and concluded "[o]rdinary human experience and a long line of cases teach that few entanglements could be more offensive to the spirit of the Constitution."[8]

## Free exercise

Local government land development regulations typically apply to places of religious assembly such as churches, synagogues, and mosques. However, the free exercise of religion is a fundamental right.[9] Substantive due process requires reviewing such regulations using either the fairly debatable standard or strict scrutiny.

First, as is the case with all land use regulations, a land use rule that applies to places of religious assembly generally must only meet the permissive fairly debatable standard to satisfy substantive due process.

Second, a government regulation that is a *substantial burden* on religious exercise must meet strict scrutiny[10] to satisfy substantive due process. This quote from the U.S. Court of Appeals for the Second Circuit explains what is a substantial burden on religious exercise:

> [U.S.] Supreme Court precedents teach that a substantial burden on religious exercise exists when an individual is required to "choose between following the precepts of her religion and forfeiting benefits, on the one hand, and abandoning one of the precepts of her religion ... on the other hand." ... In the context in which this standard is typically applied—for example, a state's denial of unemployment compensation to a Jehovah's Witness who quit his job because his religious beliefs prevented him from participating in the production of war materials—it is not a difficult standard to apply. By denying benefits to Jehovah's Witnesses who follow their beliefs, the state puts undue pressure on the adherents to alter their behavior and to violate their beliefs in order to obtain government benefits, thereby imposing a substantial burden on religious exercise.[11]

Therefore, a substantial burden is not just a government rule that makes religious exercise more difficult. Instead, it is government pressure—or coercion—targeted to peoples' behavior around their religious practice.

Third, the Supreme Court has also applied strict scrutiny to government rules that single-out religious practices for regulation:

> A law burdening religious practice that is not neutral or not of general application must undergo the most rigorous of scrutiny. To satisfy the commands of the First Amendment, a law restrictive of religious practice must advance "interests of the highest order" and must be narrowly tailored in pursuit of those interests.[12]

*Midrash Sephardi, Inc. v. Town of Surfside*[13] is a U.S. Court of Appeals for the Eleventh Circuit decision holding that a town of Surfside, Florida ordinance violated the right to the free exercise of religion.[14] The case dealt with an ordinance that prohibited places of religious assembly in the town of Surfside's business district.[15] Applying the ordinance, the city had denied two synagogues permission to operate. The court's opinion exemplifies each of the three free exercise concepts discussed to this point.

First, the decision notes that local governments may "consider factors such as size, congruity with existing uses, and availability of parking" when issuing permits to places of religious assembly.[16] These "reasonable 'run of the mill' zoning considerations do not constitute substantial burdens on religious exercise."[17] As a result, typical land use restrictions applied to religious land uses only need to meet the permissive fairly debatable standard to be constitutional.

Second, the decision evaluates whether limiting synagogues to certain zoning districts creates a substantial burden. The court gives particular attention to the fact that congregants walk to services and one effect of the city ordinance is that people will have to walk farther to reach their place of worship:

> While walking may be burdensome and "walking farther" may be even more so, we cannot say that walking a few extra blocks is "substantial," as the term is used in [free exercise jurisprudence], and as suggested by the Supreme Court. The permitted RD–1 district is

> in the geographic center of a relatively small municipality, proximate to the business, tourist and residential districts. Deposition testimony indicated that congregants wishing to practice Orthodox Judaism customarily move where synagogues are located and do not typically expect the synagogues to move closer to them. In any given congregation, some members will necessarily walk farther than others, and, inevitably, some congregants will have greater difficulty walking than others. While we certainly sympathize with those congregants who endure Floridian heat and humidity to walk to services, the burden of walking a few extra blocks, made greater by Mother Nature's occasional incorrigibility, is not "substantial" within the meaning of [free exercise jurisprudence].[18]

Finally, *Midrash Sephardi* considers that the city ordinance allows secular places of assembly—such as private clubs, lodge halls, and social clubs—in the business district, while simultaneously banning religious places of assembly:

> A zoning law is not neutral or generally applicable if it treats similarly situated secular and religious assemblies differently because such unequal treatment indicates the ordinance improperly targets the religious character of an assembly ...
>
> Surfside improperly targeted religious assemblies and violated Free Exercise requirements of neutrality and general applicability. While merely the mention of church or synagogue in a zoning code does not destroy a zoning code's neutrality, we must nevertheless be mindful of the potential for impermissible "religious gerrymanders," which may render a zoning code operatively non-neutral. As we have noted, the text of § 90–152 treats religious assemblies differently than secular assemblies by excluding religious assemblies from the business district ...[19]

Based on this conclusion that the ordinance was not generally applicable, the court applied strict scrutiny to the ordinance.[20] The court held that the ordinance failed this exacting standard.[21]

## *RLUIPA*

The Religious Land Use and Institutionalized Persons Act (RLUIPA) is a federal law that protects religious land uses. According to the U.S. Eleventh Circuit Court of Appeals,

> Congress sought, through RLUIPA, to protect religious land uses from discriminatory processes used to exclude or otherwise limit the location of churches and synagogues in municipalities across the country. As indicated during nine hearings held before both houses of Congress, RLUIPA targets zoning codes which use individualized and discretionary processes to exclude churches, especially "new, small or unfamiliar churches ... [like] black churches and Jewish shuls and synagogues." The legislative record contained statistical, anecdotal and testimonial evidence suggesting that discrimination is widespread and typically results in the exclusion of churches and synagogues even in places where theaters, meeting halls and other secular assemblies are permitted.[22]

The act includes two requirements to address these restrictions on religious liberty. First, the law requires that a substantial burden on religious exercise must meet strict scrutiny.[23] Second, the law forbids local governments from treating a religious assembly or institution differently (i.e. "on less than equal terms") from a non-religious assembly or institution.[24]

### Box 26.1 Practice problem: Lightning of the Lord Ministries

Lighting of the Lord Ministries is an organization in Collegeborough that provides religious and other services to homeless residents of Collegeborough. The organization holds meetings several times a week, where it serves meals to these homeless residents and has one of the people present lead a prayer and informal religious service for all the folks present. The ministry is growing and Lighting of the Lord Ministries purchases a newer and larger building from the Moose Lodge of Collegeborough.

When the Moose Lodge of Collegeborough owned the building, it used the building to hold several meetings a week of its membership and to host communal meals among the membership. The organization had done this for years without conflict between itself and its neighbors or the city of Collegeborough.

As soon as Lighting of the Lord Ministries begins to use the building, however, the neighbors become upset. Homeless people now congregate on the property. Neighbors report that these people are disheveled and unsightly, and their presence is leading to declining property values. One neighbor complains that he has been aggressively panhandled while walking his dog. Another neighbor becomes afraid that she may be the victim of a sexual assault at the hands of vagrants. These residents, and other neighbors, contact the city of Collegeborough and ask it to address these issues with the growing homeless population in their neighborhood.

A Collegeborough planning professional checks the applicable zoning code and discovers that the Moose Lodge of Collegeborough was a "fraternal organization" whose activities were allowed under the Collegeborough zoning code. However, Lighting of the Lord Ministries is a "homeless food distribution center" whose activities are not allowed in the applicable zoning category. This planner prepares a letter to the organization which says Lighting of the Lord Ministries must stop serving food to homeless persons or face fines for its violation of the zoning code.

Lighting of the Lord Ministries sees itself in a tight spot. The organization believes that sharing food is an important part of spiritual fellowship. The organization also believes that welcoming the poor into its services is essential to its religious observance. Most importantly, Lighting of the Lord Ministries cannot afford to pay fines or to relocate to a building in a different zoning district.

Fortunately for Lighting of the Lord Ministries, a law professor from the law school at State University supports them and offers to provide the organization with free legal representation. This law professor sues the city of Collegeborough, alleging that the city is violating Lighting of the Lord Ministries' right to the free exercise of religion.

Evaluate Lighting of the Lord Ministries' claim.

## Notes

1 U.S. Const. amend. I.
2 Larkin v. Grendel's Den, Inc., 459 U.S. 116, 122 (1982).
3 *Id.* at 122–23.
4 *See Larkin*, 459 U.S. 116 (1982).
5 *Id.* at 117–19.
6 *Id.* at 123 (citations omitted).
7 *Id.* at 125–26.
8 *Id.* at 127.
9 *See* Espinoza v. Mont. Dep't of Revenue, 140 S. Ct. 2246, 2254–55 (2020); Trinity Lutheran Church of Columbia, Inc. v. Comer, 137 S. Ct. 2012, 2024 (2017) (requiring a compelling government interest, of the "highest order," to justify a substantial burden on religious exercise).

10 As with equal protection and the substantive due process right to free speech, the strict scrutiny standard in the context of the substantive due process right to free exercise requires government to narrowly tailor its regulation to meet a compelling public purpose. This test is different from the strict scrutiny standard used to evaluate a quasi-judicial decision.

11 Westchester Day Sch. v. Vill. of Mamaroneck, 504 F.3d 338, 348 (2d Cir. 2007) (citations omitted).

12 Church of the Lukumi Babalu Aye, Inc. v. City of Hialeah, 508 U.S. 520, 546 (1993) (citations omitted).

13 Midrash Sephardi, Inc. v. Town of Surfside, 366 F.3d 1214, 1232–35 (11th Cir. 2004).

14 The court in *Midrash Sephardi* did not actually decide that the Town of Surfside ordinance was a violation of the substantive due process right to the free exercise of religion. Instead, the court evaluated whether the ordinance violated the Religious Land Use and Institutionalized Persons Act. *Id.* at 1225–26. I have reproduced the court's analysis here, however, to serve as an example of a challenge to a local ordinance that follows the similar free exercise analysis as when the substantive, First Amendment right is violated.

15 *Midrash Sephardi* at 1219–20.

16 *Id.* at 1227 n.11.

17 *Id.*

18 *Id.* at 1228 (citations omitted).

19 *Id.* at 1232–33 (citations omitted).

20 *Id.* at 1232.

21 *Midrash Sephardi* at 1235.

22 *Id.* at 1236 (citations omitted).

23 42 U.S.C. § 2000cc(a)(1).

24 42 U.S.C. § 2000cc(b)(1).

# Table of cases

Case names and page spans in **bold** indicate that the case is reprinted in the book.

# Index

Page numbers in **bold** indicate that the referenced term is present in a table.

9780367622602